THESAURUS

Since 1996 third graders in Denver, Colorado, have discovered word treasures when using their own thesaurus. The students' first lesson is about the friendly dinosaur Thesaurus. The dinosaur has a big head, big feet, big arms, big body, big legs, big mouth, big teeth!!!!
(True, but boring.)
What are other words for BIG?
How many similar words do you know?
Now look up BIG in your thesaurus and see other words that mean the same.
Synonyms!

Now what does your sentence about Thesaurus the dinosaur sound like?

Using the thesaurus for speaking or writing changes boring to interesting and leads to an expanded vocabulary.

Words are like little treasures. They are like the bones an archaeologist digs up. They may sometimes seem all mixed up, but when you find out how they can work together, you may discover something amazing and exciting, like a dinosaur skeleton that no one has ever seen before.

The thesaurus with its treasury of words can soon become a student's favorite writing tool.

This book is dedicated to all students and their family members who see learning as an adventure and are ready to discover new ideas as they build their vocabularies.

Cathee Fisher

Printed and made in the U.S.A.

ISBN 0-934669-10-5

THESAURUS

written by Sarah Hilgendorf

"The difference between the right word and the wrong word is the difference between lightning and the lightning bug."

Mark Twain

Imagine for a moment that you are in the middle of writing a story. Your character has been frantically searching all over town for his lost dog. Finally, he sees a familiar tail peeking out from behind a neighbor's shrubs. You write...

Exhausted and ready to give up, Bobby finally spotted Dozer's wagging tail behind Mrs. London's prized azalea bushes. In a flash, his weariness was gone and he felt_____!

Everyone has experienced a moment when the right word just does not come to mind. We then have two options: settle for a simply satisfactory word, or seek out the word that will express precisely what we want to say. Words are tools, and sometimes we have to do a little work to find the right one. You could use a ping-pong paddle to play tennis, but is it really the best tool for the job? Likewise, when writing the story above, you could use the word *happy* to describe how Bobby felt after finding Dozer, but *ecstatic*, *elated*, and *overjoyed* may be more descriptive alternatives.

It is in moments like this that the thesaurus shines! The word *thesaurus* is Greek for "storehouse." That is exactly what you will find in the next three hundred pages. This book is meant to be a treasure trove of options, possibilities, WORDS! It is an alphabetical listing of words presented with their **synonyms** (words with similar meanings) and **antonyms** (words with opposite meanings). While it is virtually impossible to find two words in the English language with absolutely identical meanings, it can be quite helpful to scan a list of words with similar meanings in order to find the one that carries the specific message you wish to convey. What a superb opportunity for creativity, expression, and learning. Want to know the best part? This particular thesaurus was written especially with you, the student, in mind. All of the words contained in this book were chosen to grow your vocabulary and help you give shape to your thoughts and ideas. After all, the words you choose are a projection of who you are and how you want the world to see you.

Remember, this book has been given to you today because someone in your community believes deeply in two things: the power of words and ***YOU***.

Sarah Hilgendorf

How to use this thesaurus

A thesaurus does not serve the same purpose as a dictionary. Instead of providing the proper pronunciation and definitions of words, a thesaurus suggests alternative word choices. A thesaurus is a useful tool for expanding your vocabulary and adding variety to your written projects and speech. Let's talk about each part of the following example entry from this thesaurus:

THE HEADWORD: In this example, the headword is **courteous.** This means that this entry will provide synonyms (and in many cases antonyms) for this word.

courteous (SYN) polite, mannered, gracious, considerate, respectful
(ANT) rude, impolite, discourteous, ill-mannered

THE SYNONYMS: In this book, we have used the abbreviation (SYN) to indicate synonyms for the headword. *Synonyms are words that have similar meanings.* In this example, the synonyms given for courteous are **polite, mannered, gracious, considerate,** and **respectful**.

THE ANTONYMS: The majority of the entries in this thesaurus will also have antonyms given. *Antonyms are words with opposite meanings.* In this book, we have used the abbreviation (ANT) to indicate antonyms for the headword. In this example, the antonyms given for courteous are **rude, impolite, discourteous,** and **ill-mannered.**

A

abandon (SYN) leave, desert, strand, surrender, relinquish, recklessness (ANT) keep, preserve, maintain, continue, self-control

abate (SYN) lessen, diminish, fade, subside, reduce (ANT) increase, intensify, strengthen

abbreviate (SYN) shorten, condense, summarize, abridge, compress (ANT) lengthen, prolong, expand

abdicate (SYN) resign, renounce, step down, give up, forsake (ANT) claim, assert

abduct (SYN) kidnap, seize, capture

aberration (SYN) anomaly, variation, peculiarity, deviation, irregularity

abet (SYN) help, assist, support

abhor (SYN) detest, hate, loathe, despise, dislike (ANT) love, admire

abide (SYN) endure, bear, suffer, tolerate, continue, persist, dwell, reside

ability (SYN) skill, capability, aptitude, power, means (ANT) inability, limitation

able (SYN) competent, qualified, capable, adept, proficient (ANT) unable, incompetent, inept

abnormal (SYN) unusual, strange, extraordinary, aberrant, anomalous (ANT) typical, common, expected, natural, representative

abode (SYN) home, dwelling, residence, domicile

abolish (SYN) cancel, rescind, stop, put an end to (ANT) establish, promote, sustain

abolition (SYN) ending, termination, elimination

abominable (SYN) terrible, detestable, loathsome, atrocious, appalling, vile (ANT) good, admirable, likable

abortive (SYN) futile, vain, failed, unsuccessful, unproductive (ANT) successful, fruitful

abound (SYN) thrive, flourish, teem

about (SYN) regarding, concerning, relating to, near, beside, almost, roughly (ANT) exactly, precisely

above (SYN) over, beyond, higher than, upon (ANT) below, under, underneath

abrasion (SYN) scrape, scratch, gash, laceration, erosion, wearing away

abridge (SYN) shorten, abbreviate, edit, prune, truncate (ANT) extend, lengthen, expand

abroad (SYN) overseas

abrupt (SYN) sudden, unforeseen, blunt, impatient, curt (ANT) gradual, slow, warm, courteous

absence (SYN) lack, want, shortage, unavailability (ANT) presence absent (SYN) missing, away, elsewhere, preoccupied, vacant (ANT) present, alert, attentive

absent-minded (SYN) distracted, unaware, forgetful, scatter-brained

absolute (SYN) complete, downright, thorough, supreme, unrestricted, partial, limited, qualified

absolve (SYN) forgive, pardon, excuse, release, exonerate, acquit (ANT) convict, blame

absorb (SYN) soak up, take in, engage, engross, rivet, grip (ANT) emit, expel

absorbent (SYN) permeable, porous, assimilating, spongy

abstain (SYN) restrain, forego, resist, renounce, avoid (ANT) indulge

abstinence (SYN) avoidance, self-restraint, temperance (ANT) indulgence

abstract (SYN) indefinite, theoretical, conceptual, summary, synopsis (ANT) actual, concrete, applied

absurd (SYN) ridiculous, illogical, irrational, ludicrous, foolish (ANT) sensible, reasonable, logical

absurdity (SYN) folly, nonsense, silliness, insanity

abundance (SYN) bounty, profusion, plenty, plethora, riot (ANT) scarcity

abundant (SYN) ample, copious, plentiful, teeming, prolific (ANT) scarce, sparse, rare, insufficient

abuse (SYN) harm, maltreatment, exploitation, desecration, dishonor, violate, insult (ANT) respect, honor

abusive (SYN) offensive, disparaging, derogatory, violent, cruel, oppressive (ANT) polite, kind, respectful

abysmal (SYN) dreadful, terrible, dire, woeful, awful, infinite, deep

abyss (SYN) void, pit, gulf, chasm, hole

academic (SYN) scholarly, educational, intellectual, studious (ANT) illiterate, ignorant

academy (SYN) school, institute, college

acceleration (SYN) hastening, quickening, speeding up (ANT) deceleration, slowing, retardation

accent (SYN) inflection, pronunciation, emphasis, stress, accentuate, underscore

accept (SYN) receive, gain, admit, recognize, believe (ANT) decline, reject, refuse

acceptance (SYN) acknowledgement, acquiescence, compliance, receipt, taking (ANT) denial, refusal, rejection

access (SYN) entry, admission, admittance

accessible (SYN) open, approachable, comprehensible, attainable, nearby, handy (ANT) inaccessible, closed, unreachable

accessory (SYN) addition, attachment, associate, accomplice, co-conspirator accident (SYN) mishap, calamity, collision, crash, chance, luck, coincidence

acclaim (SYN) celebrate, applaud, salute, commendation, praise (ANT) criticize, berate, ridicule, criticism

acclimate (SYN) adapt, adjust, habituate

accommodate (SYN) house, lodge, assist, oblige, comply, modify (ANT) hinder, inconvenience

accommodation (SYN) housing, board, shelter

accompany (SYN) join, escort, attend, come with, go together with

accomplice (SYN) assistant, partner, collaborator, henchman, partner in crime

accomplish (SYN) complete, achieve, execute, realize, attain

accomplishment (SYN) triumph, exploit, achievement, conclusion, fulfillment

accord (SYN) agreement, unison, conform, correspond, tally (ANT) opposition, disagreement, differ

accost (SYN) greet, salute, confront, hail

account (SYN) report, description, explanation, value, significance, ledger, statement, register

accrue (SYN) increase, accumulate, collect, gather, grow (ANT) decrease, lessen

accumulate (SYN) amass, store, build up, stockpile (ANT) disperse

accumulation (SYN) collection, pile, stock, hoard, concentration

accuracy (SYN) exactness, precision, correctness, authenticity, truth (ANT) inaccuracy

accurate (SYN) correct, unerring, exact, certain, precise (ANT) inaccurate, incorrect, false

accusation (SYN) allegation, charge, indictment, incrimination, assertion

accuse (SYN) blame, charge, implicate, incriminate (ANT) absolve, exonerate

accustom (SYN) adapt, familiarize, acclimate, habituate

ache (SYN) hurt, cramp, throb, pain, soreness, tenderness

achieve (SYN) attain, fulfill, gain, obtain, realize, accomplish

achievement (SYN) accomplishment, feat, realization, completion, triumph

acknowledge (SYN) concede, grant, admit, recognize (ANT) deny, ignore, reject

acknowledgement (SYN) acceptance, confession, greeting, salutation, appreciation, credit (ANT) denial, repudiation

acquaint (SYN) inform, familiarize, introduce

acquaintance (SYN) associate, contact, association, relationship, knowledge, experience

acquiesce (SYN) submit, comply, yield, assent, surrender (ANT) object, protest

acquire (SYN) receive, get, gain, secure, obtain (ANT) lose, forfeit, give up

acquisition (SYN) purchase, addition, possession, earning, obtaining (ANT) loss

acquit (SYN) clear, release, vindicate, exonerate, absolve, pardon (ANT) blame, condemn, convict

acquittal (SYN) absolution, liberation, release, pardoning, forgiveness

acrimony (SYN) rancor, bitterness, resentment, malevolence (ANT) kindness, tenderness, goodwill

act (SYN) behave, conduct oneself, move, take steps, deed, performance, pretense

action (SYN) movement, activity, act, exploit, undertaking, conduct (ANT) inaction, idleness

active (SYN) energetic, alert, lively, in operation, working (ANT) inactive, inert, idle

activity (SYN) action, exercise, movement, pursuit, diversion

actor (SYN) player, thespian, performer

actual (SYN) real, tangible, genuine, definite, concrete (ANT) imaginary, false, unreal

actually (SYN) really, indeed, literally, truly, as a matter of fact

acumen (SYN) insight, cleverness, judgment, wisdom, discernment

acute (SYN) sharp, severe, critical, urgent, keen, perceptive (ANT) dull, mild, chronic, obtuse

adage (SYN) saying, proverb, maxim

adamant (SYN) firm, resolute, uncompromising, stubborn, persistent (ANT) yielding, flexible, wavering, unresolved

adapt (SYN) adjust, change, conform, accommodate, modify, alter

adaptation (SYN) modification, transformation, adjustment, familiarization, acclimatization

add (SYN) count up, total, include, augment, increase, compound (ANT) subtract, remove, deduct

addict (SYN) fan, devotee, enthusiast, abuser, junkie

addiction (SYN) dependence, obsession, craving, habit

additional (SYN) extra, added, further, supplementary, spare

address (SYN) location, whereabouts, speech, lecture, oration, hail, speak to

adept (SYN) skillful, accomplished, proficient, expert, consummate (ANT) inept, awkward, unskilled

adequate (SYN) enough, sufficient, satisfactory, passable, acceptable (ANT) insufficient, inadequate, useless, lacking adhere (SYN) cling, hold fast, stick, bond (ANT) separate, loosen

adherent (SYN) follower, disciple, fan, devotee

adhesive (SYN) sticky, cohesive, glue, paste, cement

adieu (SYN) goodbye, farewell

adjacent (SYN) next, beside, neighboring, touching, bordering (ANT) distant, far, separate

adjoin (SYN) connect, link, meet, attach

adjourn (SYN) suspend, delay, interrupt, postpone, recess

adjust (SYN) alter, modify, rearrange, adapt, assimilate, attune

adjustable (SYN) flexible, movable, alterable, variable, versatile (ANT) inflexible, rigid, immovable

adjustment (SYN) alteration, tuning, tailoring, adaptation

ad-lib (SYN) improvise, make up, extemporize (ANT) recite

administer (SYN) give, dispense, perform, manage, supervise, run

administration (SYN) direction, control, management, regulation, leadership, government

administrator (SYN) executive, manager, official, director, coordinator

admirable (SYN) commendable, praiseworthy, exemplary,

respectable, deserving (ANT) deplorable, despicable, dishonorable, abominable

admiration (SYN) esteem, appreciation, regard, respect, approval (ANT) contempt, disregard, scorn

admire (SYN) value, marvel at, delight in, prize, respect, revere (ANT) dislike, abhor, detest, loathe

admissible (SYN) acceptable, allowable, tolerable, approved, passable (ANT) inadmissible, wrong, unjust, unfair

admission (SYN) entry, admittance, access, confession, disclosure, revelation

admit (SYN) receive, take in, divulge, concede, acknowledge (ANT) exclude, reject, refuse, deny

admonish (SYN) chide, berate, reprimand, rebuke, punish

ado (SYN) excitement, commotion, fuss

adolescent (SYN) juvenile, young, immature, teenager, minor (ANT) mature

adopt (SYN) foster, choose, embrace, assume, accept (ANT) reject, refuse

adore (SYN) love, cherish, prize, worship, treasure (ANT) hate, despise, detest

adorn (SYN) decorate, festoon, embellish, ornament, enhance

adrift (SYN) afloat, unmoored, aimless, lost, disoriented

adult (SYN) grown-up, mature, ripe
(ANT) child, adolescent, immature

advance (SYN) progress, breakthrough,
headway, proceed, boost, evolve
(ANT) retreat, regress, hinder, halt,
cessation

advantage (SYN) benefit, bonus,
blessing, edge, upper hand (ANT)
disadvantage, obstacle

advantageous (SYN) helpful, valuable,
worthwhile, beneficial, useful (ANT)
useless, disadvantageous, harmful

advent (SYN) approach, arrival

adventure (SYN) expedition, experience,
exploit, excitement, thrills, action

adversary (SYN) enemy, rival,
opponent, foe, competitor (ANT)
friend, ally

adverse (SYN) negative, hostile,
unfavorable, harmful, opposing
(ANT) favorable, beneficial,
encouraging

adversity (SYN) difficulty, affliction,
hardship, misfortune, trouble

advertise (SYN) announce, promote,
publicize, broadcast, tout

advertisement (SYN) commercial,
announcement, promotion, plug

advice (SYN) guidance, counsel,
recommendation, suggestion,
instruction

advisable (SYN) sensible, wise, prudent,
recommendable, proper (ANT)
inadvisable, unwise, ill-considered

advise (SYN) counsel, suggest,
recommend, caution, urge, appraise,
inform, report

advisor (SYN) confidante, counselor,
guide, mentor, consultant

advocate (SYN) support, champion,
encourage, proponent, defender,
spokesman (ANT) oppose, advise
against, critic

aesthetic (SYN) artistic, tasteful (ANT)
distasteful, crude

affair (SYN) event, happening, incident,
matter, business

affect (SYN) influence, impact, alter,
move, touch, feign, adopt, simulate

affectation (SYN) insincerity, pretense,
show, posturing, airs

affection (SYN) tenderness, fondness,
warmth, love, attachment, friendship
(ANT) aversion, animosity,
indifference, antipathy

affectionate (SYN) kind, doting, tender,
adoring, demonstrative (ANT) cold,
distant, apathetic, uncaring

affiliate (SYN) join, associate, link,
unite, connect, align, merge (ANT)
divide, separate

affiliation (SYN) connection,
association, union, bond

affinity (SYN) attraction, partiality,
relationship, similarity, empathy,
rapport (ANT) difference,
dissimilarity, aversion

affirm (SYN) confirm, declare, state, attest, swear (ANT) deny, refute, oppose, contradict

affirmation (SYN) testimony, certification, confirmation, oath

affirmative (SYN) positive, concurring, assenting, favorable, corroborative (ANT) negative, unfavorable

afflict (SYN) trouble, distress, plague, burden, beset

affliction (SYN) suffering, adversity, ordeal, trial, misfortune (ANT) comfort, relief

affluence (SYN) wealth, prosperity, riches, opulence (ANT) poverty, need

afford (SYN) spare, manage, provide, offer, render, supply

afraid (SYN) fearful, scared, nervous, apprehensive, reluctant, hesitant, sorry (ANT) bold, confident, brave, fearless, glad

after (SYN) following, later, behind, subsequently (ANT) before, ahead

aftermath (SYN) effects, wake, result, consequences, repercussions

again (SYN) once more, anew, another time, also, moreover

against (SYN) opposed to, averse to, abutting, in contact with

age (SYN) mature, grow old, era, period, senility, seniority (ANT) youth

aged (SYN) old, antique, ancient, elderly (ANT) young

agency (SYN) business, organization, firm, bureau, office

agenda (SYN) schedule, plan, program, timetable, calendar

agent (SYN) representative, emissary, vehicle, instrument, force

aggravate (SYN) inflame, irritate, worsen, annoy, provoke (ANT) soothe, relieve, improve

aggregate (SYN) total, sum, combination, composite, combination (ANT) part, individual

aggression (SYN) hostility, belligerence, violence, force, attack, assault

aggressive (SYN) offensive, militant, confrontational, pugnacious, quarrelsome, assertive, pushy, forceful (ANT) shy, retiring, peaceful

agile (SYN) nimble, spry, swift, alert, clever, sharp (ANT) clumsy, awkward, dull

agitate (SYN) upset, fluster, unnerve, stir, shake (ANT) calm, soothe, quiet

agitation (SYN) turmoil, upheaval, turbulence, commotion, disquiet

agony (SYN) suffering, anguish, torture, pain, torment (ANT) comfort, pleasure

agreeable (SYN) amenable, congenial, affable, enjoyable, gratifying (ANT) unpleasant, disagreeable, obnoxious, contentious

agreement (SYN) understanding, pact, consistency, accord, compliance, consent (ANT) disagreement, opposition, discord

agriculture (SYN) farming, cultivation

ahead (SYN) leading, in front, forward, before (ANT) behind, trailing

aid (SYN) help, assistance, relief, cooperation, serve, sustain (ANT) hindrance, hinder, obstruct

aide (SYN) helper, assistant, advisor, deputy

ailment (SYN) illness, affliction, malady, complaint, disorder

aim (SYN) intend, attempt, point, direct, target, objective, purpose, aspiration

air (SYN) atmosphere, sky, draft, breeze, manner, appearance, voice, publicize, ventilate, freshen

airborne (SYN) flying, hovering (ANT) grounded

aisle (SYN) corridor, passageway, path, lane

ajar (SYN) open, askew (ANT) closed

alacrity (SYN) readiness, eagerness, enthusiasm, zeal, speed

alarm (SYN) panic, anxiety, alert, siren, warning, startle, disconcert (ANT) composure, security, calmness, reassure

alcoholic (SYN) strong, intoxicating, distilled, fermented, brewed (ANT) non-alcoholic

alert (SYN) watchful, attentive, prepared, warn, notify, signal (ANT) asleep, unobservant

alias (SYN) pseudonym, nom de plume, pen name, stage name, assumed name

alibi (SYN) excuse, explanation, justification, story

alien (SYN) exotic, strange, unfamiliar, foreigner, stranger, extraterrestrial (ANT) familiar, ordinary, kindred, native

alienate (SYN) estrange, isolate, distance, separate

alight (SYN) descend, disembark, land, perch, flaming, blazing, brilliant

alignment (SYN) adjustment, straightening up, unison, affiliation

alike (SYN) similar, analogous, identical, uniformly, comparably (ANT) different, unlike, dissimilar

alive (SYN) living, existing, animated, vivacious (ANT) dead, deceased, lifeless

all (SYN) whole, entire, every, each, completely, utterly

allegation (SYN) claim, accusation, charge, assertion, contention

allege (SYN) state, declare, claim, accuse, present (ANT) deny, refute, contradict allegiance (SYN) loyalty, fidelity, devotion, faithfulness, adherence (ANT) disloyalty, treachery, treason

allegory (SYN) symbol, myth, parable, story, fable

allergy (SYN) sensitivity, susceptibility

alleviate (SYN) ease, lessen, relieve, moderate, allay (ANT) intensify, aggravate

alley (ANT) passageway, lane

alliance (SYN) union, coalition, confederation, league, marriage, partnership

allocate (SYN) allot, designate, earmark, distribute, dole out

allot (SYN) divide, apportion, budget, assign, dispense, deal

allotment (SYN) portion, allocation, ration, quota

allow (SYN) permit, approve, sanction, concede, acknowledge, set aside, reserve (ANT) forbid, prevent, deny, refuse

allowance (SYN) quota, share, limit, ration

alloy (SYN) mixture, amalgam, composite, hybrid, combination

allude (SYN) mention, refer, hint, imply, intimate

allusion (SYN) reference, suggestion, insinuation

ally (SYN) partner, accomplice, associate, unite, collaborate (ANT) opponent, enemy, split

almighty (SYN) supreme, omnipotent, absolute, all-powerful (ANT) weak, powerless, feeble

almost (SYN) nearly, just about, not quite, practically, virtually (ANT) exactly, completely

alms (SYN) donation, charity, contribution

alone (SYN) isolated, solitary, unaccompanied, solo, lonely (ANT) together, accompanied, loved

aloof (SYN) distant, unfriendly, withdrawn, detached, unapproachable (ANT) involved, warm, cordial, outgoing

aloud (SYN) audibly, intelligibly, out loud (ANT) silently, quietly, noiselessly

already (SYN) before, previously, earlier

also (SYN) in addition, further, moreover, as well, too

alter (SYN) change, amend, revise, adjust, transform (ANT) preserve, keep, retain

alteration (SYN) modification, alteration, change, amendment

alternate (SYN) rotate, fluctuate, take turns, switch, interchange

alternative (SYN) choice, option, possibility, substitute, different although (SYN) even though, albeit, while, despite the fact that

altitude (SYN) height

altogether (SYN) completely, entirely, collectively, as a whole, all told (ANT) partly, partially, somewhat

altruistic (SYN) generous, charitable, humanitarian, benevolent, selfless

always (SYN) continually, forever, perpetually, eternally, unfailingly (ANT) never, sometimes

amass (SYN) collect, gather, accumulate, compile, assemble (ANT) disperse, scatter, spend

amateur (SYN) beginner, apprentice, novice (ANT) professional, expert

amaze (SYN) astonish, surprise, stun, astound, stagger (ANT) bore

amazement (SYN) wonder, bewilderment, astonishment, awe, speechlessness

ambassador (SYN) envoy, diplomat, agent, representative

ambience (SYN) atmosphere, surroundings, mood, air

ambiguous (SYN) vague, unclear, obscure, cryptic, uncertain (ANT) clear, explicit, definite, plain, unmistakable

ambition (SYN) goal, objective, drive, zeal, desire (ANT) indifference, resignation, laziness, apathy

ambitious (SYN) motivated, eager, striving, determined, challenging, formidable (ANT) satisfied, content, indifferent

ambivalent (SYN) wavering, uncertain, equivocal, indecisive, unsure

ambush (SYN) trap, attack, ensnare, surprise

ameliorate (SYN) improve, better (ANT) worsen, deteriorate

amenable (SYN) receptive, agreeable, responsive, acquiescent (ANT) resistant

amend (SYN) fix, remedy, repair, improve, correct (ANT) harm, impair

amendment (SYN) change, reform, modification, clarification, addendum

amenity (SYN) luxury, comfort, convenience, service, courtesy

amiable (SYN) pleasant, friendly, cordial, likeable, affable (ANT) hostile, unfriendly, rude, morose, surly, cross

amid (SYN) amongst, in the middle of, surrounded by

ammunition (SYN) explosives, rounds, shells, armaments, bullets

amnesty (SYN) forgiveness, absolution, dispensation, reprieve, release, pardon

among (SYN) in the midst of, amid, between, in the company of

amount (SYN) quantity, number, magnitude, sum, total

ample (SYN) plenty, abundant, profuse, sufficient, lavish, full (ANT) meager, insufficient, inadequate, limited

amplify (SYN) magnify, intensify, strengthen, expand, elaborate (ANT) condense, reduce, decrease

amputate (SYN) remove, sever, cut off, remove, separate (ANT) join, fasten, connect

amulet (SYN) good luck charm, talisman

amuse (SYN) entertain, delight, please, occupy, distract (ANT) bore, tire, irritate

amusement (SYN) enjoyment, entertainment, leisure, relaxation, diversion, fun

analogous (SYN) similar, alike, parallel, corresponding, akin (ANT) incomparable, unlike, unrelated, different, incongruous

analogy (SYN) comparison, resemblance correlation, similarity

analysis (SYN) examination, scrutiny, investigation, study, evaluation

analyze (SYN) research, evaluate, dissect, inspect, probe

anarchist (SYN) rebel, insurgent, revolutionary, terrorist

anarchy (SYN) turmoil, riot, lawlessness, disorder, commotion (ANT) peace, calm, order, regulation

anatomy (SYN) structure, framework, composition, inquiry, examination

ancestor (SYN) predecessor, forefather, parent

anchor (SYN) secure, fasten, attach, fix

ancient (SYN) old, antique, timeworn, elderly, primitive (ANT) new, modern, young, contemporary

anecdote (SYN) story, tale, yarn, narrative, reminiscence

anemic (SYN) pale, ashen, colorless, sickly, weak (ANT) ruddy, flushed, healthy, sanguine

anesthetic (SYN) painkiller, analgesic, numbing, dulling, sedative

angel (SYN) cherub, seraph (ANT) demon, devil

anger (SYN) rage, fury, wrath, displease, infuriate, rile (ANT) pleasure, patience, placate, pacify

angle (SYN) corner, point, slope, approach, standpoint, position,

angry (SYN) mad, furious, incensed, irate, seething (ANT) pleased, calm

anguish (SYN) agony, torment, pain, misery, heartache (ANT) comfort, joy, pleasure, happiness, relief

animal (SYN) creature, beast, barbarian, savage, monster, carnal

animate (SYN) stimulate, enliven, rouse, energize, living, alive, breathing (ANT) depress, inanimate, dead animosity (SYN) enmity, hostility, hatred, malice, resentment (ANT) friendship, goodwill, affability

annals (SYN) records, archives, history, chronicles, accounts

annex (SYN) join, connect, acquire, addition, supplement

annihilate (SYN) destroy, decimate, eradicate, obliterate, extinguish (ANT) save, preserve, create

announce (SYN) proclaim, broadcast, reveal, declare, advertise (ANT) suppress, conceal, stifle

announcement (SYN) report, statement, declaration, bulletin, message

annoy (SYN) bother, irritate, disturb, trouble, vex (ANT) console, please, soothe, gratify

annoyance (SYN) nuisance, irritation, bother, hassle

annual (SYN) yearly, once a year

annul (SYN) cancel, invalidate, negate, repeal

anoint (SYN) sanctify, consecrate, bless, baptize, oil

anomaly (SYN) exception, inconsistency, irregularity, oddity, aberration, quirk (ANT) normality

anonymous (SYN) nameless, unknown, unidentified, unsigned (ANT) known, named, identified

answer (SYN) reply, explanation, solution, retort, rejoinder (ANT) question, ask

antagonist (SYN) rival, opponent, foe

antagonize (SYN) offend, annoy, provoke, alienate, intimidate (ANT) pacify, disarm, soothe, befriend

antecedent (SYN) cause, precedent, past

anthem (SYN) song, hymn, carol

anticipate (YSN) expect, await, look forward to, predict, forecast

antidote (SYN) cure, remedy, countermeasure, palliative

antipathy (SYN) aversion, enmity, hatred, repulsion, animus, loathing (ANT) affinity, liking, fondness, admiration, sympathy

antiquated (SYN) old, dated, outmoded, behind the times, obsolete (ANT) modern, new, fresh

antique (SYN) heirloom, relic, antiquity, vintage, collectable, classic (ANT) modern, recent, new

antiseptic (SYN) hygienic, pure, sterile, sanitary, purifier, disinfectant

antisocial (SYN) withdrawn, uncommunicative, disruptive, menacing, rebellious (ANT) outgoing, friendly, gregarious, sociable, acceptable

antithesis (SYN) opposite, inverse, reverse, contrary

anxiety (SYN) uneasiness, apprehension, dread, angst, misgiving, trepidation (ANT) calm, security, confidence

anxious (SYN) concerned, nervous, impatient, eager, worried (ANT) certain, assured, unconcerned, tranquil

anyway (SYN) nevertheless, in any case

apart (SYN) separate, aside, solitary, unique, to pieces, asunder (ANT) together

apartment (SYN) room, flat, quarters, suite, residence

apathy (SYN) indifference, passivity, unconcern, cool, lack of enthusiasm (ANT) interest, passion, emotion

ape (SYN) imitate, mimic, copy

apex (SYN) pinnacle, climax, crown, peak, summit (ANT) depth, base, nadir

aplomb (SYN) confidence, composure, poise, self-possession (ANT) uncertainty, apprehension

apocalyptic (SYN) visionary, prophetic

apologetic (SYN) sorry, remorseful, contrite, repentant, penitent (ANT) unremorseful

apologize (SYN) say sorry, express regret, ask for pardon

apology (SYN) regrets, excuse, confession, acknowledgment

apostle (SYN) evangelist, missionary, supporter, advocate, follower, disciple

apotheosis (SYN) transformation, exultation, deification

appall (SYN) horrify, shock, dismay, disgust, offend (ANT) please, enchant, delight

apparatus (SYN) equipment, mechanism, device, system, structure

apparel (SYN) clothing, clothes

apparent (SYN) obvious, evident, discernable, seeming, superficial (ANT) unclear, invisible, indistinct, real

apparently (SYN) seemingly, outwardly, ostensibly

apparition (SYN) ghost, spirit, phantom

appeal (SYN) request, plead, attraction, allure, charm

appear (SYN) emerge, turn up, surface, seem, look (ANT) vanish, disappear

appearance (SYN) air, looks, impression, illusion, manifestation, arrival, development (ANT) departure, absence, disappearance

appease (SYN) placate, satisfy, mollify, ease, placate (ANT) provoke, inflame

appendix (SYN) supplement, adjunct, addendum

appetite (SYN) hunger, desire, craving, longing, eagerness, enthusiasm applaud (SYN) clap, cheer, praise, compliment, salute (ANT) boo, condemn, disapprove, criticize

applause (SYN) cheers, hand, ovation

appliance (SYN) machine, device, mechanism, tool, apparatus

applicable (SYN) relevant, fitting, suitable, pertinent, appropriate (ANT) useless, irrelevant

applicant (SYN) candidate, inquirer

application (SYN) request, petition, effort, dedication, diligence, use, implementation

apply (SYN) put on, smear, paint, pertain, relate, employ, utilize, bid, solicit, seek

appoint (SYN) delegate, nominate, elect, choose, establish, furnish

appointment (SYN) meeting, engagement, selection, assignment, position

appraisal (SYN) assessment, evaluation, estimate, opinion

appraise (SYN) value, judge, gauge, consider, review, rate

appreciate (SYN) value, treasure, prize, realize, understand, increase, gain, grow (ANT) scorn, disparage, depreciate, decrease

appreciation (SYN) gratitude, acknowledgement, thankfulness, recognition, growth (ANT) ingratitude, disapproval

apprehend (SYN) arrest, capture, seize, grasp, understand, comprehend

apprehension (SYN) anxiety, disquiet, trepidation, awareness, perception (ANT) confidence, composure

apprentice (SYN) beginner, novice, student, trainee

apprise (SYN) inform, notify, acquaint (ANT) hide, conceal

approach (SYN) move towards, come near, method, technique, strategy, advance, proposal, appeal (ANT) leave, depart

approachable (SYN) friendly, affable, welcoming, accessible, reachable (ANT) aloof, cold, distant, inaccessible

appropriate (SYN) fitting, suitable, opportune, allocate, apportion (ANT) inappropriate, wrong, improper

approval (SYN) consent, endorsement, acceptance, blessing, respect, admiration (ANT) disapproval, refusal, rejection, censure

approve (SYN) allow, authorize, permit, favor, regard highly (ANT) disapprove

approximate (SYN) estimated, rough, inexact, approach, reach (ANT) precise, exact

approximately (SYN) about, almost, nearly, more or less (ANT) exactly, precisely, just

apropos (SYN) appropriate, fitting

apt (SYN) inclined, disposed, bright, gifted, talented, suitable, relevant (ANT) unlikely, slow, inappropriate

aptitude (SYN) talent, capability, girt, proficiency

aqueduct (SYN) waterway, pipe, canal

arbiter (SYN) judge, referee, mediator, authority

arbitrary (SYN) random, whimsical, unpredictable, subjective, capricious (ANT) reasoned, logical, objective

arbitration (SYN) judgment, determination, intervention, mediation

arch (SYN) curve, arc, bend, bow, span, bridge

archaic (SYN) ancient, antique, primitive, obsolete, out-dated (ANT) modern, new, updated, contemporary

architect (SYN) designer, planner, creator, author, inventor

architecture (SYN) building, design, construction, style, structure, framework

archive (SYN) repository, registry, records, files, history

ardent (SYN) passionate, intense, enthusiastic, zealous (ANT) indifferent, half-hearted, apathetic, nonchalant

ardor (SYN) fervor, spirit, eagerness, zeal, avidity (ANT) coolness, indifference, disinterest

arduous (SYN) tough, difficult, strenuous, challenging, grueling (ANT) easy, simple

area (SYN) region, zone, space, section, realm, sector

arena (SYN) ring, stadium, amphitheater, domain, territory, scene

argue (SYN) debate, dispute, claim, contend, quarrel, bicker (ANT) agree, harmonize, concur

argument (SYN) disagreement, feud, altercation, controversy, discussion, logic, reasoning, grounds

arid (SYN) dry, desert, parched (ANT) humid, damp, wet, moist

arise (SYN) happen, ensue, surface, occur, result, get up, stand up (ANT) disappear, sink

aristocrat (SYN) noble, patrician, lord, lady (ANT) commoner, peasant

arm (SYN) limb, appendage, equip, furnish, provide, supply, division, branch (ANT) disarm

armaments (SYN) weapons, ammunition, guns, weaponry

armistice (SYN) truce, ceasefire, peace

armor (SYN) protection, shield, covering

arms (SYN) weaponry, guns, artillery, munitions

army (SYN) troops, soldiers, military, infantry, crowd, horde, throng, multitude aroma (SYN) scent, smell, fragrance, perfume, bouquet, nose

around (SYN) encircling, surrounding, about, approximately, roughly, nearby (ANT) distant, precisely

arouse (SYN) stimulate, excite, kindle, cause, agitate, awaken (ANT) allay, pacify, calm, alleviate

arrange (SYN) contrive, organize, position, sort, out, score, orchestrate

arrangement (SYN) plan, provision, deal, agreement, structure, organization, version, interpretation

array (SYN) arrange, display, parade, decorate, adorn, range, assortment

arrest (SYN) capture, apprehend, stop, halt, obstruct, detention, seizure (ANT) release, let go, free

arrival (SYN) entrance, appearance, approach, advent, dawn (ANT) departure, end, disappearance

arrive (SYN) come, appear, reach, attain (ANT) leave, depart

arrogance (SYN) pride, conceit, insolence, disdain, superiority (ANT) humility, modesty

arrogant (SYN) haughty, condescending, self-important, cocky, presumptuous, cavalier (ANT) modest, humble, self-effacing

arrow (SYN) dart, shaft, pointer, indicator

arsenal (SYN) storehouse, stockpile, armory, store, supply

art (SYN) skill, craft, mastery, design, aesthetics, composition

artful (SYN) cunning, crafty, sly, wily (ANT) artless, innocent, naive

article (SYN) object, thing, report, account, feature

articulate (SYN) express, voice, communicate, eloquent, persuasive (ANT) inarticulate, clumsy, unintelligible

artifice (SYN) trick, tactic, subterfuge, cleverness, ingenuity, skill (ANT) sincerity, honesty

artificial (SYN) fake, synthetic, contrived, insincere, phony, imitation (ANT) real, genuine, natural

artillery (SYN) canons

artisan (SYN) craftsman, artist

artistic (SYN) creative, expressive, imaginative, aesthetic, ornamental, beautiful, tasteful

artless (SYN) frank, candid, straightforward, guileless, innocent, natural (ANT) deceptive, craft, cunning, skilled, insincere

ascend (SYN) climb, mount, scale, progress, rise (ANT) descend, lower, fall

ascension (SYN) rising

ascent (SYN) upward movement, climb, gradient, incline, rise (ANT) descent, fall ascertain (SYN) discover, learn, establish, deduce, determine

ascetic (SYN) self-disciplined, austere, abstinent, self-denying

ashamed (SYN) mortified, embarrassed, humiliated, remorseful, contrite (ANT) pleased, proud

ashore (SYN) aground, on land

aside (SYN) apart, privately, annotation, parenthesis

ask (SYN) inquire, question, request, plead, invite, summon (ANT) answer, order

askew (SYN) crooked, off-center, awry, disordered, out of place (ANT) orderly, neat, straight

asleep (SYN) sleeping, slumbering, dormant (ANT) awake

aspect (SYN) feature, facet, detail, perspective, standpoint, appearance, air, expression

asphyxiate (SYN) suffocate, smother, strangle, choke

aspiration (SYN) aim, goal, objective, ambition, target, dream

aspire (SYN) seek, hope, aim, wish

assassinate (SYN) kill, slay, murder, eliminate

assault (SYN) attack, beat, strike, onslaught, invasion

assemble (SYN) build, construct, gather, collect, muster, convene (ANT)

scatter, disperse, disassemble, dismantle

assembly (SYN) conference, gathering, congress, construction, fabrication

assert (SYN) declare, claim, affirm, insist, uphold

assertive (SYN) confident, forceful, bold, decisive, commanding (ANT) timid, meek, unassuming, passive

assess (SYN) evaluate, appraise, judge, estimate, determine, value

assessment (SYN) appraisal, valuation, rating, opinion, charge, fee, toll

asset (SYN) property, possession, resource, capital, benefit, advantage, blessing (ANT) liability

assign (SYN) designate, choose, allocate, attribute, ascribe

assignment (SYN) task, duty, appointment, mission, responsibility

assimilate (SYN) absorb, incorporate, adjust, adapt, habituate, conform

assist (SYN) help, aid, support, facilitate, encourage (ANT) hinder, impede

assistance (SYN) aid, cooperation, backing, reinforcement (ANT) discouragement

assistant (SYN) helper, aide, associate

associate (SYN) partner, colleague, companion, attach, affiliate, connect, mingle, consort (ANT) separate, avoid association (SYN) alliance, group, bond, organization, relationship, connection

assortment (SYN) variety, medley, array, mixture, selection

assuage (SYN) relieve, pacify, ease, moderate, alleviate (ANT) intensify, worsen, increase

assume (SYN) presume, infer, suppose, feign, adopt, affect (ANT) know, doubt

assumption (SYN) conjecture, belief, hypothesis, taking, shouldering (ANT) knowledge, certainty, proof

assurance (SYN) confidence, certainty, conviction, poise, pledge, guarantee,

assure (SYN) vow, certify, confirm, secure, convince, persuade

astonish (SYN) amaze, astound, stun, confound, surprise (ANT) bore, tire

astonishment (SYN) awe, bewilderment, wonderment, consternation

astound (SYN) impress, stagger, surprise, dumbfound, flabbergast

astray (SYN) adrift, lost, off course, missing

astronomical (SYN) huge, vast, immense

astute (SYN) clever, intelligent, sharp, perceptive, shrewd, bright (ANT) unintelligent, stupid

asylum (SYN) refuge, harbor, sanctuary, shelter, protection, immunity

atheism (SYM) disbelief, skepticism, incredulity (ANT) faith, belief

athletic (SYN) fit, active, strong, muscular, powerful (ANT) puny, weak, frail, feeble

atom (SYN) particle, molecule, bit, speck, trace

atrocious (SYN) cruel, brutal, barbaric, monstrous, savage, dreadful, miserable (ANT) admirable, kind, benevolent, superb

atrocity (SYN) crime, outrage, wickedness, viciousness, inhumanity

attach (SYN) fasten, connect, secure, assign, attribute (ANT) disconnect, remove, detach

attachment (SYN) fondness, affinity, affection, accessory, supplement

attack (SYN) assault, raid, criticize, abuse, violate (ANT) protect, defend

attain (SYN) achieve, obtain, fulfill, reach, accomplish, realize

attempt (SYN) try, endeavor, strive, venture, aim

attend (SYN) be present at, tend, accompany, wait on

attendance (SYN) presence, appearance, turnout, crowd

attendant (SYN) assistant, aide, companion, servant

attention (SYN) concentration, thought, notice, regard, concern, care (ANT) disregard, neglect, omission, oversight

attentive (SYN) observant, aware, mindful, thoughtful, considerate (ANT) inattentive, distracted, unaware

attire (SYN) clothing, garb, garments, apparel

attitude (SYN) disposition, outlook, perspective, stance, viewpoint

attract (SYN) allure, charm, entice, appeal to, tempt (ANT) repel, repulse

attraction (SYN) fascination, magnetism, pull, draw, affinity

attractive (SYN) appealing, fetching, lovely, handsome, stunning (ANT) unattractive, ugly, unpleasant, uninviting

attribute (SYN) feature, trait, element, characteristic, ascribe, credit

audacity (SYN) courage, bravery, daring, recklessness, nerve, impertinence

audible (SYN) perceptible, distinct, discernable, clear (ANT) faint, inaudible, imperceptible

audience (SYN) crowd, gallery, public, interview, meeting

augment (SYN) increase, enhance, expand, supplement (ANT) decrease, reduce, abate

augur (SYN) predict, prophesy, foretell

auspicious (SYN) bright, encouraging, promising, fortunate, felicitous (ANT) inauspicious, hopeless, unfavorable

austere (SYN) stern, solemn, forbidding, plain, simple, stark (ANT) friendly, luxurious, ornate

authentic (SYN) genuine, real, legitimate, valid, truthful (ANT) inauthentic, fake, counterfeit

authenticate (SYN) validate, verify, certify, substantiate (ANT) disprove, discredit

author (SYN) writer, creator, producer, architect

authoritative (SYN) reliable, accurate, definitive, dependable, commanding, assertive (ANT) questionable, dubious, timid

authority (SYN) power, influence, control, influence, expert, specialist

authorize (SYN) sanction, permit, warrant, allow, approve (ANT) forbid, prohibit

autocrat (SYN) dictator, tyrant, absolutist

automatic (SYN) mechanized, involuntary, unconscious, instinctive (ANT) manual, deliberate, conscious

autonomous (SYN) independent, sovereign, self-governing, free

auxiliary (SYN) reserve, secondary, supporting, additional, emergency (ANT) primary, regular, main, chief available (SYN) on hand, accessible, ready, free, unoccupied (ANT) unavailable, busy

avalanche (SYN) landslide, deluge, barrage, wave, torrent

avarice (SYN) greed, materialism, covetousness, self-seeking (ANT) giving, selflessness, generosity

avenge (SYN) retaliate, repay, pay back, settle, vindicate (ANT) forgive, pardon

avenue (SYN) street, road, course, path, route

average (SYN) normal, standard, typical, mean, norm (ANT) abnormal, unusual, extraordinary, exceptional

aversion (SYN) dislike, loathing, abhorrence, disinclination, distaste (ANT) love, affection, attachment

avert (SYN) turn away, avoid, prevent, ward off (ANT) allow

avid (SYN) enthusiastic, eager, fanatical, passionate, ardent (ANT) apathetic, indifferent

avocation (SYN) hobby, leisure activity

avoid (SYN) dodge, shirk, elude, escape, (ANT) encounter, face, confront

await (SYN) anticipate, expect, look forward to

awake (SYN) wakeful, conscious, alert, vigilant, rouse, wake up (ANT) asleep, oblivious, unaware

award (SYN) recognition, prize, bestow, give, grant

aware (SYN) knowledgeable, alert, mindful, cognizant, informed (ANT) unaware, unconscious, ignorant

away (SYN) off, elsewhere, absent, gone

awe (SYN) wonder, amazement, reverence, impress, astonish, dread

awesome (SYN) breathtaking, staggering, imposing, formidable, magnificent

awful (SYN) horrible, appalling, dreadful, horrendous, abominable (ANT) delightful, excellent, superb, wonderful

awkward (SYN) clumsy, uncoordinated, unmanageable, cumbersome, embarrassing, delicate (ANT) graceful, lithe, dexterous, coordinated, comfortable

axiom (SYN) rule, precept, principle, aphorism, adage, truism

axle (SYN) shaft, rob, pin, pivot, spindle

B

babble (SYN) chatter, gibberish, nonsense, prattle

baby (SYN) infant, newborn, child, miniature, small (ANT) adult, grown-up, large, full-sized

back (SYN) rear, reverse, posterior, support, aid, sponsor (ANT) front, fore, face, oppose, inhibit background (SYN) history, circumstances, scene, setting, environment, record, experience (ANT) foreground

backward (SYN) reverse, rearward, downhill, negative, regressive, primitive (ANT) forward, ahead, progressive, developed

bacteria (SYN) microorganisms, pathogens, germs, viruses

bad (SYN) dangerous, harmful, unpleasant, corrupt, wicked, rotten, decayed, unfortunate, distressing (ANT) good, beneficial, virtuous, fresh

badge (SYN) identification, symbol, hallmark, pin, button

baffle (SYN) confound, puzzle, bewilder, stump, confuse (ANT) explain, enlighten, assist

bag (SYN) sack, catch, arrest, trap

baggage (SYN) luggage, belongings, suitcases, history

bail (SYN) security, pledge, guarantee

bait (SYN) lure, incentive, enticement, taunt, goad, tease

balance (SYN) footing, stability, fairness, uniformity, proportion, remainder, difference, level, steady, compare, evaluate (ANT) imbalance, instability, bias, inequity

balcony (SYN) terrace, veranda, gallery, deck

bald (SYN) hairless, smooth, shaven (ANT) hairy

balk (SYN) resist, hesitate, foil, frustrate, thwart

ball (SYN) globe, orb, sphere

ballad (SYN) song, poem

ballast (SYN) counterweight, stabilizer

ballot (SYN) vote, election, polling

balm (SYN) salve, ointment, lotion, comfort, palliative

balmy (SYN) mild, gentle, temperate, summery (ANT) stormy, tempestuous

ban (SYN) bar, prohibit, forbid, restriction, moratorium, expulsion (ANT) permit, allow, legalize

banal (SYN) stale, unimaginative, overused, insipid, trite (ANT) fresh, novel, original, stimulating

band (SYN) group, ensemble, company, posse, strap, cord

bandage (SYN) gauze, dressing, compress, bind, swathe, cover

bandit (SYN) thief, marauder, villain, robber, outlaw

bane (SYN) scourge, curse, ruin, torment

bang (SYN) clap, explosion, blow, slam, hit

banish (SYN) expel, evict, remove, dismiss, exile (ANT) welcome, receive

banister (SYN) railing, handrail,
balustrade

bank (SYN) storehouse, repository,
reserve, stockpile, deposit, shore,
brink, incline, slope, tilt

bankrupt (SYN) ruined, insolvent, broke

banner (SYN) flag, pennant, streamer,
sign

banquet (SYN) feast, meal, dinner

banter (SYN) wordplay, repartee,
teasing, kidding, joke, kid

baptism (SYN) christening, purification

baptize (SYN) bless, consecrate,
christen, initiate, name

bar (SYN) rod, pole, stick, block, hinder,
obstruct, exclude, tavern, saloon
(ANT) allow, permit, include, aid

barb (SYN) spike, quill, thorn, bristle,
insult, gibe, affront

barbaric (SYN) brutal, fierce, savage,
cruel, inhuman, uncivilized, wild
(ANT) gentlemanly, gentle, civilized

bare (SYN) naked, nude, uncovered,
stark, plain, unadorned (ANT)
dressed, covered, decorated,
embellished

barely (SYN) scarcely, only just, hardly

bargain (SYN) giveaway, good value,
negotiate, haggle, agreement, pact

bark (SYN) yap, woof, bellow, yell,
covering, skin (ANT) whisper

baroque (SYN) ornate, elaborate,
adorned (ANT) simple, plain,
unembellished

barracks (SYN) quarters, garrison,
encampment, fort

barrage (SYN) hail, onslaught,
bombardment, shower, avalanche

barren (SYN) sterile, infertile, desolate,
empty, arid (ANT) fertile,
productive, fruitful

barricade (SYN) barrier, obstruction,
roadblock, fortify, defend, seal off

barrier (SYN) fence, wall, blockade,
hurdle, impediment

barter (SYN) trade, exchange, swap,
bargain, negotiate

base (SYN) foundation, bottom,
pedestal, build, ground, locate,
station, low, immoral, shameful
(ANT) top, noble, honorable,
respected

bashful (SYN) shy, timid, reserved,
inhibited (ANT) bold, confident

basic (SYN) simple, elementary,
fundamental, primary, essential
(SYN) secondary, advanced, extra,
supplemental

basin (SYN) bowl, tub, sink, depression

basis (SYN) ground, foundation,
support, rationale, justification,
premise, core

bask (SYN) sunbathe, loll, relax, loaf,
luxuriate

bass (SYN) deep, low-pitched, resonant (ANT) high, shrill

bastion (SYN) fortress, stronghold, citadel

bat (SYN) swing, strike, hit, whack, swat

batch (SYN) quantity, group, cluster, bundle

bath (SYN) soak, cleansing, tub

bathe (SYN) wash, cleanse, soak, cover, flood, envelop, pervade

baton (SYN) stick, club, staff, wand

batter (SYN) beat, pummel, thrash, pound

battery (SYN) artillery, guns

battle (SYN) fight, combat, dispute, struggle, clash (ANT) peace, amnesty

bay (SYN) inlet, cove, sound, gulf, nook, alcove

bazaar (SYN) market, souk, mart, sale

be (SYN) exist, live

beach (SYN) shore, coast, seaside, run ashore, ground

beacon (SYN) signal, sign, flare, lighthouse

bead (SYN) droplet, bubble, pearl, drip, pill

beak (SYN) bill

beam (SYN) shine, radiate, grin, ray, shaft, joist, rafter

bear (SYN) carry, transport, produce, bring forth, support, tolerate, endure (ANT) avoid, evade

beast (SYN) animal, brute, barbarian, monster, fiend, savage

beat (SYN) strike, batter, pound, throb, pulse, rhythm, cadence

beautiful (SYN) gorgeous, attractive, exquisite, lovely, fetching, stunning (ANT) ugly, plain, unattractive, homely

beauty (SYN) charm, attractiveness, loveliness, appeal, belle, vision, bombshell (ANT) ugliness, plainness

because (SYN) since, owing to, on account of

beckon (SYN) summon, motion, gesture, call, entice, lure

become (SYN) change into, develop into, suit, fit, flatter (ANT) remain, stay

bed (SYN) bunk, cot, divan, bottom, foundation, groundwork

bedlam (SYN) chaos, confusion, turmoil, mayhem, confusion (ANT) order, serenity, calm, harmony, accord

before (SYN) earlier than, prior to, previously, formerly, ahead of, in front of (ANT) after, later, subsequently, afterwards

beforehand (SYN) already, ahead of
time, earlier, previously; in
anticipation (ANT) afterwards

beg (SYN) beseech, request, implore,
petition, supplicate (ANT) earn

beggar (SYN) pauper, needy person,
supplicant, vagrant, vagabond

begin (SYN) start, commence, initiate,
emerge, originate (ANT) complete,
finish, end

beginning (SYN) outset, origin, opening,
inception, germ, root (ANT) end,
conclusion, termination

beguile (SYN) mislead, charm, distract,
deceive, fool

behave (SYN) act, conduct oneself,
comport, function, operate

behavior (SYN) manner, actions,
demeanor, performance, working

behemoth (SYN) giant, monster,
leviathan (ANT) dwarf

behind (SYN) in back of, following,
supporting, backing, responsible for,
guilty of, after (ANT) in front of,
ahead, before

being (SYN) creature, living thing,
individual, entity, existence, reality,
life

belabor (SYN) repeat, reiterate, harp on

belated (SYN) late, overdue, tardy,
delayed (ANT) early, punctual, on
time

beleaguered (SYN) persecuted, plagued,
badgered, besieged, surrounded,
encircled

belie (SYN) refute, distort, misrepresent
(ANT) clarify

belief (SYN) assurance, conviction,
confidence, opinion, principle,
doctrine (ANT) disbelief, doubt,
skepticism

believe (SYN) trust, accept, have faith
in, think, reckon (ANT) doubt,
question

belittle (SYN) scorn, disparage,
humiliate, minimize, trivialize
(ANT) praise, magnify, flatter, exult

bellicose (SYN) warlike, belligerent
(ANT) peaceful, nonviolent

belligerent (SYN) aggressive,
confrontational, antagonistic, hostile,
combative (ANT) peaceful,
easygoing

bellow (SYN) howl, roar, bawl, cry

belly (SYN) stomach, abdomen, gut,
middle, paunch

belonging (SYN) acceptance,
association, inclusion, fellowship

belongings (SYN) possessions, things,
personal property, effects

beloved (SYN) dear, prized, precious,
treasured, cherished (ANT) hated,
neglected, despised

below (SYN) less than, lower than,
beneath, underneath (ANT) above,
over, more than

belt (SYN) waistband, sash, girdle, strip, zone, stretch

bemoan (SYN) lament, regret, morn, rue

bench (SYN) seat, pew

bend (SYN) arc, curve, angle, arch, twist, stoop, bow, hunch (ANT) straighten

beneath (SYN) under, below, unbefitting, unworthy of, inferior to (ANT) above

benediction (SYN) blessing, prayer

benefactor (SYN) sponsor, patron, backer, supporter, contributor

beneficent (SYN) generous, charitable (ANT) greedy, stingy, selfish

beneficial (SYN) advantageous, helpful, useful, valuable, profitable (ANT) useless, harmful, damaging, detrimental

beneficiary (SYN) recipient, heir, payee (ANT) benefactor

benefit (SYN) advantage, help, enhance, profit, serve (ANT) disadvantage, harm, detriment

benevolence (SYN) kindness, charity, sympathy, philanthropy, tenderness (ANT) inhumanity, cruelty, malevolence

benevolent (SYN) caring, altruistic, compassionate, kind-hearted (ANT) unkind, harsh, cruel

benign (SYN) genial, friendly, harmless, non-malignant (ANT) hostile, cancerous

bent (SYN) crooked, curved, angled, stooped, hunched, inclination, tendency (ANT) straight

bequest (SYN) legacy, gift, inheritance, estate, endowment

berate (SYN) rebuke, scold, chide, reprimand (ANT) honor, praise, commend

bereavement (SYN) death, loss

bereft (SYN) devoid, deprived, lacking, robbed of

berserk (SYN) crazy, frenzied, raging, hysterical, manic (ANT) calm, composed, sane

beseech (SYN) plead, beg, implore, ask, appeal

beside (SYN) next to, along side, neighboring, adjacent to, parallel to

besides (SYN) in addition, furthermore, what's more, not counting

besiege (SYN) surround, encircle, hem in, overwhelm, inundate, swamp

best (SYN) finest, leading, unrivalled, unsurpassed, ultimate (ANT) worst

bestow (SYN) present, impart, confer on, award, give

bet (SYN) gamble, venture, wager, chance, hazard, risk

betray (SYN) be disloyal to, expose, reveal, unmask (ANT) be faithful to, keep

better (SYN) superior, surpassing, preferable, well, cured, improve, raise (ANT) worse, worsen, inferior

between (SYN) among, in the middle of, betwixt, connecting, uniting

beverage (SYN) drink, liquid, refreshment, libation

bevy (SYN) group, collection, assembly

beware (SYN) be cautious, guard against, mind, take heed, be alert

bewildered (SYN) confused, perplexed, puzzled, bemused, mystified (ANT) enlightened

bewitch (SYN) enchant, captivate, fascinate, hypnotize, dazzle (ANT) repulse

beyond (SYN) past, exceeding, surpassing, upwards of

bias (SYN) prejudice, favoritism, partiality, influence, distort, skew (ANT) impartiality, fairness, justice

bicker (SYN) quarrel, argue, fight, squabble, dispute (ANT) agree

bid (SYN) offer, propose, tender, attempt, endeavor, greet, wish

big (SYN) large, sizable, extensive, important, momentous (ANT) small, tiny, diminutive, minor, insignificant

bigotry (SYN) racism, prejudice, intolerance, narrow-mindedness,

discrimination (ANT) impartiality, open-mindedness, tolerance

bill (SYN) invoice, charges, proposal, measure, beak, mandible

billow (SYN) cloud, mass, balloon, swirl, pour, flow

bind (SYN) fasten, secure, tether, compel, force, require (ANT) loosen, untie, free

binge (SYN) spree, bout, spell

birth (SYN) childbirth, delivery, emergence, dawning, genesis, ancestry, descent (ANT) death, end

bit (SYN) piece, fragment, morsel, speck

bite (SYN) chew, gnaw, nip, sting, snack, refreshment

bitter (SYN) harsh, sharp, unsweetened, spiteful, resentful, sullen, freezing, icy (ANT) sweet, pleasant, amicable, content

bizarre (SYN) strange, outlandish, peculiar, curious, weird (ANT) normal, common, expected

black (SYN) dark, raven, ebony, inky (ANT) white, bright, light

blackmail (SYN) extortion, intimidation, threaten, compel, pressure

blame (SYN) accuse, condemn, hold accountable, guilt, liability, responsibility (ANT) absolve, exonerate bland (SYN) dull, flat, uninteresting, tasteless, flavorless (ANT) tangy, spicy, inspiring

blank (SYN) bare, empty, void, expressionless, vacant, gap

blanket (SYN) cover, cloak, envelop, shroud

blasphemy (SYN) impiety, profanity, sacrilege, irreverence, desecration

blast (SYN) explosion, bang, outburst, blare, gust, demolish, shatter

blatant (SYN) obvious, flagrant, glaring, overt, brazen (ANT) inconspicuous, hidden, subtle

blaze (SYN) fire, flames, inferno, glare, glow, burn

bleach (SYN) whiten, fade, lighten

bleak (SYN) dismal, cheerless, somber, stark, desolate, dim, depressing (ANT) cheerful, optimistic, rosy

bleed (SYN) gush, ooze, extract, drain

blemish (SYN) mar, damage, spot, mark, flaw, imperfection

blend (SYN) combine, mix, merge, harmonize, complement, mixture, compound (ANT) separate

bless (SYN) dedicate, consecrate, sanctify, bestow, give, sanction (ANT) curse, denounce

blessing (SYN) grace, invocation, dedication, approval, consent, help, godsend, benefit (ANT) condemnation, denunciation, misfortune, affliction

blight (SYN) scourge, plague, infestation, destroy, damage, wreck (ANT) blessing, help

blind (SYN) unsighted, visionless, indiscriminate, heedless, inattentive (ANT) sighted, seeing, perceptive, mindful

blink (SYN) wink, flutter, flash, twinkle

bliss (SYN) contentment, joy, delight, pleasure, elation (ANT) misery, unhappiness, sorrow, sadness, grief

blister (SYN) sore, swelling, welt, boil

blizzard (SYN) snowstorm

block (SYN) brick, hunk, obstacle, barrier, obstruct, clog, halt, impede (ANT) clear, allow, aid, promote, advance

blockade (SYN) barricade, wall, obstruction, impediment

blond or blonde (SYN) fair, flaxen, light, yellow, golden (ANT) dark, brunette

blood (SYN) ancestry, lineage, birth

bloom (SYN) flower, flower, open, flourish, thrive (ANT) wilt, die

blot (SYN) spot, smudge, blotch, absorb, soak up

blow (SYN) breathe, puff, exhale, waft, flutter, punch, thump, disaster, setback

blue (SYN) cobalt, sapphire, navy, low,
downcast, depressed, gloomy (ANT)
upbeat, happy, elated

bluff (SYN) cliff, precipice, pretend,
feign, deceit, fraud

blunder (SYN) mistake, error, oversight,
botch, bungle, stumble, flounder

blunt (SYN) dull, worn, rounded,
straightforward, frank (ANT) sharp,
pointed, subtle, delicate, tactful

blur (SYN) cloud, obscure, make
indistinct, dim, smudge (ANT)
sharpen, focus, clear

blush (SYN) flush, redden, color, glow,
ruddiness

board (SYN) plank, panel, lodge, harbor,
mount, ascend, council, committee

boast (SYN) brag, gloat, possess, be
proud of (ANT) belittle, minimize,
apologize

boat (SYN) ship, vessel

bode (SYN) predict, signify, portend,
indicate

body (SYN) physique, build, shape,
collection, bulk, corpse, cadaver

bog (SYN) marsh, swamp, mire,
wetlands

bogus (SYN) fake, artificial, imitation,
fraudulent (ANT) genuine, legitimate

boil (SYN) froth, bubble, blister,
swelling

bold (SYN) fearless, daring, confident,
brazen, confident, insolent (ANT)
timid, meek, shy, cowardly

bolt (SYN) bar, latch, pin, peg, lock,
secure, rush, dart, hurry

bomb (SYN) shell, explosive, projectile,
attack, assail, blast

bombard (SYN) bomb, shell, assault,
hound, besiege

bond (SYN) relationship, affiliation,
attachment, pledge, oath, join, fuse
(ANT) separate, sever, disconnect

bondage (SYN) confinement, captivity,
imprisonment, slavery (ANT)
liberty, freedom

bonus (SYN) extra, benefit, plus, prize,
reward, incentive (ANT)
disadvantage

book (SYN) publication, volume,
reserve, schedule

boorish (SYN) crude, vulgar, churlish,
uncivilized, coarse (ANT) refined,
civilized, polite

boost (SYN) elevate, increase, amplify,
encouragement, uplift (ANT)
decrease, lower, hinder

boot (SYN) kick, punt, drive

border (SYN) boundary, edge,
perimeter, frontier, hem, flank,
adjoin (ANT) inside, interior

bore (SYN) drill, perforate, pierce,
weary, fatigue, nuisance (ANT)
interest

boredom (SYN) monotony, tediousness, ennui, repetitiveness (ANT) excitement, stimulation, amusement

boring (SYN) tiresome, dull, dreary, uneventful, mind-numbing (ANT) interesting, exciting

borrow (SYN) have use of, acquire, embrace, adopt, copy (ANT) lend, return

bosom (SYN) chest, breast, dear, cherished, close

boss (SYN) supervisor, leader, chief, domineer, order, bully

bother (SYN) disturb, irritate, annoy, inconvenience, mind, worry (ANT) aid, comfort

bottom (SYN) base, floor, foundation, underside, backside, rear, rump, lowest (ANT) top, height, pinnacle, peak

bounce (SYN) bound, leap, spring, jump

bound (SYN) tied, restrained, limit, confine, bounce, hurdle, skip, certain, destined, united, interdependent (ANT) free, unfettered, loose, unbound

boundary (SYN) margin, fringe, border, limits, outline, division (ANT) center, inside, interior

bountiful (SYN) plentiful, lavish, generous, ample, liberal (ANT) lacking, scarce

bout (SYN) spell, period, stint, contest, match

bow (SYN) comply, surrender, bend, stoop, kneel, genuflect, front, prow (ANT) stand, refuse

bowl (SYN) dish, vessel, throw, pitch, hurl

box (SYN) container, carton, crate, package, wrap, bundle

boycott (SYN) avoid, reject, refuse, shun, ban, embargo (ANT) support, embrace

brace (SYN) support, reinforce, truss, crutch, prop, prepare, fortify, steel

bracket (SYN) division, class, category, rack, frame

brag (SYN) boast, gloat, exaggerate, crow (ANT) deprecate, minimize

braid (SYN) plait, intertwine, lace, weave

brain (SYN) mind, intellect, intelligence, wisdom

brake (SYN) stop, slow, halt, restraint, limit, control (ANT) accelerator, accelerate

branch (SYN) bough, limb, section, wing, offshoot, subdivision

brand (SYN) label, logo, trademark, kind, class, variety, burn, scar

brandish (SYN) wave, flourish, wield, swing, swish

brash (SYN) brazen, bold, pushy, arrogant, audacious, presumptuous (ANT) meek, subdued, subtle bravado (SYN) swagger, cockiness, confidence, assertiveness, boastfulness

brave (SYN) courageous, valiant, heroic, dauntless, intrepid, endure, withstand, defy (ANT) fearful, cowardly, timid, succumb to

bravery (SYN) nerve, valor, boldness, mettle, fortitude (ANT) weakness, fear

brawl (SYN) fight, altercation, skirmish, riot, dispute

breach (SYN) rift, violation, infraction, trespass

breadth (SYN) width, span, wideness, extent, scope (ANT) length

break (SYN) shatter, fracture, opening, malfunction, disobey, violate, reveal, announce, interruption, rest (ANT) mend, repair, join, obey

breakthrough (SYN) advance, discovery, find, innovation, revolution (ANT) setback, regression

breast (SYN) chest, bust, bosom

breath (SYN) breathing, respiration

breathe (SYN) inhale and exhale, respire, gulp, whisper, sigh

breed (SYN) reproduce, procreate, foster, cultivate, type, strain, species

breeding (SYN) upbringing, rearing, training, refinement, polish

breeze (SYN) wind, air, gust, draft, flit, glide, sweep

brevity (SYN) briefness, economy, succinctness (ANT) length, verbosity, elaboration

brew (SYN) steep, prepare, gather, loom, mixture, cocktail

bribe (SYN) corrupt, reward, inducement, payoff

bridal (SYN) wedding, matrimonial, nuptial, marital

bridge (SYN) arch, overpass, span, connect, link

bridle (SYN) control, rein, curb, check (ANT) free, liberate, loosen

brief (SYN) short, fleeting, temporary, concise, inform, prime, summary, synopsis (ANT) long, protracted, permanent, lasting, exhaustive

brigade (SYN) troop, company, squad

bright (SYN) radiant, glowing, luminous, vivid, clever, intelligent, sunny (ANT) dull, dark, dim, gloomy

brilliant (SYN) dazzling, shining, gifted, smart, exceptional, impressive (ANT) dim, dull, unintelligent, undistinguished

brim (SYN) rim, lip, edge, verge, margin

bring (SYN) carry, bear, transport, escort, guide, cause, occasion

brink (SYN) edge, threshold, frontier, fringe, boundary

brisk (SYN) quick, energetic, lively, rapid, hurried

bristle (SYN) prickle, seethe, rage, take offense

brittle (SYN) fragile, delicate, frail, breakable (ANT) solid, supple

broach (SYN) mention, bring up, raise the subject, open, put forth, air

broad (SYN) wide, spacious, general, inclusive, comprehensive, open (ANT) thin, narrow, limited, detailed

broadcast (SYN) transmit, relay, announce, advertise, transmission, program

broaden (SYN) expand, stretch, swell, extend, develop (ANT) narrow, restrict

brochure (SYN) booklet, pamphlet, advertisement

broke (SYN) impoverished, penniless, poor (ANT) wealthy, rich, affluent

broker (SYN) dealer, agent, intermediary

brood (SYN) family, offspring, young, ponder, muse, dwell on

brook (SYN) stream, creek, rivulet

browse (SYN) peruse, skim, scan, look over (ANT) examine

bruise (SYN) discolor, injure, damage, contusion, mark

brush (SYN) undergrowth, shrubs, graze, sweep, encounter, confrontation

brusque (SYN) discourteous, curt, short, terse, blunt (ANT) polite, gentle, courteous

brutal (SYN) vicious, cruel, savage, ferocious, merciless (ANT) kind, gentle, forgiving, sensitive

brute (SYN) barbarian, beast, monster, animal, savage

bubble (SYN) gurgle, froth, fizz, effervesce, foam

buckle (SYN) collapse, crumple, fold, fastener, clip

bucolic (SYN) rustic, country, pastoral (ANT) urban, modern

bud (SYN) grow, develop, sprout, burgeon

budge (SYN) move, shift, dislodge, reposition

budget (SYN) allowance, resources, financial plan, allocate, designate

buffer (SYN) cushion, barrier, safeguard

buffet (SYN) batter, pummel, strike, lash

buffoon (SYN) clown, fool, joker, jester

bug (SYN) insect, spy, tap, eavesdrop, defect, glitch, illness, ailment

build (SYN) construct, assemble, make, physique, shape, strengthen, increase, amass (ANT) destroy, demolish, dismantle

building (SYN) structure, property, establishment

bulge (SYN) bump, lump, protrusion, swell, distend

bulk (SYN) size, dimensions, magnitude, most, majority

bullet (SYN) ball, shot, pellet, slug

bulletin (SYN) announcement, communication, message, dispatch

bully (SYN) intimidator, tormentor, oppress, persecute, coerce, tyrant, thug

bulwark (SYN) fortress, bastion, defense, security

bump (SYN) knock, collide into, jolt, bounce, lump, contusion

bunch (SYN) cluster, bundle, group, collect

bundle (SYN) parcel, roll, clump, wrap, tie

buoy (SYN) marker, guide, boost, cheer, raise

buoyant (SYN) floating, weightless, carefree, light-hearted, joyful, sunny (ANT) gloomy, morose, melancholy

burden (SYN) strain, responsibility, liability, trouble, distress, weigh down (ANT) lighten, ease, mitigate, unload

bureau (SYN) service, office, agency, branch, division

bureaucracy (SYN) government, administration, red tape, protocol

burgeon (SYN) escalate, flourish, rocket, boom, thrive (ANT) sink, wilt, decrease

burglar (SYN) thief, robber

burial (SYN) internment, funeral, committal

burn (SYN) blaze, smolder, ignite, torch, scorch, singe (ANT) extinguish, put out

burrow (SYN) tunnel, den, lair, dig, excavate, channel

burst (SYN) explode, pop, split, surge, storm, outbreak

bury (SYN) conceal, cover, hide, embed

bush (SYN) shrub, hedge

business (SYN) occupation, profession, industry, company, firm, concern

busy (SYN) active, occupied, engaged, hectic, eventful (ANT) idle, free

but (SYN) however, on the other hand, besides, nonetheless

butcher (SYN) annihilate, murder, destroy, slaughter, carve

buttress (SYN) support, brace, uphold, bolster, strengthen

buy (SYN) purchase, obtain, acquire, bargain, deal, believe (ANT) sell

by (SYN) beside, next to, via, by way of, near, past

bypass (SYN) avoid, go round, circumvent, skirt (ANT) encounter, face

bystander (SYN) onlooker, eyewitness, spectator

C

cab (SYN) taxi

cabin (SYN) room, compartment, hut, cottage, lodge

cabinet (SYN) cupboard, case, dresser, locker

cable (SYN) rope, cord, line, wire

cache (SYN) hoard, store, stockpile, reserve, hide, conceal

cackle (SYN) laugh, exclaim

cacophonous (SYN) loud, jarring, noisy, discordant (ANT) harmonious

cafeteria (SYN) lunchroom, restaurant, snack bar, mess hall

cage (SYN) enclosure, pen, trap, enclose, confine, coop up

cajole (SYN) persuade, coax, lure, beguile

cake (SYN) loaf, slab, bar, encrust, congeal

calamity (SYN) disaster, tragedy, mishap, distress, ruin (ANT) fortune, blessing, benefit

calculate (SYN) compute, figure, reckon, consider, weigh, plan, intend

calculation (SYN) estimation, judgment, prediction, projection

caliber (SYN) worth, merit, quality, ability, level, stature

call (SYN) shout, exclaim, summon, hail, name, designate, phone, invitation, reason, justification (ANT) answer, listen

callous (SYN) heartless, insensitive, uncaring, indifferent, hard (ANT) kind, compassionate, sympathetic

calm (SYN) composed, unexcited, relaxed, dispassionate, peace, stillness, hush, soothe (ANT) agitated, nervous, stormy, emotional, upset, disturb

camouflage (SYN) disguise, mask, subterfuge, cover, conceal, obscure (ANT) show, reveal, display

camp (SYN) encampment, base, settlement, faction, group

campaign (SYN) operation, movement, push, lobby, effort, strategy

canal (SYN) channel, duct, waterway

cancel (SYN) revoke, call, off, eliminate, erase, annul (ANT) confirm, enforce

cancellation (SYN) revocation, abandonment, elimination

cancer (SYN) tumor, malignancy, growth, corruption, sickness candid (SYN) honest, blunt, straightforward, truthful, frank (ANT) insincere, guarded, hidden, shrewd

candidate (SYN) nominee, applicant, contender, entrant

candor (SYN) openness, directness, sincerity, frankness

cane (SYN) rod, pole, stick, staff, club

canopy (SYN) awning, covering, tent, shade

cant (SYN) hypocrisy, pretense, jargon, lingo, tilt, slant

cantankerous (SYN) grumpy, irritable, disagreeable, bad-tempered, contrary (ANT) friendly, happy, sanguine

canvas (SYN) examine, study, poll, survey, solicit

canyon (SYN) gorge, ravine, gulch, abyss, chasm

cap (SYN) lid, top, ceiling, limit, crown

capable (SYN) able, qualified, competent, proficient, skilled (ANT) incapable, inexperienced, incompetent

capacity (SYN) size, room, aptitude, facility, role, position

cape (SYN) point, promontory, peninsula, cloak, mantle

capital (SYN) money, funds, resources, vital, major, principal

capitalism (SYN) private enterprise, free market (ANT) communism, socialism

capitulate (SYN) relent, submit, yield, surrender (ANT) refuse, withstand

caprice (SYN) whim, impulse, fancy

capsize (SYN) overturn, invert, upset, tip over

capsule (SYN) pill, tablet, pod, vessel, module

captain (SYN) leader, commander, chief, supervisor, skipper

captivate (SYN) charm, enthrall, fascinate, mesmerize, allure (ANT) repel, bore

captive (SYN) prisoner, hostage, detainee, incarcerated, confined (ANT) free

capture (SYN) ensnare, catch, apprehend, trap, arrest, seizure (ANT) release, liberate, free, abandon

car (SYN) vehicle, automobile

carcass (SYN) body, cadaver, corpse, remains

cardinal (SYN) primary, central, fundamental, essential, leading (ANT) secondary, auxiliary

care (SYN) caution, heed, concern, worry, supervision, responsibility, tend, affection (ANT) neglect, carelessness

career (SYN) occupation, vocation,
    calling, profession, trade

careful (SYN) cautious, vigilant,
    attentive, prudent, scrupulous (ANT)
    careless, casual, reckless, negligent

careless (SYN) thoughtless, insensitive,
    negligent, irresponsible, impetuous
    (ANT) deliberate, thoughtful, wary,
    meticulous

caress (SYN) stroke, touch, skim, brush

cargo (SYN) freight, baggage, shipment

caricature (SYN) parody, cartoon,
    distortion, mockery

carnage (SYN) slaughter, bloodshed,
    murder, holocaust, massacre

carnival (SYN) festival, celebration,
    revelry, fair

carnivorous (SYN) meat-eating

carol (SYN) song, tune, hymn

carouse (SYN) party, celebrate, revel

carp (SYN) complain, criticize, scold,
    berate, gripe, whine (ANT) praise,
    compliment

carpet (SYN) rug, mat, blanket, cover

carriage (SYN) coach, vehicle, bearing,
    posture, comportment

carry (SYN) transport, haul, lug,
    transmit, relay (ANT) leave, drop

carton (SYN) box, container, package,
    case

cartoon (SYN) drawing, sketch,
    caricature, animation

cartridge (SYN) shell, round, capsule

carve (SYN) cut, sculpt, etch, whittle

cascade (SYN) waterfall, torrent, flood,
    flow, gush, pour

case (SYN) instance, occasion, situation,
    context, holder, container, covering

cash (SYN) money, currency, resources,
    assets, funds

cashier (SYN) clerk, teller

casket (SYN) coffin

cast (SYN) throw, toss, pitch, form,
    mold, actors, characters, distribute,
    radiate

caste (SYN) class, stratum, status, social
    order

castle (SYN) fortress, citadel, chateau,
    palace

casual (SYN) informal, relaxed, careless,
    offhand, nonchalant, chance, random
    (ANT) formal, serious, intentional,
    deliberate

casualty (SYN) victim, loss, death,
    fatality

catacombs (SYN) vault, tomb, crypt

catalog (SYN) list, directory, roster,
    classify, archive, index

catalyst (SYN) accelerator, motivation,
    impetus, driving force

catapult (SYN) sling, shoot, hurl, propel

catastrophe (SYN) disaster, fiasco, calamity, tragedy, debacle

catch (SYN) capture, seize, snare, apprehend, understand, disadvantage, complication, clasp, fastener, haul

category (SYN) division, grouping, sort, classification

cater (SYN) provide, furnish, supply, serve, consider

catharsis (SYN) cleansing, purge, purification

cattle (SYN) cows, livestock, bovines

cause (SYN) origin, root, conviction, belief, grounds, justification, objective, produce, prompt (ANT) outcome, result, effect

caustic (SYN) burning, corrosive, harsh, malicious, scathing (ANT) kind, mellow

caution (SYN) concern, care, watchfulness, warning, admonition, advise, urge (ANT) carelessness, indiscretion

cautious (SYN) guarded, prudent, tentative, wary, careful, circumspect (ANT) reckless, foolish, heedless

cave (SYN) hole, grotto, cavern, chamber, hollow

caveat (SYN) warning, limitation, stipulation

cavern (SYN) cave, hollow, pothole

cavity (SYN) hole, pit, crater, depression

cease (SYN) stop, conclude, halt, terminate, quit, discontinue (ANT) begin, continue, persist

ceaseless (SYN) continual, everlasting, incessant, perpetual, unremitting (ANT) temporary, terminal, ending, brief

celebrate (SYN) rejoice, honor, observe, commemorate (ANT) ignore, dishonor

celebration (SYN) party, festival, commemoration, remembrance, merrymaking

celebrity (SYN) fame, distinction, prominence, stardom, prestige, star, VIP (ANT) obscurity, nobody

celestial (SYN) heavenly, ethereal, divine, supernatural (ANT) earthly, mortal, terrestrial

celibacy (SYN) chastity, purity

cell (SYN) room, chamber, unit, group

cellar (SYN) basement, crypt

cement (SYN) adhesive, glue, paste, affix

cemetery (SYN) graveyard, churchyard

censor (SYN) cut, delete, suppress, ban

censure (SYN) disapproval, criticism, reproach, blame, denounce, scold

center (SYN) middle, interior, heart, focus, concentrate (ANT) edge, periphery central (SYN) middle, inner, focal, dominant, principal, main (ANT) side, outer, secondary, incidental

cerebral (SYN) intellectual, mental (ANT) physical, carnal

ceremonial (SYN) formal, ritualistic, solemn, stately

ceremony (SYN) rite, ritual, service, pomp, formalities, decorum

certain (SYN) assured, confident, positive, conclusive, inevitable, fixed (ANT) uncertain, indefinite, doubtful, unlikely, possible

certainty (SYN) conviction, faith, trust, fact, reality (ANT) uncertainty, doubt

certificate (SYN) document, authentication, credentials, accreditation

certify (SYN) confirm, verify, authenticate, affirm, guarantee

chafe (SYN) rub, abrade, scrape, irritate, annoy (ANT) soothe

chagrin (SYN) shame, embarrassment, mortification, humiliation (ANT) pride

chain (SYN) series, string, progression, bind, restrain, shackle

challenge (SYN) dare, opposition, confrontation, trial, difficulty, question, contest

chamber (SYN) room, compartment

champion (SYN) victor, winner, hero, defender, upholder, support, advocate (ANT) loser, oppose

chance (SYN) probability, likelihood, luck, coincidence, fortune, risk, hazard, opportunity

change (SYN) alteration, modification, revolution, variety, departure, swap, trade, amend, adapt, evolve (ANT) stability, keep, preserve, maintain

changeable (SYN) erratic, variable, irregular, unstable, fickle (ANT) constant, steady, settled, unwavering

channel (SYN) route, avenue, approach, strait, canal, direct, guide

chant (SYN) sing, intone, recite, song, chorus

chaos (SYN) bedlam, tumult, confusion, pandemonium, disorder (ANT) order, peace, harmony, tranquility

chaperone (SYN) escort, guardian, accompany, protect, safeguard

chapter (SYN) section, phase, division, episode, stage

char (SYN) scorch, burn

character (SYN) disposition, personality, nature, reputation, integrity, eccentric, original, symbol, letter

characteristic (SYN) attribute, feature, quality, peculiarity, typical, representative (ANT) abnormal, atypical

characterize (SYN) typify, indicate, identify, distinguish, call

characterization (SYN) portrayal, depiction, classification

charade (SYN) pretense, parody, act, masquerade, facade

charge (SYN) rush, storm, attack, accuse, blame, price, expense, command, entrust, custody, responsibility

charisma (SYN) charm, allure, magnetism, influence, attraction

charitable (SYN) generous, munificent, altruistic, tolerant, lenient, forgiving (ANT) selfish, stingy, strict, intolerant

charity (SYN) compassion, kindness, goodwill, giving, philanthropy, foundation, charitable organization, aid, assistance (ANT) business, misanthropy, selfishness, cruelty

charm (SYN) enchant, fascinate, charisma, appeal, loveliness, spell, incantation, amulet, talisman (ANT) repel, repulse, disgust

charming (SYN) captivating, delightful, endearing, winning, likable (ANT) unattractive, unpleasant, repulsive

chart (SYN) diagram, graph, plot, draft, outline, trace, document

charter (SYN) hire, lease, rent, book, authorize, permit, contract, dispensation

chase (SYN) pursue, trail, hunt, follow, race, pursuit

chasm (SYN) gulf, crater, abyss, gorge

chaste (SYN) pure, innocent, virtuous (ANT) corrupt, defiled, sinful, impure

chat (SYN) talk, converse,

chauvinism (SYN) bias, prejudice, jingoism, partisanship (ANT) tolerance, liberalism, objectiveness

cheap (SYN) inexpensive, economical, inferior, tasteless, mediocre, frugal (ANT) expensive, dear, elegant, steep

cheat (SYN) deceive, defraud, swindle, dupe, fleece, beguile, crook, trickster (ANT) support, protect, repay

check (SYN) scrutinize, review, examine, inspect, probe, halt, block, impediment, tick mark (ANT) overlook, disregard, neglect, promote, continue

cheek (SYN) nerve, audacity, impertinence, flippancy, gall, disrespect (ANT) respect, timidity, deference

cheer (SYN) restore, brighten, gladden, applaud, whimsy, glee, liveliness, jubilation (ANT) depress, sadden, dishearten, antagonize, sadness, boo

cheerful (SYN) happy, animated, sunny, perky, carefree, effervescent (ANT) cheerless, gloomy, mournful, sullen, melancholy, somber

cherish (SYN) treasure, value, adore, appreciate, revere, esteem (ANT) scorn, neglect, abandon, hate, disdain

chest (SNY) bust, bosom, box, case, container, commode, cabinet, dresser chew (SYN) gnaw, munch, nosh, nibble, bite, chomp

chic (SYN) stylish, tasteful, trendy, sophisticated, modish, current (ANT) unfashionable, frumpy, dowdy

chide (SYN) scold, reprove, rebuke, admonish, reprimand, disparage(ANT) praise, commend, applaud, approve, flatter

chief (SYN) main, foremost, supreme, key, paramount, primary, greatest, leader, commander (ANT) incidental, inessential, petty, superfluous, minor, follower, underling

chiefly (SYN) mainly, particularly, over all, especially, predominantly, largely, above all (ANT) lastly, unimportantly, least of all

childish (SYN) immature, juvenile, silly, inexperienced, frivolous, naive, petty (ANT) mature, adult, grown up, sophisticated

childlike (SYN) innocent, unaffected, simple, natural, uninhibited, spontaneous, naive (ANT) experienced, worldly, hardened, complicated, wise

chill (SYN) refrigerate, freeze, cool, numb, brisk, shiver, frighten, indifference, hostile, relax (ANT) warm, heat, warmth, hearten

chirp (SYN) peep, warble, tweet, sing, whistle

chivalrous (SYN) gentlemanly, gallant, polite (ANT) rude, impolite, uncivil, crude

choice (SYN) variety, range, assortment, alternative, prime, finest, preferred, inclination, selection, vote (ANT) inferior, common, rough, flawed

choke (SYN) gag, cough, sputter, strangle, smother, stifle, constrict, suffocate

choler (SYN) anger, rage, bitterness, hostility, combativeness, hot-temper (ANT) serenity, peace, tranquility, composure, affection

choose (SYN) elect, pick, select, favor, single-out, prefer (ANT) reject, shun, spurn, decline, rebuff, snub

chop (SYN) sever, cut, cleave, rent, split, hack, fell, trim, reduce, abridge

chore (SYN) burden, job, duty, task, drudgery, responsibility, grind (ANT) privilege, recreation, relaxation, fun

chortle (SYN) laugh, chuckle, snicker, cackle, snort, crow

christen (SYN) baptize, anoint, dedicate, consecrate, name, call, dub

chronic (SYN) persistent, lingering, habitual, rooted, lifelong, protracted (ANT) acute, fleeting, temporary, casual

chronicle (SYN) history, account, narrative, report, recount, tell, relate (ANT) hide, misrepresentation, parody, distortion

chuckle (SYN) laugh, giggle, chortle, guffaw

chunk (SYN) piece, hunk, lump, fragment, portion (ANT) whole

churn (SYN) disturb, agitate, whisk, whip, beat, mix, shake, heave, swirl (ANT) calm, pacify, compose

cinder (SYN) ash, ember

cinema (SYN) movies, motion pictures, films

circle (SYN) ring, loop, clique, group, set, encircle, surround, cycle, circumnavigate

circuit (SYN) lap, turn, course, route, revolution, orbit

circuitous (SYN) indirect, meandering, roundabout, winding, labyrinthine (ANT) direct, straightforward, candid, forthright

circular (SYN) round, cyclical, rhythmic, complete, indirect, illogical, flier, handbill, pamphlet, advertisement (ANT) straight, logical, linear, explicit

circulate (SYN) spread, broadcast, distribute, disseminate, flow, mingle, socialize (ANT) conceal, hide, suppress

circulation (SYN) flow, current, motion, transmission, spread, distribution (ANT) standstill, blockage, concealment, obstruction

circumference (SYN) perimeter, outline, border, edge, contour, boundary (ANT) contents, interior, core, center

circumlocution (SYN) wordiness, redundancy, digression, ambiguity, vagueness, evasion, protraction (ANT) candor, frankness, straightforwardness

circumspection (SYN) caution, consideration, discretion, calculation, vigilance (ANT) indifference, laxity, carelessness, inattention, dereliction

circumstance (SYN) occurrence, situation, predicament, state, occasion

circumstantial (SYN) inconclusive, inferential, uncertain, presumptive, contingent, debatable (ANT) concrete, indisputable, certain

circumvent (SYN) avoid, evade, dodge, bypass, encircle (ANT) confront, face, aid

circus (SYN) carnival, spectacle, fair

citadel (SYN) fortress, castle, stronghold, keep

citation (SYN) quotation, mention, excerpt, ticket, summons

cite (SYN) quote, mention, reference, reproduce, allege (ANT) contradict, refute, challenge, negate

citizen (SYN) inhabitant, dweller, native, national, denizen

city (SYN) metropolis, town, metropolitan, urban (ANT) rural, suburban

civic (SYN) communal, city, public, local, municipal

civil (SYN) polite, courteous, diplomatic, secular, public (ANT) rude, impertinent, condescending

civility (SYN) courtesy, manners, grace, decency, tact, decorum (ANT) discourtesy, impropriety, incivility

civilization (SYN) society, community, people, culture, progress, illumination (ANT) degeneration, barbarism, savagery, wildness

civilize (SYN) tame, cultivate, refine, enlighten, domesticate, advance, polish (ANT) stunt, neglect, impair

claim (SYN) declaration, right, request, assert, contend (ANT) deny, refute, contradict

claimant (SYN) owner, petitioner, applicant, accuser

clairvoyant (SYN) psychic, visionary

clammy (SYN) sweaty, moist, dank, damp (ANT) dry, arid, parched

clamor (SYN) disturbance, outcry, commotion, ruckus, shout (ANT) calm, quiet, peace, serenity

clan (SYN) family, line, clique, circle, association, brotherhood

clandestine (SYN) hidden, secret, undercover, surreptitious, shrouded (ANT) obvious, open, apparent, evident

clang (SYN) ring, jangle, reverberation, clink, toll

clap (SYN) thump, peal, crack, applaud, cheer (ANT) boo, jeer, deride, heckle

clarify (SYN) explain, interpret, simplify, decipher, filter, purify (ANT) confuse, obscure, complicate, cloud

clarion (SYN) clear, resounding, deafening, loud, sharp (ANT) muted, soft, muffled

clarity (SYN) transparency, simplicity, definition, precision, intelligibility (ANT) obscurity, vagueness, cloudiness

clash (SYN) collision, confrontation, argument, clang, mismatch (ANT) agree, harmonize, blend, match, jibe

clasp (SYN) grasp, clutch, embrace, fastener, secure, possess (ANT) relinquish, surrender, drop, withdraw

class (SYN) rank, category, division, status, standing, dashing

classic (SYN) typical, quintessential, characteristic, ageless, masterpiece (ANT) uncharacteristic, inferior, radical

classical (SYN) elegant, refined, understated, well-known, established (ANT) modern, avant-garde

classification (SYN) grouping, allocation, arrangement, category, taxonomy

classify (SYN) arrange, label, type, distribute, categorize, pigeonhole (ANT) disorder, jumble, dishevel

clause (SYN) section, chapter, article, condition, qualification, catch

claw (SYN) nail, talon, tear, scratch, rip

clean (SYN) spotless, sterile, chaste, cleanse, purify (ANT) dirty, used, polluted, contaminated

cleanliness (SYN) neatness, tidiness, orderliness, sanitation, purity (ANT) filth, dirtiness, pollution, contamination

cleanse (SYN) bathe, purify, purge, disinfect, absolve (ANT) soil, defile, pollute

clear (SYN) transparent, unclouded, open, explicit, acquit (ANT) clouded, ambiguous, congested, guilty, uncertain

clearance (SYN) removal, demolition, permission, consent, space, leeway

clearly (SYN) obviously, undeniably, plainly, observably, audibly, certainly (ANT) questionably, indistinctly, unclearly, inaudibly

cleave (SYN) split, divide, rend, adhere, cling (ANT) join, attach, unite, forsake, abandon

cleft (SYN) split, fissure, crack, crevice, breach, separated (ANT) joined, united

clemency (SYN) mercy, compassion, forgiveness, leniency, benevolence (ANT) punishment, cruelty, vindictiveness, vengeance, retribution

clench (SYN) grip, grasp, hold, clasp, lock (ANT) loosen, release

clergy (SYN) cleric, priest, rector, minister, preacher, rabbi

clerk (SYN) salesperson, cashier, teller, bookkeeper

clever (SYN) smart, intelligent, shrewd, crafty, adept (ANT) senseless, stupid, awkward, clumsy, slow

cliché (SYN) commonplace, trite, saying, stereotype, platitude (ANT) innovation, fresh, profundity

click (SYN) snap, clack, be compatible, match (ANT) clash, conflict

client (SYN) customer, patron, buyer, shopper, patient (ANT) seller, vendor, owner, seller

cliff (SYN) bluff, overhang, ledge, escarpment, precipice

climactic (SYN) peak, paramount, crucial, dramatic, pivotal, momentous (ANT) anticlimactic, dull, trivial

climate (SYN) weather, atmosphere, environment, ambiance, conditions, milieu

climax (SYN) peak, culmination, top, pinnacle, turning point (ANT) bottom, low

climb (SYN) ascend, rise, mount, surmount, progress (ANT) descend, drop, lower, decline

clime (SYN) conditions, climate, weather

cling (SYN) stick, adhere, embrace, hug, clutch (ANT) release, detach, repel

clinging

clinging (SYN) sticking, adhering, embracing, hugging (ANT) separating, loosening

clinic (SYN) hospital, infirmary, medical center

clinical (SYN) cold, stark, institutional, impersonal, scientific (ANT) warm, welcoming, personable, emotional, passionate

clip (SYN) snip, cut, crop, decrease, graze, nudge, clasp, fasten, excerpt, abridge (ANT) lengthen, extend, supplement

clique (SYN) group, circle, gang, club, organization (ANT) adversary, rival

cloak (SYN) coat, cape, mask, shroud, disguise, envelop (ANT) reveal, divulge, bare

clog (SYN) obstruct, congest, crowd, hinder, plug (ANT) free, liberate

close (SYN) shut, secure, end, complete, nearby, intimate, detailed (ANT) open, commence, distant

closed (SYN) shut, sealed, restricted, resolved, withdrawn, (ANT) open, communicative

closet (SYN) cabinet, cupboard, wardrobe, recess, vault

clot (SYN) blockage, lump, coagulate, thicken, glob (ANT) opening, flow, loosen

cloth (SYN) material, fabric, textile, rag

clothing (SYN) apparel, attire, garments, vestments, gear

cloud (SYN) mist, gloom, swarm, overshadow, obscure, confuse (ANT) clear, unveil, explain

cloudy (SYN) overcast, obscured, vague, murky, dismal (ANT) clear, sunny, transparent, bright, uplifting

clout (SYN) influence, power, authority, sway, hit (ANT) servitude, subjugation

clown (SYN) joker, jester, fool, prankster, idiot

club (SYN) group, association, bludgeon, baton, nightspot

clue (SYN) hint, indication, evidence, trace, tip

clumsy (SYN) awkward, graceless, uncoordinated, klutzy, inept (ANT) graceful, dexterous, polished

cluster (SYN) clump, knot, gathering, assemble, congregate (ANT) part, separate, individual, disperse

clutch (SYN) clasp, grip, embrace, grasp, control (ANT) release, loose

clutter (SYN) mess, disorder, litter, junk, tangle (ANT) order, tidiness, organization

coach (SYN) instruct, train, teacher, mentor, carriage (ANT) player, pupil, learn, follow, obey

coagulate (SYN) clot, thicken, congeal, solidify, set (ANT) liquefy, thin, dilute coalesce (SYN) blend, fuse, integrate, join, consolidate (ANT) separate, divide, disperse, split

coalition (SYN) alliance, merger, partnership, association, league (ANT) nonalignment, discord

coarse (SYN) rough, unrefined, vulgar, indecent, harsh, scratchy (ANT) soft, polite, polished

coast (SYN) seashore, beach, cruise, glide

coat (SYN) fur, pelt, jacket, layer, cover, overlay

coax (SYN) persuade, encourage, sweet-talk, influence, manipulate (ANT) discourage, deter, force, coerce

cobbler (SYN) shoemaker

cock (SYN) rooster, set, ready, alert

cocky (SYN) arrogant, haughty, brash, boastful, overconfident (ANT) modest, humble, meek, self-effacing

cocoon (SYN) chrysalis, pupa, envelop, swaddle, wrap

coddle (SYN) indulge, spoil, pamper, caress, humor (ANT) neglect, ignore

code (SYN) laws, regulations, cipher, encrypt, signal

coerce (SYN) force, compel, bully, threaten, draft (ANT) prevent, convince, foil, permit, allow

coercion (SYN) pressure, duress, enforcement, insistence, intimidation (ANT) free will, volition, persuasion

coexistence (SYN) harmony, accord, order, peace, synchronicity

coffin (SYN) casket, pall, box, sarcophagus

cog (SYN) tooth, catch, projection

cognition (SYN) understanding, awareness, knowledge, recognition, discernment (ANT) ignorance, unawareness

cognizant (SYN) aware, conscious, knowing, acquainted, enlightened (ANT) unaware, oblivious, unconscious, ignorant

coherent (SYN) rational, logical, sound, comprehensible, clear (ANT) illogical, ambiguous, irrational

cohesion (SYN) attachment, fusion, unity (ANT) incongruity

coil (SYN) wind, twirl, wrap, spiral (ANT) straighten, unwind

coin (SYN) money, currency, invent, conceive, concoct, mint

coincide (SYN) agree, correspond, match, harmonize, jibe (ANT) differ, disagree, conflict, clash

coincidence (SYN) agreement, luck, fortune, chance, congruence (ANT) plan, design

cold (SYN) chilly, frigid, unwelcoming, stark, indifferent, illness, thoroughly, callous, off-track (ANT) hot, sweltering, passionate, emotional, enthusiastic

collaborate

collaborate (SYN) cooperate, join, conspire, fraternize consort (ANT) disagree, part

collaboration (SYN) teamwork, partnership, cooperation, alliance, collusion (ANT) independence

collapse (SYN) crumple, fold, cave, dissolve, failure, breakdown (ANT) mount, rise, success, triumph

collar (SYN) seize, capture, apprehend, neckband

collate (SYN) compile, match, compare, examine, assemble (ANT) disorder, disorganize

collateral (SYN) guarantee, pledge, insurance, secondary, dependant (ANT) chief, principle, prime

colleague (SYN) coworker, associate, partner, ally, companion (ANT) foe, adversary, stranger, antagonist, opponent

collect (SYN) save, assemble, gather, raise, fetch (ANT) distribute, pitch, dispense, scatter, give

collection (SYN) set, hoard, group, offering, compilation

collective (SYN) combined, unified, shared, joint, common (ANT) individual, separate, particular

college (SYN) university, higher education, academy, school

collide (SYN) clash, crash, conflict, bump, disagree (ANT) avoid, dodge, miss

collision (SYN) clash, accident, impact, encounter, discord (ANT) harmony, avoidance

colloquial (SYN) informal, local, conversational, vernacular, slang (ANT) formal, literary, pedantic

colonial (SYN) provincial, new, transplanted, quaint (ANT) modern

colonist (SYN) pilgrim, settler, pioneer, immigrant, expatriate (ANT) native

colonization (SYN) settlement, migration, establishment, expansion, occupation, invasion

colony (SYN) territory, settlement, cluster, group, hive

color (SYN) hue, shade, pigment, decorate, influence, affect, flush (ANT) discolor, pale, whiten

colossal (SYN) huge, enormous, vast, monumental (ANT) diminutive, tiny, trivial, insignificant

column (SYN) pillar, post, row, file, editorial, article, feature

columnist (SYN) journalist, reporter, correspondent, press

coma (SYN) unconsciousness, lethargy, trance, oblivion, stupor

comb (SYN) untangle, tidy, groom, forage, sweep

combat (SYN) battle, warfare, fight, defy, resist (ANT) peace, pacify, surrender combination (SYN) mixture, composite, blend, league, association (ANT) separation, division, dissolution

combine (SYN) mix, integrate, blend, fuse, join, (ANT) disconnect, separate, detach, split, sever

combustible (SYN) flammable, burnable, explosive, touchy, irritable (ANT) non-explosive, passionless, indifferent

come (SYN) arrive, advance, appear, occur, arise, transpire (ANT) go, leave, withdraw, retire, depart

comedy (SYN) humor, jokes, laughs, fun, farce (ANT) drama, tragedy

comely (SYN) becoming, suitable, lovely, appealing, beautiful (ANT) homely, plain, ugly, unattractive

comfort (SYN) consolation, support, console, soothe, luxury (ANT) discomfort, distress, agitate, upset

comfortable (SYN) pleasant, cozy, contented, prosperous, opulent (ANT) miserable, troubled, destitute, cramped

comic (SYN) funny, humorous, amusing, playful, farcical, jocular, clown, comedian (ANT) sober, somber, dull, subdued, grave, grim

command (SYN) order, supervise, decree, instruction, power, rank, grasp (ANT) obey, follow, beg, plead

commandeer (SYN) take, seize, confiscate, sequester, requisition (ANT) request, liberate, release

commemorate (SYN) recognize, mark, acknowledge, honor, celebrate (ANT) forget, neglect, ignore, disregard, overlook

commencement (SYN) beginning, launch, inception, threshold, graduation (ANT) end, termination, finale

commend (SYN) praise, compliment, congratulate, approve, recommend (ANT) blame, criticize, condemn, disparage, knock

commensurate (SYN) level, equivalent, corresponding, adequate, sufficient (ANT) disproportionate, divergent, inconsistent

comment (SYN) remark, observation, review, opinion, statement (ANT) refrain

commerce (SYN) business, trade, exchange, trafficking, economics (ANT) charity, hobby

commercial (SYN) trading, materialistic, business, profitable, advertisement (ANT) noncommercial, personal

commiserate (SYN) sympathize, pity, console

commission (SYN) mission, errand, fee, committee, delegation, contract (ANT) salary, retract

commit (SYN) perform, perpetrate, accomplish, entrust, confine (ANT) fail, free

commitment (SYN) dedication, devotion, obligation, vow, duty (ANT) disavowal

committee (SYN) board, task force, delegation, panel, council

commodity (SYN) merchandise, product, belonging, stock

common (SYN) ordinary, customary, collective, unrefined, public grounds (ANT) unique, rare, distinctive, individual, polished

commonwealth (SYN) nation, state, republic, federation, population

commotion (SYN) disturbance, fuss, excitement, altercation, hubbub (ANT) peace, order, serenity, calm

commune (SYN) cooperative, community, share, meditate, converse

communicable (SYN) contagious, transmittable, infectious, informative, open (ANT) noncommunicable, noninfectious, reserved

communicate (SYN) talk, convey, transmit, disclose, express (ANT) withhold, avoid, retain, suppress

communication (SYN) talk, contact, correspondence, message, news (ANT) secret

communion (SYN) fellowship, harmony, partaking, Eucharist, reflection (ANT) solitude, isolation, privacy

communism (SYN) socialism, collectivism, Marxism (ANT) capitalism

communist (SYN) collectivist, socialist, Marxist, radical, communal (ANT) capitalist

community (SYN) society, people, neighborhood, commonality, association (ANT) solitude, individual

commute (SYN) travel, drive, reduce, decrease, substitute (ANT) lengthen, increase, remain

compact (SYN) agreement, dense, small, brief, flatten (ANT) bulky, lengthy, expand, loose, unabridged

companion (SYN) friend, escort, partner, associate, attendant (ANT) stranger, enemy, rival, adversary

company (SYN) business, corporation, guests, presence, unit (ANT) isolation, solitude, host

comparable (SYN) alike, relative, similar, equivalent, on par (ANT) incomparable, different, dissimilar, unlike

compare (SYN) liken, rival, weigh, contrast, juxtapose, parallel

comparison (SYN) similarity, resemblance, distinction, relation, analogy (ANT) difference, dissimilarity

compass (SYN) range, scope, extent, limits, reach (ANT) fail

compassion (SYN) sensitivity, sympathy, empathy, mercy, condolence (ANT) cruelty, brutality, callousness, indifference compatible (SYN) harmonious, agreeable, suited, consonant, correspondent (ANT) incompatible, discordant, incongruous, unsuited

compel (SYN) force, oblige, pressure, coerce, constrain (ANT) persuade, convince, coax, sway

compendium (SYN) summary, abstract, synopsis, brief, epitome (ANT) enlargement, expansion

compensate (SYN) repay, reimburse, atone, offset, balance (ANT) deprive

compensation (SYN) amends, atonement, reimbursement, repayment (ANT) gift, present, award, loss

compete (SYN) play, participate, contend, vie, challenge (ANT) cooperate

competent (SYN) able, qualified, skillful, expert, proficient (ANT) incompetent, inept, unprofessional, clumsy, unskilled

competition (SYN) contest, match, sport, rivalry, challengers, opposition (ANT) partnership, teamwork, cooperation

competitor (SYN) opponent, rival, participant, challenger (ANT) partner, ally, teammate

compile (SYN) collect, gather, organize, assemble, amass (ANT) separate, scatter

complacency (SYN) contentment, satisfaction, smugness (ANT) discomfort, modesty, reserve

complacent (SYN) pleased, unconcerned, egotistic, smug (ANT) concerned, insecure, uneasy

complain (SYN) criticize, whine, lament, disapprove, grumble (ANT) approve, sanction, accept, endorse, bless

complaint (SYN) illness, malady, accusation, charge, objection (ANT) compliment, praise, health

complement (SYN) companion, quota, enhance, complete, suit, counterpart (ANT) contrast, conflict, diminish, reduce

complete (SYN) finish, thorough, intact, absolute, unabridged (ANT) begin, neglect, lacking, short, partial

complex (SYN) complicated, involved, difficult, structure, obsession (ANT) basic, simple, straightforward, clear

complexion (SYN) skin, coloring, tone, appearance, character

compliance (SYN) obedience, assent, acquiescence, submission, conformity (ANT) defiance, dissent, noncompliance, disobedience

complicate (SYN) confuse, muddle, compound, hamper, involve (ANT) simplify, streamline, clarify

compliment (SYN) flattery, praise, congratulate, commend, admiration (ANT) disapproval, insult, criticize, disparage

comply (SYN) obey, follow, submit, correspond, acquiesce (ANT) differ, disobey, disregard, rebuff component (SYN) part, piece, element, ingredient, inherent, intrinsic (ANT) whole, overall

comport (SYN) behave, conduct, act, agree, match (ANT) misbehave

compose (SYN) write, produce, arrange, steady, calm (ANT) destroy, excite, agitate

composite (SYN) compound, amalgamate, motley, blended, conglomerate (ANT) unmixed, part

composition (SYN) creation, design, anatomy, constitution, essay (ANT) decomposition

compost (SYN) fertilizer, organic waste, compound

composure (SYN) poise, serenity, calm, balance, self-control (ANT) passion, exuberance, agitation

compound (SYN) combination, fusion, combine, aggravate, complex (ANT) simple, separate, reduce, soothe, element

comprehend (SYN) understand, grasp, fathom, know, discern (ANT) ignore, mistake, misinterpret, exclude

comprehensive (SYN) thorough, complete, sweeping, broad (ANT) limited, finite, small, inadequate

compress (SYN) condense, squash, summarize, consolidate, bandage (ANT) expand, increase, spread, augment

comprise (SYN) make up, form, embrace, consist of, include (ANT) exclude, lack, need

compromise (SYN) deal, agreement, concede, damage, jeopardize (ANT) contention, disagreement, quarrel, differ

compulsion (SYN) urge, obsession, preoccupation, pressure, coercion (ANT) persuasion

compulsory (SYN) required, mandatory, imperative, necessary, enforced (ANT) optional, elective, voluntary, discretionary

compute (SYN) calculate, reckon, figure, count, tally (ANT) guess, estimate, speculate

comrade (SYN) friend, ally, partner, confidante, associate (ANT) enemy, stranger, adversary, rival

con (SYN) crook, criminal, swindle, scam, cheat, downside (ANT) enlighten, inform

concave (SYN) sunken, hollow, indented, curved, dented (ANT) convex, swollen, raised, protuberant

conceal (SYN) hide, obscure, mask, camouflage, disguise (ANT) reveal, broadcast, leak, disclose

concede (SYN) acknowledge, admit, surrender, relinquish, permit (ANT) resist, refuse, deny, fight

conceit (SYN) arrogance, narcissism, pride, whim, affectation (ANT) modesty, humility, respect, deference

conceivable (SYN) imaginable,
believable, credible, convincing,
likely (ANT) far-fetched,
unconvincing, inconceivable

conceive (SYN) imagine, grasp,
compose, create, become pregnant
(ANT) duplicate, imitate, forge,
reproduce

concentrate (SYN) focus, contemplate,
gather, congregate, reduce (ANT)
disperse, scatter

concentration (SYN) density, reduction,
cluster, attention, rumination (ANT)
distraction, absentmindedness,
dispersal

concept (SYN) notion, theory, idea,
abstraction, image (ANT) sensation,
concrete

conception (SYN) idea, realization,
origin, genesis, pregnancy (ANT)
ending, termination

concern (SYN) interest, affair, worry
distress, affect, consideration (ANT)
indifference, disinterest, calm

concert (SYN) agreement, accord,
cooperation, recital, symphony,
collaborate

concession (SYN) allowance,
compromise, reduction, permit
(ANT) insistence, protest, refusal

conciliate (SYN) reconcile, win over,
placate, ingratiate, beguile (ANT)
aggravate, annoy, provoke

conciliatory (SYN) pacifying,
peacemaking, winning, soothing,

placatory (ANT) antagonistic,
aggressive, stubborn, defiant

concise (SYN) succinct, brief, abridged,
compact, abbreviated (ANT)
lengthy, wordy, protracted

conclude (SYN) finish, close, settle,
decide, surmise (ANT) begin,
initiate, commence

conclusion (SYN) ending, resolution,
judgment, outcome, close (ANT)
start, commencement, beginning

concoct (SYN) devise, hatch, brew,
invent, imagine

concordant (SYN) agreeable,
harmonious, accordant, compatible,
amicable (ANT) discordant,
troubled, disagreeable

concrete (SYN) specific, tangible,
conclusive, definite, cement (ANT)
abstract, imaginary, conceptual

concur (SYN) agree, approve, grant,
assent, concede (ANT) disagree,
refute,
protest

condemn (SYN) disapprove, reproach,
criticize, doom, sentence (ANT)
commend, praise, pardon, absolve,
condone

condemnation (SYN) disapproval,
denunciation, blame, shame,
punishment

condensation (SYN) compression,
digest, synopsis

condense (SYN) shorten, abridge, thicken, contract, consolidate (ANT) expand, increase, swell, augment

condescend (SYN) patronize, deign, stoop, oblige, humble (ANT) respect

condiment (SYN) sauce, dressing, relish

condition (SYN) situation, circumstance, stipulation, health, malady, prepare

conditioning (SYN) preparation, instruction, priming

condolence (SYN) comfort, sympathy, solace, commiseration (ANT) indifference, detachment, unconcern, congratulation

condone (SYN) pardon, excuse, allow, forgive, justify (ANT) condemn, criticize, censure

conducive (SYN) helpful, useful, contributive, beneficial (ANT) counter, unfavorable, adverse

conduct (SYN) behavior, demeanor, manage, orchestrate, escort, transmit

conductor (SYN) conduit, channel, leader, trainman

conduit (SYN) channel, gutter, trough, passage

confection (SYN) sweet, candy, cake

confederate (SYN) assistant, collaborator, consort, organized, united (ANT) adversary, opponent

confederation (SYN) league, union, alliance, partnership (ANT) discord, hostility

confer (SYN) discuss, deliberate, chat, grant, bestow (ANT) take, withdraw

conference (SYN) convention, meeting, forum, discussion, gathering

confess (SYN) acknowledge, disclose, admit, profess, reveal (ANT) deny, refute, contest, conceal

confession (SYN) admission, disclosure, contrition, penance, memoir (ANT) denial, secret

confidant (SYN) friend, comrade, companion, advisor, crony (ANT) foe, adversary

confide (SYN) tell, reveal, whisper, declare, confess (ANT) conceal, hide, deny

confidence (SYN) faith, trust, conviction, aplomb, privately (ANT) mistrust, modesty, suspicion

confident (SYN) sure, satisfied, assertive, bold, self-assured (ANT) meek, timid, reserved

confidential (SYN) private, classified, secret, hush-hush (ANT) public, known, obvious, open

configuration (SYN) shape, structure, form

confine (SYN) restrict, limit, incarcerate, cage, restrain (ANT) loose, free, release, liberate

confines (SYN) limits, boundaries, boundaries, extent, scope, range

confirm (SYN) verify, prove,
substantiate, assert, endorse (ANT)
deny, disprove, cancel, contradict

confirmation (SYN) proof, evidence,
validation, approval, ratification
(ANT) question, contradiction

confiscate (SYN) seize, impound,
commandeer, usurp, sequester
(ANT) release, return

conflict (SYN) disagreement, hostility,
quarrel, war, differ (ANT)
agreement, peace, concord, harmony

confluence (SYN) junction, meeting,
convergence, assembly, congregation

conform (SYN) comply, adapt, agree,
obey, fit in (ANT) rebel, flout, defy,
revolt, challenge

conformity (SYN) similarity,
resemblance, uniformity,
compliance, orthodoxy (ANT)
rebellion, disobedience,
nonconformity, noncompliance

confront (SYN) face, defy, challenge,
tackle, address (ANT) evade, avoid,
dodge, bypass

confuse (SYN) confound, mistake,
perplex, disorient, complicate (ANT)
guide, enlighten, simplify

confusion (SYN) disorder, chaos,
uncertainty, perplexity, ambiguity
(ANT) certainty, order, regularity

congeal (SYN) stiffen, thicken, solidify,
set, coagulate (ANT) dissolve,
liquefy

congenial (SYN) friendly, pleasant,
hospitable, affable, kindred (ANT)
rude, unpleasant, irksome,
unsociable

congestion (SYN) crowding, jam, press,
concentration, gridlock (ANT)
emptiness

conglomeration (SYN) mix, mass,
collection, aggregate, mishmash

congratulations (SYN) salute,
compliments, felicitations (ANT)
derision, criticism, disregard

congregate (SYN) meet, gather, rally,
huddle, convene (ANT) scatter,
disperse, disband, spread

congregation (SYN) assembly, gathering
fellowship, parish, flock

congress (SYN) legislature, parliament,
assembly, caucus

congruent (SYN) equal, consistent,
compatible, identical, harmonious
(ANT) unequal, incongruent,
disagreeable

conjecture (SYN) assumption
speculation, hypothesis, guess, hunch
(ANT) fact, certainty

conjunction (SYN)combination,
connection, union, agreement,
concurrence (ANT) contrast,
division, separation

conjure (SYN) evoke, create, recollect,
magic, summon

connect (SYN) attach, link, couple,
relate, correlate (ANT) disconnect,
separate, divide, separate, disjoin

connection (SYN) bond, association, relevance, relationship, contact (ANT) disconnect, distance, separation, breach, enemy

connive (SYN) conspire, plot, scheme, disregard, consent (ANT) expose

connoisseur (SYN) expert, authority, aficionado, buff, enthusiast (ANT) novice, amateur, apprentice

connotation (SYN) implication, insinuation, intent, meaning, significance (ANT) denotation

conquer (SYN) defeat, best, overpower, obtain, capture, ascend (ANT) surrender, fall, succumb, forfeit

conquest (SYN) takeover, subjugation, defeat, victory, success (ANT) loss, surrender

conscience (SYN) honor, scruples, morality, ethics, superego (ANT) indifference

conscientious (SYN) thoughtful, diligent, particular, meticulous, scrupulous (ANT) casual, careless, irresponsible

conscious (SYN) aware, awake, responsive, deliberate, calculated (ANT) unconscious, comatose, insensible, unintentional

consciously (SYN) knowingly, deliberately, freely, wittingly (ANT) unconsciously, unawares, accidentally

consecrate (SYN) devote, dedicate, sanctify, hallow, exalt (ANT)

desecrate, abuse, pollute, defile, condemn

consecutive (SYN) sequential, running, straight, uninterrupted (ANT) random, irregular, intermittent, disordered

consensus (SYN) agreement, unanimity, unity, solidarity, popular opinion (ANT) disagreement, discord

consent (SYN) permission, approval, sanction, allow, authorize (ANT) forbid, dissent, protest

consequence (SYN) effect, outcome, repercussion, importance, significance (ANT) cause, source, insignificance

consequential (SYN) significant, grave, weighty, important, paramount (ANT) trivial, insignificant, unimportant, inessential

conservation (SYN) preservation, safekeeping, protection, upkeep, restoration (ANT) waste, destruction, squandering

conservative (SYN) traditional, conventional, right-wing, old fashioned, moderate (ANT) liberal, radical, left-wing, progressive

conservatory (SYN) greenhouse, hothouse, arboretum, academy

conserve (SYN) preserve, save, sustain, hoard, skimp (ANT) squander, discard, exhaust, waste

consider (SYN) contemplate, weigh, respect, remember, deem (ANT) ignore, dismiss, forget, disregard considerate (SYN) thoughtful, unselfish, courteous, attentive, sensitive (ANT) rude, impolite, disrespectful, inconsiderate

consideration (SYN) thought, deliberation, factor, kindness, fee (ANT) disregard, negligence, thoughtlessness, oversight

consign (SYN) entrust, authorize, deliver, remand, transfer (ANT) keep, receive

consignment (SYN) shipment, batch, delivery, assignment, relegation (ANT) receiving

consist (of) (SYN) contain, incorporate, involve, include (ANT) exclude, omit

consistent (SYN) regular, uniform, congruous, steady, compatible, like (ANT) erratic, incongruous, irregular, inconsistent

consolation (SYN) sympathy, condolence, encouragement, cheer, second (ANT) discouragement, sorrow, deprecation, disparagement

console (SYN) comfort, hearten, commiserate, empathize, soothe (ANT) upset, hurt, discourage, depress, worry

consolidate (SYN) combine, unite, condense, pool, fortify (ANT) divide, separate, weaken

consonant (SYN) harmonious, suitable, consistent, uniform, agreeable (ANT) incompatible, discordant, dissonant, disagreeing

conspicuous (SYN) obvious, blatant, noticeable, apparent, prominent (ANT) inconspicuous, hidden, concealed, unremarkable, unnoticeable

conspiracy (SYN) scheme, plot, treachery, collusion (ANT) loyalty

constant (SYN) continuous, perpetual, unrelenting, sustained, loyal (ANT) intermittent, variable, fluctuating, irregular, wavering

constellation (SYN) cluster, galaxy, pattern

consternation (SYN) dismay, anxiety, fear, alarm, panic (ANT) composure, tranquility, happiness, calm

constitute (SYN) comprise, represent, establish, create, authorize

constitution (SYN) character, disposition, health, composition, temperament, code

constrain (SYN) force, oblige, restrict, inhibit, restrain (ANT) free, release, liberate

construct (SYN) make, build, produce, assemble, formulate (ANT) demolish, destroy, dismantle, raze

construction (SYN) formation, building, structure, interpretation, analysis (ANT) destruction, demolition

constructive (SYN) helpful, useful, valuable, productive (ANT) hurtful, negative, useless construe (SYN) interpret, explain, infer, deduce, spin (ANT) misconstrue, mislead, confuse

consult (SYN) refer, consider, confer, discuss, check (ANT) disregard, ignore

consultant (SYN) specialist, advisor, expert, authority

consume (SYN) devour, gobble, destroy, spend, absorb (ANT) save, accumulate, fast, create, emit

consumer (SYN) shopper, customer, purchaser, buyer, user (ANT) seller, marketer

consummate (SYN) complete, end, perfect, supreme, absolute (ANT) begin, initiate, inadequate, deficient, mediocre

consumption (SYN) use, depletion, expenditure, waste, eating (ANT) conservation, preservation

contact (SYN) touch, communication, connection, reach, meeting (ANT) avoid, evade

contagious (SYN) infectious, catching, spreading, virulent, communicable (ANT) noninfectious

contain (SYN) have, embody, hold, compose, include, stifle (ANT) except, exclude, release, vent

container (SYN) holder, receptacle, vessel

contaminant (SYN) pollutant, toxin, poison, blight

contaminate (SYN) pollute, corrupt, taint, spoil, poison (ANT) clean, purify, cure

contamination (SYN) infection, pollution, corruption, impurity, taint (ANT) decontamination

contemplate (SYN) ponder, reflect, consider, plan, examine (ANT) disregard, ignore, forget, neglect

contemporary (SYN) modern, current, present-day, peer, concurrent (ANT) old, outdated, archaic, obsolete, past, future

contempt (SYN) hatred, scorn, derision, disdain, disrespect (ANT) respect, admiration, regard, esteem

contemptible (SYN) detestable, despicable, shameful, low, abhorrent (ANT) admirable, honorable, worthy, dignified, commendable

contend (SYN) argue, assert, maintain, compete, fight (ANT) agree, surrender, cede, comply

content (SYN) meaning, significance, volume, satisfied, happy, comfort (ANT) restless, miserable, upset, discontent

contention (SYN) argument, controversy, dissent, quarrel, explanation (ANT) accord, agreement, harmony

contentious (SYN) argumentative, controversial, testy, belligerent, combative (ANT) agreeable, passive, calm, peaceful contest (SYN) dispute, challenge, struggle, competition, match, fight (ANT) accept, accede, acquiesce, cooperation

context (SYN) circumstances, situation, background, scene, framework

contiguous (SYN) bordering, adjacent, meeting, neighboring, beside (ANT) apart, remote, removed, separated

contingent (SYN) conditional, dependant, reliant, uncertain, tentative (ANT) unconditional, certain

continual (SYN) constant, regular, unremitting, frequent, chronic (ANT) interrupted, periodic, rare

continue (SYN) persist, proceed, remain, resume, persevere (ANT) stop, desist, cease, finish

continuous (SYN) constant, unceasing, uninterrupted, incessant, steady (ANT) ceasing, intermittent, interrupted, broken

contortion (SYN) distortion, mutilation, twist, grimace, convolution (ANT) straightness, accuracy, truth

contour (SYN) curve, figure, silhouette, border, delineation (ANT) center, inside, core

contraband (SYN) unlawful, taboo, smuggled, prohibited, illicit (ANT) legal, permitted, authorized

contract (SYN) shorten, condense, acquire, agreement, pact, tighten (ANT) extend, loosen, expand, relax, elongate

contraction (SYN) shortening, tightening, abbreviation, decline (ANT) lengthening, relaxation, swelling, expansion

contradict (SYN) deny, challenge, rebut, dispute, counter (ANT) agree, comply, verify, confirm

contraption (SYN) device, gadget, instrument, appliance, gizmo

contrary (SYN) opposite, incompatible, contradictory, hostile, antagonistic (ANT) similar, consistent, correspondent, compatible

contrast (SYN) difference, disparity, opposite, distinguish, compare (ANT) likeness, similarity, agreement

contribute (SYN) give, donate, add, help, chip in (ANT) withhold, ignore, oppose, deny

contribution (SYN) donation, grant, offering, present, gift

contrite (SYN) sorry, regretful, repentant, remorseful, apologetic (ANT) unrepentant, proud, self-righteous, arrogant

contrive (SYN) arrange, maneuver, scheme, concoct, create (ANT) ruin, fail

control (SYN) authority, command, restraint, manage, subdue (ANT) resign, risk, servitude

controversy (SYN) debate, dispute, argument, contention, storm (ANT) agreement, harmony, unity contusion (SYN) bruise, bump, injury, swelling, discoloration

convalescent (SYN) recovery, healing, recuperation, rehabilitation, mending (ANT) regressing, worsening, sickly

convene (SYN) meet, gather, assemble, congregate, call (ANT) disperse, scatter, cancel

convenience (SYN) advantage, benefit, availability, utility, amenity (ANT) inconvenience

convenient (SYN) handy, useful, suitable, accessible, available (ANT) inconvenient, troublesome, ineffectual, inaccessible

convent (SYN) abbey, cloister, nunnery

convention (SYN) conference, assembly, custom, protocol

conventional (SYN) customary, traditional, standard, predictable (ANT) new, original, unconventional, irregular, unorthodox

converge (SYN) meet, intersect, join, gather, merge (ANT) disperse, divide, scatter

conversant (SYN) knowledgeable, acquainted, versed, proficient (ANT) ignorant, unfamiliar, inexperienced

conversation (SYN) talk, discussion, dialogue, chat, gossip

converse (SYN) chat, confer, opposite, contrary, reverse

conversion (SYN) change, transformation, adaptation, reorganization

convert (SYN) change, transform, adapt, remodel, reform, disciple (ANT) remain, stay, preserve

convex (SYN) rounded, bulging, swollen, arched, raised (ANT) concave, sunken

convey (SYN) tell, communicate, express, transfer, move (ANT) retain, keep, refrain

convict (SYN) condemn, sentence, criminal, felon (ANT) acquit, exonerate, clear

conviction (SYN) belief, position, faith, certainty, confidence (ANT) disbelief, doubt

convince (SYN) persuade, sway, assure, coax, win over (ANT) discourage, dispel

convoluted (SYN) complex, involved, puzzling, tangled (ANT) simple, straightforward, clear

convulsion (SYN) spasm, contraction, seizure, fit

cook (SYN) prepare, make, bake, chef, baker

cool (SYN) chilly, chill, composure, relaxed, aloof, hip (ANT) warm, friendly, excited, agitated

coop (SYN) cage, imprison, fence, corral (ANT) free, liberate cooperate (SYN) unite, collaborate, team up, participate (ANT) obstruct, impede, hinder, part

cooperation (SYN) teamwork, unity, assistance, alliance, partnership (ANT) rivalry, autonomy, competition

cooperative (SYN) helpful, obliging, willing, shared, collective (ANT) divided, ungracious, unwilling

coordinate (SYN) match, harmonize, orchestrate, organize, correlate (ANT) mismatch, disorganize, disrupt

coordination (SYN) agility, dexterity, administration, planning, organization (ANT) clumsiness, awkwardness, disorganization

cope (SYN) manage, endure, handle, weather, deal (ANT) panic, collapse, succumb, avoid

copious (SYN) full, abundant, extensive, ample, liberal (ANT) meager, lacking, skimpy, incomplete

copy (SYN) duplicate, replica, forge, reproduce, mimic (ANT) original, invent, produce, master, originate

cord (SYN) rope, line, twine, corduroy

cordial (SYN) polite, warm, friendly, earnest, tender (ANT) distant, cold, unwelcoming, hostile, surly

core (SYN) center, crux, heart, middle, substance (ANT) exterior, peripheral

corner (SYN) angle, bend, retreat, nook, trap, monopolize, tight spot

corny (SYN) cliché, old-fashioned, sentimental, unoriginal (ANT) fresh, unique, deep, original

corollary (SYN) consequence, result, end, culmination, analogy

coronation (SYN) inauguration, installment, instatement, ordination, crowning

corporation (SYN) company, business, firm, partnership, enterprise

corps (SYN) squad, team, company, division, regiment, unit

corpse (SYN) body, cadaver, remains

corpulent (SYN) fat chubby, flabby, hefty, rotund (ANT) skinny, slender, underweight, slight

corral (SYN) enclosure, cage, pen, confine, fence (ANT) set free

correct (SYN) accurate, proper, suitable, repair, fix, reprimand (ANT) wrong, indecent, flawed, incorrect

correction (SYN) alteration, remedy, discipline, editing, revisal (ANT) reward

correlate (SYN) relate, compare, correspond, connect, parallel (ANT) differ, disconnect

correlation (SYN) connection, match, reciprocity, relationship, correspondence (ANT) opposition, contradiction

correspond (SYN) agree, coincide, conform, communicate, write (ANT) differ, clash, disagree correspondence (SYN) letters, communication, correlation, similarity, consistency (ANT) incongruity, divergence, imbalance, disagreement

correspondent (SYN) journalist, reporter, writer, contributor

corridor (SYN) hallway, passage, alley, lane, channel

corroborate (SYN) affirm, support, endorse, substantiate, verify (ANT) refute, deny, contradict, negate

corrosive (SYN) caustic, wearing, acrid, destructive, sarcastic (ANT) fortifying, strengthening, mild

corrugated (SYN) creased, furrowed, channeled, grooved (ANT) smooth, flat

corrupt (SYN) dishonest, unlawful, distorted, bribe, pervert (ANT) honorable, sound, decent, purify

corruption (SYN) misconduct, immorality, vice, extortion, distortion (ANT) honesty, virtue, scruples

cosmetic (SYN) superficial, surface, beautifying, restorative (ANT) genuine, legitimate

cosmic (SYN) huge, vast, infinite, universal, stellar (ANT) finite, infinitesimal

cosmopolitan (SYN) sophisticated, global, cultivated, worldly, urban (ANT) insular, narrow-minded, rustic

cost (SYN) price, charge, loss, sacrifice, expenditure, value, fetch

costume (SYN) outfit, apparel, garb, garments, dress

cot (SYN) bed, pallet, stretcher

cottage (SYN) house, cabin, hut, lodge, bungalow

couch (SYN) sofa, lounge, settee, bed, frame, phrase

cough (SYN) bark, hack, ahem, choke

council (SYN) committee, panel, board, assembly

counsel (SYN) attorney, advocate, guidance, advise, recommend, urge, steer (ANT) betray, deceive

counselor (SYN) advisor, mentor, guide

count (SYN) tally, calculate, matter, consider, include, number (ANT) guess, dismiss, exclude, be insignificant

countenance (SYN) expression, appearance, looks, calmness, approval

counter (SYN) against, conversely, retaliate, oppose (ANT) accept, yield, consistent

counteract (SYN) negate, offset, thwart, check, nullify (ANT) support, assist, promote

counterfeit (SYN) fake, forgery, copy, fraudulent, imitate (ANT) real, genuine, actual counterpart (SYN) complement, equal, opposite, foil, match

country (SYN) nation, realm, homeland, rural, unrefined (ANT) urban, metropolitan

coup (SYN) rebellion, takeover, accomplishment, exploit, success (ANT) failure, defeat

couple (SYN) pair, duo, two, link, join, wed (ANT) single, detach, separate, divide

coupon (SYN) voucher, slip, certificate, rain check

courage (SYN) bravery, heroism, nerve, fearlessness, guts (ANT) fear, cowardice, timidity

courageous (SYN) brave, valiant, bold, intrepid, daring (ANT) fearful, cowardly, timid, fainthearted, wimpy

courier (SYN) messenger, carrier, bearer, envoy, herald, guide (ANT) sender, receiver

course (SYN) route, path, technique, approach, class, program, flow, duration

court (SYN) date, woo, flatter, pursue, invite, entourage, tribunal, courtyard, castle (ANT) avoid, reject, spurn

courteous (SYN) polite, mannered, gracious, considerate, respectful (ANT) rude, impolite, discourteous, ill-mannered

courtesy (SYN) civility, politeness, respect, consideration,

thoughtfulness (ANT) discourtesy, unkindness, rudeness

courtship (SYN) dating, pursuit, wooing, flirtation, seduction

cove (SYN) inlet, bay, lagoon, estuary, cave

covenant (SYN) promise, pact, agreement, contract, pledge, deal

cover (SYN) hide, conceal, coat, blanket, facade, consider, include, wrapper, shelter, cross (ANT) reveal, expose, omit

covert (SYN) hidden, furtive, stealthy, surreptitious, clandestine (ANT) open, overt, public

covet (SYN) envy, desire, crave, lust after, fancy (ANT) ignore, reject, renounce

covetous (SYN) envious, greedy, jealous, avaricious, selfish (ANT) generous, benevolent, giving

cow (SYN) intimidate, bully, terrorize, subdue, rattle (ANT) encourage, embolden

coward (SYN) wimp, alarmist, baby, sissy (ANT) hero, daredevil

cowardice (SYN) fearfulness, weakness, timidity, apprehension (ANT) bravery, courage

cowardly (SYN) fearful, anxious, shrinking, timorous, scared (ANT) bold, dauntless, courageous, brave

cowboy (SYN) cowhand, wrangler, rancher, bronco, buckaroo

cower (SYN) shrink, crouch, flinch, tremble, grovel (ANT) intimidate, strut

coy (SYN) bashful, demure, modest, self-effacing, coquettish (ANT) brazen, aggressive, cheeky, forward, immodest

cozy (SYN) snug, comfortable, intimate, warm, secure (ANT) uncomfortable, cold, unwelcoming

crack (SYN) cleft, fissure, split, clap, splinter, collapse, decipher, jibe

cradle (SYN) crib, birthplace, source, nestle, hold

craft (SYN) occupation, skill, cunning, vessel, artwork, create (ANT) incompetence, honesty

crafty (SYN) sly, shrewd, wily, devious, dishonest (ANT) naive, honest, guileless

cram (SYN) stuff, force, squeeze, gorge, study (ANT) empty, loosen

crane (SYN) winch, lift, stretch, reach, strain

crank (SYN) wind, gear, wheel, grouch, crab

crash (SYN) accident, collision, clatter, collapse, collide (ANT) silence, avoid, restore, rise, avert

crass (SYN) insensitive, gross, rude, vulgar, uncouth (ANT) polite, polished, delicate, tactful, tasteful

crate (SYN) box, container, chest

crater (SYN) dip, hollow, depression, hole, basin

crave (SYN) desire, want, yearn for, hanker after (ANT) renounce

crawl (SYN) creep, inch, swarm, teem, grovel (ANT) dash, hasten, hurry, walk

craze (SYN) rage, trend, vogue, mania, fashion (ANT) custom, tradition

crazy (SYN) absurd, nonsensical, devoted, wild, demented (ANT) sane, sensible, rational, stable, practical

creak (SYN) squeak, groan, screech

cream (SYN) lotion, salve, best, finest, ivory (ANT) dregs, worst

crease (SYN) fold, wrinkle, line, rumple, groove (ANT) flatten, smooth, press

create (SYN) make, produce, devise, cause, establish (ANT) destroy, terminate, abolish

creation (SYN) generation, inception, achievement, concoction, universe (ANT) destruction, annihilation, failure, flop

creative (SYN) inventive, original, innovative, ingenious, inspired, visionary (ANT) unimaginative, uninspired, mindless, dull

creativity (SYN) imagination, inventiveness, ingenuity, vision

creature (SYN) animal, beast, person, critter, being

credentials (SYN) references, testimonial, qualifications, experience, documentation

credible (SYN) believable, plausible, likely, reliable, sincere (ANT) doubtful, incredible, unbelievable

credit (SYN) acknowledgement, recognition, kudos, reliance, believe (ANT) discredit, disapproval, deny, doubt

credo (SYN) belief, doctrine, creed, dogma, ideology

credulous (SYN) gullible, accepting, trusting, simple, unsuspecting (ANT) cynical, suspicious, wary, incredulous, skeptical

creed (SYN) belief, faith, doctrine, religion, principles

creek (SYN) stream, brook, inlet, spring, tributary

creep (SYN) sneak, skulk, steal, crawl, pervert (ANT) hurry, leave

crescendo (SYN) swell, intensification, escalation, culmination

crest (SYN) top, ridge, summit, emblem, tuft (ANT) base, bottom, trough

crevice (SYN) gap, opening, crack, cleft, split

crew (SYN) company, team, sailors, troupe

crib (SYN) cradle, bed, house, abode

crime (SYN) transgression, violation, offense, corruption, infraction (ANT) innocence, good deed, kindness

criminal (SYN) convict, offender, illegal, illicit, deplorable (ANT) lawful, legal, innocent, honest, virtuous

cringe (SYN) shrink, flinch, wince, shy, crouch

cripple (SYN) disable, paralyze, incapacitate, damage, impair (ANT) support, strengthen, heal, fortify, enable

crisis (SYN) emergency, meltdown, plight, crux, culmination (ANT) calm, equilibrium, serenity

crisp (SYN) brisk, clean, crunchy, firm, brittle (ANT) flexible, soft, balmy, sloppy

criterion (SYN) standard, measure, test, gauge, barometer

critic (SYN) expert, authority, reviewer, detractor, analyst (ANT) advocate, champion, supporter, admirer, fan

critical (SYN) crucial, urgent, serious, disparaging, vital, analytical (ANT) trivial, approving, insignificant

criticism (SYN) disapproval, censure, assessment, evaluation, critique (ANT) praise, commendation, raves

criticize (SYN) condemn, knock, attack, chastise, scrutinize (ANT) applaud, praise, compliment, cheer

croak (SYN) squawk, wheeze, gasp, grunt

crooked (SYN) curved, twisting, bent, askew, corrupt (ANT) straight, direct, legal, honorable

crop (SYN) harvest, yield, prune, trim, cut, nibble

cross (SYN) bridge, traverse, intersect, betray, blend, crucifix, burden, grumpy (ANT) agreeable, remain, divide, aid

crouch (SYN) hunch, stoop, bend, squat, duck (ANT) stretch, straighten

crow (SYN) brag, gloat, trumpet, strut, whoop

crowd (SYN) swarm, group, audience, gather, cram (ANT) scatter, disperse

crown (SYN) coronet, pinnacle, top, honor, complete (ANT) bottom, dishonor, commence

crucial (SYN) critical, vital, pressing, key, paramount (ANT) insignificant, trivial, incidental, mild, unimportant

crucifixion (SYN) torture, execution, persecution, martyrdom

crude (SYN) primitive, rudimentary, vulgar, tasteless, raw (ANT) refined, clean, sophisticated, finished, tasteful

cruel (SYN) callous, vicious, sadistic, ruthless, traumatic (ANT) benevolent, compassionate, gentle, merciful

cruelty (SYN) depravity, brutality, savagery, malignity, rancor (ANT) consideration, heart, humanity, tenderness, kindness

cruise (SYN) voyage, sail, coast, drift, mosey

crumble (SYN) crush, grind, disintegrate, collapse, deteriorate (ANT) build, develop, thrive

crusade (SYN) cause, campaign, movement, battle, fight

crush (SYN) press, squash, quell, crowd, demoralize, infatuation (ANT) repair, expand, encourage, promote

crust (SYN) shell, covering, coating, topping, surface

crux (SYN) meaning, essence, gist, substance, thrust (ANT) extra, secondary, trivial

cry (SYN) weep, sob, shriek, appeal, lament (ANT) laugh, whisper, murmur

crypt (SYN) vault, tomb, grave, chamber, sepulcher

cryptic (SYN) vague, ambiguous, puzzling, enigmatic, veiled (ANT) clear, obvious, explicit, direct

crystal (SYN) transparent, clear, luminous (ANT) opaque, cloudy

crystallize (SYN) develop, arise, materialize, take shape (ANT) dissolve, disperse

cub (SYN) young, offspring, child, youngster

cue (SYN) signal, reminder, prompting, hint, intimation

cull (SYN) choose, pluck, mark, collect, gather

culminate (SYN) conclude, finish, close, end, crown (ANT) commence, begin, open, undertake

culpable (SYN) responsible, guilty, answerable, accountable, blameworthy (ANT) innocent, guiltless, inculpable, exempt

culprit (SYN) offender, wrongdoer, villain, guilty party, convict (ANT) innocent

cult (SYN) sect, faction, idolization, clan, faddism

cultivate (SYN) encourage, foster, refine, court, farm (ANT) pollute, neglect

cultural (SYN) enlightening, civilizing, aesthetic, social, anthropological (ANT) wild, ignorant

culture (SYN) customs, heritage, society, refinement, development (ANT) degeneration, regression, vulgarity

cumbersome (SYN) awkward, bulky, unwieldy, inconvenient, unmanageable (ANT) compact, manageable, easy, slight

cumulative (SYN) collective, combined, amassed, aggregate, growing (ANT) individual, separate, decreasing

cunning (SYN) crafty, sly, devious, trickery, cleverness (ANT) honest, sincere, naive, insipid

cup (SYN) glass, mug, chalice, contain, hold

cupboard (SYN) closet, cabinet, shelf, pantry, storeroom

curator (SYN) caretaker, director, conservator, administrator, steward

curb (SYN) barrier, limitation, restrain, control, restrict (ANT) encouragement, push, foster, facilitate

curdle (SYN) sour, spoil, thicken, condense, ferment (ANT) thin, liquefy

cure (SYN) heal, restore, preserve, remedy, treatment (ANT) malady, illness, harm, injure, poison

curiosity (SYN) interest, inquisitiveness, oddity, spectacle, novelty (ANT) indifference, boredom, disinterest, commonality

curious (SYN) questioning, intrigued, bizarre, peculiar, extraordinary (ANT) apathetic, uninterested, typical, conventional

curl (SYN) twirl, coil, spiral, wind, wrap (ANT) straighten, uncurl, unwind

curmudgeon (SYN) grouch, malcontent, miser, crab

currency (SYN) money, tender, cash, popularity, exposure

current (SYN) contemporary, topical, common, valid, flow, progression (ANT) antiquated, dated, past

curriculum

curriculum (SYN) program, schedule, course of study, syllabus

curry (SYN) flatter, kiss up, cajole, fawn over

curse (SYN) swear, obscenity, expletive, jinx, affliction, trouble (ANT) bless, blessing, advantage

curt (SYN) blunt, terse, succinct, abrupt, sharp (ANT) courteous, diplomatic, lengthy, loquacious

curtail (SYN) diminish, reduce, truncate, restrict, limit (ANT) lengthen, extend, prolong, increase

curtain (SYN) drapery, hanging, screen, shade, blind

curtsy (SYN) bow, bend, genuflect

curvature (SYN) arc, bend, trajectory, curve, shape

curve (SYN) bend, loop, turn, swerve, arch (ANT) straighten

curved (SYN) bent, arched, rounded, crescent, crooked (ANT) straight, linear, direct

cushion (SYN) buffer, shield, protect, soften, pillow (ANT) hurt

custodian (SYN) janitor, caretaker, guardian, steward, overseer

custody (SYN) care, supervision, responsibility, imprisoned, arrest (ANT) freedom, liberty

custom (SYN) tradition, convention, habit, routine (ANT) deviation, irregularity

customary (SYN) common, established, familiar, traditional, habitual (ANT) abnormal, original, offbeat, different

customer (SYN) client, consumer, patron, shopper, regular (ANT) merchant, seller, vendor

cut (SYN) chop, sever, mow, abridge, insult, laceration, dilute (ANT) addition, increase, compliment, reattach, enhance

cute (SYN) sweet, endearing, dear, adorable, charming (ANT) ugly, homely, unappealing

cycle (SYN) loop, pattern, rhythm, period, bicycle, circuit, sequence

cyclone (SYN) hurricane, tempest, typhoon, tropical storm

cynic (SYN) skeptic, pessimist, misanthrope, doubter, detractor (ANT) idealist, believer, devotee, optimist

cynicism (SYN) disbelief, doubt, skepticism, suspicion, disenchantment (ANT) idealism, optimism

cyst (SYN) growth, blister, pouch, vesicle, tumor

D

dad (SYN) father, pop, daddy

daft (SYN) foolish, crazy, silly, absurd, stupid (ANT) sensible, sound, sane

dagger (SYN) knife, blade, glower, scowl

daily (SYN) everyday, day-to-day, diurnal, common, habitual (ANT) nightly, sporadic, intermittent

dainty (SYN) delicate, petite, fragile, charming, fine, choosy (ANT) weighty, substantial, unparticular

dais (SYN) platform, podium, terrace, stage

dally (SYN) dawdle, idle, tarry, procrastinate, flirt, frolic (ANT) hurry, hasten, speed, expedite

dam (SYN) barrier, obstruction, wall, barricade, restrict (ANT) release, unblock, loosen

damage (SYN) harm, injure, destruction, impairment, expense (ANT) safeguard, improve, repair, mend, benefit

damp (SYN) moist, dank, humid, soggy, saturated (ANT) dry, parched, arid

dance (SYN) boogie, prance, gyrate, sway, ball, social

danger (SYN) risk, jeopardy, peril, threat, vulnerability (ANT) security, safety, defense

dangerous (SYN) treacherous, hazardous, menacing, precarious, dodgy (ANT) safe, harmless, unthreatening

dangle (SYN) hang, swing, trail, jingle, flourish, suspend

dappled (SYN) checkered, variegated, brindled, speckled, flecked (ANT) solid, monochrome

dapper (SYN) neat, trim, elegant, debonair, natty (ANT) scruffy, disheveled, unkempt, untidy, sloppy

dare (SYN) challenge, provoke, risk, hazard, venture (ANT) avoid, pass, refrain

daring (SYN) bold, adventurous, intrepid, audacity (ANT) timid, afraid, wimpy, cowardice

dark (SYN) unlit, bleak, sinister, somber, black (ANT) light, bright, illuminated, joyful, virtuous

darkness (SYN) night, gloom, shadow, wickedness, ignorance (ANT) lightness, comprehension, cheer

darling (SYN) adorable, dear, beloved, charming, delightful (ANT) detestable, foe

darn (SYN) repair, mend, patch, stitch, reinforcement (ANT) tear, worsen

dart (SYN) dash, race, scamper, direct, missile, projectile (ANT) mosey, plod, trudge, dawdle

dash (SYN) hurry, bolt, throw, shatter, bit, pinch, flamboyance (ANT) linger, amble, stroll, raise, gob, encourage

data (SYN) information, statistics, particulars, evidence, figures

date (SYN) day, time, court, escort, appointment, chronicle

daub (SYN) smear, coat, dab, cover, paint

daunt (SYN) terrorize, intimidate, bully, discourage, thwart (ANT) encourage, embolden, urge, aid

dauntless (SYN) fearless, intrepid, unflinching, audacious, valiant (ANT) timid, cowardly, afraid, daunted

dawdle (SYN) linger, amble, mosey, idle, loiter, procrastinate (ANT) hurry, hasten, rush

dawn (SYN) sunrise, daybreak, beginning, arrive, emerge (ANT) dusk, twilight, conclusion

day (SYN) date, era, height, daytime, light (ANT) night, dark

daze (SYN) shock, bewilder, trance, muddle, confusion (ANT) clarify, explain, enlighten

dazzle (SYN) astonish, impress, overwhelm, disorient, magnificence (ANT) bore, disenchant

dead (SYN) departed, late, deceased, inactive, numb, exhausted, dull, utterly (ANT) alive, lively, animated, working, partially

deadline (SYN) due date, time limit, target date

deadlock (SYN) impasse, gridlock, stalemate, standstill, draw (ANT) breakthrough, resolution

deadly (SYN) fatal, lethal, toxic, mortal, dangerous (ANT) harmless, benign, innocuous

deaf (SYN) unhearing, oblivious, unconcerned (ANT) hearing, listening, attentive, aware

deafening (SYN) booming, thunderous, ear-piercing, resounding (ANT) low, soft, faint, inaudible

deal (SYN) arrangement, understanding, bargain, negotiate, handle, examine, distribute (ANT) disagreement, neglect, collect

dealer (SYN) merchant, purveyor, supplier, peddler, vendor

dear (SYN) beloved, treasured, prized, intimate, expensive (ANT) despised, rival, cheap

dearly (SYN) greatly, extremely, profoundly, fondly (ANT) little, hatefully

death (SYN) passing, demise, end, destruction, ruin (ANT) life, birth, existence, inception, beginning

debacle (SYN) disaster, fiasco, collapse, breakdown (ANT) success, triumph

debatable (SYN) arguable, doubtful, controversial, contestable, questionable (ANT) certain, definite, unequivocal, inarguable

debate (SYN) dispute, contention, discuss, argue, consider (ANT) agreement, concur

debilitate (SYN) weaken, disable, incapacitate, undermine, harm (ANT) strengthen, aid, energize, invigorate

debit (SYN) debt, claim, liability,
obligation

debrief (SYN) question, probe,
interrogate, quiz

debris (SYN) rubble, remains, wreckage,
ruins, fragments

debt (SYN) bill, charges, deficit,
commitment, gratitude (ANT)
excess, assets

debtor (SYN) borrower

debut (SYN) introduction, beginning,
opening, launching (ANT) closing,
finale, farewell

decadence (SYN) corruption,
degradation, decline, self-indulgence

decay (SYN) deteriorate, crumble, wane,
decompose, disintegration (ANT)
flourish, grow, thrive, vigor

deceased (SYN) dead, lifeless, departed,
expired (ANT) alive

deceit (SYN) dishonesty, fraud, guile,
deception, trickery (ANT) honesty,
truth, openness

deceitful (SYN) false, untrustworthy,
insincere, duplicitous, sneaky (ANT)
sincere, upright, straightforward,
honest

deceive (SYN) trick, mislead, dupe,
swindle, fool (ANT) advise, help,
enlighten, inform

decency (SYN) courtesy, etiquette,
respectability, virtue, consideration
(ANT) indecency, impropriety

decent (SYN) proper, satisfactory,
pleasant, generous, ethical (ANT)
lewd, improper, inappropriate,
inadequate

deception (SYN) lying, treachery,
pretense, subterfuge, cunning (ANT)
honesty, integrity, veracity, candor

decide (SYN) conclude, resolve,
determine, settle, judge (ANT)
hesitate, defer, fluctuate, waver

decimate (SYN) devastate, ravage,
destroy, massacre, annihilate (ANT)
preserve, restore, construct,
surrender

decipher (SYN) decode, interpret, read,
solve, analyze (ANT) encode,
scramble

decision (SYN) conclusion, verdict,
determination, resolve, fortitude
(ANT) tie, stalemate, draw,
indecision

decisive (SYN) firm, resolute,
purposeful, pivotal, key (ANT)
indefinite, inconclusive, dependant,
inconsequential

decisively (SYN) certainly, easily,
categorically, unconditionally (ANT)
doubtfully, questionably, probably

deck (SYN) decorate, adorn, dress

declaration (SYN) assertion, testimony,
announcement, statement

declare (SYN) state, proclaim, articulate,
express, reveal (ANT) conceal, deny,
retract

decline

decline (SYN) diminish, decrease, ebb, worsen, abstain, drop (ANT) rise, improvement, strengthen

decompose (SYN) rot, decay, disintegrate, dissect, separate (ANT) grow, develop, improve, combine

decomposition (SYN) breakdown, dissolution, decay, rot, division

decorate (SYN) ornament, trim, adorn, honor (ANT) strip, simplify, spoil, disrespect

decoration (SYN) trimming, embellishment, beatification, ornament, award

decorous (SYN) dignified, proper, becoming, refined (ANT) inappropriate, unsuitable, impolite

decoy (SYN) lure, trap, enticement, seduce, tempt (ANT) dissuade, repel

decrease (SYN) lessen, diminish, abate, dwindle, reduction (ANT) increase, expansion, growth, enlarge, heighten

decree (SYN) law, command, edict, proclamation, dictate, pronounce

decrepit (SYN) weak, infirm, feeble, dilapidated, battered (ANT) fit, sound, powerful, robust

decry (SYN) criticize, belittle, condemn, disparage, denounce (ANT) support, praise, compliment, applaud

dedicate (SYN) devote, commit, consecrate, bless, inscribe (ANT) keep, withhold, desecrate, dishonor

dedication (SYN) allegiance, devotion, faithfulness, loyalty, sanctification, inscription (ANT) apathy, disloyalty

deduce (SYN) glean, infer, conclude, gather (ANT) misinterpret

deduct (SYN) subtract, debit, dock, diminish, reduce (ANT) add, increase, grow, amplify

deed (SYN) action, feat, exploit, title, contract (ANT) failure, deliberation

deep (SYN) abysmal, cavernous, intense, profound, immersed, resonant (ANT) shallow, high, shrill, superficial, distracted

deface (SYN) damage, tarnish, vandalize, ruin (ANT) mend, restore, freshen

defamation (SYN) libel, aspersion, detraction, vilification (ANT) laudation, commendation, admiration, approval

default (SYN) failure, neglect, dereliction, lapse, dodge (ANT) payment, satisfy

defeat (SYN) conquer, beat, frustrate, derail, loss, setback (ANT) triumph, victory, surrender, lose

defect (SYN) flaw, shortcoming, imperfection, desert, abandon (ANT) excellence, faultlessness, remain

defective (SYN) faulty, unsound, deficient, broken, lacking (ANT) perfect, intact, flawless defend (SYN) protect, guard, secure, justify, explain (ANT) criticize, forsake, attack, renounce

defendant (SYN) offender, defense, the accused (ANT) accuser, prosecution

defense (SYN) security, protection, armaments, shield, justification, excuse (ANT) offense, attack, prosecution

defensive (SYN) watchful, protective, vigilant, uptight, paranoid (ANT) offensive, negligent, inattentive, relaxed

defer (SYN) comply, yield, suspend, delay, shelve (ANT) dissent, hasten, expedite

deference (SYN) consideration, regard, respect, compliance, acquiescence (ANT) defiance, opposition, disrespect, contempt

defiance (SYN) confrontation, insolence, resistance, rebellion, insubordination (ANT) obedience, submission, passivity, surrender

defiant (SYN) bold, disobedient, obstinate, uncooperative, unruly (ANT) conforming, respectful, obedient, submissive

deficient (SYN) lacking, insufficient, flawed, inadequate, meager (ANT) ample, adequate, sufficient, perfect, complete

deficit (SYN) debt, shortage, loss, lack, deficiency (ANT) surplus, profit, plenty, excess

defile (SYN) soil, tarnish, corrupt, debase, desecrate, violate (ANT) cleanse, purify, honor, sanctify

define (SYN) characterize, describe, delineate, outline, exemplify (ANT) confuse, distort, obscure, complicate

definite (SYN) clear, precise, fixed, explicit, decisive (ANT) ambiguous, uncertain, vague, indeterminate

definitely (SYN) surely, absolutely, undeniably, categorically, decidedly (ANT) possibly, perhaps, indefinitely, doubtfully, maybe

definition (SYN) meaning, interpretation, explanation, clarity, resolution (ANT) distortion, blurriness, ambiguity

definitive (SYN) conclusive, decisive, authoritative, ultimate, exhaustive (ANT) debatable, unreliable, inconclusive, provisional, contestable

deflate (SYN) collapse, shrink, flatten, humiliate, dispirit (ANT) inflate, swell, expand, boost, flatter

deflect (SYN) divert, distract, deviate, ricochet, avert, parry (ANT) confront, face

deformity (SYN) abnormality, malformation, distortion, warp, asymmetry (ANT) normality, perfection

defraud (SYN) cheat, fleece, trick, swindle, deceive, beguile (ANT) support, repay, help

defray (SYN) pay, fund, finance

defrost (SYN) thaw, unfreeze, warm, soften (ANT) freeze

deft (SYN) able, dexterous, proficient, skillful, expert (ANT) inept, awkward, bumbling, unqualified

defunct (SYN) inoperative, obsolete, deceased (ANT) existing, working, thriving

defy (SYN) challenge, disregard, flout, resist, confront (ANT) surrender, yield, obey, relent, comply

degenerate (SYN) decline, deteriorate, depraved, immoral, perverted (ANT) improve, flourish, upright, virtuous

degrade (SYN) demean, shame, debase, belittle, demote (ANT) dignify, promote, elevate, admire

degree (SYN) unit, level, extent, magnitude, proportion, recognition

deify (SYN) exalt, venerate, idolize, worship, idealize (ANT) dishonor, lower, reduce, humble

dejection (SYN) despair, gloom, melancholy, despondency, depression (ANT) joy, bliss, happiness, euphoria

delay (SYN) postpone, impede, linger, stall, hesitate, interruption (ANT) hurry, assist, acceleration, advancement

delectable (SYN) delicious appetizing, scrumptious, delightful, exquisite (ANT) disgusting, sickening, unpleasant, nauseating

delegate (SYN) representative, ambassador, envoy, entrust, designate

delete (SYN) erase, remove, cancel, excise, expunge (ANT) add, insert, include

deliberate (SYN) calculated, intentional, measured, contemplate, debate (ANT) accidental, careless, impulsive, spontaneous

deliberately (SYN) willfully, knowingly, purposely, intentionally, voluntarily (ANT) unwittingly, unintentionally, accidentally

delicacy (SYN) indulgence, rarity, luxury, fragility, elegance, sensitivity (ANT) durability, toughness, necessity, ordinary, dull

delicate (SYN) slight, feeble, awkward, diplomatic, insubstantial (ANT) healthy, robust, durable, strong, inconsiderate

delicious (SYN) tasty, savory, pleasing, delectable, piquant (ANT) bland, distasteful, gross, unappetizing

delight (SYN) charm, enchant, thrill, enjoyment, bliss (ANT) dismay, distress, displeasure, misery, discontent

delightful (SYN) pleasurable, rapturous, lovely, amusing, captivating (ANT) disappointing, unhappy, objectionable, repulsive

delinquent (SYN) criminal, offender, hooligan, overdue, derelict (ANT) dutiful, lawful delirious (SYN) incoherent, frenzied, ecstatic, lunatic, irrational (ANT) lucid, sane, composed, rational, stable

deliver (SYN) convey, transport, pronounce, administer, liberate (ANT) keep, retain, confine, withhold

delivery (SYN) transport, distribution, shipment, articulation, childbirth

delude (SYN) deceive, fool, betray, misguide, dupe (ANT) enlighten, explain, inform, advise

delusion (SYN) illusion, misapprehension, error, fantasy, hallucination (ANT) reality, truth

deluxe (SYN) superior, luxurious, grand, opulent, choice (ANT) inferior, ordinary, cheap

delve (SYN) explore, research, search, investigate, inquire

demagogue (SYN) agitator, instigator, incendiary, dissident, troublemaker, malcontent (ANT) peacemaker, pacifier

demand (SYN) command, order, dictate, request, necessitate grant, offer, supply

demean (SYN) lower, shame, humiliate, humble, abase (ANT) elevate, honor, cherish, enhance, dignify

demeanor (SYN) conduct, bearing, manner, carriage, attitude, presence, disposition

demented (SYN) deranged, insane, crazy, psychotic, maniacal (ANT) sane, rational, stable

demerit (SYN) fault, error, misdeed, shortcoming, flaw (ANT) perfection, sufficiency

demise (SYN) ruin, downfall, death, collapse, disintegration (ANT) birth, beginning

democratic (SYN) autonomous, popular, egalitarian, representative, elected (ANT) dictatorial, intolerant, communistic, authoritarian, tyrannical

demolish (SYN) destroy, raze, dismantle, wreck, obliterate, annihilate (ANT) build, fortify, construct, restore, preserve

demolition (SYN) leveling, destruction, bulldozing, explosion, wrecking (ANT) creation, construction, building, restoration

demonic (SYN) evil, diabolic, satanic, infernal, wicked (ANT) angelic, saintly, virtuous, good, heavenly

demonstrate (SYN) manifest, exhibit, illustrate, teach, protest (ANT) conceal, confuse

demonstration (SYN) presentation, explanation, proof, confirmation, march

demoralize (SYN) dishearten, discourage, undermine, weaken, daunt, deprave, pervert (ANT) boost, encourage, uplift, purify demur (SYN) dispute, challenge, vacillation, pause (ANT) concur, accept, acquiesce, agree, concede

demure (SYN) modest, sedate, coy, reserved, unassuming (ANT) bold, brazen, aggressive, brash, confident

den (SYN) cave, lair, hideout, sanctuary, shelter

denial (SYN) retraction, contradiction, rebuttal, rejection, refusal (ANT) admission, affirmation, approval

denigrate (SYN) malign, slander, ridicule, disparage, scandalize, impugn (ANT) flatter, compliment, respect, honor

denomination (SYN) creed, sect, church, unit, value

denounce (SYN) condemn, attack, revile, accuse, censure, implicate (ANT) praise, commend, laud

dense (SYN) crowded, tight, compact, impenetrable, foolish, obtuse (ANT) sparse, porous, scant, clever, intelligent

density (SYN) bulk, mass, thickness, consistency

dent (SYN) depression, indentation, nick, hollow, knock, mark

denunciation (SYN) blame, incrimination, reprobation, accusation, censure (ANT) compliment, appreciation, blessing

deny (SYN) contradict, refute, contest, repudiate, refuse, recant (ANT)

affirm, acknowledge, confirm, allow, assert

depart (SYN) leave, retire, vanish, deviate, stray (ANT) arrive, abide, come, linger, remain

department (SYN) division, section, branch, agency, jurisdiction

departure (SYN) withdrawal, exodus, divergence, anomaly, innovation (ANT) arrival, entrance, regularity, conformity, norm

depend (SYN) count on, rely upon, expect, hinge on, bank on, contingent

dependable (SYN) reliable, trustworthy, reputable, steadfast, loyal (ANT) irresponsible, unreliable, erratic, arbitrary

dependant (SYN) ward, charge, minor, child

dependent (SYN) reliant, incapable, vulnerable, conditional, addicted (ANT) independent, autonomous, strong, self-reliant, absolute

depict (SYN) describe, represent, portray, draw, render, detail (ANT) distort, confuse, confound

deplete (SYN) consume, exhaust, reduce, diminish, squander (ANT) augment, increase, replenish, add

deplorable (SYN) grievous, dire, shameful, pitiable, abominable (ANT) agreeable, commendable, desirable, pleasant, appealing deplore (SYN) abhor, condemn, hate, eschew, regret (ANT) endorse, sanction, accept, fancy, admire

deploy (SYN) post, install, position, utilize, exploit (ANT) recall

deport (SYN) banish, expel, oust, extradite (ANT) admit

depose (SYN) demote, remove, overthrow, supplant, topple (ANT) install, empower, crown

deposit (SYN) sediment, accumulation, layer, store, retainer, lodge

deposition (SYN) removal, dismissal, testimony, declaration, statement

depot (SYN) terminal, station, storehouse, arsenal, repository

depraved (SYN) evil, wicked, corrupt, debased, nefarious (ANT) moral, noble, chaste, virtuous, pure

depreciate (SYN) lessen, cheapen, devalue, deride, belittle (ANT) grow, increase, cherish, esteem

depreciation (SYN) deflation, drop, slump, fall, reduction, shrinkage

depredation (SYN) devastation, desecration, pillaging, marauding, robbery

depress (SYN) sadden, discourage, press, lower, inhibit, deflate (ANT) cheer, hearten, raise, heighten, uplift

depression (SYN) despair, melancholy, recession, stagnation, indentation, hollow (ANT) joy, elation, boom, recovery, bulge

deprive (SYN) withhold, rob, deny, dispossess, strip (ANT) provide, give, endow, offer

depth (SYN) extent, scope, profundity, deepness, drop (ANT) height, triviality, shallowness

deranged (SYN) demented, irrational, crazy, unhinged, lunatic (ANT) balanced, calm, stable, sane, lucid

derelict (SYN) deserted, dilapidated, negligent, delinquent, vagrant (ANT) attended, prized, conscientious

deride (SYN) mock, ridicule, taunt, jeer, disparage (ANT) commend, compliment, flatter, respect

derision (SYN) insults, disdain, contempt, scorn, affront (ANT) esteem, respect, flattery

derivative (SYN) acquired, by-product, unoriginal, transmitted (ANT) original

derive (SYN) obtain, glean, procure, determine, deduce (ANT) create, issue

derogatory (SYN) critical, slanderous, negative, unfavorable, demeaning (ANT) complimentary, approving, appreciative, positive, exalting

descend (SYN) plummet, sink, plunge, deteriorate, slope, disembark (ANT) ascend, climb, rise, mount, upgrade

descendant (SYN) heir, offspring, children (ANT) ancestor, predecessor, parent descent (SYN) drop, fall, slant, ancestry, lineage (ANT) elevation, rise, ascension

describe (SYN) explain, communicate, report, characterize, portray (ANT) distort, falsify, confuse, misrepresent

description (SYN) account, narrative, sketch, classification, category

descriptive (SYN) detailed, graphic, illustrative, explanatory, clear

desecrate (SYN) defile, abuse, pollute, contaminate, pervert (ANT) consecrate, protect, honor, sanctify, nurture

desert (SYN) wasteland, abandon, strand, forsake, defect (ANT) stay, remain, support

desertion (SYN) flight, betrayal, defection, abandonment, absconding

deserve (SYN) justify, warrant, earn, merit, rate

design (SYN) plan, outline, pattern, invent, intention

designate (SYN) specify, appoint, nominate, classify, label

designer (SYN) creator, originator, producer, architect

desirable (SYN) attractive, alluring, beneficial, advisable, popular (ANT) ugly, repulsive, worthless, imprudent, detrimental

desire (SYN) crave, want, hope, longing, passion (ANT) distaste, aversion, reject, abhor

desist (SYN) end, stop, pause, refrain, suspend (ANT) continue, persist, persevere

desolate (SYN) barren, bleak, miserable, wretched, destroy, pillage (ANT) crowded, inhabited, joyful, cheerful, build

desolation (SYN) devastation, ruin, isolation, gloom, anguish (ANT) construction, happiness, glee

despair (SYN) depression, hopelessness, woe, resign, surrender (ANT) hope, cheer

desperate (SYN) distressed, distraught, frantic, reckless, grave, extreme (ANT) cautious, rational, casual, optimistic, hopeful

desperation (SYN) agony, trouble, hopelessness, recklessness, impetuosity (ANT) optimism, hope, confidence, caution, prudence

despicable (SYN) shameful, wicked, vile, sordid, contemptible (ANT) honorable, praiseworthy, ethical, respectable, virtuous

despise (SYN) loathe, revile, scorn, hate,

deplore (ANT) adore, respect, prize, treasure, love

despite (SYN) in spite of, even with, notwithstanding, regardless of

despoil (SYN) destroy, devastate, raid, loot, wreck (ANT) protect, improve, construct, preserve despondent (SYN) sorrowful, glum, dejected, morose, melancholy (ANT) spirited, euphoric, elated, upbeat, gay

despotic (SYN) domineering, oppressive, tyrannical, dictatorial (ANT) democratic, submissive, compliant

despotism (SYN) tyranny, totalitarianism, autocracy, oppression

destination (SYN) stop, goal, aim, end, objective (ANT) start, beginning

destiny (SYN) fate, fortune, future, providence (ANT) accident, chance

destitute (SYN) poor, impoverished, penurious, bankrupt, indigent (ANT) wealthy, prosperous, affluent, rich

destroy (SYN) demolish, level, blight, eradicate, dissolve (ANT) preserve, spare, build, create, restore

destruction (SYN) demolition, havoc, carnage, devastation, elimination (ANT) preservation, reparation, creation

destructive (SYN) damaging, harmful, injurious, catastrophic, ruinous (ANT) productive, constructive, helpful

detach (SYN) separate, disconnect, sever, dismantle, remove (ANT) connect, attach, link, unite, fasten

detached (SYN) disinterested, impersonal, impartial, removed, disengaged, discrete (ANT) attached, connected, compassionate, biased, friendly

detail (SYN) component, feature, triviality, identify, specify (ANT) total, aggregate

detain (SYN) hinder, delay, impede, confine, apprehend (ANT) free, release, liberate, discharge

detect (SYN) observe, note, perceive, identify, discover, discern (ANT) overlook, miss, ignore

detective (SYN) investigator, sleuth, private eye, police officer

detergent (SYN) cleaner, soap, cleanser

deteriorate (SYN) worsen, degenerate, decline, decay, regress (ANT) improve, strengthen, grow, build

deterioration (SYN) corrosion, atrophy, crumbling, drop, descent (ANT) enhancement, improvement, development

determination (SYN) resolve, tenacity, dedication, persistence, will power, pluck (ANT) hesitation, disinterest, apathy

determine (SYN) conclude, deduce, ascertain, learn, choose (ANT) waver, question, disregard, delay, procrastinate

deterrent (SYN) obstacle, hindrance, impediment, check, discouragement (ANT) incentive, catalyst

detest (SYN) despise, loathe, abominate, revile, shun (ANT) love, relish, appreciate, admire, fancy

detonate (SYN) explode, trigger, blow up, discharge (ANT) diffuse detour (SYN) bypass, diversion, deviation, runaround, circumvention (ANT) direct route

detract (SYN) diminish, reduce, lower, minimize, discredit (ANT) enhance, increase, intensify

detrimental (SYN) harmful, adverse, destructive, negative (ANT) advantageous, beneficial, helpful, positive

devastate (SYN) demolish, wreck, ruin, shatter, traumatize (ANT) help, aid, fix, build

develop (SYN) evolve, cultivate, mature, generate, expand (ANT) regress, halt, cease, shrivel, narrow

development (SYN) progress, growth, evolution, event, incident (ANT) stagnation, recession, withering, deterioration

deviate (SYN) differ, stray, wander, swerve, vary, digress (ANT) conform, stay, remain

device (SYN) gadget, contraption, tool, maneuver, scheme

devil (SYN) Satan, demon, beast, scoundrel, villain (ANT) God, god, angel

devious (SYN) sly, insincere, surreptitious, indirect, circuitous (ANT) honest, trustworthy, open, direct, aboveboard

devise (SYN) conceive, formulate, invent, hatch, concoct

devoid (SYN) empty, deficient, wanting, lacking, bereft (ANT) full, replete, supplied

devote (SYN) dedicate, allocate, pledge, commit, reserve (ANT) withhold, keep

devotion (SYN) loyalty, allegiance, fondness, piety, spirituality (ANT) indifference, disloyalty

devour (SYN) inhale, gobble, gulp, consume, destroy, relish (ANT) abstain, avoid, nibble

devout (SYN) pious, religious, reverent, committed, loyal (ANT) atheistic, irreverent, impious

dexterity (SYN) finesse, proficiency, deftness, ability, skill, aptitude (ANT) clumsiness, inability, ineptness, incompetence

diabolical (SYN) monstrous, infernal, appalling, dreadful, evil (ANT) holy, saintly, angelic, good

diagnosis (SYN) identification, recognition, analysis, conclusion, pronouncement

diagonal (SYN) angled, slanting, crosswise, oblique (ANT) square, straight, flat

diagram (SYN) figure, drawing, chart, representation, graph

dialect (SYN) vernacular, language, jargon, idiom, slang

dialogue (SYN) conversation, discussion, chat, discourse, exchange (ANT) monologue, soliloquy diameter (SYN) breadth, width

diary (SYN) journal, chronicle, memoir, account, record, log

diatribe (SYN) criticism, tirade, onslaught, castigation, reproach

dichotomy (SYN) difference, division, split

dictate (SYN) utter, command, impose, edict, decree (ANT) request, ask, obey, follow, record

dictator (SYN) tyrant, oppressor, boss, autocrat, magnate (ANT) democrat

diction (SYN) articulation, enunciation, delivery, inflection, eloquence

dictionary (SYN) wordlist, lexicon, vocabulary, glossary

didactic (SYN) educational, instructive, enlightening, pedantic, moralizing

die (SYN) expire, perish, dwindle, fade, fail, halt (ANT) live, survive, thrive, develop, flourish

diet (SYN) food, provisions, rations, sustenance, fast, abstain (ANT) binge, gorge, overindulge

differ (SYN) vary, diverge, contradict, disagree, dissent (ANT) agree, resemble, match, correspond, conform

difference (SYN) dissimilarity, disparity, variation, conflict, remainder (ANT) similarity, likeness, agreement, harmony

different (SYN) disparate, incompatible, altered, distinct, unfamiliar (ANT) similar, alike, identical, ordinary, united

difficult (SYN) demanding, strenuous, arduous, complicated, ambitious, formidable (ANT) easy, simple, manageable, accommodating, amenable

difficulty (SYN) strain, tribulation, dilemma, quandary, impediment (ANT) ease, simplicity, accommodation

diffidence (SYN) shyness, timidity, hesitancy, constraint, reluctance (ANT) confidence, boldness

diffuse (SYN) diluted, scattered, disseminated, radiate, strew (ANT) concentrated, limited, restricted

diffusion (SYN) circulation, spread, dispersal, dissipation (ANT) concentration

dig (SYN) burrow, dredge, excavate, delve, investigate, insult (ANT) cover, fill, compliment

digest (SYN) absorb, dissolve, contemplate, assimilate, synopsis (ANT) misinterpret, expand, lengthen

digestion (SYN) ingestion, incorporation, absorption, conversion

dignify (SYN) distinguish, honor, glorify, magnify, ennoble (ANT) belittle, insult, condemn, lower

dignitary (SYN) official, celebrity, V.I.P.

dignity (SYN) pride, self-esteem, eminence, rank, decorum, integrity (ANT) indecency, impropriety, humility

digression (SYN) detour, departure, deviation, straying, divergence (ANT) consistency, regularity, conformity

dilapidated (SYN) ruined, crumbling, decrepit, neglected, unkempt (ANT) tidy, sound, ordered, prized

dilate (SYN) enlarge, stretch, widen, expand, broaden (ANT) constrict, shrink, contract

dilatory (SYN) delaying, slow, procrastinating, lingering, tarrying (ANT) prompt, ready, timely, diligent

dilemma (SYN) puzzle, predicament, plight, conflict, impasse (ANT) solution, resolution

diligence (SYN) industry, perseverance, earnestness, vigor, exertion (ANT) laziness, idleness, lethargy, indolence

diligent (SYN) hard-working, tireless, conscientious, laborious, unrelenting (ANT) negligent, lazy, sluggish, languid

dilute (SYN) thin, weaken, adulterate, diffuse, lessen, temper (ANT) concentrate, thicken, strengthen

dim (SYN) faint, muted, dismal, dull, darken, fade, vague, obtuse (ANT) bright, illuminated, lighten, clear, distinct, intelligent

dimension (SYN) measurement, proportion, size, volume, aspect, facet

diminish (SYN) dwindle, subside, decrease, reduce, wane, demean (ANT) develop, increase, expand, flatter

diminution (SYN) lessening, decay, cutback, abatement, decline (ANT) increase, growth, expansion

dimple (SYN) dent, indentation, hollow, pit, depression

din (SYN) racket, commotion, ruckus, cacophony, pandemonium, roar

dine (SYN) eat, feast, consume (ANT) fast

dingy (SYN) dreary, drab, dirty, tarnished, soiled (ANT) clean, immaculate, sparkling, bright

dinner (SYN) meal, feast, supper, spread

dip (SYN) plunge, submerge, sink, descend, plummet, reduction (ANT) increase, rise, ascend, lift

diplomacy (SYN) tact, delicacy, discretion, sensitivity, negotiation, politics (ANT) indiscretion, thoughtlessness

diplomat (SYN) negotiator, politician, ambassador, envoy, mediator

diplomatic (SYN) polite, subtle, tactful, delicate, judicious (ANT) rude, tactless, blunt, uncivil, artless dire (SYN) grim, grave, desperate, disastrous, ominous (ANT) fortunate, wonderful, trivial

direct (SYN) straight, uninterrupted, frank, straightforward, conduct, lead, aim, instruct (ANT) indirect, ambiguous, interrupted, roundabout, follow

direction (SYN) orientation, route, leadership, supervision, administration, instruction

directly (SYN) straight, immediately, exactly, candidly, frankly (ANT) eventually, late, equivocally, indirectly

directory (SYN) guide, list, index, register

dirge (SYN) lament, elegy, requiem, song, keen

dirty (SYN) filthy, contaminated, foul, vulgar, explicit (ANT) clean, immaculate, wholesome

disability (SYN) handicap, impairment, inability, incapacity, weakness (ANT) ability, strength, advantage

disable (SYN) immobilize, damage, incapacitate, deactivate, disarm (ANT) assist, rehabilitate, enable, arm

disadvantage (SYN) inconvenience, nuisance, drawback, snag, detriment (ANT) advantage, benefit, assistance, gain

disagree (SYN) challenge, dispute, quarrel, contradict, nauseate (ANT) agree, concur, match, consent, assent

disagreeable (SYN) displeasing, obnoxious, offensive, surly, irritable (ANT) easygoing, pleasant, inoffensive, delightful, acquiescent

disagreement (SYN) argument, altercation, squabble, discord, incompatibility (ANT) agreement, harmony, compatibility, accord

disappear (SYN) vanish, depart, dissolve, fade, exit, perish (ANT) appear, arrive, materialize

disappoint (SYN) fail, sadden, discontent, frustrate, dissatisfy (ANT) please, delight, satisfy, encourage, succeed

disappointment (SYN) displeasure, regret, chagrin, letdown, blow (ANT) fulfillment, pleasure, happiness, satisfaction, surprise

disapprove (SYN) object, disfavor, condemn, frown on, denounce (ANT) sanction, approve, accept, endorse, agree

disarm (SYN) charm, persuade, placate, disable, defuse (ANT) arm, fortify

disarray (SYN) confusion, chaos, disorder, clutter, unruliness (ANT) order, harmony, cleanliness, tranquility

disaster (SYN) tragedy, ruin, catastrophe, calamity, failure (ANT) success, miracle, blessing, fortune, prosperity

disastrous (SYN) devastating, fatal, tragic, catastrophic, ruinous, (ANT) fortunate, lucky, successful disbelief (SYN) distrust, skepticism, incredulity, doubt, suspicion (ANT) belief, trust, faith, confidence, certainty

disburse (SYN) divide, partition, spend, defray, outlay (ANT) hoard, keep, acquire, gather

disbursement (SYN) expenditure, payment, outlay (ANT) income

discard (SYN) abandon, reject, toss, throw out, jettison (ANT) keep, save, preserve, cherish, retain

discern (SYN) detect, recognize, perceive, differentiate, apprehend (ANT) disregard, overlook, miss, ignore, neglect

discharge (SYN) dismiss, expel, release, fire, launch (ANT) recruit, assign, hold, capture, imprison

disciple (SYN) pupil, follower, devotee, apostle, admirer (ANT) leader, skeptic, cynic, rival, adversary

discipline (SYN) regulation, training, obedience, subject, punish, reprimand (ANT) chaos, permissiveness, reward, indulgence

disclose (SYN) communicate, divulge, reveal, expose, impart (ANT) conceal, cover, hide, retain, withhold

discomfort (SYN) pain, hardship, awkwardness, embarrassment, distress (ANT) comfort, pleasure, ease

disconcerting (SYN) alarming, bothersome, unnerving, distracting, upsetting (ANT) calming, soothing, comfortable, settling

disconnect (SYN) detach, divide, separate, uncouple, sever, disengage (ANT) attach, link, hook, connect, join

disconsolate (SYN) dejected, forlorn, inconsolable, melancholy, somber (ANT) cheerful, joyous, content, upbeat, elated

discontent (SYN) displeasure, dissatisfaction, unease, unrest, fretfulness (ANT) happiness, contentment, satisfaction, serenity

discontented (SYN) displeased, vexed, frustrated, exasperated, disgruntled (ANT) satisfied, pleased, happy, content

discontinue (SYN) stop, terminate, cease, abandon, interrupt (ANT) start, resume, continue

discord (SYN) dissension, friction, division, strife, animosity (ANT) agreement, harmony, accord, peace, amicability

discount (SYN) disregard, overlook, deduction, reduce, lower (ANT) believe, notice, credit, increase, hike

discourage (SYN) deter, inhibit, daunt, dishearten, depress (ANT) encourage, persuade, embolden, inspire

discourse (SYN) discussion, conversation, dialogue, communication, speech (ANT) monologue, soliloquy discourteous (SYN) rude, impolite, ungracious, abrupt, disrespectful (ANT) civil, polite, refined, courteous, mannered

discover (SYN) uncover, detect, realize, notice, determine (ANT) hide, conceal, cover, overlook, ignore

discovery (SYN) revelation, finding, exploration, breakthrough, innovation (ANT) concealment

discredit (SYN) slander, disparage, compromise, doubt, challenge (ANT) credit, commend, laud, verify, support

discreet (SYN) tactful, guarded, considerate, prudent, sensitive, delicate (ANT) reckless, thoughtless, careless, conspicuous

discrepancy (SYN) difference, contradiction, variation, deviation, mismatch (ANT) consistency, agreement, uniformity, correspondence, resemblance

discretion (SYN) diplomacy, tact, delicacy, option, inclination (ANT) indiscretion, foolishness

discriminate (SYN) distinguish, separate, favor, differentiate, victimize

discrimination (SYN) intolerance, prejudice, bias, discernment, refinement (ANT) impartiality, acceptance, thoughtlessness

discuss (SYN) debate, explore, consider, converse, weigh

discussion (SYN) dialogue, conversation, deliberation, consultation, analysis (ANT) silence, lecture

disdain (SYN) derision, scorn, condescension, arrogance, despise (ANT) respect, regard, reverence, value, praise

disease (SYN) illness, disorder, malady, sickness, ailment (ANT) health, wellness

disenchantment (SYN) disappointment, delusion, discontent, dissatisfaction (ANT) contentment, felicity, satisfaction, gratification

disengage (SYN) loosen, release, disentangle, liberate, unfasten (ANT) connect, join, engage, attach, couple

disfigure (SYN) deform, distort, mutilate, deface, maim (ANT) enhance, beautify, improve

disgrace (SYN) shame, degradation, dishonor, scandal, outrage (ANT) esteem, honor, respect, glory, dignity

disgraceful (SYN) contemptible, reprehensible, shameful, embarrassing ignominious (ANT) dignified, respectable, admirable, exalted, virtuous

disgruntled (SYN) irritated, displeased, annoyed, discontented, vexed (ANT) satisfied, happy, contented, delighted, gratified

disguise (SYN) mask, facade, camouflage, shroud, falsify (ANT) reveal, display, expose, show, revelation

disgust

disgust (SYN) repulsion, aversion, loathing, revolt, appall (ANT) delight, admiration, attract, entice, charm

disgusting (SYN) sickening, foul, offensive, objectionable, loathsome (ANT) appetizing, pleasant, desirable, appealing, enjoyable

dish (SYN) plate, platter, food, fare, vessel

disheveled (SYN) untidy, rumpled, tousled, unkempt, disarrayed, slovenly (ANT) tidy, groomed, ordered, neat

dishonest (SYN) deceitful, corrupt, underhanded, fraudulent, devious (ANT) honest, scrupulous, straightforward, truthful, open

disintegrate (SYN) crumble, separate, splinter, fragment, collapse (ANT) combine, connect, unite, join

disinterested (SYN) impartial, neutral, detached, objective, impersonal (ANT) passionate, concerned, riveted, involved

dislike (SYN) hate, despise, animosity, hostility, enmity (ANT) affection, love, approval, fancy, like

disloyal (SYN) subversive, unfaithful, traitorous, perfidious, two-faced (ANT) dependable, faithful, true, constant, unfailing

dismal (SYN) gloomy, bleak, forlorn, melancholy, morose (ANT) cheerful, bright, lively, sunny, optimistic

dismantle (SYN) demolish, disassemble, take apart, decimate, level (ANT) build, assemble, construct, erect

dismay (SYN) anxiety, trepidation, disquiet, distress, unnerve (ANT) relief, calm, pleasure, encourage, assurance

dismiss (SYN) release, discharge, banish, disregard (ANT) keep, appoint, maintain, welcome, entertain

disobedient (SYN) defiant, disorderly, naughty, unruly, rebellious (ANT) obedient, compliant, good, dutiful, peaceful

disobey (SYN) defy, flout, disregard, transgress, contravene (ANT) submit, accept, yield, obey, acquiesce, defer

disorder (SYN) clutter, chaos, disarray, commotion, turmoil, illness, malady (ANT) serenity, calm, order, tranquility, health

disorganized (SYN) confused, haphazard, muddled, messy, unsystematic (ANT) prepared, neat, ordered, tidy, organized

disparage (SYN) belittle, malign, deride, discredit, ridicule (ANT) compliment, acclaim, recommend, flatter, approve

disparate (SYN) different, contrary, inconsistent, various, divergent (ANT) similar, comparable, analogous, matching, equivalent

disparity (SYN) gap, discrepancy, imbalance, incongruity,

disproportion (ANT) equality, parity, consistency, equivalence

dispatch (SYN) send, dismiss, message, communication, speed, hustle (ANT) hold, detain, silence, dawdle, procrastination

dispel (SYN) eliminate, banish, dismiss, allay, quell (ANT) form, give rise to, gather, collect, increase

dispense (SYN) share, distribute, administer, apportion, allocate (ANT) withhold, retain, keep, receive, take

disperse (SYN) strew, diffuse, scatter, disseminate, disband, dissipate (ANT) assemble, gather, form, congregate, concentrate, collect

dispersion (SYN) dispersal, dissolution, scattering, spread, radiation (ANT) centralization, concentration, gathering, collecting

displace (SYN) move, shift, transpose, dislodge, supplant (ANT) arrange, adjust, sort, replace, reinstate

display (SYN) demonstrate, exhibit, presentation, spectacle, expression (ANT) hide, conceal, disguise, mask, camouflage

displease (SYN) disappoint, dissatisfy, exasperate, irk, pique (ANT) delight, satisfy, please, placate, gratify

dispose (SYN) distribute, discard, settle, ditch (ANT) keep, preserve, jumble, obtain, displace

disposition (SYN) temperament, constitution, inclination, placement, classification

disproportionate (SYN) unbalanced, unequal, excessive, asymmetric, lopsided (ANT) proportionate, even, equal, balanced

disprove (SYN) discredit, negate, expose, invalidate, debunk (ANT) support, confirm, validate, prove, illustrate

dispute (SYN) quarrel, altercation, contention, challenge, squabble (ANT) agreement, understanding, concur, surrender, yield

disqualify (SYN) ban, prohibit, preclude, exclude (ANT) allow, permit, qualify

disregard (SYN) discount, overlook, neglect, indifference, apathy (ANT) heed, emphasize, notice, thoughtfulness, consideration

disreputable (SYN) notorious, ignominious, despicable, scandalous, unrespectable (ANT) noble, ethical, reputable, decent, respected

disrespectful (SYN) impertinent, rude, insolent, flippant, defiant (ANT) polite, gracious, reverent, courteous, respectful

disrupt (SYN) disturb, upset, interrupt, obstruct, agitate, intrude (ANT) arrange, organize, pacify

dissatisfaction (SYN) disquiet, vexation, frustration, chagrin, discontent (ANT) enjoyment, contentment, satisfaction, bliss, pleasure

dissatisfied

dissatisfied (SYN) unhappy, disappointed, disgruntled, critical, malcontent (ANT) fulfilled, content, pleased, satisfied

dissect (SYN) analyze, explore, scrutinize, divide, section (ANT) connect, join

dissection (SYN) examination, autopsy, critique, inspection, study

disseminate (SYN) circulate, broadcast, distribute, spread, publicize (ANT) gather, collect, withhold, contain

dissemination (SYN) circulation, broadcasting, publication, diffusion, telling

dissension (SYN) dissent, friction, disagreement, discord, dissidence (ANT) agreement, harmony, accord, friendliness

dissent (SYN) argument, resistance, opposition, protest, differ (ANT) agreement, conformity, compliance, acceptance

dissimilar (SYN) different, unrelated, heterogeneous, diverse, various (ANT) alike, same, equal, similar

dissipate (SYN) evaporate, vanish, consume, expend, deplete (ANT) appear, absorb, conserve, save, collect

dissociate (SYN) detach, distance, isolate, disconnect, segregate (ANT) join, associate, relate, connect

dissolve (SYN) melt, disintegrate, discontinue, terminate, revoke

(ANT) solidify, harden, congeal, appear, continue

dissonance (SYN) jarring, cacophony, antagonism, controversy, conflict (ANT) harmony

dissuade (SYN) thwart, deter, discourage, prevent, divert (ANT) encourage, persuade, coax

distance (SYN) span, extent, interval, afar, restraint, aloofness (ANT) proximity, intimacy, closeness, associate, sympathy

distant (SYN) remote, faraway, ancient, vague, faint, unapproachable (ANT) near, adjacent, recent, clear, alert, kind

distaste (SYN) aversion, disgust, dislike, abhorrence, disfavor (ANT) desire, attraction, liking

distend (SYN) swell, bulge, inflate, balloon, amplify (ANT) deflate, shrink, contract, flatten

distinct (SYN) obvious, evident, pronounced, different, individual (ANT) indefinite, unclear, similar, confused, ambiguous

distinction (SYN) merit, renown, excellence, variation, differentiation, characteristic (ANT) similarity, resemblance, mediocrity

distinguish (SYN) perceive, discern, characterize, differentiate, ascertain (ANT) combine, confuse, mistake distinguished (SYN) noted, renowned, acclaimed, eminent, illustrious (ANT) ordinary, common, unknown

distort (SYN) twist, misrepresent, warp, contort, alter (ANT) correct, right

distract (SYN) sidetrack, divert, amuse, entertain, occupy (ANT) explain, clarify, soothe, focus

distraction (SYN) interruption, diversion, interference, confusion, entertainment

distraught (SYN) frantic, agitated, desperate, hysterical, overwhelmed (ANT) calm, serene, tranquil, relaxed, composed

distress (SYN) worry, grief, suffering, adversity, upset, harass (ANT) comfort, relief, ease, fortune, console, calm

distribute (SYN) circulate, disseminate, deal, allot, dole (ANT) keep, amass, hoard, accumulate, gather

distribution (SYN) dealing, sharing, allocation, supply, dispersal (ANT) concentration

district (SYN) area, sector, region, territory, zone, turf

distrust (SYN) suspicion, wariness, skepticism, misgiving, suspect, doubt (ANT) believe, depend, entrust, confidence, faith

disturb (SYN) bother, agitate, pester, fluster, rearrange (ANT) settle, calm, comfort, quiet, order

disturbing (SYN) alarming, unsettling, upsetting, harrowing, chilling (ANT) soothing, comforting, pleasing, agreeable, calming

ditch (SYN) channel, drain, trench, pitch, dump, abandon (ANT) keep, posses, claim, pursue

dive (SYN) plummet, plunge, descend, lunge, crash (ANT) rise, ascent, increase, skyrocket

diverge (SYN) differ, clash, separate, part, split (ANT) agree, conform, coincide, meet, join, converge

diverse (SYN) assorted, various, distinct, discrete, different (ANT) similar, alike, identical, like, equivalent

diversion (SYN) game, distraction, recreation, play, detour

diversity (SYN) range, distinctiveness, mixture, variation, medley (ANT) uniformity, conformity, similarity, monotony, homogeneity

divert (SYN) redirect, deflect, switch, distract, amuse (ANT) bore, irritate, maintain, focus

divest (SYN) seize, deprive, strip, bankrupt, plunder

divide (SYN) spit, partition, share, distribute, estrange (ANT) collect, unify, unite, join, fuse

dividend (SYN) gain, bonus, surplus, proceeds, profit, returns

divine (SYN) holy, heavenly, sacred, splendid, glorious, guess, surmise

(ANT) profane, imperfect, mortal, infernal

divisible (SYN) separable, dividable (ANT) indivisible

division (SYN) separation, dividing, distribution, branch, category, disagreement, rupture (ANT) union, marriage, whole, understanding

divorce (SYN) separation, dissolution, disconnect, part, split (ANT) marriage, union, marry, join

divulge (SYN) confess, tell, reveal, disclose, declare (ANT) conceal, cover, hide, withhold

do (SYN) perform, undertake, create, design, act, behave, suffice (ANT) fail, neglect, undo, pass, dissatisfy

docile (SYN) compliant, submissive, obedient, mellow, tame (ANT) aggressive, defiant, unruly, obstinate, vicious

dock (SYN) harbor, pier, anchor, land, join, deduct, reduce (ANT) set sail, detach, unfasten, increase

doctor (SYN) physician, medic, change, alter, misrepresent, dilute

doctrine (SNY) creed, belief, ideology, teaching, principle

document (SYN) record, paper, support, verify, chronicle

dodge (SYN) duck, swerve, evade, elude, avoid (ANT) confront, face, encounter

dog (SYN) canine, hound, mutt, pooch

dogged (SYN) tireless, persistent, resolute, determined, tenacious (ANT) yielding, indifferent, compromising

dogma (SYN) doctrine, teachings, opinion, canon, tenet (ANT) doubt

doldrums (SYN) depression, gloom, dumps, inactivity, slump (ANT) joy, happiness, elation, high spirits

dole (SYN) assign, distribute, allocate, share, grant

domain (SYN) territory, land, realm, filed, discipline

dome (SYN) arch, bulge, roof, bubble

domestic (SYN) home, household, family, national, internal (ANT) public, professional, foreign, imported

dominant (SYN) assertive, superior, controlling, primary, crucial (ANT) subordinate, humble, submissive, inferior, secondary

dominate (SYN) rule, control, govern, command, influence (ANT) follow, submit, yield, cave, defer

domineering (SYN) bossy, oppressive, overbearing, arrogant, imperial (ANT) timid, submissive, complacent

donate (SYN) give, contribute, gift, endow, bequeath (ANT) keep, take, withhold

donation (SYN) gift, offering, grant, philanthropy, handout, contribution, aid donor (SYN) giver, benefactor, contributor, patron, sponsor (ANT) beneficiary, recipient

doom (SYN) ruin, destruction, catastrophe, condemn, sentence (ANT) choice, hope, redeem

door (SYN) entry, exit, opening, portal, entryway

dormant (SYN) inactive, inert, hibernating, latent, sleeping, suspended (ANT) active, awake, alive, dynamic

dose (SYN) quantity, amount, dosage, measure, prescription

dot (SYN) spot, speck, mark, dab, sprinkle

doting (SYN) indulgent, adoring, admiring, affectionate, loving (ANT) indifferent, detached, aloof, cold, impartial

double (SYN) twice, paired, dual, duplicate, magnify, clone (ANT) single, lone

doubt (SYN) uncertainty, hesitation, misgiving, suspicion, suspect, question (ANT) trust, certainty, conviction, belief

doubtful (SYN) dubious, unclear, unlikely, debatable, ambiguous (ANT) confident, probable, certain, clear, sure

douse (SYN) drench, drown, immerse, smother, snuff

down (SYN) depressed, sad, swallow, drain, descending, declining (ANT) cheery, up, jolly, animated

downward (SYN) sliding, descending, declining, slipping, falling (ANT) upward, rising, climbing, mounting

doze (SYN) nap, sleep, snooze, slumber

drab (SYN) dull, dismal, dingy, colorless, boring (ANT) vibrant, bright, brilliant, colorful, exciting

draft (SYN) outline, sketch, version, order, compose, formulate

drafty (SYN) breezy, windy, airy, gusty, blustery (ANT) stuffy, still, calm

drag (SYN) haul, lug, heave, resistance, annoyance, delay (ANT) push, propel, speed

drain (SYN) pipe, channel, strain, withdraw, seep (ANT) fill, replenish, supply

drama (SYN) play, show, theater, spectacle, excitement

dramatic (SYN) theatrical, powerful, moving, climactic, suspenseful (ANT) normal, unexciting, familiar, routine

dramatically (SYN) suddenly, boldly, abruptly, arrestingly, grandly

drape (SYN) cover, wrap, swathe, envelop, shroud

drastic (SYN) extreme, radical, dire, momentous, substantial (ANT) modest, slight, moderate, inconsiderable, trivial

draw (SYN) sketch, depict, tug, attract, stalemate (ANT) repel, shove, alienate

drawback (SYN) flaw, snag, disadvantage, downside, deficiency (ANT) advantage, bonus, aid

drawn (SYN) tense, worn, fraught, taut, haggard (ANT) refreshed, vigorous, relaxed, energetic

dread (SYN) foreboding, fear, trepidation, horror, disquiet (ANT) confidence, bravery, courage, reassurance, welcome

dreadful (SYN) terrible, appalling, deplorable, shocking, atrocious (ANT) pleasant, agreeable, marvelous

dream (SYN) fantasy, ambition, reverie, delusion, invent (ANT) reality

dreamer (SYN) idealist, optimist, visionary, romantic, radical

dreary (SYN) dull, tedious, bleak, forlorn, dismal (ANT) bright, cheery, lively, pleasant, spirited

drench (SYN) soak, saturate, swamp, wet, bathe (ANT) dry, drain

dress (SYN) gown, frock, apparel, clothe, deck, decorate, bandage (ANT) undress

drift (SYN) float, stray, wander, digress, gist, significance

drill (SYN) training, repetition, rehearse, bore, penetrate

drink (SYN) swallow, swig, guzzle, beverage, liquid

drip (SYN) trickle, dribble, drop, leak, run (ANT) pour, surge, flow

drive (SYN) pilot, operate, excursion, jaunt, chauffeur, propel, compel, motivation, tenacity

droll (SYN) comical, amusing, eccentric, ludicrous, campy (ANT) serious, dramatic, boring, tiring, grave

drone (SYN) hum, buzz, vibrate, chant, intone

droop (SYN) sink, wilt, sag, slouch, dangle, slump (ANT) rise

drop (SYN) fall, descend, plummet, omit, abandon, bead, droplet (ANT) increase, rise, arise, continue, lift

dross (SYN) debris, garbage, rubbish, refuse, litter

drought (SYN) dry spell, dryness, scarcity, aridity, insufficiency (ANT) rain, wetness, abundance

drown (SYN) submerge, immerse, muffle, stifle, suffocate

drowsy (SYN) tired, sleepy, lethargic, dopey, languid (ANT) lively, awake, animated, alert, energetic

drudgery (SYN) labor, grind, work, chore, toil (ANT) relaxation

drug (SYN) remedy, medication, opiate, medicate, numb, dope, lace

drum (SYN) beat, rap, reverberate, thump, barrel, tank

drunk (SYN) intoxicated, inebriated, tipsy, under the influence, alcoholic (ANT) sober

dry (SYN) arid, dehydrated, monotonous, sarcastic, wry, wipe, towel (ANT) wet, humid, moist, fascinating, moisten

dual (SYN) double, twofold, duplicate, coupled, binary (ANT) single, lone, individual

dubious (SYN) suspicious, hesitant, skeptical, unreliable, shady (ANT) definite, positive, settled, trustworthy

duck (SYN) avoid, evade, dip, crouch, dodge, lower (ANT) face, meet, confront, straighten

duct (SYN) tube, canal, pipe, conduit, shaft

due (SYN) payable, outstanding, scheduled, anticipated, owed, deserved, fee, straight, directly (ANT) paid, settled, indirectly, undue

duel (SYN) fight, contest, clash, rivalry, struggle

dull (SYN) unsharpened, blunt, dense, unintelligent, unimaginative, flat, gloomy, indistinct, alleviate, deaden (ANT) sharp, bright, smart, captivating

dumb (SYN) silent, mute, speechless, stupid, ignorant (ANT) talkative, intelligent, witty, clever, bright

dumbfounded (SYN) stunned, astonished, astounded, speechless, bewildered (ANT) apathetic, cool, grounded, nonchalant, unflappable

dump (SYN) deposit, unload, pitch, discard, junkyard, slum

dune (SYN) heap, mound, bank, drift

dungeon (SYN) cell, cage, prison, vault

dupe (SYN) fool, baffle, swindle, outwit, beguile (ANT) inform, protect, tip, forewarn

duplicate (SYN) copy, replicate, clone, facsimile, identical (ANT) create, original, different

durable (SYN) reliable, tough, sturdy, long-lasting, resilient (ANT) flimsy, delicate, weak, fragile

duration (SYN) length, span, spell, extent, term

duress (SYN) coercion, threat, pressure, force, compulsion (ANT) liberty, freedom

dusk (SYN) twilight, dark, evening, nightfall, sunset (ANT) dawn, morning, daybreak

dust (SYN) particles, grit, wipe, clean, sift

dutiful (SYN) devoted, reverent, conscientious, obedient, faithful (ANT) disobedient, irresponsible

duty (SYN) responsibility, obligation, allegiance, task, function (ANT) treachery, choice dwarf (SYN) midget, dominate, overshadow, miniature, diminutive (ANT) huge, large, giant, magnify

dwell (SYN) live, inhabit, reside, consider, linger

dwelling (SYN) house, lodging, residence, domicile, abode

dwindle (SYN) lessen, diminish, decline, wane, subside (ANT) increase, expand, grow, surge, intensify

dye (SYN) pigment, stain, tint, coloring

dynamic (SYN) vital, lively, aggressive, energetic, intense (ANT) boring, static, lifeless, weak, idle

dynasty (SYN) empire, lineage, house, rule, regime

dysfunctional (SYN) wounded, maladjusted, flawed, unfit, undermined (ANT) functional, healthy, sustaining, conducive

E

each (SYN) every, all, apiece (ANT) none

eager (SYN) willing, keen, enthusiastic, hungry, motivated (ANT) apathetic, indifferent, diffident, uninterested

ear (SYN) perception, taste, sensitivity, discrimination

early (SYN) prematurely, too soon, primitive, young, initial (ANT) late, tardy, timely, modern

earn (SYN) make, net, gain, merit, deserve, warrant (ANT) steal, beg, lose, forfeit

earnest (SYN) sincere, thoughtful, determined, grave, fervent (ANT) careless, frivolous, negligent, flippant

earth (SYN) ground, land, turf, world, globe

earthly (SYN) worldly, mortal, human, bodily, material (ANT) divine, celestial, spiritual, ethereal

ease (SYN) simplicity, content, serenity, leisure, alleviate, soothe, slip, maneuver (ANT) difficulty, strife, aggravate, intensify

easily (SYN) simply, readily, effortlessly, surely, dexterously (ANT) difficultly, arduously, barely, awkwardly, gruelingly

easy (SYN) straightforward, simple, effortless, elementary, carefree, tranquil (ANT) difficult, complicated, involved, trying, harsh

eat (SYN) consume, ingest, munch, dissolve, decay

eavesdrop (SYN) spy, snoop, overhear, monitor, listen

ebb (SYN) recede, retreat, subside, diminish, fade (ANT) increase, surge, mount, grow

eccentric (SYN) peculiar, quirky, unconventional, bizarre, anomalous (ANT) conventional, normal, mainstream ecclesiastic (SYN) religious, spiritual, clergy, minister, father

echo (SYN) repeat, imitate, mimic, mirror, reflection, reverberation

eclipse (SYN) darkening, obscuring, surpass, outshine, transcend

economic (SYN) financial, commercial, lucrative, viable, profitable

economical (SYN) thrifty, frugal, efficient, inexpensive, sensible (ANT) extravagant, expensive, lavish, costly

economy (SYN) restraint, thrift, frugality, wealth, finances (ANT) extravagance, spending, squandering

ecstasy (SYN) rapture, elation, euphoria, bliss, fervor (ANT) misery, despair, sorrow, anguish, torment

edge (SYN) boundary, perimeter, verge, brink, sharpness, advantage (ANT) middle, interior, center, kindness, handicap, disadvantage

edible (SYN) eatable, palatable, harmless, nourishing, tasty (ANT) disgusting, inedible, gross, unappetizing, poisonous

edict (SYN) decree, command, proclamation, mandate, directive

edifice (SYN) building, structure, monument, construction

edify (SYN) guide, nurture, enlighten, instruct, improve

edit (SYN) polish, adapt, correct, check, modify, abridge (ANT) expand, lengthen, compose, write

edition (SYN) version, issue, volume, copy, printing

educate (SYN) teach, instruct, train, inform, cultivate

education (SYN) development, tutoring, guidance, literacy, scholarship (ANT) ignorance, illiteracy

educational (SYN) academic, instructive, informative, didactic, edifying, scholastic

eerie (SYN) mysterious, uncanny, strange, creepy, sinister (ANT) ordinary, silly, familiar, natural

efface (SYN) cancel, erase, expunge, obliterate, fade

effect (SYN) outcome, conclusion, result, impact, repercussions (ANT) cause, reason

effective (SYN) successful, competent, valuable, convincing, productive, dynamic (ANT) ineffective, useless, futile, ineffectual

effeminate (SYN) womanly, delicate, tender, feminine (ANT) macho, manly, virile, masculine

effervescence (SYN) bubbling, foaming, vivaciousness, animation, exuberance (ANT) dullness, flatness, lifelessness

efficacious (SYN) productive, potent, effective, adequate, capable (ANT) inefficient, incapable, inefficient

efficiency

efficiency (SYN) competence, adeptness, proficiency, prowess, pragmatism (ANT) inefficiency, incompetence

efficient (SYN) organized, economic, methodical, skilled, effective, deft (ANT) inefficient, ineffectual, inept, unable, lacking

effigy (SYN) likeness, representation, statue, dummy, model

effort (SYN) endeavor, exertion, striving, attempt, enterprise (ANT) ease, laziness, inaction

effusion (SYN) outpouring, diffusion, gushing, stream, emanation (ANT) restraint, stoppage

ego (SYN) personality, character, self, pride, self-esteem

egocentric (SYN) selfish, self-centered, individualistic, conceited, narcissistic (ANT) humble, selfless, giving, altruistic, modest

egotism (SYN) vanity, self-absorption, arrogance, overconfidence, presumption, superiority (ANT) humility, submission, self-abasement, insecurity

egotist (SYN) narcissist, braggart, boaster, show-off, exhibitionist (ANT) shrinking violet, mouse

egress (SYN) exit, departure, escape, exodus (ANT) entry, ingress, entrance, arrival

eject (SYN) remove, expel, oust, emit, escape (ANT) admit, accept, include

elaborate (SYN) detailed, intricate, involved, expand, embellish (ANT) simple, plain, ordinary, condense

elapse (SYN) lapse, pass, go by, expire

elastic (SYN) stretchy, pliant, springy, adaptable, adjustable (ANT) fixed, stiff, inflexible, rigid

elation (SYN) bliss, delight, ecstasy, exhilaration, euphoria, glee (ANT) gloom, depression, misery, apathy

elbow (SYN) knock, nudge, jostle, crowd, shove

elder (SYN) older, senior, big, leader (ANT) younger, little, junior

elect (SYN) vote, select, choose, decide, opt (ANT) reject, refuse, oust

election (SYN) selection, voting, poll, choice, preference

electric (SYN) charged, dynamic, exciting, thrilling, tense (ANT) dull, boring, unexciting

electrify (SYN) shock, thrill, excite, galvanize, stimulate (ANT) bore, tire, weary

elegant (SYN) cultivated, exquisite, tasteful, polished, fine (ANT) rough, crude, tasteless

element (SYN) unit, component, ingredient, detail, aspect (ANT) whole, compound

elementary (SYN) simple, basic, rudimentary, introductory, fundamental (ANT) complicated, advanced, involved, difficult, hard elevate (SYN) lift, heighten, promote, exalt, boost, hoist (ANT) lower, demote, denounce

elevation (SYN) height, altitude, promotion, upgrading, glorification (ANT) depression, degradation, lowering

elicit (SYN) extract, prompt, trigger, evoke, summon (ANT) hide, suppress

eligible (SYN) fit, suitable, qualified, entitled, able (ANT) ineligible, unqualified, unfit, unsuitable

eliminate (SYN) remove, eradicate, omit, purge, exclude, discard (ANT) restore, maintain, accept, include

elite (SYN) best, privileged, choice, exclusive, prime, world-class (ANT) common, ordinary, low-class

elope (SYN) escape, disappear, abscond, bolt

eloquence (SYN) expressiveness, persuasiveness, lucidity, fluency, articulation (ANT) incoherence, mumbling, vagueness

else (SYN) other, different

elsewhere (SYN) away, abroad, gone, removed (ANT) here

elude (SYN) dodge, evade, foil, confound, thwart (ANT) succumb, confront, encounter, face, embrace, seek

elusive (SYN) fleeting, transient, subtle, shifty, slippery, ambiguous (ANT) tangible

emaciated (SYN) gaunt, undernourished, lean, starved, wasted (ANT) plump, heavy, overfed, fat

emanate (SYN) stem, issue, originate, emit, exude

emancipate (SYN) free, liberate, release, deliver (ANT) enslave, bind, imprison, shackle

emancipation (SYN) deliverance, freedom, liberation, redemption (ANT) enslavement, incarceration

embalm (SYN) preserve, mummify, conserve, prepare

embargo (SYN) ban, bar, prohibit, restriction, block (ANT) sanction

embark (SYN) board, commence, launch, undertake, venture, set out (ANT) disembark, conclude, finish

embarrass (SYN) shame, fluster, mortify, humiliate, perturb (ANT) comfort, calm, encourage, soothe

embarrassment (SYN) bashfulness, self-consciousness, awkwardness, bind, predicament (ANT) pride, assurance, relief

embed (SYN) implant, deposit, insert, lodge, set (ANT) dig up, excavate

embellish (SYN) decorate, ornament, enhance, beautify, garnish (ANT) deface, spoil, mar

embezzle (SYN) steal, cheat, misappropriate, pilfer, filch

emblem (SYN) symbol, logo, insignia, trademark, crest

embody (SYN) represent, personify, symbolize, comprise, include (ANT) exclude

embrace (SYN) hug, clasp, adopt, welcome, comprise, include (ANT) release, reject, renounce

embryonic (SYN) budding, beginning, developing, evolving, immature

emerge (SYN) appear, surface, materialize, unfold, arise (ANT) disappear, leave, fade, vanish, cease

emergency (SYN) crisis, plight, danger, catastrophe, urgent (ANT) solution, stability

emigrant (SYN) foreigner, fugitive, pilgrim, refugee, migrant (ANT) native

emigrate (SYN) move, migrate, relocate, resettle (ANT) immigrate, remain, stay

eminent (SYN) prominent, celebrated, notable, acclaimed, renowned (ANT) obscure, common, unimportant, humble

emission (SYN) discharge, radiation, release, outflow, leak

emotion (SYN) feeling, sentiment, warmth, reaction, passion (ANT) apathy, insensibility

emotional (SYN) stirring, passionate, poignant, sensitive, sentimental (ANT) cold, unemotional, clinical, insensitive

empathize (SYN) understand, relate, share, appreciate, grasp

empathy (SYN) insight, compassion, comprehension, warmth, compassion (ANT) antagonism, disregard, indifference

emperor (SYN) ruler, king, monarch, sovereign

emphasis (SYN) importance, stress, weight, significance, prominence, value

emphasize (SYN) highlight, spotlight, accentuate, point out, focus on (ANT) downplay, understate, ignore

empire (SYN) realm, kingdom, territory, corporation

empirical (SYN) factual, observed, observational, experimental, pragmatic (ANT) theoretical, unproven, hypothetical

employ (SYN) hire, appoint, utilize, practice, occupy (ANT) fire, release, terminate, dismiss

employee (SYN) worker, hand, staff member, agent (ANT) boss, employer, owner

employer (SYN) boss, company, firm (ANT) worker, employee

employment (SYN) profession, job, occupation, trade, post

empower (SYN) permit, authorize, allow, entitle, enable (ANT) disallow

empty (SYN) hollow, vacant, blank, meaningless, drain, unload (ANT) full, complete, worthwhile, fill, replace emulate (SYN) imitate, mimic, rival, mirror, follow, contend (ANT) ignore, differ

enable (SYN) allow, sanction, permit, equip, qualify (ANT) oppose, prevent, block, hinder, forbid

enact (SYN) establish, proclaim, portray, depict, perform (ANT) repeal, veto, revoke

enamored (SYN) charmed, fond, smitten, devoted, bewitched (ANT) repelled, sickened

enchant (SYN) enthrall, fascinate, captivate, beguile, charm (ANT) offend, disgust, repel

enchantment (SYN) allure, enticement, fascination, draw, interest (ANT) repulsion, aversion, disinterest

enclose (SYN) surround, fence, circle, include, insert (ANT) release, free

enclosure (SYN) pen, compound, ring, coop, yard

encompass (SYN) circle, envelop, surround, cover, involve, contain

encore (SYN) repeat, return, reappearance

encounter (SYN) meet, confront, happen upon, meeting, clash (ANT) avoid, retreat, miss, evade

encourage (SYN) cheer, inspire, motivate, reassure, prompt, urge (ANT) dishearten, discourage, deflate, deter, inhibit

encouragement (SYN) support, enticement, persuasion, coaxing, incentive (ANT) discouragement

encroachment (SYN) intrusion, invasion, imposition

end (SYN) conclusion, finish, border, periphery, target, objective (ANT) start beginning, middle, center, means, begin

endanger (SYN) threaten, imperil, risk, compromise, expose (ANT) safeguard, defend, protect

endeavor (SYN) attempt, strive, venture, effort, enterprise (ANT) surrender, yield, neglect

endless (SYN) eternal, continual, incessant, boundless, perpetual (ANT) finite, limited, ending

endorse (SYN) support, approve, champion, recommend, sign (ANT) oppose, denounce, reject

endowment (SYN) grant, legacy, donation, provision, funding, subsidy

endurance (SYN) stamina, perseverance, tenacity, fortitude, patience (ANT) weakness, faltering

endure (SYN) withstand, tolerate, bear, suffer, persist, survive (ANT) fade, subside, fail, succumb, break

enemy (SYN) rival, opponent, adversary, foe, competition (ANT) ally, friend, accomplice, partner

energize (SYN) animate, motivate, enliven, vitalize, electrify (ANT) bore, weaken, tire, exhaust energy (SYN) vigor, strength, zest, liveliness, exuberance, drive, power (ANT) lethargy, weakness, inertia

enfeeble (SYN) deplete, weaken, fatigue, exhaust, undermine (ANT) strengthen, fortify, rejuvenate, empower

enfold (SYN) embrace, enclose, wrap, surround, envelop

enforce (SYN) implement, invoke, impose, compel, administer (ANT) neglect, relax, disregard

engage (SYN) absorb, grip, occupy, recruit, participate, encounter (ANT) release, dismiss, cancel, surrender

engagement (SYN) appointment, involvement, battle, betrothal, commitment

engender (SYN) produce, create, induce, generate, provoke (ANT) prevent, finish, halt

engine (SYN) motor, generator, turbine

engineer (SYN) devise, mastermind, contrive, organize

engrave (SYN) carve, etch, inscribe, imprint, ornament

engrossed (SYN) absorbed, immersed, preoccupied, riveted, rapt (ANT) disinterested, bored, distracted, inattentive

engulf (SYN) submerge, envelop, bury, overwhelm, inundate

enhance (SYN) improve, boost, augment, intensify, flatter (ANT) diminish, reduce

enigma (SYN) puzzle, mystery, riddle, teaser

enjoy (SYN) savor, relish, appreciate, adore, posses (ANT) dislike, detest, loathe, lack, need

enjoyable (SYN) pleasurable, entertaining, agreeable, satisfying, delightful (ANT) disagreeable, tiresome, boring, tedious

enjoyment (SYN) pleasure, fun, amusement, merriment, indulgence (ANT) aversion, displeasure, disgust

enlarge (SYN) grow, increase, amplify, magnify, swell (ANT) decrease, reduce, shrink

enlighten (SYN) inform, teach, illuminate, counsel, apprise (ANT) confuse, bewilder, cloud

enlightened (SYN) aware, knowledgeable, cultivated, educated, sophisticated (ANT) ignorant, uninformed

enlist (SYN) join, enter, enroll, volunteer, recruit, obtain (ANT) avoid, resign, dodge

enmity (SYN) hostility, hatred, malice, animosity, rancor (ANT) affection, love, kindness, amity, friendship

enormity (SYN) magnitude, immensity, vastness, horror, atrocity (ANT) triviality, unimportance, virtue, goodness enormous (SYN) massive, gigantic, colossal, mighty, tremendous (ANT) tiny, small, minute

enough (SYN) ample, sufficient, plenty, adequate, abundant (ANT) insufficient, scant, deficient

enrage (SYN) anger, madden, infuriate, provoke, antagonize (ANT) calm, sooth, pacify, please

enrich (SYN) refine, enhance, improve, better, augment (ANT) spoil, deplete, reduce, cheapen

enroll (SYN) register, enlist, apply, join, volunteer (ANT) reject, pass, withdraw

enrollment (SYN) admission, matriculation, acceptance, recruitment

ensemble (SYN) whole, total, sum, chorus, band, outfit, costume

ensue (SYN) arise, result, follow, develop, stem, emerge (ANT) precede

ensure (SYN) guarantee, confirm, check, assure, establish

entail (SYN) involve, require, demand, imply, mean (ANT) exclude

entangle (SYN) trap, ensnare, catch, complicate, muddle (ANT) free, release, clarify, disentangle, simplify

enter (SYN) go into, arrive, pierce, commence, join (ANT) exit, leave, depart, go out, stop

enterprise (SYN) company, business, project, endeavor, venture, initiative (ANT) idleness, inactivity, lethargy

entertain (SYN) interest, charm, divert, capture, consider, contemplate, host (ANT) bore, displease, tire, banish, forget, ignore

entertainment (SYN) enjoyment, pleasure, leisure, relaxation, delight (ANT) work

enthrall (SYN) captivate, grip, enchant, spellbind, rivet, intrigue (ANT) weary, bore, repel, disillusion

enthusiasm (SYN) passion, zeal, eagerness, fervor, commitment (ANT) apathy, lethargy, indifference, passivity

enthusiastic (SYN) keen, eager, passionate, zealous, committed (ANT) apathetic, disinterested

entice (SYN) coax, persuade, draw, tempt, lure (ANT) repulse, repel, scare

entire (SYN) whole, total, complete, full (ANT) partial, unfinished, incomplete

entitle (SYN) qualify, allow, enable, permit

entity (SYN) being, creature, thing, organism, individual

entourage (SYN) associates, followers, staff, attendants

entrance (SYN) doorway, opening, arrival, admittance, captivate, enthrall (ANT) exit, departure, egress, bore, repel

entrepreneur (SYN) businessman, businesswoman, tycoon, self-starter

entrust (SYN) assign, commit, deliver, delegate, give, charge

entry (SYN) door, access, gateway, introduction, record, listing

enumerate (SYN) list, number, itemize, count, cite, mention

enunciate (SYN) articulate, vocalize, utter, pronounce, utter

envelop (SYN) wrap, enclose, cocoon, swathe, surround (ANT) release, unwrap, uncover

envelope (SYN) case, jacket, wrapper

envious (SYN) jealous, resentful, covetous, begrudging (ANT) contented, satisfied

environment (SYN) surroundings, habitat, setting, situation, context

envy (SYN) jealousy, ill will, resentment, lusting, covet (ANT) generosity

ephemeral (SYN) brief, passing, transient, momentary, temporary (ANT) eternal, lasting, permanent, enduring

epic (SYN) legend, saga, tale, poem

epidemic (SYN) outbreak, eruption, spread, illness, plague

epidermis (SYN) skin

epigram (SYN) witticism, quip, aphorism

epilogue (SYN) postscript, conclusion, afterward, summation (ANT) prologue, preface, forward, introduction

episode (SYN) event, incident, installment, chapter, phase

epitaph (SYN) inscription, elegy, memorial, sentiment

epitome (SYN) essence, embodiment, personification, archetype, example

epitomize (SYN) illustrate, represent, symbolize, capture, typify

epoch (SYN) era, period, time, stage

equal (SYN) identical, equivalent, impartial, balanced, amount to (ANT) different, unlike, disproportioned, biased

equality (SYN) uniformity, fairness, impartiality, justice, balance (ANT) inequality, discrimination, disparity, irregularity

equalize (SYN) level, square, balance, even up

equation (SYN) comparison, parallel

equestrian (SYN) jockey, horse rider

equilibrium (SYN) harmony, balance, symmetry, stability, rest (ANT) instability, unevenness

equip (SYN) supply, furnish, provide, stock, prepare, train

equipment (SYN) gear, supplies, implements, utensils, apparatus

equitable (SYN) fair, impartial, just, honest, reasonable (ANT) inequitable, unjust, unfair, biased

equity (SYN) integrity, honest, fairness

equivalent (SYN) comparable, equal, alike, interchangeable, tantamount (ANT) unlike, different, dissimilar, unequal

equivocate (SYN) mislead, evade, hedge, dodge, shuffle (ANT) confront, face, address

era (SYN) age, generation, period, epoch

eradicate (SYN) remove, extinguish, eliminate, obliterate, wipe out (ANT) build, create, propagate, fix

erase (SYN) delete, expunge, blot, cancel, remove (ANT) create, write, replace

erect (SYN) construct, raise, establish, perpendicular, straight (ANT) demolish, level, topple, slouching, flat

erode (SYN) corrode, deteriorate, consume, wear down, weaken (ANT) strengthen, reinforce, fix, rebuild

erosion (SYN) attrition, disintegration, destruction, consumption, wearing away (ANT) strengthening

err (SYN) miscalculate, slip up, blunder, deviate, stumble

errand (SYN) mission, task, job, duty

erratic (SYN) variable, unstable, unpredictable, arbitrary, volatile (ANT) consistent, dependable, steady, reliable

erroneous (SYN) wrong, false, unsound, flawed, amiss, untrue (ANT) valid, correct, accurate, factual

error (SYN) mistake, oversight, inaccuracy, glitch, omission (ANT) accuracy

ersatz (SYN) artificial, bogus, counterfeit, simulated, fake (ANT) genuine, real, actual

erudite (SYN) scholarly, learned, knowledgeable, cultivated, educated (ANT) ignorant, uneducated, illiterate

erupt (SYN) explode, spout, gush, burst, emit, rupture (ANT) contain, hold

escalate (SYN) increase, heighten, mount, intensify, soar, accelerate

escapade (SYN) antic, caper, mischief, stunt, adventure

escape (SYN) elude, flee, avoid, bolt, seep, exit (ANT) return, stay, capture

eschew (SYN) avoid, renounce, forgo, shun, abstain (ANT) indulge, like, choose, seek out

escort (SYN) companion, guide, accompany, chaperon, lead (ANT) neglect, leave, abandon

esoteric (SYN) mysterious, cryptic, inscrutable, profound, subtle (ANT) familiar, plain, obvious, simple, concrete especially (SYN) notably, unusually, remarkably, chiefly, particularly

espionage (SYN) spying, surveillance, intelligence, reconnaissance

esprit de corps (SYN) camaraderie, team spirit, solidarity, alliance

espouse (SYN) support, champion, promote, uphold (ANT) deny, desert, detract

essay (SYN) piece, article, composition, endeavor, undertake

essence (SYN) base, core, nature, quintessence, extract, concentrate

essential (SYN) vital, requisite, necessary, intrinsic, basic (ANT) secondary, auxiliary, unimportant, incidental

establish (SYN) set up, ground, initiate, prove, demonstrate (ANT) unsettle, invalidate, abolish, repeal

establishment (SYN) organization, business, institution, foundation, inception

estate (SYN) property, holdings, assets, possessions, wealth

esteem (SYN) regard, respect, admiration, admire, value (ANT) loathe, despise, contempt, disdain

estimate (SYN) guess, evaluate, approximate, opinion, surmise (ANT) measure, compute

et cetera (SYN) and so forth, and others, and the rest

etch (SYN) engrave, carve, mark, cut, inscribe

eternal (SYN) everlasting, unceasing, abiding, permanent, unbroken (ANT) temporary, fleeting, brief, finite

eternity (SYN) infinity, forever, all time, ages, the afterlife

ethical (SYN) right, moral, decent, honest, principled (ANT) unethical, corrupt, dishonest, inappropriate

ethics (SYN) morality, standards, principles, ideals, convention

ethnic (SYN) cultural, native, traditional, indigenous, racial

etiquette (SYN) decorum, manners, protocol, civility, social graces

eulogy (SYN) acclaim, commendation, praise, tribute

euthanasia (SYN) mercy killing, assisted suicide

euphoria (SYN) elation, ecstasy, joy, delight, bliss (ANT) misery, sorrow, depression, despair, unhappiness

evacuate (SYN) clear, vacate, desert, flee, empty (ANT) occupy, load

evade (SYN) elude, dodge, avoid, skirt, bypass (ANT) confront, meet, face, acknowledge

evaluate (SYN) assess, gauge, reckon, appraise, rate, judge

evaporate (SYN) vaporize, dry up, disappear, vanish, fade (ANT) condense, materialize, solidify, crystallize

evaporation (SYN) dehydration, dissipation, vanishing, evanescence

evasive (SYN) elusive, shifty, deceptive, cagey, indirect, misleading (ANT) straightforward, candid, honest, direct, forthright

eve (SYN) night before, verge, brink, threshold

even (SYN) flat, level, flush, uniform, steady (ANT) bumpy, rough, irregular, unequal

evening (SYN) dusk, twilight, nightfall, sunset (ANT) morning, dawn, daybreak

evenly (SYN) uniformly, equally, identically (ANT) differently, unevenly

event (SYN) happening, affair, occasion, occurrence, function

eventually (SYN) ultimately, one day, finally, in the end, in due course (ANT) immediately, promptly, at once

ever (SYN) at any time, always, constantly, perpetually

every (SYN) each, all, every single, all possible (ANT) none

everybody (SYN) each person, all people (ANT) nobody

everyday (SYN) common, routine, mundane, ordinary, ongoing (ANT)

unusual, strange, uncommon, occasional, special

everyone (SYN) every person, one and all, everybody (ANT) no one

everything (SYN) all, the lot, the works (ANT) nothing

everywhere (SYN) all around, in every place, all over, far and wide (ANT) nowhere

evidence (SYN) proof, confirmation, substantiation, testimony, indication, hints

evident (SYN) visible, unmistakable, apparent, obvious, plain (ANT) obscure, puzzling, questionable

evil (SYN) wicked, vile, immoral, depravity, wrongdoing (ANT) good, moral, virtuous, upright, righteousness

evoke (SYN) awaken, summon, recall, invoke, elicit (ANT) repress, silence, quiet

evolution (SYN) progress, development, maturation, adaptation (ANT) regression, decline, deterioration

evolve (SYN) develop, grow, elaborate, advance, mature (ANT) regress, halt, die, stagnate

exacerbate (SYN) aggravate, intensify, worsen, madden, provoke (ANT) soothe, placate, assuage, appease

exact (SYN) accurate, correct, precise, literal, true (ANT) approximate, rough, imprecise, inexact, wrong exactly (SYN) precisely, absolutely, totally, perfectly, completely (ANT) roughly, approximately, around

exaggerate (SYN) amplify, embellish, overstate, magnify, inflate, stretch (ANT) understate, minimize, downplay, lessen, reduce

exalt (SYN) raise, promote, glorify, praise, extol (ANT) degrade, debase, humiliate, ridicule, condemn

examination (SYN) analysis, investigation, inquiry, exploration, perusal

examine (SYN) study, inspect, view, scrutinize, survey (ANT) ignore, disregard

example (SYN) instance, sample, illustration, archetype, deterrent

exasperate (SYN) madden, incense, anger, infuriate, pique (ANT) calm, soothe, placate, please, appease

exceed (SYN) surpass, overreach, eclipse, go beyond, top (ANT) fall short, fail

excel (SYN) shine, be skillful in, be talented at, outdo, best (ANT) be inferior

excellence (SYN) distinction, greatness, superiority, brilliance, quality (ANT) mediocrity, inferiority

excellent (SYN) superb, world-class, outstanding, splendid, terrific (ANT) inferior, negligible, inadequate

except (SYN) besides, barring, excluding, apart from, not counting (ANT) including

exception (SYN) oddity, deviation, irregularity, exclusion, anomaly (ANT) the norm

exceptional (SYN) remarkable, phenomenal, extraordinary, rare, unusual (ANT) common, usual, frequent

excerpt (ANT) passage, fragment, quotation, selection, clip

excess (SYN) extra, surplus, overload, extravagance, abundance (ANT) lack, shortage, deficiency, moderation, temperance

excessive (SYN) extreme, undue, immoderate, unwarranted, unreasonable (ANT) moderate, reasonable, frugal

exchange (SYN) trade, swap, substitution, dialogue, discussion

excite (SYN) thrill, inspire, provoke, stimulate, rouse (ANT) bore, calm, soothe, placate

excitement (SYN) action, commotion, agitation, anticipation, exhilaration (ANT) boredom, disinterest, inertia, lethargy

exciting (SYN) stirring, dramatic, compelling, invigorating, gripping (ANT) dull, boring, tedious, unexciting

exclaim (SYN) shout, yell, proclaim, cry, blurt (ANT) whisper, keep silent exclude (SYN) ban, bar, keep out, omit, reject (ANT) include, admit, welcome, allow

exclusive (SYN) sole, restricted, unique, select, fashionable (ANT) inclusive, public, shared, unrestrictive, admissive

exclusively (SYN) completely, entirely, wholly, singularly (ANT) partly

excruciating (SYN) severe, unbearable, agonizing, intense

excursion (SYN) trip, outing, jaunt, tour, expedition

excuse (SYN) explanation, reason, apology, forgive, relieve (ANT) punish, blame, reprimand

execute (SYN) kill, put to death, perform, accomplish, implement

execution (SYN) killing, capital punishment, administration, realization

executive (SYN) administrative, governing, director, manager, authority

exemplary (SYN) ideal, praiseworthy, admirable, faultless, impeccable (ANT) awful, lousy, reprehensible

exemplify (SYN) demonstrate, embody, exhibit, represent, epitomize

exempt (SYN) spare, absolve, immune, excused, not liable (ANT) oblige, bound, liable

exercise (SYN) activity, exertion, practice, task, apply

exert (SYN) wield, employ, utilize

exertion (SYN) effort, endeavor, struggle, industry, toil (ANT) rest, relaxation, lethargy, idleness

exhale (SYN) breathe, expel, respire (ANT) inhale

exhaust (SYN) weaken, fatigue, deplete, finish, drain (ANT) energize, refresh, conserve, replenish

exhaustion (SYN) weariness, fatigue, tiredness, debilitation, depletion (ANT) energy, vitality

exhaustive (SYN) thorough, extensive, in-depth, complete, all-encompassing, sweeping (ANT) superficial, incomplete, rough, lacking

exhibit (SYN) display, show, demonstrate, reveal, express (ANT) hide, cover, conceal

exhibition (SYN) presentation, showing, exposition, display

exhilaration (SYN) liveliness, invigoration, elation, delight, uplift (ANT) dejection, melancholy, gloom

exigency (SYN) crisis, difficulty, plight, necessity, requirement

exile (SYN) eviction, banishment, deportation, outcast, refugee

exist (SYN) be, live, survive, endure, subsist. prevail (ANT) die, perish, pass away

existence (SYN) life, actuality, survival, subsistence, lifestyle exit (SYN) door, departure, farewell, retreat, retire (ANT) enter, entrance, arrive

exodus (SYN) flight, migration, retreat, departure, evacuation (ANT) entrance, influx

exonerate (SYN) clear, acquit, absolve, pardon, liberate (ANT) convict, condemn, incriminate

exorcise (SYN) purify, cast out, expel

exotic (SYN) unfamiliar, foreign, mysterious, strange, unconventional (ANT) native, familiar, ordinary, usual

expand (SYN) spread, widen, elaborate, broaden, develop (ANT) condense, shrink, abridge, lessen

expanse (SYN) space, area, extent, range

expatriate (SYN) emigrant, exile, refugee

expect (SYN) anticipate, envision, assume, await, demand

expectation (SYN) suspense, anticipation, assumption, belief, presumption

expediency (SYN) utility, convenience, usefulness, advisability, practicality

expedition (SYN) mission, trek, voyage, journey, quest

expel (SYN) eject, remove, drive out, banish, evict (ANT) admit, welcome, allow, invite

expenditure (SYN) cost, payment, output, spending (ANT) income

expense (SYN) cost, loss, price, fees, spending

expensive (SYN) costly, lavish, luxurious, pricey, steep (ANT) inexpensive, cheap, economical, reasonable

experience (SYN) undergo, endure, practice, exposure, episode (ANT) immaturity, inexperience

experiment (SYN) trial, observation, research, try, evaluate

expert (SYN) authority, specialist, professional, skillful, adept, proficient (ANT) novice, amateur, incompetent, inexperienced

expertise (SYN) command, mastery, ability, prowess, capability (ANT) weakness, ineptness, inadequacy

expiration (SYN) death, closing, end, termination

expire (SYN) cease, conclude, stop, perish (ANT) begin, commence, live

explain (SYN) clarify, resolve, expound, interpret, excuse (ANT) bewilder, confuse, complicate, befuddle, perplex

explanation (SYN) reason, justification, excuse, description, definition

expletive (SYN) curse, oath, swear, cuss

explicit (SYN) clear, frank, precise, unambiguous, graphic, uncensored (ANT) vague, unclear, implicit, tasteful, decent explode (SYN) blow up, detonate, shatter, blast, discharge (ANT) fizzle

exploit (SYN) abuse, manipulate, take advantage of, achievement, stunt (ANT) honor, cherish, respect, nurture

exploration (SYN) study, examination, scrutiny, expedition, travel

explore (SYN) inquire, delve, probe, scout, consider

explorer (SYN) traveler, seeker, pioneer, trailblazer, adventurer

explosion (SYN) bang, blast, detonation, outburst, fit

explosive (SYN) volatile, unstable, violent, touchy, combustible (ANT) passive, peaceful, relaxed

export (SYN) trade, ship, transport (ANT) import

expose (SYN) reveal, disclose, uncover, make aware of, acquaint with (ANT) hide, conceal, cover up

exposition (SYN) composition, discourse, editorial, fair, bazaar

exposure (SYN) discovery, unveiling, publicity, exhibition, vulnerability (ANT) cover, shelter, shield

express (SYN) convey, communicate, intimate, specific, singular, rapid, swift (ANT) uncertain, vague, slow, unhurried, leisurely

expression (SYN) appearance, look, phrase, sign, manifestation, declaration

expulsion (SYN) banishment, removal, purge, ejection, ousting (ANT) welcoming

expunge (SYN) delete, cancel, obliterate, discard (ANT) restore

exquisite (SYN) striking, beautiful, lovely, refined, discerning (ANT) imperfect, flawed, coarse, horrible

extend (SYN) enlarge, prolong, stretch, offer, present (ANT) decrease, curtail, abridge, shorten, reduce, withdraw

extension (SYN) addition, annex, supplement, development, lengthening (ANT) contraction, reduction, shrinkage

extensive (SYN) vast, far-reaching, wide, substantial, comprehensive (ANT) narrow, limited, superficial, confined

extent (SYN) degree, size, length, proportions, scope, magnitude

extenuate (SYN) diminish, lessen, mitigate, excuse, minimize

exterior (SYN) outside, surface, facade, external (ANT) interior, inside

exterminate (SYN) eliminate, destroy, rid, decimate, eradicate (ANT) generate, produce, create, originate

external (SYN) outer, peripheral, outermost, alien, outside (ANT) internal, inside, intrinsic

extinct (SYN) dead, gone, vanished, lost (ANT) alive, thriving extinguish (SYN) quench, douse, abolish, suppress, stifle, wipe out (ANT) ignite, light, create

extort (SYN) blackmail, bully, coerce, squeeze, force

extortion (SYN) fraud, pressure, blackmail, demand, swindle

extra (SYN) additional, surplus, superfluous, added, extremely, especially (ANT) enough, sufficient, basic

extract (SYN) remove, derive, obtain, extricate, essence, concentrate (ANT) add, insert, whole

extradition (SYN) deportation

extraneous (SYN) unrelated, irrelevant, unconnected, needless, nonessential (ANT) basic, necessary, integral, essential

extraordinary (SYN) sensational, astonishing, fantastic, uncommon, bizarre, singular (ANT) common, ordinary, normal

extraterrestrial (SYN) alien

extravagant (SYN) excessive, wasteful, lavish, outrageous, unrestrained (ANT) moderate, plain, economical, parsimonious

extreme (SYN) ultimate, drastic, radical, farthest, edge (ANT) slight, safe, near, sober, moderate

extremity (SYN) limb, arm, leg, boundary, frontier, limit (ANT) middle

extricate (SYN) free, release, rescue, extract, disentangle (ANT) involve, embroil, entangle

extrinsic (SYN) external, outside, outward, acquired (ANT) intrinsic, internal, inner, integral

exuberant (SYN) spirited, lively, animated, buoyant, energetic (ANT) downcast, sad, depressed, defeated, austere, blue

exude (SYN) leak, radiate, emit, issue, secrete (ANT) conceal, hide

exultation (SYN) celebration, triumph, joy, elation, reveling (ANT) misery, sadness

eye (SYN) judgment, taste, discrimination, scrutinize, survey, observe

F

fable (SYN) story, parable, allegory, tale, fantasy, legend

fabric (SYN) cloth, textile, material, framework, structure

fabricate (SYN) build, produce, manufacture, feign, concoct (ANT) break, ruin, dismantle

fabulous (SYN) superb, brilliant, incredible, fantastic, excellent (ANT) routine, ordinary, common

facade (SYN) front, exterior, appearance, pretense, mask (ANT) interior face (SYN) encounter, challenge, meet, expression, countenance, surface (ANT) retreat, evade, hide, back

facet (SYN) plane, side, aspect, phase, element

facetious (SYN) funny, flippant, playful, jocular, sarcastic (ANT) somber, serious, grave

facile (SYN) easy, obvious, flexible, clever, adept (ANT) difficult, hard, complicated

facilitate (SYN) enable, promote, hasten, aid, expedite (ANT) slow, impede, block, hamper, delay

facsimile (SYN) copy, duplicate, replica, print

fact (SYN) certainty, actuality, truth, detail, aspect (ANT) lie, fiction, illusion, possibility

faction (SYN) splinter group, party, dissension, division, friction (ANT) whole, peace, unity

factious (SYN) broken, rival, quarrelsome, hostile, sectarian (ANT) harmonious, united, agreeing, cooperative

factor (SYN) element, part, circumstance, component, influence

factory (SYN) mill, plant, industry, shop

factual (SYN) truthful, correct, genuine, accurate, authentic (ANT) fictitious, untrue, false, wrong, hypothetical

faculty (SYN) capacity, ability, aptitude, teachers, staff, employees (ANT) incapacity, inability, students

fad (SYN) trend, rage, fashion, craze

fade (SYN) dissolve, disappear, decline, deteriorate, crumble (ANT) brighten, recover, strengthen, energize

fail (SYN) falter, collapse, disappoint, fold, flunk (ANT) succeed, triumph, improve, thrive, pass

failure (SYN) defeat, downfall, ruin, disaster, negligence (ANT) success, achievement, accomplishment, winner

faint (SYN) dim, distant, muffled, pass out, collapse, dizzy (ANT) clear, distinct, strong

fair (SYN) just, unbiased, average, decent, pale, lovely (ANT) unfair, partial, exceptional, inferior, dark

fairy (SYN) sprite, pixie, nymph

faith (SYN) belief, assurance, creed, religion, persuasion (ANT) disbelief, mistrust, skepticism

faithful (SYN) loyal, reliable, resolute, accurate, authentic (ANT) disloyal, unreliable, untrue

fake (SYN) pretend, falsify, imposter, artificial, forgery (ANT) genuine, real, authentic

fall (SYN) autumn, drop, topple, plunge, subside (ANT) rise, increase, climb, ascend fallacy (SYN) falsehood, error, mistake, untruth, misconception (ANT) truth

fallible (SYN) erring, imperfect, unsound, weak, faulty (ANT) strong, perfect, sure

false (SYN) mistaken, incorrect, wrong, bogus, artificial, misleading, deceptive (ANT) correct, right, genuine, true, valid

falsehood (SYN) lie, untruth, fib, fabrication, deceit, dishonesty (ANT) truth, fact

falter (SYN) waver, stumble, hesitate, delay, be on the fence (ANT) commit, persist

fame (SYN) repute, celebrity, popularity, prominence, renown (ANT) obscurity, anonymity

familiar (SYN) customary, recognizable, friendly, intimate, aware, acquainted (ANT) unfamiliar, unknown, strange, foreign, formal

family (SYN) relatives, kin, lineage, loved ones, clan (ANT) stranger

famine (SYN) scarcity, starvation, food shortage, lack (ANT) feast, abundance, plenty

famished (SYN) starving, ravenous, empty (ANT) full, satiated

famous (SYN) noted, prominent, distinguished, popular, acclaimed (ANT) unknown, obscure

fan (SYN) cool, refresh, ventilator, admirer, follower

-fanatic (SYN) extremist, zealot, enthusiast, devotee

fancy (SYN) ornate, elaborate, notion, whim, desire, crave (ANT) plain, simple, conviction

fang (SYN) tooth

fantastic (SYN) outlandish, unlikely, implausible, incredible, surreal (ANT) rational, normal, commonplace

fantasy (SYN) daydream, illusion, creativity, invention, make-believe (ANT) reality, realism, actuality

far (SYN) a great distance, distant, remote, greatly, easily (ANT) near, close by, little, almost

farce (SYN) satire, comedy, joke, parody, charade

fare (SYN) food, rations, manage, cope, price, fee

farewell (SYN) good-bye, parting, so long, departure, adieu, sendoff (ANT) hello, greeting, welcome

farm (SYN) homestead, ranch, plantation, cultivate, plant

farmer (SYN) agriculturalist, cultivator, harvester, tender

farther (SYN) more distant, more remote (ANT) nearer, closer

fascinate (SYN) intrigue, absorb, rivet, enthrall, charm (ANT) displease, bore, tire, disinterest fascination (SYN) interest, appeal, preoccupation, lure, pull (ANT) boredom, disenchantment

fashion (SYN) style, custom, trend, method, mold, shape

fast (SYN) abstain, rapid, speedy, hurried, swift, deeply, soundly (ANT) feast, slow, lightly

fasten (SYN) secure, join, bind, connect (ANT) unfasten

fat (SYN) overweight, stout, portly, thick, lard, grease (ANT) thin, slender, lean, light

fatal (SYN) deadly, lethal, mortal, terminal, disastrous (ANT) harmless, benign, healthy, nourishing

fatalities (SYN) deaths, casualties, losses

fate (SYN) destiny, providence, fortune, predestination (ANT) accident

father (SYN) parent, dad, predecessor

fathom (SYN) grasp, understand, comprehend, apprehend, unravel

fatigue (SYN) tiredness, lethargy, drain, exhaust, weaken (ANT) energy, strength, invigorate

fault (SYN) flaw, defect, shortcoming, blunder, lapse, blame, criticize (ANT) merit, virtue, excuse

favor (SYN) service, courtesy, kindness, prefer, approval (ANT) disfavor, dislike

favorite (SYN) preferred, popular, chosen, cherished, dearest, darling (ANT) hated, despised

fear (SYN) dread, suspect, terror, alarm, anxiety, fright (ANT) bravery, courage, fearlessness

fearful (SYN) timid, cowardly, petrified, frightening, ghastly (ANT) pleasant, calm, fearless, unafraid

feasible (SYN) possible, viable, attainable, doable, practical (ANT) unfeasible, impossible, unlikely, impracticable

feast (SYN) banquet, festival, spread, dine, indulge (ANT) snack, fast, starve

feat (SYN) achievement, exploit, accomplishment, triumph, endeavor (ANT) failure, inaction

feature (SYN) trait, characteristic, article, column, spotlight, emphasize (ANT) downplay, disregard

fee (SYN) charge, bill, cost, payment, rate

feeble (SYN) frail, weak, tenuous, delicate, ineffective, flimsy (ANT) strong, well, vigorous, brave

feed (SYN) food, fodder, nourish, provide for, eat (ANT) starve, deprive

feel (SYN) touch, handle, perceive, experience, believe, texture

feign (SYN) pretend, affect, fake

feisty (SYN) fiery, spunky, ornery, tough, spirited (ANT) tame, meek, amenable, docile

felicity (SYN) bliss, mirth, happiness, jubilation, cheerfulness

fell (SYN) cut down, flatten, raze, tumble (ANT) build, construct, raise

fellow (SYN) man, person, associate, companion, colleague

fellowship (SYN) companionship, friendship, solidarity, alliance, brotherhood

felon (SYN) criminal, crook, convict, offender

feminine (SYN) womanly, ladylike, delicate, gentle, pretty (ANT) masculine, manly, virile

fence (SYN) wall, barricade, confine, enclose, dodge, parry (ANT) release

ferment (SYN) brew, concoct, agitate, excite, provoke (ANT) quiet, soothe

ferocious (SYN) fierce, violent, savage, brutal, dangerous (ANT) gentle, tame, docile, tender

ferret (SYN) discover, unearth, dig up, trace

fertile (SYN) abundant, rich, prolific, productive, lush (ANT) barren, sterile, unproductive

fervent (SYN) earnest, heartfelt, ardent, vehement, intense (ANT) indifferent, cool, apathetic, dispassionate

fester (SYN) decay, putrefy, intensify, smolder (ANT) diminish, lessen, dissipate

festival (SYN) carnival, celebration, gala, feast, holiday

fetch (SYN) collect, bring, retrieve, earn, make

fetish (SYN) fixation, obsession

feud (SYN) quarrel, dispute, conflict, rivalry, squabble (ANT) peace, harmony, accord

fever (SYN) delirium, excitement, frenzy, mania, agitation

few (SYN) not many, a small number, scant (ANT) many, lots

fiasco (SYN) mess, disaster, debacle, flop, catastrophe (ANT) success

fib (SYN) lie, story, untruth, fiction (ANT) truth

fiber (SYN) thread, filament, strand, essence, nature

fickle (SYN) changeable, erratic, unsteady, inconsistent, capricious (ANT) resolute, steadfast, stubborn, constant

fiction (SYN) fantasy, myth, nonsense, tale, invention, literature (ANT) fact, non-fiction, reality, history

fictitious (SYN) false, made-up, untrue, imaginary, fabricated (ANT) truthful, genuine, real

fiddle (SYN) fidget, finger, tamper with, tinker, violin

fidelity (SYN) loyalty, devotion, allegiance, faithfulness, commitment, authenticity (ANT) infidelity, betrayal, disloyalty, inaccuracy

fidget (SYN) squirm, fiddle, twitch

field (SYN) pasture, meadow, subject, domain, competition, catch, retrieve

fiend (SYN) brute, monster, maniac, fanatic

fierce (SYN) savage, vicious, cruel, relentless, vehement (ANT) gentle, mild, harmless, tame

fiery (SYN) burning, blazing, passionate, spirited, fervid (ANT) dispassionate, dull, monotonous, smothered

fight (SYN) clash, struggle, battle, contend, brawl, campaign, contest (ANT) retreat, agree, surrender, yield, accord

figment (SYN) dream, illusion, fancy, whimsy (ANT) reality, fact, actuality

figurative (SYN) symbolic, descriptive, metaphorical, illustrative, allegorical (ANT) literal

figure (SYN) calculate, compute, character, diagram, outline, body, proportions, fathom, comprehend

figure head (SYN) front man, puppet, mouthpiece

filament (SYN) thread, fiber, strand, hair, tendril, gossamer

filch (SYN) steal, take, pilfer, embezzle

file (SYN) documents, folder, register, record, march, smooth, polish, arrange, classify

filial (SYN) dutiful, obedient, respectful

fill (SYN) load, pack, supply, saturate, satisfy (ANT) empty, drain, clear, leave

film (SYN) movie, motion picture, covering, membrane, photograph, video

filthy (SYN) dirty, foul, unclean, grimy, obscene, lewd (ANT) clean, pleasant

filtration (SYN) purification, cleansing, refinement (ANT) contamination

final (SYN) last, ultimate, closing, absolute, binding (ANT) first, beginning, initial, provisional

finale (SYN) conclusion, ending, close, culmination, denouement (ANT) introduction, prelude, opening, beginning

finally (SYN) eventually, in the end, in conclusion, lastly, decisively (ANT) initially, partly

finance (SYN) fund, subsidize, back, economics, commerce

find (SYN) discover, locate, detect, pinpoint, acquisition (ANT) lose, misplace

fine (SYN) exceptional, delicate, satisfactory, sunny, fair, subtle, flimsy, penalty, fee (ANT) unrefined, poor, thick finesse (SYN) skill, acumen, delicacy, discretion, tact (ANT) clumsiness, thoughtlessness

finger (SYN) touch, handle, manipulate, fiddle with, digit

finicky (SYN) picky, particular, critical, fussy, choosy (ANT) accepting, easygoing

finish (SYN) complete, conclude, consume, surface, texture (ANT) start, begin, commence, initiate

finite (SYN) limited, restricted, bound, fixed, demarcated (ANT) infinite, free, unlimited

fire (SYN) flame, blaze, zest, enthusiasm, dismiss, discharge (ANT) laziness, hire

firm (SYN) hard, stiff, secure, stable, inflexible, determined, company, partnership (ANT) soft, yielding, unreliable, indefinite

firmly (SYN) securely, staunchly, tightly, unshakably, adamantly (ANT) weakly

first (SYN) foremost, principal, fundamental, earliest, top, greatest (ANT) last, final, later, lowest

first aid (SYN) emergency care

fish (SYN) angle, trawl, delve, grope, hunt

fissure (SYN) fracture, split, crevice, breach, rift

fist (SYN) hand

fit (SYN) appropriate, proper, equipped, trim, robust, match (ANT) unfit, unhealthy, ill-suited

fitness (SYN) good health, stamina, athleticism, readiness, competence

fix (SYN) position, embed, fasten, mend, correct, focus, dilemma, plight (ANT) loosen, remove, break, damage

fixture (SYN) equipment, institution

flabbergasted (SYN) shocked, amazed, stunned, astounded, speechless

flaccid (SYN) drooping, limp, soft, slack (ANT) taut, firm

flag (SYN) banner, pennant, hail, wave, tire, ebb, label (ANT) revive

flagrant (SYN) blatant, glaring, bold, outrageous, shameless (ANT) slight, subtle, inconspicuous

flail (SYN) thrash, strike, beat, whale

flair (SYN) knack, mastery, talent, gift, style, panache

flake (SYN) layer, scale, sliver, peel, chip

flamboyant (SYN) glitzy, theatrical, extravagant, glamorous, colorful, exuberant (ANT) restrained, plain

flame (SYN) fire, blaze, flair, sweetheart, beau

flammable (SYN) combustible

flank (SYN) side, haunch, edge, border

flap (SYN) flutter, flail, beat, fly, stir

flare (SYN) flame, blast, flicker, signal, widen, splay

flash (SYN) instant, moment, shimmer, spark, flaunt, expose

flat (SYN) level, even, horizontal, tiresome, dull (ANT) sloping, vertical, curved, lively, animated

flattery (SYN) fawning, sweet-talk, obsequiousness, compliment, praise

flaunt (SYN) parade, display, show off, sport (ANT) hide, deny, conceal

flavor (SYN) taste, essence, season, infuse, feeling

flaw (SYN) shortcoming, imperfection, weakness, fault, glitch (ANT) strength

flay (SYN) lash, slash, criticize, scathe

flee (SYN) bolt, escape, run away, retreat, scram (ANT) remain, stay

fleece (SYN) wool, exploit, overcharge, swindle

fleet (SYN) armada, navy, convoy, flotilla

fleeting (SYN) passing, temporary, brief, momentary (ANT) lasting, permanent, lasting, stable

flex (SYN) bend, display (ANT) extend

flexible (SYN) stretchy, pliant, limber, elastic, adaptable, adjustable (ANT) rigid, unbending, stubborn, inflexible

flicker (SYN) twinkle, flutter, spark, dance, tremble, twitch

flight (SYN) aviation, trip, departure, exodus, flock

flimsy (SYN) fragile, rickety, sheer, feeble, weak (ANT) strong, sturdy, thick, sound, substantial

flinch (SYN) wince, recoil, shrink, start, dodge (ANT) face

fling (SYN) cast, throw, toss, heave, romance

flip (SYN) toss, flick, bold, cheeky, sassy (ANT) polite, unassuming, serious, grave

flippant (SYN) disrespectful, irreverent, rude, insolent, nervy (ANT) courteous, mannerly, polite

flirt (SYN) toy, tease, consider, dabble in, heartbreaker (ANT) ignore, reject

float (SYN) bob, sail, hover, drift, launch (ANT) sink, drop

flock (SYN) herd, swarm, flight, gather, throng, stream (ANT) avoid

flog (SYN) whip, beat, lash, flay, cane

flood (SYN) torrent, deluge, submerge, immerse, abundance (ANT) drought, drain, starve, trickle

floor (SYN) ground, level, tier, throw, perplex, disconcert

floral (SYN) flowery

florid (SYN) flushed, ruddy, flowery, ornate, flamboyant (ANT) plain, simple, basic, unadorned

flotilla (SYN) navy, armada, fleet

flounder (SYN) fumble, struggle, thrash, flail, grope

flourish (SYN) thrive, prosper, blossom, wave, brandish, embellishment (ANT) die, decline, wither, weaken, decay

flout (SYN) defy, mock, spurn, disobey, violate (ANT) obey, observe, heed, follow

flow (SYN) course, surge, circulate, spring, arise

flower (SYN) blossom, bloom, unfold, mature

fluctuate (SYN) change, vary, veer, waver, alternate, shift (ANT) persist, abide, stay, sustain

fluctuation (SYN) change, variance, oscillation (ANT) stability, constancy

fluent (SYN) effortless, natural, smooth, articulate, flowing

fluid (SYN) liquid, runny, watery, graceful, continuous (ANT) solid, jerky

fluke (SYN) chance, coincidence, lucky break, accident

flurry (SYN) fuss, commotion, whirl, spell, fit

flush (SYN) blush, redden, cleanse, purge, level, square (ANT) pale, uneven, rough

fluster (SYN) upset, agitate, rattle, unnerve, embarrass (ANT) calm, soothe, pacify

flutter (SYN) beat, flap, flit, vibration, confusion (ANT) remain, stand

flux (SYN) tide, drift, current, change

fly (SYN) soar, wing, rush, dart, pilot

foam (SYN) bubbles, froth, lather, fizz, suds

focal (SYN) central, foremost (ANT) peripheral

focus (SYN) center, emphasis, heart, essence, aim, pinpoint (ANT) periphery

foe (SYN) enemy, rival, adversary, opponent, adversary (ANT) friend, pal, mate, confidant, teammate

fog (SYN) mist, smog, cloud, haze, gloom

foil (SYN) thwart, frustrate, hinder, complement, contrast (ANT) assist, aid

foliage (SYN) leaves, plants

fold (SYN) bend, crease, overlap, fail, collapse (ANT) unfold, spread, open, succeed, triumph

folder (SYN) file, binder, envelope

folk (SYN) people, inhabitants, family, relatives, kin

follow (SYN) chase, pursue, imitate, heed, observe, result, develop (ANT) lead, disregard, ignore, flout

folly (SYN) nonsense, foolishness, recklessness (ANT) wisdom

fond (SYN) affectionate, dear, tender, loving, partial to (ANT) uncaring, indifferent, spiteful, hateful

fondle (SYN) cuddle, caress, pet, stroke

food (SYN) sustenance, fare, cuisine, rations, nourishment

fool (SYN) dupe, deceive, trick, dunce, idiot, (ANT) clarify, genius

foolish (SYN) silly, absurd, mindless, rash, imprudent (ANT) sensible, wise, logical

forage (SYN) search, rummage, hunt, scour

foray (SYN) raid, invasion, attempt, stab, trail

forbear (SYN) refrain, abstain, withhold (ANT) indulge, revel, satisfy

forbearance (SYN) restraint, patience, tolerance, abstinence (ANT) excess, indulgence

forbid (SYN) ban, exclude, disallow, prohibit, outlaw (ANT) permit, allow, consent, tolerate, sanction

force (SYN) power, strength, muscle, pressure, compel, intimidation (ANT) weakness, ineffectiveness, persuasion

foreboding (SYN) dread, misgiving, fear, apprehension, anxiety

forecast (SYN) predict, foresee, anticipate, prediction, conjecture

foreign (SYN) strange, exotic, alien, external, remote (ANT) local, domestic, native

foreigner (SYN) immigrant, stranger, alien, outsider (ANT) native

foreman (SYN) manager, overseer, boss, supervisor, spokesman

foremost (SYN) leading, chief, primary, supreme, paramount (ANT) minor, secondary, incidental

foreseeable (SYN) predictable, anticipatable (ANT) unknown

foresight (SYN) anticipation, preparedness, precaution

forest (SYN) woods, grove

forestall (SYN) prevent, avert, thwart, preclude

foretell (SYN) predict, prophesy, forecast, warn of, divine (ANT) ignore

forever (SYN) always, evermore, eternally, constantly, perpetually (ANT) never, occasionally

forfeit (SYN) lose, relinquish, surrender, sacrifice, renounce (ANT) keep, retain

forge (SYN) create, mold, falsify, copy, fake

forgery (SYN) fraud, counterfeit, fake, replica (ANT) genuine, original

forget (SYN) omit, overlook, neglect, disregard, leave behind (ANT) remember

forgive (SYN) excuse, acquit, pardon, condone, absolve (ANT) blame, accuse, charge, resent

forgiveness (SYN) mercy, absolution, amnesty, pardon

forgo (SYN) waive, do without, abandon

forgotten (SYN) past, left behind, lost (ANT) remembered

fork (SYN) divide, split, branch, separate, diverge (ANT) join, connect

forlorn (SYN) miserable, hopeless, desperate (ANT) happy, contented, cheerful

form (SYN) shape, figure, structure, mold, conceive, document (ANT) shapelessness, dissolve, ruin, destroy

formal (SYN) orderly, ritualistic, official, conventional, stiff (ANT) informal, casual, friendly, intimate, habitual

formality (SYN) custom, procedure, etiquette, decorum, reserve (ANT) informality, ease, friendliness, spontaneity

formation (SYN) production, establishment, pattern, arrangement, configuration (ANT) destruction, dissolution, chaos

former (SYN) previous, past, earlier, prior (ANT) latter, current, future

formidable (SYN) daunting, intimidating, awesome, impressive (ANT) comforting, inviting, welcoming

formula (SYN) recipe, method, blueprint, procedure

formulate (SYN) express, define, specify, devise, frame

fort (SYN) castle, stronghold, garrison, citadel, bastion

forte (SYN) gift, talent, specialty, strength, strong suit (ANT) weakness, vulnerability

forthright (SYN) blunt, straightforward, candid, open, upfront (ANT) guarded, secretive, furtive, sneaky, surreptitious

fortify (SYN) protect, strengthen, secure, invigorate, bolster (ANT) weaken, subdue

fortitude (SYN) bravery, courage, valor, resolution, mettle (ANT) faint-heartedness

fortress (SYN) castle, stronghold, garrison

fortunate (SYN) lucky, favorable, opportune, blessed, advantageous (ANT) unfortunate, unlucky, unhappy, dire

fortune (SYN) wealth, affluence, luck, destiny (ANT) poverty, hardship forum (SYN) meeting, rally, gathering, symposium, assembly

forward (SYN) ahead, first, leading, advance, bold, pushy (ANT) backward, rear, final, shy, reserved

foster (SYN) nurture, promote, encourage, stimulate, raise (ANT) neglect, suppress, quell, squash

foul (SYN) filthy, putrid, obscene, profane, unfair, dishonest, pollute, defile (ANT) clean, tidy, upright, polite, pleasant

found (SYN) discovered, establish, begin, institute, launch (ANT) dissolve, lost

foundation (SYN) groundwork, substructure, footing, evidence, basis

founder (SYN) architect, originator, sink, fail, stumble (ANT) raise up, succeed

foundry (SYN) factory, plant, refinery

fountain (SYN) font, spring, source, wellspring

fowl (SYN) poultry, chicken, rooster, turkey, pheasant

foyer (SYN) lobby, vestibule, entryway, atrium

fraction (SYN) piece, segment, share, snippet, trifle (ANT) whole

fracture (SYN) break, crack, split, splinter, fissure (ANT) join, connect

fragile (SYN) brittle, delicate, weak, flimsy, breakable (ANT) strong, sturdy, durable, tough

fragment (SYN) portion, shred, bit, particle, shatter (ANT) whole, entire, unite

fragrance (ANT) smell, perfume, scent, aroma, bouquet

frail (SYN) infirm, delicate, vulnerable, insubstantial, weak (ANT) strong, robust, vigorous, potent, sound

frame (SYN) casing, shell, figure, build, mount

frank (SYN) direct, sincere, outspoken, candid, obvious (ANT) evasive, deceptive, insincere, disguised

frantic (SYN) frenzied, wild, mad, hysterical, berserk, hectic (ANT) calm, tranquil, placid, serene

fraternity (SYN) brotherhood, league, union, fellowship, companionship, solidarity

fraud (SYN) trickery, deceit, cheat, imposter, swindler (ANT) honesty, integrity, genuine

fraudulent (SYN) treacherous, dishonest, crooked, duplicitous, deceitful (ANT) honest, upstanding, righteous, ingenuous

fray (SYN) wear, unravel, tatter, discord, commotion

freak (SYN) oddity, anomaly, abnormal, unusual, enthusiast (ANT) normal, usual, common freckle (SYN) spot

free (SYN) independent, liberated, release, emancipate, complimentary (ANT) captive, enslaved, detain, trap, expensive

freedom (SYN) liberty, independence, sovereignty, opportunity, discretion (ANT) slavery, captivity, subjection, obligation, liability

freeze (SYN) chill, harden, ice, stand still, become motionless (ANT) thaw, move

freezer (SYN) icebox

freight (SYN) shipment, transportation, cargo, merchandise, goods

frenzy (SYN) passion, rage, fury, hysteria, delirium, agitation

frequent (SYN) recurrent, habitual, repeated, common, continual (ANT) rare, isolated, sporadic, occasional

fresh (SYN) current, novel, new, healthy, innovative, invigorating, rude (ANT) old, stale, trite, tired, respectful

fret (SYN) worry, brood, agonize, concern oneself (ANT) relax

friction (SYN) rubbing, chaffing, scraping, abrasion, hostility, animosity (ANT) harmony, accord

friend (SYN) companion, buddy, pal, playmate, confidant (ANT) stranger, enemy, rival, adversary

friendship (SYN) familiarity, goodwill, intimacy, relationship, bind (ANT) hostility, unfamiliarity

fright (SYN) fear, panic, trepidation, dread, jolt

frighten (SYN) alarm, startle, scare, intimidate, terrorize (ANT) comfort, encourage, reassure, soothe

frigid (SYN) cold, arctic, aloof, forbidding, unresponsive (ANT) warm, temperate, affectionate, accessible, welcoming

frill (SYN) trim, extra, embellishment, fuss, bells and whistles (ANT) basic

fringe (SYN) edging, trimming, edge, outskirts, unofficial (ANT) middle, mainstream, official

frisky (SYN) lively, playful, sportive, high-spirited, animated (ANT) bored, lethargic

fritter (SYN) waste, squander, misspend, idle away

frivolous (SYN) flippant, joking, inane, silly, trivial (ANT) serious, weighty

frolic (SYN) play, romp, cavort, revel, antic

front (SYN) facade, head, beginning, start, pretense, disguise (ANT) back, behind, rear, posterior

frontier (SYN) boundary, verge, limit, perimeter, borderline

frost (SYN) freeze, ice

froth (SYN) foam, bubbles, head, suds, lather

frown (SYN) scowl, glare, glower, sulk (ANT) smile, grin, beam

frozen (SYN) solid, icy, chilled, frigid, numb (ANT) thawed, warm, liquefied

frugal (SYN) sparing, thrifty, cheap, parsimonious, economical, prudent (ANT) lavish, wasteful, spendthrift, extravagant

fruit (SYN) produce, harvest, yield, outcome, reward

fruitful (SYN) productive, worthwhile, valuable, beneficial (ANT) barren, futile, pointless

fruition (SYN) ripeness, attainment, fulfillment, completion, realization

frustrate (SYN) baffle, hinder, halt, derail, exasperate, dishearten (ANT) assist, facilitate, further, satisfy

fudge (SYN) hedge, dodge, evade, beat around the bush

fuel (SYN) power, drive, incite, ammunition, provocation

fugitive (SYN) runaway, escapee, refugee, absconder, deserter

fulfill (SYN) meet, comply with, perform, achieve, realize (ANT) fail, fall short, ignore, disappoint

full (SYN) brimming, loaded, ample, extensive, comprehensive (ANT) empty, hungry, selective, incomplete

fullness (SYN) plenty, saturation, richness, strength

fumes (SYN) smoke, gas, vapor, exhaust

fumigate (SYN) cleanse, purify, disinfect

fuming (SYN) angry, seething, enraged, furious

fun (SYN) pleasure, play, entertainment, agreeable, enjoyable (ANT) boredom, misery

function (SYN) purpose, role, operate, work, celebration, gathering (ANT) malfunction

fund (SYN) reserve, supply, finance, subsidize, support

fundamental (SYN) basic, essential, primary, rule, law (ANT) dispensable, secondary, incidental

funeral (SYN) burial, internment, laying to rest

fungus (SYN) mold, mushrooms

funnel (SYN) channel, conduct, direct, move

funny (SYN) comical, witty, humorous, peculiar, bizarre, suspicious (ANT) serious, normal, trustworthy

fur (SYN) hair, pelt

furious (SYN) livid, enraged, inflamed, ranting, heated, tempestuous (ANT) pleased, calm, docile, civil

furnish (SYN) decorate, equip, supply, offer, provide (ANT) strip, dismantle furniture (SYN) furnishings, possessions, household goods

furor (SYN) uproar, commotion, hullabaloo, brouhaha, outcry, stir

further (SYN) additionally, moreover, assist, advance, beyond (ANT) existing, impede

furtive (SYN) sly, sneaky, stealthy, clandestine, hidden (ANT) open

fury (SYN) wrath, frenzy, outrage, violence, savagery (ANT) pleasure

furry (SYN) fuzzy, fluffy, hairy

fuse (SYN) mix, merge, join, mingle, combine (ANT) separate

fusion (SYN) mixture, blend, merger, amalgam

fuss (SYN) excitement, stir, protest, objection, fret, worry

futile (SYN) useless, worthless, vain, ineffectual, unsuccessful (ANT) successful, productive, beneficial, useful

future (SYN) hereafter, outlook, prospect, later, forthcoming (ANT) past, previous

G

gadget (SYN) device, contraption, tool, instrument, doodad

gaffe (SYN) blunder, faux pas, mistake, slip

gag (SYN) quiet, stifle, retch, choke, joke

gaiety (SYN) glee, merriment, cheerfulness, joy, mirth, liveliness (ANT) sadness, melancholy, gloom

gain (SYN) obtain, secure, earn, benefit, profit, increase (ANT) lose, loss

gait (SYN) walk, stride, step, carriage

gala (SYN) party, ball, celebration

gale (SYN) storm, wind, tornado, tempest, outburst

gall (SYN) nerve, hostility, insolence, irritate, vex (ANT) humility, modesty, manners, pacify, please

gallant (SYN) brave, valiant, courageous, heroic, noble, chivalrous (ANT) fearful, cowardly, impolite

gallery (SYN) corridor, passageway, exhibition, studio

gallivant (SYN) wander, roam, gad, flirt

gallop (SYN) run, rush, bolt, trot

galore (SYN) aplenty, to spare, in abundance

galvanize (SYN) inspire, stir, electrify, stimulate, rouse

gamble (SYN) bet, wager, speculate, chance, risk (ANT) insure, certainty

game (SYN) pastime, recreation, diversion, contest, prey, willing, eager (ANT) work, drudgery, hesitant gamut (SYN)scope, scale, range, field

gang (SYN) mob, pack, crew, clique

gangling (SYN) tall, lanky, awkward

gap (SYN) space, opening, hole, pause, lull, disparity, difference (ANT) closure

gape (SYN) stare, gawk, ogle, open, split

garbage (SYN) trash, litter, waste, rubbish, refuse

garish (SYN) loud, tasteless, flashy, vulgar, harsh (ANT) subdued, tasteful, drab, sober, discreet

garment (SYN) dress, clothes, garb, outfit, attire

garner (SYN) store, amass, collect, accumulate, hoard (ANT) squander

garnish (SYN) decorate, adorn, embellish, trim, enhancement

garrison (SYN) troops, unit, fort, base, post

garrulous (SYN) talkative, chatty, babbling, verbose, rambling (ANT) quiet, withdrawn, taciturn

gaseous (SYN) vaporized

gash (SYN) cut, slit, wound, laceration

gasp (SYN) gulp, pant, heave, wheeze, exclamation

gate (SYN) door, passageway, portal, entryway, exit

gather (SYN) collect, assemble, assume, surmise, intensify, grow, pleat (ANT) distribute, spread, scatter, disperse

gauche (SYN) tactless, awkward, unsophisticated, clumsy (ANT) refined, elegant, sophisticated

gaudy (SYN) flashy, bright, bold, tacky, cheap (ANT) plain, tasteful, subdued

gauge (SYN) measure, determine, estimate, assess, indicator, standard

gaunt (SYN) bony, lean, scrawny, emaciated, haggard (ANT) fat, obese, portly, stout, heavy

gay (SYN) cheerful, carefree, jovial, light-hearted, homosexual (ANT) sad, grouchy, sullen, heterosexual, straight

gaze (SYN) watch, look, stare, gape, scrutinize

gear (SYN) cog, machinery, equipment, tools, clothing, possessions

gelatinous (SYN) gummy, jelly-like, glutinous

gem (SYN) jewel, precious stone, masterpiece, prize treasure (ANT) worthless

general (SYN) widespread, prevalent, customary, vague, approximate (ANT) localized, exceptional, rare, particular, infrequent

generality (SYN) cliché, platitude

generally (SYN) normally, usually, typically, universally, as a rule

(ANT) uncommonly, rarely,
occasionally

generate (SYN) create, cause, produce,
induce, prompt (ANT) destroy,
oppose, resist

generation (SYN) era, period, formation,
genesis, wave

generosity (SYN) charity, kindness,
unselfishness, magnanimity, altruism
(ANT) greed, selfishness, meanness

generous (SYN) liberal, free, giving,
ungrudging, plentiful, ample (ANT)
selfish, uncharitable, meager, sparing

generously (SYN) open-handedly,
liberally, munificently (ANT)
selfishly

genesis (SYN) beginning, origin, root,
inception, creation (ANT) end,
termination, death

genial (SYN) friendly, amiable, cheerful,
pleasant, gracious (ANT) sorrowful,
unhappy, moody

genius (SYN) mastermind, whiz,
prodigy, intellect, brilliance (ANT)
moron, simpleton, stupidity,
ignorance

genre (SYN) type, sort, style, variety

gentility (SYN) nobility, refinement,
upper-class, elite, aristocracy

gentle (SYN) tender, mild, soothing,
compassionate, gradual,
imperceptible (ANT) rough, course,
mean, harsh, brutal, steep

gentlemanly (SYN) polite, courteous,
civil, honorable (ANT) rude,
impolite

gently (SYN) softly, carefully, quietly,
sensitively (ANT) roughly, harshly,
callously

genuflect (SYN) bow, curtsey, grovel

genuine (SYN) real, authentic,
legitimate, reliable, sincere (ANT)
misleading, false, erroneous

genuinely (SYN) truly, actually, really

germ (SYN) microbe, virus, bacterium,
bug, origin, bud

germinate (SYN) sprout, grow, develop,
originate, swell

gestation (SYN) pregnancy

gesticulate (SYN) signal, motion,
gesture, indicate

gesture (SYN) sign, motion, indication,
action, deed

get (SYN) obtain, acquire, receive,
secure, become, comprehend (ANT)
give, lose, release, surrender

ghastly (SYN) horrible, dreadful,
frightful, vile, detestable (ANT)
pleasant, endearing, welcoming

ghost (SYN) apparition, spirit, phantom,
trace, suggestion (ANT) reality,
substance

giant (SYN) ogre, monster, huge,
colossal, immense (ANT) tiny,
small, miniature, dwarf

gibberish (SYN) babble, nonsense, incoherence

giddy (SYN) reeling, dizzy, silly, gleeful, light-hearted (ANT) solemn, calm, serious

gift (SYN) talent, capability, present, donation, bequest

gigantic (SYN) enormous, tremendous, vast, massive, gargantuan (ANT) little, teeny, diminutive, wee

giggle (SYN) laugh, titter, chuckle, chortle, snicker

gild (SYN) brighten, enhance, ornament, embellish

gimmick (SYN) stunt, ploy, device, trick, contrivance

gingerly (SYN) gently, carefully, cautiously, hesitantly, reluctantly (ANT) quickly, roughly

gird (SYN) surround, enclose, secure, bind, support

girl (SYN) young woman, female child, miss, gal

girth (SYN) size, circumference, measurement

gist (SYN) point, meaning, significance, core

give (SYN) contribute, present, furnish, supply, yield (ANT) take, withhold, get, receive

given (SYN) stated, specified, established fact

glad (SYN) contented, pleased, happy, delighted, thrilled (ANT) sad, dismayed, reluctant, disappointed

gladly (SYN) willingly, happily, eagerly, freely, readily, with pleasure (ANT) begrudgingly, reluctantly, unhappily

glamorous (SYN) dazzling, glossy, prestigious, elegant, fashionable (ANT) dowdy, dull, plain

glamour (SYN) charm, allure, style, fascination, prestige

glance (SYN) look, glimpse, peek, scan, reflect, shimmer (ANT) examine, scrutinize, study

glare (SYN) frown, scowl, dazzle, blaze, shine

glaring (SYN) obvious, conspicuous, blatant, gross (ANT) subtle, inconspicuous, minor

glaze (SYN) gloss, polish, lacquer, coat, varnish

gleam (SYN) shine, sparkle, flash, glitter, inkling, glimmer

glean (SYN) garner, extract, collect

glee (SYN) elation, exuberance, merriment, triumph, joy (ANT) sorrow, heartache, suffering, sadness

glib (SYN) vocal, suave, slick, slippery, insincere (ANT) faltering, quiet

glide (SYN) sail, skate, slide, flow, slip (ANT) stick

glimpse (SYN) glance, sighting, spot, view, notice

glitch (SYN) problem, snag, hitch, difficulty, interruption

glitter (SYN) shine, glint, sparkle, flash, twinkle

gloat (SYN) brag, triumph, boast, crow

global (SYN) universal, worldwide, international, broad, comprehensive

globe (SYN) world, sphere, ball, orb, planet

gloom (SYN) murk, shadow, depression, melancholy, blues (ANT) light, happiness, optimism

gloomy (SYN) dismal, dreary, somber, glum, morose (ANT) bright, sparkling, blithe, buoyant

glorify (SYN) elevate, magnify, exalt, adore, venerate, praise

glorious (SYN) sublime, majestic, superb, spectacular, marvelous (ANT) odious, horrid, shameful

glory (SYN) honor, recognition, fame, grandeur, revel (ANT) shame, modesty, obscurity

glossy (SYN) polished, shiny, lustrous, brilliant, glistening (ANT) dull

glow (SYN) shine, gleam, light, radiance, smolder

glower (SYN) scowl, frown, glare, dirty look

glue (SYN) adhesive, paste, cement, stick, seal

glum (SYN) sad, down, low, sullen (ANT) happy, thrilled, lively, spirited

gluttony (SYN) greed, overindulgence, voracity

gnarled (SYN) twisted, knotty, contorted, misshapen, cantankerous, crabby

gnaw (SYN) chew, bite, nibble, munch

go (SYN) depart, leave, travel, stride, attempt, elapse (ANT) come, enter, arrive

goad (SYN) prod, drive, prompt, egg on (ANT) discourage

goal (SYN) aim, target, objective, intention, ambition

gobble (SYN) eat, devour, wolf, gulp

goblin (SYN) gremlin, gnome, troll

god (SYN) deity, idol

God (SYN) Creator, Supreme Being

goddess (SYN) female deity

godsend (SYN) blessing, luck, windfall

golden (SYN) yellow, flaxen, favorite, successful

gone (SYN) away, missing, past, finished, vanished (ANT) here, present

good (SYN) pleasing, sound, quality, ethical, kind, obedient (ANT) bad, evil, mean, undesirable good-bye (SYN) farewell, parting, adieu (ANT) hello

goodness (SYN) kind-heartedness, generosity, virtue, merit, integrity (ANT) evil, corruption

goods (SYN) wares, stuff, merchandise, property, products

goodwill (SYN) friendship, amity, benevolence, compassion, decency (ANT) hostility

gore (SYN) bloodshed, carnage, wound, impale

gorge (SYN) overeat, glut, canyon, ravine, gulch

gorgeous (SYN) ravishing, stunning, beautiful, exquisite, lovely (ANT) ugly, drab, unattractive

gospel (SYN) doctrine, creed, truth, fact

gossamer (SYN) flimsy, sheer, delicate, gauzy, filmy (ANT) substantial

gossip (SYN) scandal, hearsay, rumors, scuttlebutt, busybody

gouge (SYN) hollow, scoop, groove, gash, cut

gourmet (SYN) connoisseur, epicurean, foodie, fancy, exotic

govern (SYN) rule, command, administer, lead, determine (ANT) comply, obey

government (SYN) authority, executive, regime, administration

governor (SYN) leader, commander, chief, director

gown (SYN) dress, frock, garment, robe

grab (SYN) seize, grasp, grip, snatch, clutch (ANT) release

grace (SYN) elegance, ease, poise, favor, etiquette, pardon, blessing, dignify (ANT) awkwardness

graceful (SYN) elegant, smooth, fluid, easy, nimble, lithe (ANT) awkward, ungainly, graceless

gracefully (SYN) smoothly, fluidly, elegantly, dexterously, easily

gracious (SYN) considerate, polite, courteous, obliging, thoughtful (ANT) ungracious, rude, uncivil

grade (SYN) level, rank, class, rate, sort

gradual (SYN) slow, continuous, steady, graduated, progressive (ANT) sudden, abrupt

gradually (SYN) slowly, step by step, little by little, cautiously, systematically (ANT) all at once

graft (SYN) sprout, bud, transplant, join, splice

grain (SYN) cereals, seed, kernel, texture, weave, nap

grammar (SYN) syntax, sentence structure

grand (SYN) impressive, imposing, stately, bold, dignified, terrific (ANT) humble, small, inferior, trivial grandeur (SYN) splendor, pomp, glory, greatness, magnificence

grandiose (SYN) pompous, showy, ostentatious, lofty, monumental

grant (SYN) acknowledge, concede, subsidy, award, permit (ANT) deny, oppose

granule (SYN) grain, particle, crumb, scrap

graph (SYN) chart, illustration

graphic (SYN) vivid, striking, explicit, visual, illustrative (ANT) vague, unclear, confused

grapple (SYN) struggle, confront, wrestle, grasp, seize

grasp (SYN) hold, clutch, understand, comprehend, possession, clutches (ANT) release, miss, overlook, misunderstand

grate (SYN) shred, grind, scrape, irritate, annoy

grateful (SYN) thankful, appreciative, gratified, indebted, obliged (ANT) ungrateful, thankless

gratify (SYN) please, satisfy, gladden, humor (ANT) disappoint

gratitude (SYN) thanks, appreciation, gratefulness, recognition

gratuitous (SYN) free, voluntary, complimentary, unwarranted, needless

gratuity (SYN) tip, gift, reward

grave (SYN) serious, somber, critical, severe, crypt, tomb (ANT) flippant, comic, inconsequential

gravity (SYN) importance, significance, urgency, magnitude, sobriety

gray (SYN) dismal, dreary, drab, ashen colorless (ANT) bright

graze (SYN) feed, crop, brush, skim, scratch

grease (SYN) lubricate, oil, fat, slime

great (SYN) huge, gigantic, tremendous, crucial, outstanding (ANT) small, petty, ordinary, minor

greater (SYN) better, more, larger

greatest (SYN) ultimate, best, top

greed (SYN) avarice, selfishness, desire, hunger, voracity (ANT) generosity, selflessness, temperance

green (SYN) conservationist, ecologically sound, non-polluting, naive, inexperienced, envious, jealous, turf, lawn

greet (SYN) welcome, meet, receive

greeting (SYN) salutation, address, welcome

gregarious (SYN) outgoing, social, friendly, cordial (ANT) shy, reserved, introverted, antisocial

gridlock (SYN) standstill, stalemate, impasse

grief (SYN) anguish, suffering, woe, heartache, misery, agony, desolation (ANT) elation, joy, glee, ecstasy

grievance (SYN) complaint, gripe, objection, resentment

grieve (SYN) mourn, weep, rue, sadden, distress (ANT) rejoice, celebrate

grievous (SYN) dreadful, painful, injurious, shameful, atrocious

grim (SYN) harsh, stern, terrible, grisly, bleak (ANT) pleasant, cheerful, favorable

grimace (SYN) scowl, frown, sneer

grin (SYN) smile, beam, smirk (ANT) frown, scowl

grind (SYN) crush, pulverize, sand, labor, toil

grip (SYN) hold, clasp, control, power, grasp, command, fascinate, rivet

grisly (SYN) gruesome, appalling, shocking, ghastly, macabre

grit (SYN) dust, sand, spirit, tenacity, courage, clench

groan (SYN) moan, cry, sigh, grumble, creak

groggy (SYN) dazed, confused, unsteady, dizzy (ANT) focused, clear-headed

groom (SYN) brush, comb, prepare, train, prime

groove (SYN) indentation, hollow, channel, furrow, rut

grope (SYN) feel, search, fumble, cast about

gross (SYN) disgusting, revolting, blatant, brazen, total, earn, fat, enormous (ANT) pleasant, acceptable, slight, delicate, thin

grotesque (SYN) freakish, unnatural, bizarre, misshapen, ludicrous (ANT) normal, ordinary, sensible

ground (SYN) earth, soil, land, floor, estate

grounds (SYN) basis, motive, justification, cause, argument

group (SYN) cluster, gang, arrange, bracket, classify

grove (SYN) wood, forest, thicket

grovel (SYN) fawn, beg, crawl, demean oneself

grow (SYN) develop, raise, increase, bloom, progress (ANT) shrink, decrease, vanish, decline

grown (SYN) mature, developed

growth (SYN) improvement, progress, expansion, tumor, lump

grub (SYN) larva, maggot, dig, search, forage, food

grudge (SYN) resentment, antipathy, ill-will, animosity, complain (ANT) forgiveness

grueling (SYN) tiring, strenuous, demanding, punishing, exhausting (ANT) easy, relaxing gruesome (SYN) horrific, hideous, sickening, grisly

grumble (SYN) grouch, complain, whine, rumble, gurgle

grunt (SYN) snort, grumble

guarantee (SYN) assurance, certainty, pledge, promise, oath, vow

guard (SYN) protect, defend, shield, lookout, sentinel (ANT) forsake, desert, abandon

guardian (SYN) keeper, custodian, caretaker, trustee, protector

guess (SYN) suppose, presume, speculate, prediction, hypothesis (ANT) fact, certainty, measure, calculate

guerilla (SYN) rebel, revolutionary, terrorist

guest (SYN) visitor, company, client, tourist, patron (ANT) host, staff

guidance (SYN) advice, leadership, counseling, teaching, direction

guide (SYN) show, conduct, lead, escort, usher, example, manual (ANT) mislead, neglect

guild (SYN) society, association, club, organization, union

guile (SYN) cunning, trickery, deceit, artifice (ANT) honesty, innocence

guilt (SYN) blame, responsibility, wrongdoing, culpability, remorse, shame, contrition (ANT) innocence, blamelessness

guilty (SYN) responsible, to blame, at fault, contrite, sheepish, regretful (ANT) innocent, pure, faultless, unrepentant

guise (SYN) pretense, semblance, demeanor, appearance, form

gulf (SYN) bay, cove, chasm, split, separation

gullible (SYN) naive, trusting, unsuspecting, simple (ANT) suspicious, wary

gully (SYN) ditch, gutter, valley, ravine

gulp (SYN) swallow, guzzle, swig, choke

gum (SYN) glue, paste, resin, cement, attach

gun (SYN) firearm, pistol, revolver, rifle, piece

guru (SYN) mentor, teacher, sage, authority

gush (SYN) cascade, pour, enthuse, chatter, overstate

gust (SYN) blast, puff, blow, breeze, rush

gut (SYN) stomach, abdomen, paunch, bravery, nerve

gutter (SYN) ditch, channel, drain, trough, trench

guttural (SYN) throaty, deep, intense, rasping, gruff

gypsy (SYN) traveler, nomad, wanderer, bohemian

H

habit (SYN) custom, tendency, practice, inclination, addiction, fixation

habitat (SYN) environment, surroundings

habitation (SYN) dwelling, home, lodging, residence

habitual (SYN) familiar, routine, standard, regular, accustomed (ANT) infrequent, unusual, occasional

hackneyed (SYN) stale, trite, commonplace, unoriginal, dull (ANT) fresh, innovative, original

haggard (SYN) gaunt, thin, worn, fatigued, exhausted (ANT) lively, healthy

haggle (SYN) argue, bargain, barter, negotiate, squabble (ANT) assent, agree, concur, cave

hail (SYN) salute, greet, welcome, pelt, shower

hair (SYN) mane, tresses, locks

halcyon (SYN) serene, peaceful, happy, tranquil, carefree (ANT) stressed, worried, fretful, disturbed

hale (SYN) fit, well, strong, healthy, robust (ANT) weak, ill

half (SYN) equal portion, section, partial, limited (ANT) whole, complete

halfhearted (SYN) apathetic, lukewarm, indifferent, unenthusiastic (ANT) passionate, enthusiastic, zealous, eager

halfway (SYN) midway, central, in the middle, in between

hall (SYN) passage, corridor, foyer, assembly room, auditorium

hallow (SYN) sanctify, venerate, consecrate (ANT) defile, spoil, mar, desecrate, curse

hallucination (SYN) delusion, mirage, imagination, fantasy, illusion (ANT) reality

halt (SYN) stop, cease, block, pause, standstill (ANT) start, continue, proceed, resumption

halve (SYN) bisect, divide, split in two

hammer (SYN) hit, knock, tap, bang, pummel

hamper (SYN) hinder, impede, obstruct, prevent, delay, inhibit (ANT) help, aid, assist

hand (SYN) pass, give, assistant, helper, applause, support (ANT) take

handicap (SYN) disability, impairment, burden, limitation, disadvantage (ANT) advantage, asset, benefit

handle (SYN) grip, hold, touch, manage, cope with

handsome (SYN) attractive, comely, good-looking, sizable, abundant (ANT) ugly, unattractive, meager, inadequate handwriting (SYN) penmanship, script, hand

handy (SYN) convenient, accessible, useful, skilled, adept (ANT) inconvenient, clumsy, inept

hang (SYN) suspend, dangle, float, execute, lynch

hap (SYN) luck, fortune, chance

haphazard (SYN) random, aimless, casual, disorganized (ANT) planned, organized

hapless (SYN) unlucky, unfortunate, ill-fated, wretched (ANT) lucky, fortunate

happen (SYN) occur, transpire, take, place, ensue, chance

happily (SYN) gladly, with pleasure, joyfully, willingly, fortunately (ANT) unhappily, dejectedly, gloomily

happiness (SYN) bliss, delight, satisfaction, contentment, well-being (ANT) sadness, sorrow, unhappiness, misery

happy (SYN) cheerful, jubilant, jolly, favorable, timely (ANT) sad, miserable, unhappy, morose, depressed

harangue (SYN) rant, exhort, speech, tirade, diatribe

harass (SYN) annoy, taunt, bother, pester, intimidate, hound (ANT) comfort, console

harbor (SYN) port, haven, shelter, hide, foster (ANT) expel

hard (SYN) firm, solid, sever, complicated, strenuous, unkind, callous, doggedly, diligently (ANT) soft, lazy, gentle, casually

harden (SYN) solidify, freeze, stiffen, set, numb, toughen (ANT) soften, melt

hardly (SYN) barely, only just, scarcely

hardship (SYN) adversity, difficulty, need, distress, suffering (ANT) ease, plenty, luxury, prosperity

hardy (SYN) tough, sturdy, rugged, strong (ANT) weak, delicate

harm (SYN) hurt, injure, damage, abuse, misfortune (ANT) heal, help, blessing

harmful (SYN) damaging, destructive, pernicious, unhealthy, hazardous (ANT) beneficial, safe, harmless

harmless (SYN) safe, innocuous, innocent, benign, inoffensive (ANT) harmful, offensive, malicious

harmonious (SYN) melodious, compatible, peaceful, cooperative, united (ANT) discordant, dissonant, conflicted

harmonize (SYN) blend, match, correspond, agree

harmony (SYN) melody, unison, concord, friendship, kinship, affinity (ANT) variance, alteration, disagreement harness (SYN) tack, gear, channel, utilize, employ

harp (SYN) nag, dwell on

harrowing (SYN) distressing, upsetting, traumatic, painful, nerve-racking

harsh (SYN) raucous, rough, cruel, drastic, bleak (ANT) soft, mild, kind

harvest (SYN) crop, yield, gather, pick (ANT) plant, scatter

hassle (SYN) bother, fuss, inconvenience, trouble, badger, aggravation

haste (SYN) speed, urgency, rush, hurry, hustle (ANT) slowness

hastily (SYN) quickly, promptly, swiftly, rashly, abruptly (ANT) slowly, cautiously, deliberately

hasty (SYN) brisk, speedy, rapid, impulsive, spur-of-the-moment

hatch (SYN) incubate, plot, invent, devise, concoct

hate (SYN) despise, loathe, abhor, aversion, enmity (ANT) like, love, approve, approval

hateful (SYN) despicable, abhorrent, loathsome, offensive, repulsive (ANT) loveable, admirable, attractive

hatred (SYN) dislike, detestation, repugnance, antipathy (ANT) love, affection

haughty (SYN) arrogant, scornful, proud, conceited, disdainful, stuck-up (ANT) modest, humble, self-effacing

haul (SYN) drag, pull, tug, tow, catch, spoils (ANT) push

haunt (SYN) plague, torment, trouble, spot, stomping ground

haunting (SYN) powerful, stirring, poignant, unforgettable, evocative

have (SYN) possess, own, hold, experience, must, should (ANT) lack, want

haven (SYN) shelter, refuge, retreat, sanctuary, asylum, oasis

havoc (SYN) chaos, mayhem, disorder, bedlam, pandemonium (ANT) serenity, peace, calm, order, tranquility

hazard (SYN) danger, risk, threat, peril, menace, venture, volunteer

hazardous (SYN) unsafe, dangerous, high-risk, precarious (ANT) safe, certain

haze (SYN) fog, mist, cloud, murk, obscurity (ANT) clarity

head (SYN) boss, commander, lead, brain, intellect, front, beginning, chief, foremost (ANT) follow, bottom, end

headache (SYN) migraine, problem, nuisance, bind, hassle

heading (SYN) title, caption, headline

headway (SYN) progress, improvement, gains

heady (SYN) potent, intoxicating, exciting, thrilling, exhilarating (ANT) weak, boring, dull

heal (SYN) cure, mend, restore, treat, recover, resolve (ANT) worsen, aggravate

health (SYN) fitness, well-being, wholeness, condition, shape (ANT) sickness, illness

healthy (SYN) well, robust, flourishing, nourishing, wholesome, hygienic (ANT) ill, frail, sick, unhealthy, unsanitary

heap (SYN) pile, mound, stack, bunch, mountain

hear (SYN) listen to, perceive, learn, discover

hearing (SYN) trial, inquiry

heart (SYN) core, essence, emotions, compassion, spirit (ANT) outside

hearth (SYN) fireplace

heartfelt (SYN) sincere, honest, profound, deep, genuine (ANT) insincere, phony, artificial, feigned

heat (SYN) warmth, warm up, passion, intensity, excitement (ANT) cold, cool

heated (SYN) fierce, angry, furious, stormy, lively (ANT) calm, somber

heathen (SYN) atheist, unbeliever, pagan, godless (ANT) believer, devout, zealot

heave (SYN) hoist, lift, fling, toss, vomit, retch

heaven (SYN) paradise, rapture, the hereafter, ecstasy, utopia (ANT) hell, misery, agony

heavenly (SYN) delightful, exquisite, sublime, celestial, angelic (ANT) dreadful, infernal, mortal

heavily (SYN) awkwardly, densely, thickly, considerably, excessively (ANT) easily, moderately, lightly

heavy (SYN) hefty, massive, weighty, considerable, excessive (ANT) light, insignificant

heckle (SYN) boo, taunt, bully, jeer, disrupt (ANT) cheer

hectic (SYN) frenetic, turbulent, active, frantic, chaotic (ANT) leisurely, slow, relaxed

hedge (SYN) barrier, boundary, insure, skirt, evade (ANT) confront

heed (SYN) consider, observe, attention, regard, respect (ANT) ignore, disregard

height (SYN) altitude, stature, elevation, peak, top, maximum (ANT) width, depth

heighten (SYN) increase, sharpen, improve, amplify, boost (ANT) reduce, decrease

heinous (SYN) wicked, atrocious, despicable, hateful, reprehensible (ANT) commendable, admirable heir (SYN) successor, beneficiary, next in line

heirloom (SYN) keepsake, antique

hell (SYN) Hades, inferno, the underworld, agony, torment (ANT) heaven, bliss

hello (SYN) welcome, greetings

helm (SYN) rudder, wheel, command, control

help (SYN) support, aid, assist, improve, guidance (ANT) hinder, worsen

helpful (SYN) useful, practical, constructive, obliging, considerate, supportive (ANT) unhelpful, useless

helping (SYN) portion, serving, ration

helpless (SYN) dependent, powerless, weak, impotent, vulnerable (ANT) independent, powerful, strong

hem (SYN) edge, fringe, enclose, restrict, confine

hence (SYN) therefore, thus, consequently, as a result

herald (SYN) announce, proclaim, messenger, sign, omen

herd (SYN) group, multitude, drove, gather, huddle

hereditary (SYN) genetic, inheritable, family, handed down, ancestral

heredity (SYN) genetics, inheritance

heresy (SYN) dissidence, unorthodoxy

heretic (SYN) apostate, nonbeliever, renegade

heritage (SYN) legacy, tradition, inheritance, roots, culture

hermit (SYN) recluse, loner

hero (SYN) champion, idol, star, protagonist, leading man (ANT) villain, loser

heroine (SYN) leading lady, darling, main character

heroism (SYN) bravery, valor, courage, daring, gallantry (ANT) cowardice, fear, weakness

hesitate (SYN) waver, delay, pause, falter, doubt (ANT) hasten, continue, jump in

hesitation (SYN) indecision, uncertainty, vacillation, reluctance, misgiving (ANT) certainty, conviction, determination, action

hew (SYN) cut, slice, chop, split, carve, shape

heyday (SYN) peak, prime, pinnacle, climax

hiatus (SYN) break, interruption, respite, pause, gap

hibernate (SYN) sleep, retire, be dormant

hidden (SYN) secluded, secret, veiled, ulterior, cryptic (ANT) open, obvious, visible hide (SYN) conceal, disguise, mask, shroud, suppress (ANT) reveal, flaunt, show, expose

hideous (SYN) ugly, grotesque, unsightly, appalling, sickening (ANT) beautiful, pleasant

hierarchy (SYN) ranking, order, scale, ladder, pecking order

high (SYN) elevated, towering, excessive, extreme, important, prominent, shrill, squeaky, intoxicated, elated (ANT) low, short, lowly, deep, inferior

highlight (SYN) feature, emphasize, stress, accentuate, focal point (ANT) downplay

hijack (SYN) commandeer, take over, seize

hike (SYN) trek, march, walk, trudge, back-pack

hilarious (SYN) entertaining, comical, uproarious, amusing, side-splitting (ANT) unfunny, serious, somber, austere

hill (SYN) mound, mount, knoll, high ground, rise (ANT) depression, valley

hind (SYN) back, rear, posterior (ANT) front

hinder (SYN) stop, encumber, thwart, foil, inhibit (ANT) aid, assist, ease, help, expedite

hindrance (SYN) obstacle, difficulty, stumbling block, snag, impediment

hinge (SYN) joint, depend, rest, be contingent

hint (SYN) imply, suggestion, clue, insinuation, trace, tinge (ANT) cover, conceal

hire (SYN) employ, engage, rent, charter, lease (ANT) dismiss, fire

hiss (SYN) fizz, whistle, jeer, boo, deride (ANT) cheer

historic (SYN) documented, notable, ground-breaking, significant, momentous (ANT) insignificant, trivial, minute

historical (SYN) factual, chronicled, authentic, past, ancient (ANT) anecdotal, contemporary

history (SYN) the past, antiquity, annals, record, narrative, background (ANT) myth, distortion

hit (SYN) strike, slap, smash, success, affect, devastate (ANT) caress, failure, flop

hitch (SYN) fasten, connect, harness, problem, catch (ANT) untie, disconnect

hoard (SYN) store, gather, amass, stockpile, reserve (ANT) give, squander, donate

hoarse (SYN) rough, gravelly, rasping, husky, harsh (ANT) smooth

hoax (SYN) fraud, trick, prank, con, scam

hobby (SYN) pastime, leisure activity, diversion, amusement, recreation (ANT) job

hobnob (SYN) mingle, socialize, schmooze, associate

hoist (SYN) lift, raise, erect, winch, crane (ANT) lower

hold (SYN) keep, retain, grasp, consider, believe, convene, control (ANT) release, drop, relinquish

hole (SYN) opening, orifice, tear, cavity, hollow, burrow

holiday (SYN) vacation, recess, break, festival

hollow (SYN) empty, void, worthless, meaningless, basin, excavate (ANT) full, solid, meaningful

holocaust (SYN) genocide, massacre, annihilation

holy (SYN) blessed, sacred, devout, pious, divine (ANT) unholy, evil, wicked, profane

homage (SYN) respect, honor, reverence, devotion, tribute (ANT) contempt

home (SYN) house, abode, residence, refuge, home town

homely (SYN) dowdy, unattractive, ugly, plain (ANT) pretty, attractive

homicide (SYN) murder, killing, assassination, manslaughter

homily (SYN) sermon, lecture

homogeneous (SYN) uniform, consistent, alike, identical (ANT) heterogeneous, diverse

hone (SYN) polish, sharpen, fine tune, file

honest (SYN) truthful, sincere, frank, forthright, ethical (ANT) dishonest, deceptive

honestly (SYN) candidly, honorably, fairly, wholeheartedly, genuinely (ANT) dishonestly, underhandedly

honesty (SYN) openness, candor, straightforwardness, integrity, virtue (ANT) dishonesty, insincerity, artifice

honor·(SYN) esteem, deference, decency, fulfill, praise (ANT) defame, shame, reproach, disgrace

honorable (SYN) reputable, principled, upright, great, distinguished (ANT) crooked, deplorable, corrupt

hook (SYN) clasp, fastener, fix, secure, ensnare

hooligan (SYN) delinquent, vandal, troublemaker

hoop (SYN) ring, loop, circle

hop (SYN) jump, bounce, leap, spring, bound, vault

hope (SYN) ambition, dream, desire, anticipate, optimism (ANT) despair, depression, pessimism

hopeful (SYN) optimistic, confident, bright, promising (ANT) discouraging hopeless (SYN) pointless, useless, lousy, forlorn, futile (ANT) competent, useful, encouraging

horde (SYN) crowd, pack, mob, throng, army

horizon (SYN) skyline

horizontal (SYN) flat, level (ANT) vertical

horrible (SYN) frightful, grim, awful, nasty, terrible, unspeakable (ANT) wonderful, pleasing, agreeable

horrid (SYN) appalling, dreadful, horrendous, unkind, hateful (ANT) splendid, lovely, enjoyable

horrify (SYN) alarm, petrify, scare, shock, scandalize (ANT) please

horror (SYN) dread, panic, terror, revulsion, abhorrence (ANT) delight, fascination, pleasure

horse (SYN) stallion, mare, colt, steed

hospitality (SYN) warmth, accommodation, welcome, sociability, generosity (ANT) unkindness

host (SYN) multitude, myriad, legion, presenter, entertainer

hostage (SYN) captive, prisoner, detainee (ANT) captor

hostility (SYN) malice, resentment, antagonism, contention, venom, malevolence (ANT) loyalty, friendship, favor

hot (SYN) heated, scalding, spicy, piquant, fiery, fresh, popular (ANT) cold, frigid, bland, mild, passionless

hotel (SYN) motel, inn

hound (SYN) pester, harass, goad, pursue, torment

house (SYN) home, residence, dynasty, contain, store

household (SYN) family, home, house

hovel (SYN) shack, hut, slum, hole, shanty

hover (SYN) float, hang, drift, linger, fluctuate (ANT) land, leave

however (SYN) nevertheless, still, yet, even so, for all that

howl (SYN) bay, wail, roar, bellow, weep (ANT) whisper, murmur

hub (SYN) nerve center, core, heart, nucleus

huddle (SYN) cluster, group, converge, crouch, discussion (ANT) disperse

hue (SYN) shade, tone, color, tint, tinge

hug (SYN) embrace, cuddle, squeeze, clasp, clutch (ANT) release

huge (SYN) giant, monumental, massive, enormous, immense, hulking (ANT) tiny, small, miniature, diminutive

hulk (SYN) oaf, lump

hull (SYN) shell, frame, casing, structure, skeleton

hum (SYN) buzz, drone, whir, bustle, pulse

human (SYN) person, individual, mortal, mankind, compassionate

humane (SYN) considerate, tolerant, merciful, humanitarian, benevolent (ANT) cruel, brutal, savage

humanity (SYN) people, mankind, human race, human nature, sympathy

humble (SYN) meek, unassuming, modest, lowly, undistinguished, humiliate (ANT) proud, ostentatious, grand, bolster

humidity (SYN) moisture, dampness, mugginess (ANT) aridity

humiliate (SYN) demean, shame, embarrass, mortify, deflate (ANT) dignify, applaud, encourage, praise

humiliation (SYN) embarrassment, dishonor, indignity, discredit, put-down (ANT) honor, accolades

humility (SYN) modesty, submissiveness, unassertiveness, respect, deference (ANT) pride, boastfulness

humor (SYN) comedy, wit, joking, mood, indulge (ANT) gravity, seriousness, provoke

humorous (SYN) funny, amusing, playful, jocular, diverting (ANT) serious, dull, depressing

hump (SYN) lump, bulge, bump, mound

hunch (SYN) gut feeling, intuition, suspicion, inking, premonition (ANT) knowledge, certainty

hunger (SYN) appetite, famine, starvation, desire, ache, crave (ANT) satisfaction, satiation

hungry (SYN) empty, ravenous, starving, eager, greedy (ANT) full, fed, replete

hunt (SYN) seek, chase, pursue, stalk, probe

hurdle (SYN) obstacle, fence, barrier, difficulty, complication

hurl (SYN) throw, launch, heave, propel, sling

hurricane (SYN) storm, gale, cyclone, tempest, typhoon

hurry (SYN) rush, scurry, speed, haste, urgency (ANT) delay, dawdle, ease

hurt (SYN) harm, injure, ache, grieve, suffering, wounded (ANT) heal, cure, comfort, pleased

hurtful (SYN) unkind, damaging, offensive, spiteful, upsetting (ANT) kind, tender, heartening

hurtle (SYN) rush, race, speed, shoot, charge

husband (SYN) spouse, partner, mate

husbandry (SYN) economy, thrift, farming, agriculture

hush (SYN) quiet, muffle, silence, mute, stillness, tranquility (ANT) excite, amplify, noise hustle (SYN) dash, hasten, zoom, swindle, cheat (ANT) procrastinate, stall, delay

hut (SYN) shack, shelter, shed, den, cabin

hybrid (SYN) cross, mixture, amalgam, composite, blend, fusion (ANT) pure

hydroplane (SYN) skip, slide, spin

hygiene (SYN) cleanliness, health, sanitation, sterility

hymn (SYN) anthem, song, carol

hype (SYN) publicity, promotion, plugging, buzz

hyperbole (SYN) exaggeration, overstatement (ANT) understatement

hypnotize (SYN) mesmerize, soothe, transfix

hypocrisy (SYN) pretense, insincerity, superiority, sham (ANT) reliability, honesty

hypocrite (SYN) fraud, imposter, pretender

hypocritical (SYN) pious, deceptive, sanctimonious, two-faced, duplicitous (ANT) truthful, frank, honest

hypothesis (SYN) theory, premise, assumption, speculation, thesis

hypothetical (SYN) imaginary, supposed, conjectural, theoretical (ANT) actual

hysterical (SYN) distraught, raving, wild, hilarious, funny (ANT) calm, sedate, serious

I

icing (SYN) frosting

icon (SYN) symbol, idol, image, representation, legend

icy (SYN) cold, bitter, slippery, distant, unfriendly (ANT) hot, welcoming

idea (SYN) thought, notion, conviction, objective, meaning

ideal (SYN) perfect, vision, consummate, model, prototype (ANT) common, actual

identical (SYN) matching, alike, twin, equal, indistinguishable, duplicate (ANT) different, separate, opposite

identification (SYN) recognition, verification, empathy, connection, rapport

identify (SYN) name, distinguish, point out, understand, relate to (ANT) confuse, mistake

identity (SYN) personality, individuality, self, character, uniqueness

ideology (SYN) beliefs, opinions, ideas, doctrine

idiom (SYN) phrase, expression, vernacular

idiosyncrasy (ANT) quirk, mannerism, peculiarity, oddity, eccentricity

idiot (SYN) fool, moron, imbecile, dope
(ANT) genius, sage

idle (SYN) lazy, slothful, unoccupied,
frivolous, trifling (ANT) active,
busy, energetic, ambitious, serious

idol (SYN) deity, graven image, effigy,
hero, celebrity, superstar

idolize (SYN) worship, revere, adore,
look up to

idyllic (SYN) ideal, charming,
unspoiled, picturesque

if (SYN) assuming, provided, whether

ignite (SYN) light, torch, burn, kindle,
galvanize (ANT) douse, quench,
extinguish, dissuade

ignoble (SYN) base, inferior, lowly,
dishonorable, contemptible, vile
(ANT) noble, honored, righteous

ignorance (SYN) inexperience,
innocence, incomprehension,
unconsciousness (ANT) awareness,
knowledge, education, literacy

ignorant (SYN) uninformed, oblivious,
unlearned, insensitive, unenlightened
(ANT) educated, knowledgeable,
informed, cultured

ignore (SYN) disregard, slight, overlook,
neglect, snub (ANT) acknowledge,
obey, recognize, heed

ill (SYN) sick, unwell, ailing, harmful,
misfortune, unfavorably (ANT) well,
healthy, beneficial, kindly

illegal (SYN) criminal, unlawful, illicit,
prohibited, corrupt (ANT) legal,
sanctioned, lawful, permitted

illegible (SYN) obscure, unreadable,
indecipherable (ANT) clear, readable

illegitimate (SYN) improper, illegal,
illicit, unauthorized (ANT)
legitimate, legal

illicit (SYN) forbidden, furtive,
clandestine, criminal, unethical
(ANT) approved, right

illimitable (SYN) limitless, boundless,
vast, far-reaching (ANT) limited,
bound, finite

illiterate (SYN) uneducated, untaught,
ignorant, unable to read (ANT)
literate, educated, schooled, learned

illness (SYN) disease, ailment,
affliction, disorder, malady (ANT)
health, vigor

illogical (SYN) insensible, absurd,
irrational, unsound, superfluous
(ANT) logical, sensible, rational,
sound

illuminate (SYN) brighten, light up,
clarify, explain, reveal (ANT)
confuse, complicate

illusion (SYN) fantasy, mirage, delusion,
hallucination, misconception (ANT)
reality

illusive (SYN) hallucinatory, illusory
(ANT) real, factual

illustrate (SYN) demonstrate, show,
portray, depict, decorate

illustration (SYN) picture, sketch, example, sample, demonstration

illustrious (SYN) famous, celebrated, distinguished, renowned, acclaimed (ANT) obscure, unknown

image (SYN) likeness, representation, appearance, impression, persona

imaginary (SYN) fake, fictional, invented, make-believe, pretend, non-existent (ANT) real, actual

imagination (SYN) creativity, inventiveness, originality, vision, illusion, fantasy (ANT) reality, actuality,

imagine (SYN) visualize, conjure up, picture, infer, surmise

imbue (SYN) inspire, influence, pervade, saturate

imitate (SYN) mimic, echo, copy, emulate, mock, parody (ANT) create, originate, modify, change

imitation (SYN) replica, substitution, artificial, synthetic, impersonation (ANT) real, genuine, original

immaculate (SYN) spotless, spruce, flawless, impeccable, pristine (ANT) dirty, damaged, flawed

immaterial (SYN) insignificant, irrelevant, extraneous, inconsequential (ANT) crucial, important, essential

immature (SYN) young, childish, juvenile, inexperienced (ANT) mature, grown

immeasurable (SYN) vast, infinite, boundless, immense, endless (ANT) limited, finite, measurable

immediate (SYN) instant, prompt, near, close, direct (ANT) delayed, distant

immediately (SYN) now, right away, directly, forthwith, at once (ANT) later, sometime, eventually

immense (SYN) huge, massive, tremendous, gigantic, whopping (ANT) tiny, small, minute, unimportant

immensity (SYN) size, magnitude, bulk, expanse, enormity

immerse (SYN) plunge, dunk, bathe, submerge, engross, engage

immigrant (SYN) settler, newcomer, foreigner, alien, non-native (ANT) native, local

immigration (SYN) migration, relocation, colonization (ANT) emigration, flight

immigrate (SYN) relocate, settle

imminent (SYN) near, coming, looming, impending, approaching, expected (ANT) distant, far off, remote, improbable

immobility (SYN) stillness, fixity, inertness, motionlessness (ANT) motion, action

immoral (SYN) unethical, wicked, depraved, wrong, sinful, lecherous (ANT) ethical, pure, moral, good immortal (SYN) eternal, enduring, everlasting, perpetual, undying (ANT) mortal, earthly, ephemeral

immortality (SYN) eternity, everlasting life, glory, fame (ANT) mortality, death

immune (SYN) exempt, invulnerable, protected, safe, clear (ANT) susceptible, liable

immunity (SYN) amnesty, exemption, release, resistance, privilege (ANT) susceptibility, subjection

immunize (SYN) safeguard, protect, vaccinate, inoculate

impact (SYN) collision, strike, contact, influence, consequence (ANT) miss, avoid, avoidance

impair (SYN) weaken, diminish, undermine, lessen, decrease (ANT) strengthen, enhance, improve

impale (SYN) lance, pierce

impart (SYN) communicate, convey, divulge, give, confer

impartial (SYN) neutral, fair, objective, unbiased, detached (ANT) partial, biased, unfair, prejudiced

impassable (SYN) closed, blocked, obstructed (ANT) passable, open, clear

impasse (SYN) standoff, stalemate, deadlock, standstill

impatience (SYN) restlessness, anxiety, haste, intolerance (ANT) patience, tolerance

impatient (SYN) edgy, eager, agitated, demanding, curt (ANT) patient, calm, reluctant

impeach (SYN) accuse, charge, indict

impeccable (SYN) flawless, perfect, irreproachable, spotless, exemplary (ANT) tarnished, imperfect, sullied, defective

impede (SYN) obstruct, hinder, disrupt, slow, delay, hamper (ANT) assist, speed, hasten, facilitate

impediment (SYN) barrier, difficulty, snag, obstacle, encumbrance

impel (SYN) push, force, drive, compel, require (ANT) permit, allow

impending (SYN) near, gathering, looming, imminent, approaching (ANT) distant

impenetrable (SYN) solid, impervious, dense, mysterious, incomprehensible (ANT) porous, soft, clear, easy

imperative (SYN) mandatory, required, unavoidable, essential, vital, pressing (ANT) optional, voluntary, unimportant, unnecessary ·

imperceptible (SYN) subtle, faint, slight, negligible (ANT) apparent, obvious, significant

imperfect (SYN) flawed, faulty, inadequate, inferior, substandard (ANT) perfect, flawless, complete

imperfection (SYN) defect, shortcoming, fault, deficiency

imperial (SYN) royal, regal, sovereign

imperil (SYN) risk, endanger, expose (ANT) protect, guard

imperious (SYN) arrogant, haughty, domineering, bossy, controlling (ANT) submissive, deferential

impermeable (SYN) impervious, dense, solid (ANT) permeable

impersonal (SYN) cold, aloof, formal, detached, dispassionate (ANT) friendly, open, sociable

impersonate (SYN) mimic, imitate, masquerade, portray, represent

impertinent (SYN) rude, disrespectful, insolent, presumptuous, irrelevant, trivial (ANT) polite, courteous, respectful, pertinent, applicable, relevant

impervious (SYN) sealed, resistant, impenetrable, untouched, invulnerable

impetuous (SYN) rash, impulsive, spontaneous, reckless, foolhardy (ANT) cautious, considerate, patient

impetus (SYN) motivation, catalyst, incentive, force, momentum

implausible (SYN) unlikely, doubtful, questionable, suspect, unbelievable (ANT) plausible, possible, credible, believable

implement (SYN) tool, device, utensil, execute, achieve (ANT) neglect, cancel

implication (SYN) suggestion, meaning, innuendo, inference, consequence, result

implicit (SYN) implied, unspoken, absolute, steadfast, firm (ANT) explicit, stated, wavering

implore (SYN) beg, plead, urge, request, entreat, beseech (ANT) grant, bestow

imply (SYN) hint, intimate, insinuate, suggest, infer (ANT) express, define, assert

impolite (SYN) ill-mannered, discourteous, rude, uncivil, impertinent (ANT) polite, respectful, courteous

import (SYN) ship in, bring in, meaning, drift, weight, consequence (ANT) export, insignificance

importance (SYN) value, concern, gravity, prestige, eminence (ANT) triviality, obscurity

important (SYN) momentous, far-reaching, meaningful, consequential, influential (ANT) unimportant, insignificant, small

importunate (SYN) insistent, dogged, urgent, demanding

impose (SYN) introduce, inflict, enforce, require, trouble, inconvenience (ANT) abolish

impossible (SYN) unattainable, impractical, hopeless, absurd, ludicrous (ANT) possible, easy, feasible, obtainable

imposter (SYN) fake, trickster, pretender, impersonator

impotent (SYN) powerless, helpless, incompetent, ineffective, harmless

(ANT) capable, powerful, strong, potent

impoverished (SYN) poor, destitute, needy, poverty-stricken (ANT) wealthy, rich, affluent

impractical (SYN) unrealistic, unworkable, unachievable, infeasible (ANT) practical, workable, pragmatic, attainable

imprecate (SYN) curse, invoke evil, wish harm (ANT) bless

imprecise (SYN) loose, vague, inexact, indeterminate, rough (ANT) exact, precise

impregnable (SYN) secure, invincible, indestructible, unbeatable (ANT) vulnerable

impress (SYN) affect, rouse, dazzle, stress, imprint (ANT) bore, disappoint

impression (SYN) feeling, sense, interpretation, influence, impact, mark, indentation

impressive (SYN) grand, moving, majestic, imposing, breathtaking (ANT) unimpressive, common

imprint (SYN) impression, stamp, indentation, engrave, emboss

imprison (SYN) incarcerate, jail, confine, detain (ANT) free, release

improbable (SYN) unlikely, implausible, far-fetched, dubious, questionable (ANT) probable, likely, believable

impromptu (SYN) spur-of-the-moment, spontaneous, unrehearsed, unprepared, unplanned (ANT) planned, rehearsed

improper (SYN) inappropriate, unseemly, immodest, suggestive, unbecoming (ANT) decent, correct, acceptable, clean

impropriety (SYN) indecency, vulgarity, bad taste (ANT) propriety, decency, suitability

improve (SYN) better, enhance, upgrade, progress, amend (ANT) worsen, impair, deteriorate

improvement (SYN) advancement, growth, refinement, boost, augmentation, rally (ANT) decline, relapse

improvise (SYN) invent, ad-lib, devise, wing it, extemporize

imprudent (SYN) careless, unwise, irresponsible, ill-advised (ANT) prudent, cautious, judicious

impudent (SYN) arrogant, audacious, presumptuous, shameless, brazen (ANT) modest, humble, courteous, deferential, timid

impulse (SYN) urge, notion, inclination, whim, compulsion

impulsive (SYN) instinctive, impatient, hasty, impetuous, rash (ANT) restrained, thoughtful, premeditated

impunity (SYN) immunity, exemption, license, dispensation

impurity (SYN) contamination, taint, defilement, corruption, immorality (ANT) purity, cleanliness, morality

impute (SYN) attribute, ascribe, charge

inability (SYN) incapacity, powerlessness, ineptitude, incapacity (ANT) capability, ability, competence

inaccessible (SYN) unreachable, unattainable, remote, out of reach (ANT) accessible, reachable, convenient

inaccuracy (SYN) error, mistake, fault, imperfection, defect (ANT) reliability, correction, precision, soundness

inadequate (SYN) sparse, paltry, insufficient, unqualified, incapable (ANT) sufficient, enough, adequate

inadvertently (SYN) accidentally, unknowingly, unwittingly, unintentionally, by mistake (ANT) intentionally, knowingly, voluntarily

inalienable (SYN) absolute, inherent, inviolable

inanimate (SYN) lifeless, inert (ANT) living

inappropriate (SYN) unfitting, unsuitable, incongruous, out of place (ANT) appropriate, seemly, becoming

inarticulate (SYN) faltering, poorly spoken, hesitant (ANT) articulate, well spoken, eloquent, expressive

inattentive (SYN) distracted, preoccupied, careless, unobservant (ANT) attentive, observant

inaudible (SYN) low, stifled, indistinct, muted, unclear (ANT) clear, audible

inaugurate (SYN) launch, commence, introduce, induct, instill (ANT) terminate, dismiss

inauspicious (SYN) ominous, unfortunate, unpromising (ANT) favorable, lucky

inborn (SYN) innate, natural, intuitive, native, hereditary (ANT) learned, taught, acquired

incandescent (SYN) glowing, luminous, aglow, brilliant, bright, dynamic (ANT) dull, muted

incantation (SYN) chant, spell, invocation

incapable (SYN) unable, ineffective, weak, helpless (ANT) competent, qualified, fit

incapacitate (SYN) disable, paralyze, immobilize

incarceration (SYN) confinement, imprisonment, detainment, jail (ANT) freedom

incarnate (SYN) embodied, personified, in the flesh

incarnation (SYN) manifestation, embodiment, epitome

incendiary (SYN) inflammatory, volatile, explosive

incense (SYN) anger, rile, infuriate, madden, antagonize (ANT) placate, please, appease

incentive (SYN) lure, motivation, enticement, encouragement, sweetener

inception (SYN) birth, beginning, start

incessant (SYN) constant, perpetual, never-ending, interminable (ANT) ending, intermittent, ceasing

incessantly (SYN) nonstop, continually, persistently, eternally

inch (SYN) scoot, creep, move slowly

incident (SYN) event, occasion, matter, circumstance, disturbance

incidentally (SYN) by the way, by chance, accidentally, fortuitously

incinerate (SYN) burn, char, sear, scorch, consume (ANT) extinguish

incision (SYN) cut, gash, slit, opening

incisive (SYN) keen, penetrating, shrewd, perceptive, discerning (ANT) obtuse, dull

incite (SYN) instigate, stimulate, provoke, kindle, trigger, prompt (ANT) deter, discourage

incitement (SYN) provocation, agitation, impetus, catalyst

inclement (SYN) stormy, severe, foul, tempestuous (ANT) fair

inclination (SYN) tendency, penchant, predisposition, leaning, preference, slope, gradient

incline (SYN) slant, tilt, grade, influence, sway

include (SYN) comprise, contain, embrace, cover, add (ANT) exclude, leave out, omit

inclusive (SYN) sweeping, full, comprehensive (ANT) exclusive, limited

incognito (SYN) disguised, unrecognized

incoherent (SYN) incomprehensible, babbling, rambling, disjointed, confused (ANT) coherent, lucid, ordered, articulate

income (SYN) salary, earnings, wages, revenue, profits (ANT) expenses, expenditures, bills

incomparable (SYN) matchless, unequaled, peerless, transcendent, unrivaled (ANT) comparable, average, common, typical

incompatible (SYN) opposed, contradictory, mismatched, irreconcilable, incongruous (ANT) harmonious, consistent, matched

incompetent (SYN) useless, inept, ineffectual, unskilled, blundering, amateurish (ANT) competent, professional, proficient, capable

incomplete (SYN) unfinished, partial, fragmentary, deficient, wanting (ANT) complete, finished, full inconceivable (SYN) unthinkable, incredible, perplexing, unfathomable, mind-boggling (ANT) understandable, believable, possible

inconclusive (SYN) undecided, ambiguous, vague, open, unconvincing (ANT) conclusive, certain

incongruous (SYN) conflicting, dissonant, incompatible, unsuitable, illogical (ANT) congruous, consistent, compatible

inconsequential (SYN) unimportant, trivial, trifling, insignificant (ANT) important, major, significant

inconsiderate (SYN) selfish, unkind, insensitive, rude (ANT) tactful, thoughtful, delicate

inconsistent (SYN) erratic, unstable, fluctuating, variable (ANT) consistent, uniform, steady

inconspicuous (SYN) hidden, unobtrusive, unnoticeable, camouflaged (ANT) obvious, conspicuous

inconvenience (SYN) disruption, nuisance, trouble, discomfort, imposition

inconvenient (SYN) bothersome, untimely, inopportune, awkward (ANT) convenient, suitable, advantageous

incorporate (SYN) merge, include, integrate, assimilate, absorb (ANT) separate

incorrect (SYN) wrong, false, inaccurate, erroneous, mistaken (ANT) correct, right, proper, true

incorrectly (SYN) faultily, wrongly, mistakenly (ANT) rightly, correctly, accurately

increase (SYN) grow, enlarge, escalate, mount, inflation, surge (ANT) decrease, reduce, deplete

incredible (SYN) improbable, unconvincing, marvelous, phenomenal, fantastic (ANT) credible, believable, realistic, unremarkable

incredulous (SYN) skeptical, disbelieving, dubious, distrustful (ANT) believing, trusting, convinced

increment (SYN) gain, increase, addition, supplement, step up

incriminate (SYN) accuse, implicate, charge, blame, involve

incriminating (SYN) harmful, accusatory

incur (SYN) earn, provoke, bring upon oneself

incurable (SYN) fatal, terminal, inoperable, irreparable (ANT) curable

incursion (SYN) invasion, attack, foray

indebted (SYN) obliged, beholden, grateful (ANT) unappreciative

indecent (SYN) obscene, filthy, offensive, improper, lewd (ANT) decent, appropriate, virtuous, respectful indecisive (SYN) hesitating, tentative, vacillating, dithering (ANT) decisive, certain, unwavering

indeed (SYN) for sure, really, actually, certainly, in truth

indefinite (SYN) unclear, imprecise, inexact, general, indistinct (ANT) definite, sure, apparent, certain

indefinitely (SYN) endlessly, continually, for ever (ANT) temporarily

indelible (SYN) permanent, enduring, indestructible, ingrained (ANT) eradicable, erasable

indemnity (SYN) insurance, protection, security, compensation, restitution

indenture (SYN) servitude

independence (SYN) autonomy, self-government, liberty, self-sufficiency, freedom (ANT) dependence, reliance, subordination

independent (SYN) separate, uncontrolled, sovereign, impartial, unbiased (ANT) dependent, biased, related

independently (SYN) alone, solo, individually, unaccompanied, single-handedly (ANT) together, with help

indestructible (SYN) unbreakable, permanent, indelible (ANT) destructible, breakable

index (SYN) list, catalog, directory, database, inventory

indicate (SYN) show, designate, mark, demonstrate, suggest, declare

indication (SYN) sign, clue, intimation, pointer, guide

indicator (SYN) gauge, signal, measure, index, mark

indict (SYN) accuse, blame, charge, arraign, prosecute

indictment (SYN) charge, citation, prosecution, accusation, impeachment

indifferent (SYN) unconcerned, impervious, nonchalance, forgettable, unexceptional (ANT) enthusiastic, sympathetic, compassionate, brilliant

indigenous (SYN) native, innate, natural, inherent (ANT) alien, foreign, imported

indigent (SYN) homeless, needy, poor, destitute, impoverished, penurious (ANT) rich, wealthy, prosperous

indigestion (SYN) heartburn, upset stomach

indignant (SYN) resentful, disgruntled, peeved, exasperated, affronted (ANT) content, affable

indignation (SYN) anger, resentment, scorn (ANT) calmness, serenity

indignity (SYN) humiliation, insult, slight, disrespect, outrage (ANT) praise, esteem, honor, respect indirect (SYN) meandering, roundabout, circuitous, unintended, incidental (ANT) direct, straightforward

indirectly (SYN) inadvertently, unintentionally, secondarily (ANT) directly, intentionally

indiscreet (SYN) tactless, imprudent, unwise, naive (ANT) discreet, tactful

indispensable (SYN) crucial, key, vital, requisite, necessary (ANT) pointless, needless, gratuitous

indisputable (SYN) incontestable, irrefutable, undeniable, unquestionable, certain (ANT) unsettled, debatable, controversial

individual (SYN) person, being, distinctive, singular, original, personal (ANT) universal, ordinary, multiple, shared

individuality (SYN) distinctiveness, personality, originality, uniqueness, character (ANT) conformity, similarity

individually (SYN) alone, separately, singly, independently (ANT) together

indolent (SYN) lazy, idle, inactive, languid, sluggish (ANT) energetic, lively, spirited, vigorous

indomitable (SYN) invincible, steadfast, unyielding, resolute, unflinching (ANT) yielding, submissive, timid, shrinking

induce (SYN) persuade, instigate, convince, cause, create (ANT) prevent, dissuade, deter

inducement (SYN) incentive, attraction, lure, reward, motivation

indulge (SYN) satisfy, gratify, concede, humor, pamper (ANT) deny, annoy, irritate

indulgence (SYN) tolerance, understanding, luxury, extravagance, fulfillment (ANT) intolerance, impatience, asceticism

industrious (SYN) productive, enterprising, diligent, hard-working, conscientious (ANT) idle, lazy, inefficient, negligent

industry (SYN) commerce, business, persistence, effort, zeal (ANT) play, sloth, idleness

inebriated (SYN) drunk, intoxicated tipsy, under the influence (ANT) sober

inefficient (SYN) disorganized, inept, ineffectual, futile, unproductive (ANT) efficient, able, practical, strong

ineligible (SYN) unfit, unqualified, unsuitable (ANT) acceptable, eligible, qualified

inept (SYN) incompetent, clumsy, unskilled, unhandy, bungling (ANT) expert, proficient, able, competent, skilled

inequality (SYN) disparity, unevenness, irregularity, disproportion, imbalance, bias (ANT) equality, regularity, justice

inequity (SYN) injustice, unfairness,
bias, preference, prejudice (ANT)
equity, equality, impartiality

inert (SYN) dormant, immobile,
motionless, still, unresponsive
(ANT) moving, lively, active, mobile

inertia (SYN) inactivity, passivity,
apathy, unresponsiveness (ANT)
motion, activity

inevitable (SYN) assured, inescapable,
certain, inexorable (ANT) avoidable,
uncertain, possible

inexcusable (SYN) indefensible,
unforgivable, outrageous,
unjustifiable (ANT) pardonable,
justifiable, forgivable

inexplicable (SYN) mysterious, baffling,
strange, incomprehensible (ANT)
explicable, understandable, obvious,
clear

infallible (SYN) dependable, foolproof,
reliable, trustworthy, unfailing
(ANT) fallible, imperfect, unreliable

infamous (SYN) notorious, disreputable,
scandalous, reprehensible,
ignominious (ANT) virtuous,
admirable, esteemed, reputable

infancy (SYN) origins, outset,
beginnings, early stages, emergence
(ANT) end

infant (SYN) baby, newborn, young
child

infatuation (SYN) obsession, passion,
crush, fascination, fixation (ANT)
sensibility, prudence

infect (SYN) contaminate, pollute,
affect, taint, transfer (ANT) cleanse,
cure, disinfect, sanitize

infection (SYN) illness, disease, virus,
disorder, ailment, contamination

infectious (SYN) catching, virulent,
contagious, transmittable,
communicable, irresistible

infer (SYN) presume, deduce, surmise,
extract, gather, guess (ANT) find,
discover, prove

inference (SYN) assumption,
conclusion, deduction

inferior (SYN) substandard,
unsatisfactory, subordinate,
mediocre, second-rate (ANT)
superior, prime, better

inferiority (SYN) deficiency,
inadequacy, imperfection,
subservience (ANT) superiority

infernal (SYN) hellish, diabolical,
devilish, cursed, satanic (ANT)
angelic, holy, blessed

infest (SYN) invade, ravage, swarm,
penetrate, overrun

infiltration (SYN) penetration,
permeation, insinuation

infinite (SYN) eternal, limitless, endless,
inexhaustible, incalculable, untold
(ANT) finite, limited, bounded,
measurable

infinitesimal (SYN) teeny, microscopic,
miniscule, unnoticeable, minute
(ANT) huge, gigantic, enormous,
large

infinity (SYN) eternity, boundlessness, forever

infirm (SYN) frail, sick, weak, debilitated, ailing, decrepit (ANT) strong, healthy, robust

infirmity (SYN) debility, ailment, frailty, malady, ill-health, vulnerability (ANT) vigor, strength, health

inflame (SYN) enrage, incense, madden, infuriate, compound (ANT) calm, placate, soothe

inflammable (SYN) combustible, incendiary, explosive, volatile

inflammation (SYN) soreness, redness, tenderness, swelling, burning, infection

inflammatory (SYN) provocative, controversial, fiery, explosive

inflate (SYN) fill, swell, expand, enlarge, increase, raise (ANT) deflate, collapse, lower

inflation (SYN) escalation, rise, increase (ANT) deflation, decrease, lowering

inflict (SYN) impose, wreak, administer, give, levy, foist (ANT) spare, retract, lift

influence (SYN) leverage, control, sway, impress, impact, shape

influential (SYN) important, authoritative, prominent, leading, guiding, instrumental (ANT) insignificant, weak, impotent

influx (SYN) rush, inundation, invasion, arrival

inform (SYN) notify, enlighten, relate, instruct, communicate (ANT) hide, cover

informal (SYN) casual, relaxed, easy, familiar, unofficial (ANT) formal, official, ceremonious

informant (SYN) source, tipster

information (SYN) facts, knowledge, data, particulars, intelligence

informative (SYN) revealing, educational, instructive, forthcoming

infraction (SYN) violation, breach, infringement, transgression

infringement (SYN) trespass, violation, breach, contravention

infuriate (SYN) madden, rile, provoke, anger, incense (ANT) please, placate, appease, soothe

infuse (SYN) instill, imbue, inspire, ingrain, steep, soak

ingenuity (SYN) originality, innovation, resourcefulness, cleverness, genius (ANT) stupidity, unoriginality

ingest (SYN) eat, consume

ingratitude (SYN) thanklessness, entitlement (ANT) gratitude, thankfulness

ingredient (SYN) component, feature, aspect, element, attribute, part

inhabit (SYN) live, abide, occupy, reside, dwell, populate (ANT) abandon, leave inhabitant (SYN) resident, tenant, occupant, dweller, citizen

inhale (SYN) breathe in, respire, gasp (ANT) exhale

inherent (SYN) innate, essential, intrinsic, natural (ANT) acquired, learned, external

inherit (SYN) be left, come into, take over, assume

inheritance (SYN) birthright, legacy, endowment, bequest

inhibit (SYN) discourage, restrain, hamper, impede, curb (ANT) encourage, assist, incite

inhibition (SYN) reserve, restraint, self-consciousness, repression, bashfulness (ANT) exhibition

inhumane (SYN) cruel, barbaric, savage, ruthless, brutal (ANT) kind, merciful, compassionate, gentle

iniquity (SYN) evil, sin, wickedness, injury, abomination (ANT) righteousness, goodness

initial (SYN) first, primary, early, basic, introductory (ANT) final, last, ending

initially (SYN) originally, first, to start with, at the onset, in the beginning (ANT) lastly, finally

initiate (SYN) open, commence, launch, establish, install (ANT) conclude, finish, terminate, expel

initiation (SYN) induction, entrance, enrollment, introduction (ANT) expulsion

initiative (SYN) lead, first step, ambition, drive, enterprise (ANT) apathy

inject (SYN) vaccinate, administer, insert, infuse, introduce

injection (SYN) inoculation, vaccination, immunization, addition, infusion

injure (SYN) hurt, harm, damage, impair, mar (ANT) heal, cure, repair, restore, boost

injurious (SYN) harmful, wounding, painful, abusive, offensive (ANT) healing, helpful, beneficial, advantageous

injury (SYN) trauma, wound, pain, damage, insult (ANT) benefit, blessing

injustice (SYN) unfairness, inequality, discrimination, oppression, exploitation, affront (ANT) justice, righteousness, equity

inkling (SYN) hint, suspicion, indication, suggestion, whisper

inland (SYN) internal, interior (ANT) coastal

inlet (SYN) bay, cove, estuary, sound, channel

inmate (SYN) prisoner, captive, patient, resident, detainee (ANT) captor

inn (SYN) motel, hotel, tavern

innate (SYN) inherent, native, hereditary, intuitive, constitutional (ANT) learned, taught, acquired

inner (SYN) internal, inside, middle, interior, intimate, hidden, underlying (ANT) outer, apparent, outward

innocence (SYN) purity, virtue, inexperience, blamelessness, uprightness (ANT) guilt, corruption, guile, worldliness

innocent (SYN) guiltless, irreproachable, clean, safe, uncorrupted, impressionable (ANT) guilty, dangerous, sophisticated, incredulous

innovation (SYN) change, novelty, departure, modernization, alteration (ANT) status quo, unoriginality

innovative (SYN) groundbreaking, radical, revolutionary, fresh, experimental (ANT) old, stale, cliché

innuendo (SYN) suggestion, insinuation, overtone, implication, aspersion

inoculate (SYN) vaccinate, inject, immunize

inopportune (SYN) inconvenient, unfortunate, untimely, inappropriate (ANT) suitable, favorable, serendipitous, appropriate

inordinate (SYN) excessive, unreasonable, undue, disproportionate, preposterous (ANT) reasonable, moderate, warranted

inorganic (SYN) artificial, man-made (ANT) organic, natural

input (SYN) data entry, opinion, contribution (ANT) output

inquest (SYN) enquiry, review, probe, investigation

inquire (SYN) examine, research, question, ask, explore (ANT) reply, respond

inquiry (SYN) investigation, survey, study, inquest, examination

inquisition (SYN) questioning, interrogation, investigation, grilling

inquisitive (SYN) curious, prying, questioning, nosy (ANT) bored, indifferent

insane (SYN) crazy, demented, deranged, maniacal, nonsensical (ANT) sane, sound, rational, well-adjusted

insatiable (SYN) ravenous, unquenchable, greedy, voracious

inscription (SYN) engraving, dedication

inscrutable (SYN) inexplicable, blank, enigmatic, impenetrable (ANT) open, readable, intelligible

insect (SYN) bug

insecure (SYN) anxious, exposed, doubtful, unstable, nervous (ANT) secure, confident, assured

insensible (SYN) unaware, impervious, apathetic, unfeeling, unconscious (ANT) aware, mindful, feeling inseparable (SYN) indivisible, devoted, intimate, close (ANT) separable, divisible

insert (SYN) enter, place, push, load, install (ANT) remove, retrieve, extract

inside (SYN) interior, core, middle, within, confidential (ANT) outside, exterior, public

insidious (SYN) stealthy, surreptitious, sneaky, deceptive, sly (ANT) artless

insight (SYN) vision, comprehension, perception, intuition, judgment (ANT) stupidity, obtuseness, ignorance

insignia (SYN) logo, emblem, symbol, crest

insignificance (SYN) irrelevance, pettiness, triviality, unimportance (ANT) worth, consequence, relevance, importance

insignificant (SYN) minor, paltry, trivial, insubstantial, negligible (ANT) significant, meaningful, relevant

insincere (SYN) dishonest, false, hypocritical, hollow, artificial (ANT) sincere, truthful, genuine, straightforward

insinuate (SYN) imply, allude, hint, purport, intimate

insipid (SYN) bland, vapid, inane, flat, unimaginative (ANT) exciting, intriguing, interesting, delicious, palatable

insist (SYN) urge, demand, pressure, order, maintain (ANT) ask, plead, request, beg

insolence (SYN) rudeness, defiance, impudence, arrogance, effrontery (ANT) civility, courtesy, manners, politeness

insolent (SYN) bold, insulting, brash, disrespectful, contemptuous (ANT) polite, considerate, thoughtful, courteous

insoluble (SYN) unaccountable, unfathomable, indecipherable

insomnia (SYN) sleeplessness, wakefulness

inspect (SYN) check, scrutinize, examine, search, monitor (ANT) ignore, overlook

inspection (SYN) check, review, exploration, once-over, examination, test

inspector (SYN) examiner, surveyor, investigator, monitor, auditor

inspiration (SYN) enthusiasm, encouragement, stimulus, insight, vision

inspire (SYN) enliven, galvanize, arouse, awaken, ignite (ANT) rebuff, bore, discourage

instability (SYN) unpredictability, fluctuation, variability, unreliability, volatility (ANT) stability, steadiness, constancy, permanence, dependability

install

install (SYN) fix, position, lodge, induct, appoint (ANT) remove

installation (SYN) placement, establishment, inauguration

installment (SYN) portion, part, payment

instance (SYN) example, occasion, illustration, occurrence, mention, cite

instant (SYN) moment, point, flash, immediate, rapid (ANT) delayed

instantaneous (SYN) immediate, prompt, speedy, swift, abrupt (ANT) gradual

instantly (SYN) immediately, at once, directly, forthwith

instead (SYN) rather, alternatively (ANT) as well

instigate (SYN) initiate, trigger, incite, provoke, activate

instill (SYN) introduce, infuse, implant

instinct (SYN) intuition, predisposition, tendency, impulse, talent, knack (ANT) reason, learning, acquisition

instinctively (SYN) naturally, automatically, involuntarily, intuitively

institute (SYN) society, foundation, college, found, initiate (ANT) abolish, end

institution (SYN) school, academy, organization, tradition, convention

instruct (SYN) teach, train, direct, command, counsel (ANT) misguide

instruction (SYN) guidance, coaching, directive, mandate, order

instructor (SYN) teacher, trainer, tutor, advisor, mentor

instrument (SYN) tool, device, apparatus, vehicle, agent

instrumental (SYN) involved, influential, active, contributory (ANT) uninvolved

insubstantial (SYN) flimsy, tenuous, slight, feeble, thin (ANT) substantial, consequential

insufferable (SYN) dreadful, intolerable, agonizing, impossible (ANT) bearable, endurable, tolerable

insufficient (SYN) lacking, scant, inadequate, incomplete, short (ANT) sufficient, plentiful, ample

insulate (SYN) cushion, shield, protect, wrap, encase

insult (SYN) abuse, malign, disparage, aspersion, offense (ANT) compliment, praise, flatter

insurance (SYN) security, assurance, protection, guarantee

insure (SYN) cover, assure, underwrite, protect

insurgent (SYN) rebel, revolutionary, disobedient, riotous

insurmountable (SYN) hopeless, overwhelming, impossible

insurrection (SYN) rebellion, uprising, revolt, coup, mutiny

intact (SYN) whole, sound, perfect, undamaged (ANT) broken, damaged, fragmented, defective

intangible (SYN) vague, elusive, incorporeal, immaterial, fleeting (ANT) tangible, material, definite

integrate (SYN) combine, blend, fuse, consolidate, assimilate (ANT) isolate, separate, seclude, segregate

integrity (SYN) honor, principle, rectitude, stability, strength

intellect (SYN) mind, intelligence, reason, brains, understanding

intellectual (SYN) cerebral, studious, scholarly, academic, analytical, erudite (ANT) physical, stupid, unlearned

intelligence (SYN) cleverness, brain power, acumen, knowledge, facts

intelligent (SYN) smart, bright, sharp, astute, insightful (ANT) unintelligent, dumb, obtuse, foolish, slow

intelligently (SYN) wisely, cleverly, smartly

intelligible (SYN) clear, distinct, lucid, coherent, accessible (ANT) incomprehensible, ambiguous

intend (SYN) aim, plan, mean, propose, design, expect, hope

intense (SYN) extreme, deep, severe, impassioned, vehement (ANT) mild, latent, apathetic, slow

intensify (SYN) heighten, sharpen, magnify, escalate, reinforce (ANT) abate, lessen, diminish, reduce

intensity (SYN) force, strength, fervor, severity, emotion

intensive (SYN) thorough, comprehensive, exhaustive, concentrated, rigorous (ANT) brief, cursory, perfunctory, limited

intent (SYN) objective, meaning, goal, motive, attentive, engrossed (ANT) distracted

intention (SYN) target, purpose, plan, aim, object, expectation

intentionally (SYN) deliberately, purposefully, willfully, consciously, knowingly (ANT) accidentally, by chance, unintentionally, involuntarily

intently (SYN) eagerly, resolvedly, raptly, designedly (ANT) distractedly

inter (SYN) bury, entomb

intercede (SYN) intervene, arbitrate, mediate

intercept (SYN) stop, interrupt, obstruct, seize

interest (SYN) attention, curiosity, concern, relevance, hobby, pursuit, intrigue, attract

interesting (SYN) absorbing, fascinating, gripping, compelling, thought-provoking, riveting (ANT) dull, boring, uninteresting, tedious, bothersome interface (SYN) link, connection, border, boundary

interfere (SYN) intrude, tamper, meddle, frustrate, inhibit (ANT) help, stand aside

interference (SYN) intervention, prying, obstruction, conflict, opposition

interim (SYN) acting, temporary, makeshift, meantime (ANT) permanent

interior (SYN) inside, center, internal (ANT) exterior, outside, border, external

interlude (SYN) break, pause, intermission, respite, hiatus

intermediate (SYN) transitional, midway, middle, halfway

interment (SYN) burial, funeral

interminable (SYN) infinite, protracted, endless, never-ending, prolonged (ANT) brief, limited, short, confined

intermission (SYN) recess, break, stoppage, rest

intermittent (SYN) sporadic, irregular, broken, occasional, random (ANT) continuous, constant

intern (SYN) detain, hold, confine, imprison

internal (SYN) inner, inside, interior, central, domestic (ANT) external, outside, foreign

international (SYN) global, universal, intercontinental, cosmopolitan (ANT) local, national

internecine (SYN) destructive, deadly, fatal, ruinous

Internet (SYN) cyberspace, World Wide, Web, the net, the web

interpret (SYN) translate, decipher, clarify, unravel, render, play (ANT) misinterpret, pervert

interpretation (SYN) analysis, explanation, commentary, presentation, rendition (ANT) distortion, misrepresentation

interpreter (SYN) translator, commentator

interrogate (SYN) question, examine, grill, pump, probe

interrupt (SYN) disturb, intrude, intervene, suspend, delay (ANT) continue, sustain, maintain

intersect (SYN) meet, join, cross (ANT) miss

intersection (SYN) junction, crossroads

interval (SYN) break, intermission, time out

intervene (SYN) get involved, intercede, happen, occur, ensue (ANT) avoid

interview (SYN) meeting, dialogue, audience, discussion, question, interrogate intimacy (SYN) closeness, affection, rapport, familiarity, attachment (ANT) formality, distance, reserve

intimate (SYN) dear, tender, personal, confidential, imply, divulge (ANT) distant, cool, formal

intimidate (SYN) bully, frighten, subdue, threaten, menace, hound (ANT) comfort, assist, inspire

intolerable (SYN) unbearable, painful, excruciating, insufferable, horrible (ANT) pleasant, charming

intolerance (SYN) bigotry, discrimination, prejudice, bias, close-mindedness (ANT) tolerance, leniency, impartiality, fairness

intonation (SYN) melody, inflection, chant

intoxicate (SYN) elate, excite, inebriate, wire (ANT) depress, sober

intractable (SYN) obstinate, unruly, adamant, unyielding, headstrong (ANT) docile, amenable, manageable

intrepid (SYN) brave, daring, audacious, fearless (ANT) timid, fearful, cautious

intricate (SYN) detailed, elaborate, complex, tangled, difficult (ANT) simple, easy, uncomplicated

intrigue (SYN) interest, titillate, plot, scheme, subterfuge

intrinsic (SYN) essential, fundamental, inherent, natural (ANT) extrinsic, foreign, extraneous

introduce (SYN) present, acquaint, initiate, submit, inject (ANT) conclude, end, remove

introduction (SYN) opening, preface, launch, foundation, institution (ANT) ending, epilogue, conclusion

introspection (SYN) meditation, contemplation, brooding, soul-searching, self-examination

introvert (SYN) loner, shy person (ANT) extrovert

intrude (SYN) interrupt, infringe, trespass, encroach, invade (ANT) leave, withdraw, vacate

intrusion (SYN) invasion, violation, infiltration, interference

intuition (SYN) instinct, insight, hunch, premonition, sixth sense (ANT) reason, logic

inundate (SYN) flood, swamp, overwhelm, engulf, immerse

inure (SYN) toughen, habituate, accustom

invade (SYN) raid, attack, storm, infest, permeate, disrupt (ANT) leave, liberate, relinquish

invalid (SYN) void, unfounded, illegitimate, feeble, bedridden (ANT) valid, true, healthy, strong

invalidate (SYN) cancel, undermine, undo, nullify (ANT) validate, establish, promote invaluable (SYN) precious, priceless, vital, crucial (ANT) dispensable, worthless

invariably (SYN) always, regularly, customarily, predictably, consistently (ANT) sometimes, occasionally, never

invasion (SYN) onslaught, assault, campaign, breach, capture

invent (SYN) create, conceive, develop, concoct, fabricate (ANT) copy, imitate

invention (SYN) resourcefulness, ingenuity, origination, discovery, contraption

inventive (SYN) innovative, new, inspired, novel, unconventional (ANT) old, outdated, antiquated, unimaginative

inventor (SYN) creator, maker, designer, architect

inventory (SYN) record, account, register, list, archive

inverse (SYN) opposite, contrary, converse, reverse

invert (SYN) transpose, reverse, overturn

invest (SYN) spend, devote, empower, vest, authorize

investigate (SYN) inspect, inquire, scrutinize, analyze, study (ANT) overlook, ignore, solve

investigation (SYN) review, examination, inspection, inquiry, probe

investment (SYN) venture, contribution, stake, financing, funding, proposition

investor (SYN) backer, underwriter

inveterate (SYN) chronic, entrenched, habitual, hardened, deep-seated (ANT) flexible, tractable

invigorate (SYN) refresh, revitalize, vitalize, enliven, energize (ANT) depress, sadden, dishearten

invincible (SYN) unbeatable, unconquerable, insurmountable (ANT) destructible, vulnerable, beatable

invisible (SYN) unseen, indiscernible, imperceptible, hidden, inconspicuous (ANT) detectible, visible, observable

invitation (SYN) request, summons, invite

invite (SYN) ask, bid, summon, encourage, solicit (ANT) deny, reject

inviting (SYN) tempting, appealing, enticing, seductive (ANT) repulsive, unattractive, repellent

invoke (SYN) call upon, pray, beseech, appeal to, petition, implore

involuntary (SYN) unconscious, reflex, automatic, spontaneous (ANT) voluntary, intentional, controlled

involve (SYN) entail, require, concern, implicate, include (ANT) exclude, separate, preclude invulnerable (SYN) safe, unassailable, impenetrable, invincible (ANT) susceptible, destructible, vulnerable

inward (SYN) internal, inner, private, innermost, secret (ANT) outward, exterior, public

inwardly (SYN) privately, secretly, deep down (ANT) outwardly

iota (SYN) bit, speck, trifle, shred, ounce

irate (SYN) angry, furious, livid, incensed, indignant (ANT) happy, calm, pleased

iridescent (ANT) shimmering, lustrous, brilliant, colorful

irksome (SYN) annoying, vexing, wearisome, irritating, disturbing (ANT) soothing, gratifying, pleasant

ironic (SYN) wry, sarcastic, incongruous, paradoxical, strange (ANT) sincere, normal

irony (SYN) satire, mockery, bitterness, paradox

irradiate (SYN) illuminate, brighten, heat, radiate

irrational (SYN) absurd, illogical, preposterous, unreasonable, groundless (ANT) rational, logical, founded, justifiable, sensible

irreconcilable (SYN) detrimental, incompatible

irrefutable (SYN) certain, undeniable, unquestionable (ANT) unsure, contestable

irregular (SYN) uneven, aberrant, inconsistent, erratic, peculiar (ANT) regular, normal, even, ordinary, symmetrical

irrelevant (SYN) immaterial, extraneous, unrelated, inapplicable, peripheral (ANT) relevant, pertinent, connected, fitting

irreparable (SYN) irreversible, beyond repair, incurable (ANT) fixable, reparable

irreproachable (SYN) innocent, perfect, blameless, unimpeachable (ANT) guilty, reproachable, faulty

irresistible (SYN) compelling, urgent, uncontrollable, overwhelming, captivating

irresponsible (SYN) immature, careless, unreliable, reckless, foolish (ANT) serious, trustworthy, accountable

irretrievable (SYN) lost, permanently gone

irreverent (SYN) flippant, disrespectful, mocking, impertinent (ANT) respectful, grave, somber

irrevocable (SYN) immutable, fixed, unalterable

irrigate (SYN) water, flood, inundate

irritable (SYN) testy, touchy, cantankerous, grouchy, short-tempered (ANT) tranquil, composed, cheerful

irritate (SYN) bother, annoy, aggravate, peeve, rub, chafe (ANT) delight, please, soothe, assuage irritation (SYN) annoyance, indignation, displeasure, chagrin (ANT) pleasure, enjoyment, delight

island (SYN) isle, key, atoll

isle (SYN) island, key

isolate (SYN) separate, segregate, cut off, alienate, seclude (ANT) integrate, combine, mix, mingle

isolation (SYN) solitude, seclusion, remoteness, inaccessibility(ANT) contact, togetherness, connection, association

issue (SYN) topic, matter, point, problem, edition, number, announce, broadcast, emanate, proceed (ANT) withdraw, retain

isthmus (SYN) strip

itch (SYN) irritation, tingling, yearning, craving, ache, pine

item (SYN) detail, particular, point, thing, object, story, article

itemize (SYN) list, enumerate, mention, specify

itinerant (SYN) vagrant, nomadic, roving, migrant, wandering (ANT) settled, permanent

itinerary (SYN) schedule, timetable, route, plan, program

J

jab (SYN) thrust, stab, poke, dig, prod

jabber (SYN) chatter, babble, ramble

jacket (SYN) coat, wrapper, covering, sleeve, sheath

jaded (SYN) tired, spent, fatigued, cynical (ANT) spirited, refreshed

jagged (SYN) uneven, ragged, spiked, serrated (ANT) smooth

jail (SYN) prison, penitentiary, slammer, imprison, confine (ANT) release, free, liberate

jam (SYN) cram, squeeze, stuff, crowd, congest, obstruct, trouble, predicament

janitor (SYN) custodian, caretaker

jar (SYN) container, jug, jolt, shake, grate (ANT) soothe

jargon (SYN) terminology, slang, lingo, idiom

jaundiced (SYN) cynical, skeptical, hostile, spiteful, resentful, yellowed

jaunt (SYN) outing, trip, excursion, stroll

jealous (SYN) envious, grudging, covetous, protective, suspicious (ANT) content, satisfied, trusting, careless

jealousy (SYN) envy, bitterness, resentment, mistrust, spite, greed (ANT) geniality, contentment

jeer (SYN) taunt, deride, scoff, ridicule, heckle, sneer, insult (ANT) cheer, applaud, flatter, compliment

jeopardize (SYN) endanger, risk, gamble, imperil, threaten,

compromise (ANT) safeguard, protect, shield

jeopardy (SYN) peril, vulnerability, danger (ANT) safety

jerk (SYN) tug, twitch, wrench, yank, lurch

jest (SYN) joke, kid, tease, quip, witticism

jet (SYN) stream, spray, surge, nozzle, spout, gush, zoom

jettison (SYN) dump, unload, scrap, abandon, discard (ANT) keep, retain

jetty (SYN) wharf, pier, breakwater

jewel (SYN) gemstone, gem, precious stone, pearl, prize, treasure

jewelry (SYN) ornaments, gems, finery, trinkets

jiffy (SYN) flash, heartbeat, second

jilt (SYN) leave, ditch, dump, slight, break up with, walk out on

jingle (SYN) tinkle, ringing, song, ditty, chime

jinx (SYN) curse, hex, bewitch, spell, bad luck

jittery (SYN) nervous, fidgety, anxious, jumpy, agitated

job (SYN) occupation, career, chore, task, function

jog (SYN) trot, canter, stir, nudge, prod

join (SYN) connect, combine, bind, enlist, enroll (ANT) sever, disconnect, separate, leave

joint (SYN) collective, shared, hinge, junction, dive, club (ANT) separate

joke (SYN) pun, gag, prank, jest, banter, buffoon (ANT) seriousness

jolt (SYN) shock, startle, bump, jostle, knock

jot (SYN) write, note, record, list

journal (SYN) diary, log, newspaper, periodical

journalism (SYN) reporting, correspondence, broadcasting, press

journalist (SYN) reporter, commentator, columnist, correspondent

journey (SYN) trip, voyage, expedition, travel, roam

jovial (SYN) jolly, merry, cheerful, lighthearted, sunny (ANT) miserable, morose, unhappy, melancholy

joy (SYN) elation, delight, gaiety, glee, gladness, euphoria (ANT) sadness, sorrow, misery, heartache

jubilant (SYN) thrilled, overjoyed, exuberant, triumphant, ecstatic (ANT) sad, dejected

judge (SYN) referee, moderator, critic, authority, decide, evaluate (ANT) defer, hesitate judgment (SYN) wisdom, sense, discernment, verdict, finding, opinion, assessment

judicial (SYN) legal, fair, official

judicious (SYN) shrewd, prudent, astute, sensible (ANT) thoughtless, foolish, ill-advised

jug (SYN) container, pitcher, vessel, urn, carafe

juggle (SYN) maneuver, manipulate

juice (SYN) liquid, fluid, extract, nectar

jump (SYN) leap, bounce, spring, ascend, surge, rise

junction (SYN) union, connection, intersection, crossroads

juncture (SYN) occasion, moment, time, point

junior (SYN) minor, secondary, subordinate, younger (ANT) older, senior

junk (SYN) trash, rubbish, litter, clutter

junket (SYN) trip, picnic, outing

jurisdiction (SYN) command, authority, scope, range

just (SYN) right, deserved, equitable, merely, simply, precisely, exactly (ANT) unfair, wrong, partial, hardly

justice (SYN) fairness, integrity, equity, legitimacy (ANT) injustice, corruption, inequality

justify (SYN) excuse, explain, support, defend, rationalize (ANT) accuse, blame, reproach

jut (SYN) protrude, bulge, project, extend, overhang (ANT) indent, cave

juvenile (SYN) minor, child, adolescent, immature, youthful (ANT) adult, mature

juxtaposition (SYN) proximity, nearness, closeness, comparison, contrast

K

keen (SYN) avid, eager, enthusiastic, sharp, clever, perceptive (ANT) reluctant, unenthusiastic, dull, stupid

keep (SYN) retain, possess, control, conserve, manage, hinder, detain (ANT) throw away, relinquish, discard

kernel (SYN) grain, pith, seed, core, essence

key (SYN) answer, solution, essential, fundamental, pivotal

kick (SYN) boot, punt, quit, give, up, thrill, buzz

kid (SYN) child, youngster, tease, joke, trick

kidnap (SYN) abduct, capture, seize, snatch

kill (SYN) murder, slaughter, terminate, slay, extinguish, smother, cancel, destroy killer (SYN) assassin, murderer, executioner

kin (SYN) family, relatives, clan

kind (SYN) considerate, tender, caring, benevolent, type, variety (ANT) unkind, cruel, harsh, cold

kindle (SYN) light, ignite, awaken, inspire, stir (ANT) quench, douse, discourage

kindness (SYN) humanity, goodwill, understanding, warmth, concern (ANT) unkindness, malevolence, bitterness

kindred (SYN) similar, matching, aligned, family, relations (ANT) opposite, dissimilar, unrelated

kingdom (SYN) realm, country, territory

kink (SYN) twist, bend, coil, eccentricity, quirk (ANT) unbend, straighten

kinship (SYN) relation, consanguinity, affinity, association

kiss (SYN) smooch, peck, graze, touch, skim

kit (SYN) gear, tools, equipment, hardware

knack (SYN) skill, aptitude, gift, talent, instinct, flair, habit

knave (SYN) scoundrel, villain, rascal

knead (SYN) massage, shape, rub, work

kneel (SYN) stoop, genuflect, grovel

knife (SYN) blade, cut, wound, slash

knit (SYN) unite, meld, blend, weave, intertwine, furrow, wrinkle

knob (SYN) lump, bump, bulge, protrusion

knock (SYN) rap, thump, strike, blow, belittle, criticize

knoll (SYN) hill, mound

knot (SYN) tie, tether, secure, connection, cluster (ANT) untie

know (SYN) understand, comprehend, realize, recognize, be aware (ANT) doubt, suspect, question

knowing (SYN) significant, meaningful, suggestive, expressive

knowingly (SYN) deliberately, willfully, consciously, intentionally (ANT) unwittingly, unintentionally

knowledge (SYN) education, wisdom, intelligence, familiarity, mastery, awareness (ANT) ignorance, inexperience

knowledgeable (SYN) learned, intelligent, cultivated, well informed, conversant (ANT) ignorant, unaware, illiterate

known (SYN) noted, famous, celebrated, notorious (ANT) unknown

kudos (SYN) praise, credit, recognition, acclaim, applause

L

label (SYN) tag, sticker, ticket, mark, stamp, categorize

labor (SYN) work, toil, endeavor, drudgery, childbirth (ANT) rest, idleness, inactivity

laborious (SYN) tough, strenuous, exhausting, grueling, punishing (ANT) easy, effortless

labyrinth (SYN) maze, jungle, puzzle

lace (SYN) cord, string, tie, fasten, bind, spike, doctor (ANT) untie, unfasten

laceration (SYN) cut, gash, wound, slash

lack (SYN) need, shortage, deficiency, want, require (ANT) abundance, have, possess

lackadaisical (SYN) listless, indifferent, lazy, dreamy, lethargic (ANT) energized, active, engaged

laconic (SYN) concise, succinct, terse, brief, curt (ANT) voluble, wordy, garrulous, rambling

lad (SYN) boy, kid, young man

laden (SYN) full, loaded, crammed, burdened, encumbered (ANT) empty

lady (SYN) woman, girl, noblewoman, gentlewoman

lag (SYN) linger, tarry, straggle, trail, loiter (ANT) hasten, dash, quicken

lagoon (SYN) pool, pond

lair (SYN) den, burrow, hole, hideout

laissez faire (SYN) nonintervention, free enterprise

lake (SYN) basin, reservoir, pool, pond, waterhole

lame (SYN) disabled, limping, unconvincing, flimsy, feeble (ANT) fit, healthy, sound, convincing

lament (SYN) bemoan, mourn, grieve, complain, weep (ANT) celebrate, welcome

lampoon (SYN) satire, parody, caricature, ridicule

lance (SYN) pierce, spear, skewer, puncture, javelin

land (SYN) ground, earth, alight, dock, region, domain (ANT) sea, sky, embark, take off

landfill (SYN) garbage dump

landlord (SYN) owner, proprietor (ANT) tenant

landmark (SYN) monument, feature, milestone, turning point, watershed

landscape (SYN) scenery, vista, panorama, terrain, countryside

lane (SYN) road, alley, path, way, track

language (SYN) speech, communication, dialect, tongue, phrasing

languish (SYN) wither, droop, weaken, suffer, rot (ANT) thrive languor (SYN) sluggishness, weakness, exhaustion, weariness, listlessness

lank (SYN) slim, spare, limp, lifeless

lap (SYN) loop, orbit, sip, drink, splash

lapse (SYN) slip, mistake, blunder, regression, interruption, gap, expire

larceny (SYN) theft, robbery, stealing

lard (SYN) fat, grease

large (SYN) big, sizable, massive, substantial, important (ANT) small, tiny, slender,

largely (SYN) mainly, mostly, generally, primarily, for the most part

largess (SYN) generosity, liberality (ANT) greed, selfishness

lash (SYN) flog, whip, strike, scold, fasten, tether (ANT) reward, soothe

last (SYN) final, closing, previous, latest, continue, endure (ANT) first, next, introductory

lasting (SYN) abiding, durable, permanent, continuing, stable, long-term (ANT) fleeting, passing, ephemeral

latch (SYN) fasten, bolt, lock, hook, secure (ANT) unfasten, unbolt

late (SYN) tardy, delayed, overdue, dead, deceased, (ANT) prompt, timely, early, punctual, alive

lately (SYN) recently, not long ago, just now, of late

latent (SYN) hidden, dormant, potential, inactive, unrealized (ANT) apparent, evident

later (SYN) afterwards, after, subsequently, next, in time (ANT) earlier, prior, before, previously

lateral (SYN) sideways

latest (SYN) most recent, up-to-date, current, newest, state-of-the-art (ANT) old

lather (SYN) suds, bubbles, froth, foam

latitude (SYN) liberty, freedom, leeway, laxity, independence, slack (ANT) restriction

latter (SYN) second, last-mentioned, closing, final, concluding (ANT) former, earlier

laud (SYN) praise, esteem, honor, extol, commend (ANT) blame, revile

laugh (SYN) giggle, chuckle, guffaw, roar, joke, hoot (ANT) cry, weep, lament

laughter (SYN) amusement, glee, mirth, giggling, chuckling

launch (SYN) propel, dispatch, begin, commence, initiate (ANT) land, close

lavatory (SYN) restroom, bathroom, toilet, washroom, water closet

lavish (SYN) abundant, excessive, profuse, luxurious, heap, shower (ANT) scarce, meager, withhold, begrudge

law (SYN) code, rule, command,
ordinance, principle

lawful (SYN) legal, sanctioned,
permissible, authorized, legitimate
(ANT) illegal, prohibited, illicit

lawn (SYN) yard

lawyer (SYN) attorney, legal advisor,
counsel, advocate

lax (SYN) relaxed, lenient, remiss,
casual, careless (ANT) strict

lay (SYN) place, deposit, set, put,
devise, formulate (ANT) pick up

layer (SYN) tier, stratum, row, level,
coat, covering

lazy (SYN) sluggish, lethargic, idle,
indolent, slothful (ANT) fast,
industrious, energetic, active

lead (SYN) guide, steer, persuade,
command, be ahead (ANT) follow,
obey, conform

leader (SYN) boss, head, director,
principal, commander (ANT)
follower, adherent, supporter

leadership (SYN) direction, guidance,
management, authority, control

leaf (SYN) blade, frond, page, sheet

leaflet (SYN) pamphlet, booklet,
brochure, handbill, flyer

league (SYN) alliance, association,
union, category, class, level

leak (SYN) hole, opening, escape, seep,
reveal, divulge

lean (SYN) prop, slant, recline, bend,
tend, slim, slender, meager (ANT)
fat, portly, abundant, plentiful

leap (SYN) jump, bound, vault, rise,
surge, soar (ANT) drop, plummet

learn (SYN) master, acquire, discover,
discern, memorize

learned (SYN) scholarly, intellectual,
academic, literary (ANT) ignorant

learning (SYN) education, knowledge,
wisdom, scholarship, study (ANT)
ignorance

leash (SYN) lead, tether, rein, restraint

least (SYN) minimum, lowest, fewest,
slightest (ANT) most, maximum,
highest

leave (SYN) depart, withdraw, forget,
abandon, entrust, commit, consent,
permission (ANT) arrive, enter, stay,
remain

lecherous (SYN) lewd, lustful, salacious,
lascivious, suggestive (ANT) pure

lecture (SYN) speech, lesson, address,
presentation, reprimand, scold
(ANT) praise, commend

ledge (SYN) shelf, sill, ridge, rim

leer (SYN) stare, ogle, smirk, sneer

leeway (SYN) license, flexibility,
freedom, liberty, elbowroom

left (SYN) left-hand, port (ANT) right,
right-hand, starboard

left-wing (SYN) liberal, radical, socialist (ANT) right-wing, conservative

leg (SYN) limb, support, upright, lap, segment

legacy (SYN) estate, gift, inheritance, consequence, result

legal (SYN) permissible, sanctioned, lawful, acceptable, judicial (ANT) illegal, illicit, unauthorized

legend (SYN) myth, story, tale, fable, celebrity, phenomenon, icon, caption, description (ANT) history

legendary (SYN) mythical, fabled, famous, renowned, illustrious (ANT) unknown, insignificant, obscure

legerdemain (SYN) magic, trickery, deceit, deception, illusion

legible (SYN) clear, distinct, readable, neat (ANT) illegible, unclear, · indecipherable

legion (SYN) army, troop, multitude, mass, throng

legislature (SYN) congress, senate, assembly, parliament

legitimate (SYN) legal, lawful, authentic, genuine, logical, valid, sound (ANT) illegitimate, illegal, invalid, unreasonable

leisure (SYN) recreation, free time, rest, relaxation, ease (ANT) work, toil

leisurely (SYN) unhurried, slow, relaxed, gentle, undemanding (ANT) rushed, hurried, frenzied

lend (SYN) loan, advance, contribute, supply, give (ANT) borrow, take ·

length (SYN) distance, span, reach, duration, segment

lengthen (SYN) extend, increase, prolong, elongate, protract (ANT) shorten, condense, abbreviate, curtail

lenient (SYN) tolerant, permissive, forgiving, indulgent, magnanimous (ANT) strict, severe, unsparing

lesbian (SYN) homosexual, gay

lesion (SYN) sore, wound, injury, blister

less (SYN) fewer, smaller, minus, subtracting (ANT) more

lessen (SYN) reduce, decrease, diminish, shrink, minimize, fade, subside (ANT) increase, enhance, boost

lesson (SYN) instruction, seminar, class, warning, example

let (SYN) allow, permit, enable, rent, lease (ANT) prevent, obstruct, keep

lethal (SYN) deadly, fatal, mortal, toxic, poisonous (ANT) harmless, safe

lethargy (SYN) sluggishness, sloth, apathy, drowsiness, inertia (ANT) energy, vitality, liveliness

letter (SYN) character, symbol, note, message, correspondence

levee (SYN) dam, embankment

level (SYN) flat, horizontal, balanced, even, equalize, flatten, demolish,

lever

position, grade (ANT) vertical, irregular, uneven, erect

lever (SYN) bar, handle, arm, pry, force, wrench

levity (SYN) happiness, silliness, frivolity, giddiness, light-heartedness (ANT) seriousness, earnestness, somberness

levy (SYN) exact, impose, collect, tax, fee

lewd (SYN) indecent, smutty, obscene, lustful, wanton, licentious (ANT) decent, pure, appropriate, G-rated

liability (SYN) responsibility, culpability, obligations, debt, burden (ANT) asset, advantage

liable (SYN) accountable, responsible, guilty, prone, likely (ANT) absolved

liaison (SYN) communication, contact, cooperation, partnership, mediator, intermediary

liar (SYN) fibber, fabricator, perjurer, storyteller, imposter

libel (SYN) defamation, misrepresentation, smear, malign, slur

liberal (SYN) progressive, open-minded, reformist, generous, copious, lavish (ANT) conservative, intolerant, strict, greedy

liberate (SYN) free, emancipate, release, deliver (ANT) enslave, imprison

liberation (SYN) freedom, emancipation, release, deliverance (ANT) imprisonment

liberty (SYN) independence, freedom, autonomy, sovereignty, privilege (ANT) oppression, bondage, constraint

license (SYN) warrant, permission, right, laxity, liberty

licentious (SYN) immoral, abandoned, promiscuous, unrestrained (ANT) lawful, principled

lick (SYN) taste, lap, flicker, defeat, trounce

lid (SYN) top, cap, cover

lie (SYN) untruth, falsehood, fib, falsify, deceive, recline, repose, rest (ANT) truth, rise, stand

life (SYN) existence, vitality, being, animation, verve (ANT) death

lift (SYN) hoist, raise, boost, revoke, cancel, ride (ANT) lower, drop

light (SYN) brighten, illuminate, ignite, radiance, glow, lamp, sunny, pale, flimsy, airy, insubstantial, undemanding (ANT) extinguish, darkness, dark, shade, heavy

light-headed (SYN) dizzy, faint, woozy, giddy (ANT) sober, clear-headed

like (SYN) similar, analogous, equivalent, admire, enjoy, relish, such as, for example (ANT) unlike, different, divergent, dislike, hate likely (SYN) probable, possible, credible, disposed, apt, (ANT) unlikely, improbable, unbelievable

likeness (SYN) resemblance, correspondence, similarity, portrait, depiction (ANT) dissimilarity

lilliputian (SYN) small, diminutive, tiny, trivial, petty (ANT) huge, gargantuan, massive, monumental

limb (SYN) extremity, appendage, arm, leg, branch, bough

limber (SYN) flexible, supple, pliant, pliable (ANT) stiff, rigid, inflexible

limbo (SYN) transition, midway, oblivion, purgatory

limelight (SYN) publicity, stardom, celebrity, scrutiny, prominence (ANT) obscurity

limit (SYN) boundary, perimeter, restrict, confine, bound, maximum

limitation (SYN) reservation, restraint, control, shortcoming, deficiency (ANT) strength

limp (SYN) floppy, slack, hobble, shuffle, stagger (ANT) firm, rigid, stride

limpid (SYN) clear, transparent, lucid, serene (ANT) obscure, troubled

line (SYN) row, file, slash, boundary, margin, cord, rope, wrinkle, furrow

linger (SYN) delay, dawdle, loiter, remain, hesitate, pause (ANT) hurry, rush, hasten, vanish

lining (SYN) padding, insulation, facing

link (SYN) connection, attachment, piece, component, fasten, associate (ANT) divide, separate, split

lint (SYN) fuzz, dust

lip (SYN) brim, edge, rim, brink

liquid (SYN) fluid, flowing, molten, runny, aqueous (ANT) solid

liquidate (SYN) settle, pay, clear, sell, dispatch

liquor (SYN) alcohol, spirit, extract, liquid

list (SYN) catalog, tally, itemize, enumerate, tilt, lean

listen (SYN) hear, concentrate, heed, observe, mind, pay attention (ANT) disregard, ignore, neglect

listless (SYN) sluggish, indifferent, lazy, languid, apathetic (ANT) energetic, animated, vigorous

literacy (SYN) knowledge, education, ability to read (ANT) illiteracy

literally (SYN) exactly, verbatim, actually, truly (ANT) figuratively, symbolically

literate (SYN) informed, educated, knowledgeable, scholarly, well-read (ANT) illiterate, ignorant

literature (SYN) writings, publications, prose, lore

lithe (SYN) limber, supple, flexible, pliable (ANT) stiff

litigant (SYN) plaintiff, claimant

litigation (SYN) lawsuit, case, prosecution

litter (SYN) debris, garbage, trash, clutter, scatter, brood, offspring

little (SYN) small, miniature, young, fragment, bit, barely, seldom, trivial (ANT) big, large, old, significant, often

live (SYN) exist, survive, reside, dwell, alive, charged (ANT) dead, die, perish, inanimate

livelihood (SYN) job, occupation, income, subsistence, living

lively (SYN) active, perky, spirited, upbeat, exuberant, vivid, bustling (ANT) gloomy, despondent, quiet, slow

livery (SYN) costume, attire, uniform, regalia, dress

livid (SYN) angry, fuming, seething, irate, incensed, discolored, bruised (ANT) calm, serene, content

living (SYN) alive, breathing, current, contemporary, subsistence, livelihood (ANT) dead, extinct

load (SYN) cargo, burden, worry, heap, pack, encumber, prime (ANT) unload

loaf (SYN) lump, cake, laze, lounge, mooch

loan (SYN) advance, credit, lend (ANT) borrow

loath (SYN) reluctant, unwilling, opposed, averse (ANT) willing, inclined

loathe (SYN) hate, despise, detest, abhor (ANT) love, admire, like, cherish

loathsome (SYN) offensive, foul, abominable, odious, revolting, vile (ANT) delightful, pleasing

lobby (SYN) foyer, entrance hall, persuade, campaign, urge, promote

local (SYN) regional, limited, confined, native, inhabitant (ANT) universal, widespread

locality (SYN) site, scene, location, place, vicinity, neighborhood

locate (SYN) find, pinpoint, establish, situate, station (ANT) lose, misplace

location (SYN) spot, position, whereabouts, venue, address

lock (SYN) bolt, clasp, fasten, secure, join, grasp, tress, strand (ANT) unlock, open

locomotive (SYN) railroad engine, train

lodge (SYN) cabin, cottage, hall, reside, board, submit, implant, wedge

loft (SYN) attic, upper room

lofty (SYN) high, soaring, grand, illustrious, proud, haughty (ANT) modest, shy, low, common

log (SYN) journal, chronicle, ledger, record, stump, lumber

logic (SYN) reason, sense, coherence, rationality (ANT) foolishness, irrationality

logical (SYN) clear, sound, reasonable, sensible, wise, understandable (ANT) illogical, weak, unlikely, incoherent

logo (SYN) emblem, symbol, trademark

loiter (SYN) linger, idle, loaf, stall, tarry, dawdle (ANT) hurry, rush

loll (SYN) lounge, relax, dangle, flop, sag

lone (SYN) single, solitary, sole, isolated (ANT) joined, together

loneliness (SYN) isolation, solitude, seclusion, friendlessness (ANT) popularity, company

lonely (SYN) forsaken, withdrawn, abandoned, deserted, uninhabited, remote (ANT) popular, crowded

long (SYN) lengthy, extended, protracted, desire, crave (ANT) short, brief, curt

longing (SYN) dream, ambition, yearning, thirst, aspiration (ANT) apathy

look (SYN) glance, view, observe, seem, appear, search, hunt, appearance, expression (ANT) ignore, disregard, miss

loom (SYN) hover, tower, menace, threaten, brew, materialize

loop (SYN) ring, coil, twist, knot, turn, wind

loophole (SYN) excuse, escape, flaw, omission, discrepancy

loose (SYN) free, unbound, slack, vague, imprecise (ANT) confined, bound, tight, taut, narrow, literal

loosen (SYN) untie, ease, detach, release, free (ANT) tighten, secure

loot (SYN) prize, spoils, plunder, raid, rob, steal, rifle

lope (SYN) canter, gallop, stride, bound

lopsided (SYN) crooked, askew, uneven, asymmetrical (ANT) balanced, proportionate, even, straight

loquacious (SYN) talkative, verbose, chatty, garrulous, wordy (ANT) quiet, brief, succinct

lord (SYN) master, leader, ruler, nobleman, domineer, oppress

lore (SYN) traditions, teachings, myth, fable, wisdom

lose (SYN) misplace, forfeit, yield, squander, be defeated, (ANT) find, recover, win

loss (SYN) failure, defeat, damage, cost (ANT) recovery, profit

lost (SYN) missing, vanished, absent, gone, adrift, disoriented (ANT) found, discovered

lot (SYN) collection, bunch, destiny, fortune, plenty (ANT) little, few

lotion (SYN) salve, cream, balm, ointment

lottery (SYN) raffle, drawing, chance, gamble

loud (SYN) noisy, clamorous, thundering, resonant, garish, gaudy, flashy (ANT) quiet, silent, subdued, tasteful

lounge (SYN) relax, recline, laze, slouch, sprawl

lousy (SYN) awful, shabby, crummy, terrible, bad (ANT) great, superior, wonderful

lovable (SYN) endearing, charming, delightful, amiable (ANT) repugnant, repulsive, unappealing, unlovable

love (SYN) adore, prize, relish, tenderness, devotion, warmth, intimacy, partiality (ANT) hatred, loathing, indifference, antipathy, hate

lovely (SYN) attractive, enchanting, charming, enjoyable, pleasant, marvelous (ANT) ugly, unattractive, horrible, disagreeable

loving (SYN) affectionate, fond, tender, doting, caring (ANT) cold, cruel, distant

low (SYN) short, squat, deep, hushed, sunken, depressed, gloomy, inferior, modest (ANT) high, elevated, respectable, cheerful, superior, expensive

lower (SYN) drop, let down, minor, inferior, reduced, diminished, lessen, slash (ANT) raise, increase, boost

lowly (SYN) humble, modest, unassuming, simple, unpretentious (ANT) proud, noble, exalted

loyal (SYN) dependable, trustworthy, devoted, faithful, reliable (ANT) disloyal, treacherous

loyalty (SYN) fidelity, steadfastness, allegiance, constancy, commitment (ANT) disloyalty, infidelity, faithlessness

lubricant (SYN) grease, oil

lubricate (SYN) oil, grease, smear

lucent (SYN) shining, translucent, clear, glowing

lucid (SYN) clear, explicit, transparent, rational, sane (ANT) obscure, confused, irrational

luck (SYN) fortune, chance, blessing, serendipity, success, fate (ANT) misfortune

lucky (SYN) fortunate, blessed, charmed, timely, fortuitous (ANT) unlucky

lucrative (SYN) profitable, rewarding, well-paid, beneficial, worthwhile (ANT) profitless, unrewarding, unprofitable

ludicrous (SYN) ridiculous, laughable, absurd, mad, preposterous (ANT) sensible, logical

luggage (SYN) baggage, gear

lukewarm (SYN) tepid, room temperature, warmish, apathetic, indifferent (ANT) hot, cold, passionate lull (SYN) calm, soothe, pacify, pause, break, quiet (ANT) rouse, agitate, activity

lullaby (SYN) song

lumber (SYN) wood, logs, shuffle, trudge

luminous (SYN) glowing, bright, radiant, lustrous, incandescent (ANT) dark, dull

lump (SYN) bump, growth, bulge, group, chunk

lunatic (SYN) irrational, crazy, insane, maniac, fool

lunge (SYN) pounce, charge, thrust, dive, rush

lure (SYN) tempt, entice, attract, bait, incentive (ANT) deter

lurid (SYN) horrible, gruesome, graphic, shocking, sensational (ANT) modest, banal

lurk (SYN) hide, sneak, prowl, loiter, skulk

luscious (SYN) appetizing, succulent, delicious, appealing, tasty (ANT) unappetizing, unpalatable, unsavory

lush (SYN) dense, flourishing, abundant, lavish, extravagant (ANT) sparse, barren, plain

lust (SYN) desire, crave, longing, appetite, passion (ANT) restraint, aversion

luster (SYN) gleam, gloss, shimmer, shine, splendor

luxurious (SYN) plush, opulent, fancy, palatial, swank (ANT) plain, simple

luxury (SYN) opulence, affluence, frill, treat, indulgence (ANT) poverty, necessity

lyrical (SYN) expressive, inspired, poetic, emotional, effusive (ANT) unenthusiastic

M

macabre (SYN) dreadful, grim, morbid, ghastly, gruesome

machination (SYN) plot, scheme, device, craft, stratagem

machine (SYN) appliance, tool, contraption, system, structure

machinery (SYN) equipment, instruments, gear, hardware, technology, workings

mad (SYN) crazy, unstable, raving, furious, livid, frenetic, foolish, wild (ANT) sane, calm, pleased, indifferent

maelstrom (SYN) whirlpool, vortex, chaos, confusion, turmoil

maestro (SYN) master, genius, virtuoso, expert

magazine (SYN) periodical, journal, arsenal, store

magic (SYN) illusion, sorcery, conjuring, charm, fascination magical (SYN) miraculous, bewitching, entrancing, spellbinding, astounding (ANT) predictable, boring, ordinary, dull

magician (SYN) illusionist, sorcerer, wizard, conjurer, prestidigitator

magistrate (SYN) judge, justice

magnanimous (SYN) generous, charitable, unselfish, honorable, kind, bountiful (ANT) selfish, stingy, cruel

magnate (SYN) mogul, tycoon, baron, chief, giant

magnetic (SYN) irresistible, hypnotic, charismatic, seductive, captivating (ANT) repellent, repulsive, unattractive

magnificence (SYN) majesty, splendor, brilliance, glory, opulence

magnificent (SYN) impressive, sublime, superb, breathtaking, dazzling (ANT) uninspiring, modest, common, ordinary

magnify (SYN) expand, amplify, enlarge, boost, exaggerate (ANT) minimize, decrease, reduce, understate, diminish

magnitude (SYN) significance, importance, weight, extent, volume (ANT) insignificance

maid (SYN) girl, maiden, servant

mail (SYN) letters, correspondence, post, send, dispatch

maim (SYN) injure, disable, wound, disfigure, incapacitate

main (SYN) primary, foremost, central, leading, dominant, fundamental (ANT) minor, secondary, subordinate, subsidiary

mainstay (SYN) pillar, anchor, prop, support

mainstream (SYN) common, conventional, prevailing, established (ANT) unorthodox, revolutionary

maintain (SYN) continue, sustain, assert, insist, preserve, look after (ANT) discard, reject, abandon

maintenance (SYN) upkeep, repairs, conservation, nurture, continuation (ANT) neglect

majestic (SYN) regal, stately, grandiose, dignified, magnificent (ANT) common, ordinary, humble, modest

major (SYN) supreme, main, crucial, significant, considerable, serious (ANT) minor, trivial, inconsequential

majority (SYN) most, larger part, lion's share (ANT) minority

make (SYN) construct, produce, prepare, force, coerce, acquire, earn, designate, appoint (ANT) destroy, demolish, lose

malady (SYN) sickness, affliction, ailment, disorder, complaint

malaise (SYN) unease, anxiety, disquiet, melancholy

male (SYN) masculine, manly, macho, virile (ANT) female, feminine

malevolent (SYN) hostile, malicious, spiteful, vindictive, mean (ANT) kind, tolerant, benevolent

malfunction (SYN) fail, breakdown, defect, glitch

malice (SYN) animosity, hatred, bitterness, ill will, rancor (ANT) generosity, kindness, sympathy

malign (SYN) slander, disparage, denigrate, vilify, discredit (ANT) compliment, celebrate, extol

malignant (SYN) harmful, destructive, dangerous, cancerous, deadly (ANT) benign, harmless

malleable (SYN) soft, workable, manageable, compliant, flexible (ANT) stiff, resolute, inflexible, unyielding

malnutrition (SYN) undernourishment, starvation

mammoth (SYN) huge, colossal, immense, gigantic, enormous (ANT) tiny, small, diminutive, little

man (SYN) human, person, male, humanity, staff, occupy

manage (SYN) run, direct, command, accomplish, cope, survive (ANT) mismanage, fail

manageable (SYN) docile, easy, submissive, amenable (ANT) unmanageable, difficult

management (SYN) administration, command, guidance, control, supervision

manager (SYN) director, supervisor, administrator, principal, head

mandate (SYN) command, decree, edict, order, directive (ANT) suggestion, request

mandatory (SYN) required, obligatory, necessary, requisite (ANT) optional

maneuver (SYN) scheme, ruse, strategy, movement, tactic, steer, navigate

mangle (SYN) ruin, crush, distort, wound, injure

maniac (SYN) lunatic, fanatic, psycho, fan, enthusiast

manifest (SYN) obvious, evident, exhibit, expose, reveal (ANT) secret, concealed, hidden, hide

manifesto (SYN) declaration, statement, pronouncement

manifold (SYN) numerous, diverse, varied, copious, assorted

manipulate (SYN) handle, use, influence, control, exploit

mankind (SYN) humanity, people, human race

manner (SYN) custom, method, conduct, behavior

manners (SYN) etiquette, propriety, civility, formalities

mannerism (SYN) habit, trait, quirk, idiosyncrasy, characteristic

manor (SYN) estate, house, mansion

mansion (SYN) manor, residence, stately home

manual (SYN) physical, hand-operated, guide, instructions

manufacture (SYN) assemble, build, invent, concoct, production

manure (SYN) dung, droppings, compost, fertilizer

manuscript (SYN) document, writing, composition

many (SYN) several, numerous, countless, plenty, scores (ANT) few, scarce

map (SYN) chart, plot, plan, atlas

mar (SYN) damage, spoil, tarnish, taint, wreck

marauder (SYN) bandit, raider, outlaw, invader

march (SYN) walk, parade, stride, progress, advancement (ANT) stay, retreat

margin (SYN) edge, border, perimeter, verge, leeway, allowance (ANT) interior, center

marginal (SYN) borderline, doubtful, slight, minimal, insignificant (ANT) considerable

marine (SYN) nautical, seafaring, maritime

maritime (SYN) nautical, naval, oceanic, coastal, seaside

mark (SYN) imprint, spot, stain, symbol, indicate, observe, grade, characteristic

market (SYN) fair, mart, sell, promote, advertise

maroon (SYN) strand, desert, abandon, leave, forsake

marriage (SYN) wedding, nuptials, match, union, fusion (ANT) divorce, separation

marry (SYN) web, unite, join, link, merge, ally, unify, blend (ANT) divorce, separate

marsh (SYN) swamp, bog, quagmire, mire, fen

marshal (SYN) escort, guide, usher, arrange, position

martial (SYN) military, belligerent, warlike, combative (ANT) peaceful, submissive

marvel (SYN) wonder, gape, sensation, prodigy, phenomenon (ANT) bore

marvelous (SYN) amazing, astonishing, spectacular, extraordinary, splendid (ANT) common, awful, normal, insignificant

masculine (SYN) manly, male, vile, robust (ANT) feminine, girly, effeminate

mash (SYN) squish, grind, crush, pulverize

mask (SYN) disguise, veil, camouflage, cloak, conceal, screen (ANT) reveal, uncover, disclose

masquerade (SYN) masked ball, pretense, disguise, pose, impersonate

mass (SYN) chunk, block, heap, bunch, magnitude, widespread, gather

massacre (SYN) slaughter, carnage, murder, extermination, holocaust, execute, kill

massage (SYN) rubdown, knead, caress, work

massive (SYN) huge, hefty, vast, mighty, mountainous (ANT) small, minute, tiny, delicate

master (SYN) ruler, lord, expert, guru, teacher, grasp, triumph (ANT) servant, pupil, disciple

mastermind (SYN) plan, devise, architect, director, genius

masterpiece (SYN) accomplishment, jewel, classic, magnum opus

mastery (SYN) skill, expertise, proficiency, command, control

match (SYN) game, contest, equal, rival, pairing, correspond

mate (SYN) partner, spouse, breed, couple, companion, friend (ANT) separate, stranger, enemy

material (SYN) substance, matter, data, information, concrete, tangible, vital, meaningful, relevant, cloth (ANT) spiritual, intangible, irrelevant

materialize (SYN) appear, occur, emerge, happen, realize (ANT) vanish, disappear

maternal (SYN) motherly, nurturing, caring

maternity (SYN) motherhood, pregnancy

matrimony (SYN) marriage, wedlock

matter (SYN) substance, material, situation, subject, count, be relevant

mature (SYN) adult, experienced, ripe, develop, age, grow up (ANT) immature, young, juvenile, inexperienced

maturity (SYN) growth, adulthood, wisdom, responsibility, sense (ANT) immaturity

maudlin (SYN) tearful, sentimental, weepy, overemotional (ANT) stoic

maul (SYN) tear, mangle, claw, abuse, man-handle, attack

maverick (SYN) rebel, individualist, radical, dissenter, non-conformist

maxim (SYN) saying, proverb, rule, adage, tenet, teaching

maximum (SYN) greatest, utmost, supreme, top, limit (ANT) minimum, lowest, least, smallest

maybe (SYN) possibly, perhaps, perchance (ANT) certainly, definitely

mayhem (SYN) chaos, disorder, havoc, anarchy, turmoil, bedlam (ANT) peace, tranquility maze (SYN) labyrinth, tangle, confusion, web, network

meadow (SYN) field, pasture, grassland

meager (SYN) measly, scant, inadequate, slight, paltry, insubstantial (ANT) abundant, sufficient, lavish

meal (SYN) feast, spread, breakfast, lunch, dinner

mean (SYN) signify, indicate, intend, plan, aim, stingy, callous, malevolent, middle, average (ANT) generous, kind, extreme

meander (SYN) wander, wind, snake, ramble, curve, twist

meaning (SYN) message, gist, significance, implication, definition, interpretation

means (SYN) money, resources, wealth, method, medium

meanwhile (SYN) for now, at the same time, simultaneously, concurrently

measure (SYN) volume, standard, rule, gauge, estimate, ruler, scale

measured (SYN) steady, regular, rhythmic, deliberate, careful

measurement (SYN) calculation, evaluation, assessment, proportion, dimension

meat (SYN) flesh, food

mechanic (SYN) repairman

mechanical (SYN) automated, impersonal, routine, instinctive (ANT) manual, thoughtful

mechanism (SYN) machine, device, apparatus, system, procedure, process

medal (SYN) award, badge, ribbon, decoration, prize

meddle (SYN) interfere, intrude, tamper, pry, butt in

median (SYN) middle, center, mid-point, central, half-way

mediate (SYN) referee, arbitrate, reconcile, moderate, settle, resolve

medical (SYN) healing, restorative, curative, therapeutic

medicinal (SYN) curative, therapeutic, healing

medicine (SYN) remedy, cure, medication, drug, treatment, prescription

mediocre (SYN) inferior, ordinary, average, unexceptional, forgettable (ANT) remarkable, distinguished, inspired, excellent

meditate (SYN) think, reflect, consider, muse, deliberate, brood, ponder

meditation (SYN) reflection, study, rumination, contemplation, thought

medium (SYN) middle, intermediate, compromise, vehicle, channel, environment (ANT) extreme medley (SYN) mixture, assortment, mishmash, jumble

meek (SYN) humble, timid, mild, submissive, docile (ANT) bold, assertive, arrogant

meet (SYN) encounter, gather, intersect, join, satisfy (ANT) avoid

meeting (SYN) introduction, assembly, convention, consultation, appointment, crossing, union

melancholy (SYN) gloomy, sad, sorrow, depression, blues (ANT) happy, gleeful, joyful, high spirits, gladness

mellow (SYN) soften, mature, relaxed, easy-going, good-natured, smooth (ANT) immature, irritable, harsh

melodramatic (SYN) sensational, overemotional, theatrical, stagy (ANT) restrained, straightforward, subdued

melody (SYN) tune, music, song, harmony, refrain

melt (SYN) thaw, liquefy, soften, relax, fade, vanish (ANT) freeze, solidify, grow

member (SYN) limb, extremity, appendage, subscriber, associate

membership (SYN) participation, enrollment, belonging, members, fellows

memento (SYN) keepsake, reminder, souvenir, token, trophy

memoir (SYN) autobiography, recollections, memories, life story, chronicle

memorable (SYN) noteworthy, unforgettable, significant, haunting, indelible (ANT) forgettable, common, ordinary, insignificant

memorandum (SYN) memo, note, reminder, message, communication

memorial (SYN) monument, remembrance, record, tribute, shrine, commemorative

memorize (SYN) learn, remember, retain (ANT) forget

memory (SYN) remembrance, recollection, retention, honor, respect

menace (SYN) threat, hazard, nuisance, pest, bully, frighten (ANT) safety, security, protect, guard

menagerie (SYN) collection, exhibition

mend (SYN) repair, fix, restore, improve, heal, recover (ANT) damage, injure, hurt, break

menial (SYN) unskilled, dull, routine, low, boring

mental (SYN) intellectual, cerebral, psychological, cognitive, rational (ANT) physical

mentality (SYN) outlook, attitude, disposition, state of mind, way of thinking

mentally (SYN) inwardly, intellectually, psychologically (ANT) physically mention (SYN) reference, allusion, refer to, point out, acknowledgement (ANT) forget, hide

mentor (SYN) instructor, advisor, guide, teacher, coach, consultant (ANT) student, pupil, follower

menu (SYN) list, bill of fare

mercenary (SYN) greedy, sordid, corrupt (ANT) generous, giving

merchandise (SYN) goods, products, wares, commodities, promote, sell

merchant (SYN) vendor, supplier, broker, salesman, dealer, distributor

merciful (SYN) lenient, forgiving, compassionate, humane, sparing, benevolent (ANT) merciless, cruel, savage, tyrannical

merciless (SYN) ruthless, cruel, heartless, barbarous, unsympathetic, remorseless (ANT) kind, merciful, gracious, tender-hearted

mercy (SYN) clemency, pity, charity, tolerance, forgiveness, magnanimity (ANT) cruelty, unkindness, intolerance

mere (SYN) simple, nothing more than, pure, sheer

merely (SYN) only, simply, just, solely, purely

merge (SYN) combine, fuse, join, consolidate, blend, integrate (ANT) separate, divide, sever

merit (SYN) worth, value, quality, deserve, warrant (ANT) fault, weakness

merry (SYN) cheerful, jolly, festive, lively, carefree (ANT) unhappy, mournful, miserable, low, glum

mesh (SYN) screen, netting, knit, connect, interlock, harmonize

mesmerize (SYN) captivate, entrance, enthrall, fascinate, hypnotize (ANT) bore

mess (SYN) clutter, disorder, dilemma, plight, dirty, pollute, interfere (ANT) order, organization, clean

message (SYN) communication, tidings, word, meaning, theme, idea, signal

messenger (SYN) herald, courier, envoy, carrier, runner, go-between

messy (SYN) untidy, cluttered, disheveled, sloppy, complex, unpleasant (ANT) clean, ordered, tidy

metamorphosis (SYN) change, transformation, alteration, conversion, mutation (ANT) stability, constancy

metaphor (SYN) figure of speech, analogy, symbol, image, comparison, allegory

method (SYN) style, manner, technique, approach, pattern, logic (ANT) disorder, confusion,

methodical (SYN) deliberate, precise, orderly, structured, systematic, efficient (ANT) loose, informal, haphazard

meticulous (SYN) thorough, painstaking, exacting, careful, detailed, conscientious (ANT) careless, casual

metropolis (SYN) major city, urban area

mettle (SYN) courage, nerve, valor, vigor, character, prowess (ANT) fear, cowardice

microcosm (SYN) world in miniature

microscopic (SYN) tiny, miniscule, infinitesimal, imperceptible, small (ANT) huge, giant, enormous, gargantuan

middle (SYN) central, halfway, average, intermediate, core, midst (ANT) edge, extreme, border, periphery

midget (SYN) little person, dwarf, pygmy (ANT) giant

midst (SYN) heart, thick, middle

might (SYN) power, strength, force, brawn, vigor, authority (ANT) weakness, feebleness

mighty (SYN) strong, powerful, robust, hefty, great (ANT) feeble, weak, delicate, placid

migrant (SYN) wanderer, itinerant, nomad, drifter, transient, mobile (ANT) fixed, stable, settled

migrate (SYN) move, travel, journey, relocate, roam

migration (SYN) travel, movement, emigration, voyage, trek

mild (SYN) gentle, docile, light, vague, bland, moderate, tranquil (ANT) harsh, rigid, strong, severe

milieu (SYN) setting, surroundings, environment, scene, background

milestone (SYN) achievement, turning point, significant event

militant (SYN) aggressive, combatant, radical, extremist, activist

military (SYN) army, defense, militia, martial, warlike (ANT) civilian

milk (SYN) pump, squeeze, exploit, extort, extract

mill (SYN) factory, plant, grind, crush, crowd

mime (SYN) gesture, simulate, act out

mimic (SYN) copy, imitate, impersonate, parody, ape

mimicry (SYN) imitation, mockery, simulation, impersonation, caricature (ANT) original

mince (SYN) grind, chop, soften, moderate, restrain

mind (SYN) intellect, reason, intentions, inclination, observe, heed, guard, watch (ANT) body, matter, neglect

mine (SYN) deposit, shaft, source, stock, treasury, excavate, unearth mingle (SYN) mix, merge socialize, hobnob, circulate (ANT) separate, sort

miniature (SYN) small, little, minute, scaled-down, diminutive (ANT) giant, massive, full-scale

minimize (SYN) reduce, lessen, decrease, belittle, downplay (ANT) maximize, exaggerate

minimum (SYN) lowest, least, smallest, slightest (ANT) maximum, most

minister (SYN) cleric, pastor, priest, tend, help, nurse

ministry (SYN) department, office, bureau, the church, service

minor (SYN) adolescent, juvenile, slight, trivial, insignificant, obscure (ANT) adult, major, important

minority (SYN) smaller part, less than half (ANT) majority

mint (SYN) coin, cast, stamp, produce

minute (SYN) moment, instant, jiffy, little, small, precise, exact, meticulous (ANT) huge

minutiae (SYN) details, particulars, trivia, fine points

miracle (SYN) marvel, wonder, sensation, phenomenon

miraculous (SYN) incredible, astonishing, unaccountable, extraordinary, spectacular (ANT) common, everyday, ordinary, believable

mirage (SYN) illusion, hallucination, phantom

mire (SYN) swamp, marsh, bog, plunge, involve, entangle

mirror (SYN) looking glass, reflector, reflect, emulate, match, echo (ANT) invent, originate

mirth (SYN) joy, merriment, laughter, revelry, fun (ANT) gloom, seriousness, dejection

misapprehend (ANT) misconstrue, mistake, misread, misinterpret

misbehave (SYN) act up, get into mischief, disobey (ANT) behave, obey

miscellaneous (SYN) random, assorted, varied, motley, diverse (ANT) similar, homogeneous

mischief (SYN) trouble, tomfoolery, naughtiness, disobedience, harm, damage

mischievous (SYN) naughty, playful, roguish, malicious, wicked

misconception (SYN) error, misunderstanding, fallacy, misapprehension

misconduct (SYN) wrongdoing, impropriety, misstep, misdeed

misconstrue (SYN) misunderstand, mistake, misinterpret, misread (ANT) comprehend, grasp, understand

miscreant (SYN) criminal, scoundrel, villain, evildoer

misdemeanor (SYN) offense, misdeed,
transgression, crime

miser (SYN) cheapskate, tightwad,
penny-pincher (ANT) spendthrift,
philanthropist

miserable (SYN) forlorn, sorrowful,
unhappy, wretched, squalid, bleak,
cheerless (ANT) happy, lighthearted,
joyful, lovely

misery (SYN) suffering, anguish,
despair, affliction, torment, woe
(ANT) ecstasy, rapture, contentment,
pleasure

misfortune (SYN) adversity, bad luck,
difficulty, trouble, disaster (ANT)
fortune, prosperity, success

misgiving (SYN) unease, worry,
suspicion, trepidation, distrust,
apprehension (ANT) confidence,
trust

misguided (SYN) unwise, ill-considered,
imprudent, unsound, deluded (ANT)
wise, sound, prudent

mishap (SYN) accident, disaster,
calamity

misinterpret (SYN) misunderstand,
distort, misconceive, confuse,
misjudge

misjudge (SYN) miscalculate,
overestimate, underestimate, err

mislead (SYN) fool, deceive, delude, lie
to, misinform, dupe (ANT) lead,
guide, advise

misleading (SYN) ambiguous,
deceptive, false, confusing,

disingenuous (ANT) honest,
straightforward, clear

misplace (SYN) lose, mislay, displace
(ANT) discover, find, locate

miss (SYN) omit, skip, avoid, overlook,
mistake, error, blunder, yearn for,
crave (ANT) catch, get, have,
succeed

missile (SYN) rocket, weapon, projectile

missing (SYN) gone, absent, astray,
unaccounted for, lost (ANT) present

mission (SYN) errand, duty, task,
activity, project, purpose

missionary (SYN) evangelist, apostle,
proselytizer

missive (SYN) letter, note, message,
communication, dispatch,
memorandum

mist (SYN) fog, cloud, spray, haze,
vapor

mistake (SYN) error, fault, slip, flaw,
oversight, misunderstand, confuse
with (ANT) fact, accuracy

mistreat (SYN) harm, abuse, maltreat,
misuse, wrong

mistress (SYN) women in charge,
girlfriend, paramour, concubine

mistrust (SYN) doubt, suspect, wariness,
misgiving, uncertainty (ANT)
assurance, confidence, trust, believe

misty (SYN) foggy, murky, dim,
indistinct, obscure (ANT) clear

184

misunderstand (SYN) misinterpret, misjudge, misapprehend, misconceive, be mistaken (ANT) understand, comprehend

misuse (SYN) waste, squandering, abuse, exploit, manipulate (ANT) respect, employ

mitigate (SYN) ease, lighten, lessen, temper, diminish (ANT) strengthen, increase, exacerbate

mix (SYN) combine, fuse, mingle, socialize, blend, compound, stir (ANT) separate, sort, divide, segregate

mixture (SYN) medley, variety, assortment, blend, jumble, brew, concoction

moan (SYN) groan, whine, lament, sob, complain, grumble, bellyache

mob (SYN) crowd, pack, horde, gang, surround, swarm, besiege

mobile (SYN) movable, portable, transportable, free, itinerant (ANT) immobile, fixed, stationary

mobilize (SYN) ready, rally, activate, prepare, organize, awaken, stir

mock (SYN) taunt, ridicule, mimic, deride, false, pretended, imitation (ANT) honor, applaud, genuine

mode (SYN) method, style, technique, fashion, craze, vogue

model (SYN) replica, imitation, archetype, standard, form, mold, display, sport

moderation (SYN) restraint, temperance, measure (ANT) extravagance, extreme

modern (SYN) contemporary, fresh, current, up-to-date, present, chic (ANT) dated, obsolete, old-fashioned, past, primitive

modest (SYN) humble, bashful, ordinary, unexceptional, simple (ANT) conceited, grand, excessive, pretentious,

modesty (SYN) reserve, timidity, humility, decency, decorum (ANT) arrogance, ego, vanity, pride, indecency

modicum (SYN) little, shred, touch, drop, fragment

modification (SYN) revision, change, alteration, adjustment, refinement

modify (SYN) adapt, convert, amend, alter, revise, transform

modulate (SYN) tune, adjust, balance, regulate

mogul (SYN) tycoon, magnate

moist (SYN) damp, soggy, wet, dewy, clammy, humid, soaked, dank (ANT) dry, arid, parched

moisture (SYN) wetness, liquid, dew

mold (SYN) fungus, mildew, cast, shape, construct, influence, control, character, type

molest (SYN) abuse, harm, maltreat, annoy, pester, disturb

molt (SYN) shed

molten (SYN) heated, melted

moment (SYN) instant, second, flash, time, juncture

momentary (SYN) brief, temporary, fleeting, short-lived, transitory (ANT) lengthy, lasting, permanent, unchanging, prolonged

momentous (SYN) important, pivotal, significant, historic, consequential (ANT) trivial, insignificant, uneventful

momentum (SYN) power, drive, force, speed, velocity, strength

monarch (SYN) ruler, sovereign, king, queen

monarchy (SYN) kingdom, realm, autocracy, sovereignty

monetary (SYN) financial, fiscal, economic, capital

money (SYN) currency, cash, legal tender, wealth, funds

monitor (SYN) supervisor, watchdog, check, observe, survey, display, screen (ANT) ignore, disregard, neglect

monk (SYN) friar, brother

monkey (SYN) primate, simian

monologue (SYN) speech, lecture, sermon, soliloquy (ANT) dialogue, conversation

monopolize (SYN) dominate, control (ANT) share

monopoly (SYN) control, corner, exclusive rights

monotonous (SYN) boring, tedious, unchanging, repetitive, mind-numbing (ANT) exciting, varied

monster (SYN) beast, freak, savage, giant, enormous, tremendous

monstrous (SYN) unnatural, frightening, outrageous, shocking, vile, massive (ANT) normal, small, expected

monument (SYN) memorial, shrine, remembrance, tribute, statue

monumental (SYN) huge, colossal, mighty, grand, defining, epic (ANT) small, tiny, insignificant

mood (SYN) temper, humor, disposition, sate of mind, atmosphere, ambiance

moon (SYN) satellite, mope, languish, daydream

moot (SYN) undecided, arguable, doubtful, debatable, unresolved (ANT) settled, indisputable, decided

mop (SYN) sponge, swab, clean, wipe, tangle, mass

moral (SYN) ethical, virtuous, principled, lesson, message (ANT) immoral, evil, indecent, dishonest

morale (SYN) confidence, heart, self-esteem, motivation

morality (SYN) integrity, goodness, standards, principles, ethics morally (SYN) righteously, ethically, virtuously, honestly (ANT) immorally, unethically, unjustly

moratorium (SYN) suspension, halt, freeze, delay

morbid (SYN) gruesome, macabre, grim, somber, sick, horrid

more (SYN) extra, additional, supplementary, further (ANT) less, fewer

mores (SYN) standards, conventions, traditions, expectations

morgue (SYN) mortuary

morning (SYN) dawn, a.m., daybreak (ANT) evening

morose (SYN) sullen, dour, moody, surly, ill-tempered (ANT) cheery, happy, joyful, optimistic

morsel (SYN) piece, crumb, scrap, bit, bite

mortal (SYN) fatal, lethal, terminal, human, temporal (ANT) immortal, eternal, everlasting

mortality (SYN) humanity, transience, death (ANT) immortality

mortify (SYN) humiliate, embarrass, crush, shame, abase (ANT) praise, commend, applaud

mortuary (SYN) morgue, funeral parlor

mother (SYN) parent, mom, nurture, tend, native, natural (ANT) neglect

motif (SYN) theme, idea, design, shape, ornament

motion (SYN) movement, mobility, gesture, signal, proposal, suggestion (ANT) immobility, stillness, inaction

motionless (SYN) still, stationary, immobile, unmoving, frozen (ANT) moving, traveling

motivate (SYN) inspire, induce, prompt, stimulate, encourage (ANT) discourage, halt

motivation (SYN) reason, incentive, stimulus, inducement

motive (SYN) purpose, incitement, grounds, cause

mottled (SYN) blotchy, spotted, dappled, speckled (ANT) uniform, solid

motto (SYN) saying, adage, slogan, maxim, catchphrase

mound (SYN) heap, pile, stack, hill, dune, knoll

mount (SYN) climb, ascend, build, intensify, frame, support, prepare (ANT) descend, decline

mountain (SYN) peak, pile, heap, abundance, stack

mourn (SYN) grieve, weep, lament, bemoan, regret (ANT) celebrate

mourning (SYN) woe, grieving, weeping, sorrowing, lamentation (ANT) celebration mouth (SYN) opening, door, entrance, gateway

move (SYN) transfer, relocate, proceed, stir, provoke, affect, influence, recommend, urge, action, ploy (ANT) stay, remain

movement (SYN) motion, stirring, transportation, shifting, campaign, crusade (ANT) stillness

movie (SYN) film, feature, motion picture

moving (SYN) touching, emotional, poignant, mobile, running (ANT) stationary, fixed

mow (SYN) trim, crop, cut, shear, clip

much (SYN) ample, considerable, substantial, plenty, greatly, considerably (ANT) little, slightly

mud (SYN) dirt, sludge, earth, soil

muddy (SYN) dirty, grimy, soiled, swampy, murky, cloudy (ANT) clean, clear

muffle (SYN) stifle, soften, suppress, swaddle, shroud (ANT) amplify

mug (SYN) cup, stein, rob, assault, face, visage

muggy (SYN) humid, sticky, moist, stuffy, sultry (ANT) dry

mull (SYN) ponder, weigh, contemplate, think over, deliberate

multiple (SYN) numerous, several, various, manifold (ANT) single

multiply (SYN) increase, expand, accumulate, snowball, reproduce (ANT) decrease

multitude (SYN) mass, myriad, throng, host, crowd

munch (SYN) chew, chomp, crunch

mundane (SYN) routine, ordinary, tedious, dull, earthly, secular (ANT) exceptional, extraordinary, heavenly, celestial

municipal (SYN) civic, public, urban, metropolitan (ANT) private, rural

municipality (SYN) town, city, district, borough

murder (SYN) homicide, killing, slay, assassinate, slaughter, execute (ANT) save, rescue

murderer (SYN) killer, butcher, assassin, hit-man

murky (SYN) clouded, dull, gloomy, dark, dismal, dirty (ANT) clear

murmur (SYN) mumble, whisper, mutter, drone, buzzing, humming

muscle (SYN) tendon, sinew, strength, might, power

muse (SYN) brood, reflect, consider, ruminate, meditate, dream, inspiration, goddess

musical (SYN) melodious, lyrical, tuneful, harmonious (ANT) jarring, discordant must (SYN) need to, obligated to, imperative, essential, requisite, necessity

mutable (SYN) inconsistent, changeable, volatile, variable, fickle (ANT) immutable, stable, inalterable

mutation (SYN) alteration, transformation, evolution, change, modification

mute (SYN) silence, silent, dumb, voiceless, mum, speechless (ANT) vocal, eloquent, talkative

mutilate (SYN) maim, mangle, disfigure, injure, desecrate (ANT) mend, heal, repair

mutinous (SYN) unruly, riotous, rebellious, disobedient, subversive

mutiny (SYN) revolt, rebellion, insurrection, uprising, rebel, revolt, strike

mutual (SYN) shared, joint, reciprocal, common, returned (ANT) individual, one-sided

muzzle (SYN) snout, gag, guard, suppress, restrain, stifle

myopic (SYN) nearsighted, shortsighted, narrow-minded

myriad (SYN) countless, innumerable, untold, incalculable, multitude (ANT) limited, few

mysterious (SYN) strange, puzzling, cryptic, bizarre, secret, evasive (ANT) distinct, straightforward, open, revealing

mystery (SYN) riddle, enigma, conundrum, paradox, secrecy, uncertainty (ANT) revelation, solution, answer

mystical (SYN) otherworldly, supernatural, paranormal, spiritual, metaphysical, transcendental (ANT) explained, clear

mystify (SYN) stump, baffle, confound, perplex, bewilder

myth (SYN) legend, fable, tale, fantasy, superstition, misconception (ANT) history, fact

N

nadir (SYN) bottom, depths, lowest point, floor

nag (SYN) badger, irritate, hassle, annoy, pester, plague, hound, trouble

naive (SYN) innocent, unsuspicious, gullible, trusting, inexperienced (ANT) worldly, sophisticated, experienced

naked (SYN) bare, nude, exposed, stripped, undressed (ANT) clothed, covered, dressed

name (SYN) title, moniker, designation, call, christen, nominate, appoint

namely (SYN) specifically, that is to say, in other words

nap (SYN) rest, sleep, doze, siesta, weave, pile, grain

napkin (SYN) cloth, wipe, linen

narcotic (SYN) drug, sedative,
painkiller, tranquilizer, anesthetic

narrate (SYN) recount, detail, recite, tell,
report, relate

narrative (SYN) story, tale, account,
chronicle

narrator (SYN) storyteller, author,
writer, presenter, commentator
(ANT) listener, audience

narrow (SYN) slender, thin, limited,
tight, tighten, constrict, intolerant,
prejudiced (ANT) wide, broad,
expansive, widen, open-minded,
liberal

nasty (SYN) unpleasant, vile, repulsive,
hurtful, malicious, serious (ANT)
delightful, pleasant, kind, slight

nation (SYN) country, society, people,
land, tribe

national (SYN) nationwide, public,
citizen, resident (ANT) local,
international

nationality (SYN) race, nation

native (SYN) local, indigenous, innate,
intrinsic, resident, local (ANT)
foreign, alien, imported, foreigner,
immigrant

natural (SYN) normal, typical,
unaffected, real, inherent (ANT)
artificial, man-made, unusual,
strange

naturally (SYN) of course, certainly,
genuinely, spontaneously, innately

nature (SYN) earth, environment,
constitution, character, sort, type

naughty (SYN) bad, wicked,
mischievous, lewd, improper (ANT)
obedient, behaved, proper,
appropriate

nausea (SYN) queasiness, sickness,
vomiting, disgust

nauseate (SYN) sicken, repulse, disgust,
offend, turn one's stomach

nautical (SYN) marine, naval, maritime,
sailing, boating

naval (SYN) nautical, seafaring,
maritime

navigate (SYN) sail, pilot, steer, guide,
direct

navigation (SYN) sailing, voyaging

navigator (SYN) pilot, mariner

navy (SYN) armada, fleet, flotilla

near (SYN) close, adjacent, neighboring,
approaching, looming, imminent
(ANT) far, remote, distant

nearby (SYN) adjacent, convenient,
close, accessible, handy (ANT)
faraway, distant

nearly (SYN) almost, practically,
virtually, just about, for all intents
and purposes, not quite

neat (SYN) tidy, orderly, clean, skillful,
clever (ANT) cluttered, disorderly,
unkempt

necessary (SYN) vital, imperative, mandatory, requisite, inevitable (ANT) unnecessary, needless

necessitate (SYN) demand, require, call for, impel, oblige

necessity (SYN) fundamental, requirement, prerequisite, need, obligation (ANT) elective

need (SYN) require, lack, poverty, destitution, requirement, necessity, emergency, crisis (ANT) possess, supply, wealth

needle (SYN) taunt, provoke, rile, annoy, goad, pester

needy (SYN) poor, destitute, underprivileged, disadvantaged, penniless (ANT) affluent, wealthy, well-off

nefarious (SYN) wicked, evil, criminal, villainous, sinister, corrupt (ANT) virtuous, noble

negate (SYN) cancel, reverse, invalidate, deny, rebut (ANT) approve, accept, affirm

negative (SYN) opposing, dissenting, contradictory, pessimistic, unenthusiastic (ANT) positive, constructive, optimistic, helpful

neglect (SYN) disregard, forget, slight, omission, inattention, carelessness (ANT) watch, concern, care, cherish, heed, remember

negligence (SYN) indifference, laxity, disregard, dereliction (ANT) attention, care, concern

negligible (SYN) trivial, minor, insignificant, unimportant, minimal (ANT) important, major, significant

negotiate (SYN) deal, bargain, haggle, clear, surmount

neighborhood (SYN) community, region, district, area, vicinity

neighboring (SYN) nearby, adjacent, bordering, connecting, next (ANT) far off, remote, distant

nemesis (SYN) enemy, opponent, rival, undoing, ruin, downfall

nepotism (SYN) bias, partiality, favoritism, preferential treatment

nerve (SYN) bravery, pluck, boldness, audacity, impudence

nerves (SYN) stress, tension, worry, anxiety, butterflies

nervous (SYN) tense, edgy, uneasy, uptight, apprehensive (ANT) calm, relaxed, serene, confident

nest (SYN) refuge, retreat, den

nestle (SYN) snuggle, huddle, cuddle, burrow, nuzzle

net (SYN) mesh, web, catch, ensnare, final, gain, earn, make (ANT) gross

nettle (SYN) vex, harass, irritate, sting

neurotic (SYN) unstable, disturbed, obsessive, overanxious, paranoid irrational (ANT) calm, stable

neuter (SYN) fix, castrate, emasculate, spay

neutral (SYN) unbiased, impartial, uninvolved, dull, indistinct, harmless (ANT) partisan, interested, aligned, colorful, provocative

neutralize (SYN) counteract, undo, nullify, counterbalance

never (SYN) at no time, under no circumstances (ANT) always

nevertheless (SYN) but, even so, still, yet, however, nonetheless

new (SYN) fresh, original, modern, recent, changed, improved, extra, additional (ANT) old, second-hand, out-dated, antique

news (SYN) information, intelligence, report, announcement, disclosure, gossip

newsworthy (SYN) important, notable, significant, remarkable, interesting

next (SYN) following, subsequent, closet, adjoining, later, afterwards (ANT) previous, before

nibble (SYN) bite, munch, peck, snack, morsel, taste

nice (SYN) kind, courteous, delightful, agreeable, friendly (ANT) mean, unpleasant, nasty

niche (SYN) nook, corner, position, function, calling

nick (SYN) chip, cut, notch, scratch

nickname (SYN) pet name, label, moniker, epithet

niggardly (SYN) stingy, miserly, mean, frugal, ungenerous (ANT) generous, giving

night (SYN) dark, darkness (ANT) day

nightmare (SYN) bad dream, torment, night terror, ordeal, trial

nil (SYN) nothing, zero, none, naught

nimble (SYN) agile, spry, deft, dexterous, shrewd, brilliant (ANT) clumsy, slow, dull

nirvana (SYN) paradise, bliss, peace, serenity

no (SYN) never, no way, refusal, negation (ANT) yes

nobility (SYN) aristocracy, elite, upper class, virtue, integrity

noble (SYN) titles, patrician, dignified, grand, lofty, worthy, lord (ANT) humble, ignoble, subservient, commoner

nobody (SYN) no one

nocturnal (SYN) nighttime, night (ANT) day, daytime

nod (SYN) indicate, acknowledge, doze, nap, signal, cue

noise (SYN) sound, racket, din, commotion, uproar (ANT) quiet, silence, calm

noisy (SYN) loud, blaring, thunderous, rowdy, boisterous (ANT) quiet, sedate nomad (SYN) wanderer, migrant, vagabond, drifter, itinerant

nominate (SYN) designate, appoint, select, propose, recommend

nomination (SYN) choice, suggestion, recommendation, proposal

nominee (SYN) runner, candidate, entrant

nonchalant (SYN) casual, indifferent, unconcerned, laid-back, relaxed, cool (ANT) enthusiastic

none (SYN) nothing, not any, nobody, zero (ANT) some

nonexistent (SYN) fictional, imaginary, unreal, mythical, fanciful (ANT) real

nonfiction (SYN) reality, true story

nonsense (SYN) rubbish, drivel, insanity, madness (ANT) sense, wisdom

nook (SYN) opening, alcove, retreat

noon (SYN) midday, twelve o'clock

normal (SYN) average, ordinary, regular, rational, well-adjusted (ANT) abnormal, unique, unusual, insane

normally (SYN) usually, generally, typically, conventionally, traditionally (ANT) unexpectedly

nose (SYN) beak, snout, ease forward, nudge, snoop, pry

nosegay (SYN) bouquet, posy

nostalgia (SYN) wistfulness, reminiscence, recollection, regret, sentimentality

nosy (SYN) curious, inquisitive, intrusive, meddlesome

notable (SYN) rare, outstanding, striking, impressive, prominent, superstar (ANT) unknown, insignificant

notation (SYN) signs, notes, symbols, script, code

notch (SYN) indentation, mark, nick, score, cut, indent

note (SYN) communication, message, reminder, symbol, observe, indicate, mention

nothing (SYN) void, nil, zero, naught, zilch (ANT) something

notice (SYN) perceive, detect, bulletin, announcement, notification, scrutiny (ANT) overlook, ignore

noticeable (SYN) obvious, evident, conspicuous, clear, apparent (ANT) unnoticeable, invisible, imperceptible

notification (SYN) statement, warning, announcement, declaration, notice

notify (SYN) inform, tell, alert, publish, advise

notion (SYN) idea, impression, thought, whim, inclination, hunch

notoriety (SYN) infamy, scandal, dishonor, disrepute

notorious (SYN) infamous, scandalous, shameful, arrant, disreputable

notwithstanding (SYN) despite, in spite of

nourish (SYN) tend, feed, sustain, cultivate, foster, encourage, enrich (ANT) deprive, deny

nourishment (SYN) food, sustenance, nutrition

novel (SYN) tale, story, fiction, narrative, new, innovative, fresh (ANT) traditional, conventional

novelty (SYN) originality, strangeness, creativity, unfamiliarity, gimmick, gadget, souvenir

novice (SYN) beginner, apprentice, amateur, pupil, rookie (ANT) expert, veteran

now (SYN) at present, at the moment, immediately, promptly, right away (ANT) later

noxious (SYN) harmful, unhealthy, poisonous, foul, destructive

nuance (SYN) subtlety, refinement

nucleus (SYN) center, core, heart, focus middle, crux

nude (SYN) naked, bare, undressed, disrobed (ANT) clothed, dressed, covered

nudge (SYN) push, elbow, touch, bump, shove, prompt, persuade

nugget (SYN) lump, chunk, hunk, piece

nuisance (SYN) problem, inconvenience, hassle, bother, burden, headache (ANT) blessing

nullify (SYN) cancel, negate, veto, invalidate

numb (SYN) unfeeling, deadened, frozen, insensitive, dull (ANT) feeling, sensitive

number (SYN) numeral, digit, quantity, amount, count, enumerate

numeral (SYN) number, integer, figure

numerous (SYN) many, plentiful, profuse, copious (ANT) few

nuptials (SYN) marriage, matrimony, wedding

nurse (SYN) treat, care for, feed, nurture, preserve, support

nursery (SYN) playroom, daycare, green house

nurture (SYN) develop, instruct, rear, strengthen, stimulate, fuel (ANT) slight, neglect, hinder

nutrition (SYN) food, nourishment, sustenance

nutritious (SYN) nourishing, healthy, wholesome, strengthening, beneficial (ANT) unhealthy

nymph (SYN) maiden, fairy, naiad, dryad

O

oaf (SYN) dolt, goon, moron

oath (SYN) pledge, bond, promise, vow, guarantee, curse, expletive

obedience (SYN) compliance, submissiveness, acquiescence, respect (ANT) disobedience, rebelliousness, insurgence, mutiny

obedient (SYN) respectful, docile, deferential, compliant, governable (ANT) rebellious, defiant, mischievous

obelisk (SYN) column, pillar, monument, monolith

obese (SYN) fat, portly, rotund, chubby, plump, corpulent (ANT) thin, slender, lean

obey (SYN) comply, conform, heed, observe, submit to (ANT) defy, ignore

obfuscate (SYN) confuse, perplex, cloud, obscure (ANT) clarify

object (SYN) thing, item, focus, intention, objective, disagree, oppose, argue (ANT) agree, accept, consent

objection (SYN) protest, opposition, doubt, complaint, disapproval (ANT) affirmation, concurrence

objective (SYN) goal, target, unbiased, fair, impartial (ANT) subjective, personal emotional

objurgate (SYN) rebuke, remonstrate, scold, admonish (ANT) commend, praise

obligation (SYN) duty, charge, liability, responsibility, commitment

obligatory (SYN) required, imperative, necessary, mandatory, compulsory (ANT) avoidable, optional

oblige (SYN) force, require, compel, accommodate, indulge, humor

oblique (SYN) angled, sloping, tilted, indirect, circuitous (ANT) straight, straightforward

obliterate (SYN) destroy, erase, annihilate, eradicate, delete (ANT) build, reconstruct

oblivion (SYN) neglect, disregard,

oblivious (SYN) unaware, unconscious, unmindful, forgetful (ANT) aware, cognizant, concerned, mindful

oblong (SYN) rectangular, oval

obnoxious (SYN) unpleasant, insufferable, offensive, displeasing (ANT) pleasant, enjoyable, agreeable

obscene (SYN) vulgar, indecent, lewd, shocking, scandalous (ANT) pure, honorable, clean, G-rated

obscure (SYN) confusing, vague, cryptic, unknown, remote, hide, conceal, complicate (ANT) clear, evident, famous, clarify, reveal

obscurity (SYN) shadows, darkness, haze, unimportance, insignificance (ANT) clarity, fame

obsequious (SYN) fawning, servile, submissive, ingratiating, sycophantic (ANT) proud, haughty, defiant

observance (SYN) compliance, honoring, notice

observation (SYN) scrutiny, study,
surveillance, comment, remark,
reflection

observe (SYN) notice, perceive, watch,
mention, comply, respect (ANT)
neglect, ignore

obsessed (SYN) haunted, preoccupied,
fixated, consumed, infatuated (ANT)
indifferent

obsession (SYN) complex, fixation,
passion, compulsion, neurosis

obsolete (SYN) out of date, old,
antiquated, defunct, extinct, archaic
(ANT) current, modern, new

obstacle (SYN) hurdle, hitch,
obstruction, impediment, difficulty
(ANT) help, aid, advantage

obstinate (SYN) stubborn, inflexible,
unyielding, willful, dogged (ANT)
compliant, flexible, bending,
obedient

obstruct (SYN) block, hinder, impede,
thwart, stop (ANT) assist, aid,
encourage, facilitate

obstruction (SYN) hindrance, difficulty,
barrier, restriction, congestion

obtain (SYN) acquire, achieve, earn,
gain, land (ANT) lose, forfeit

obtainable (SYN) available, attainable,
to be had, accessible, up for grabs

obtrusive (SYN) blatant, prominent,
obvious, noticeable (ANT)
unobtrusive, subtle

obtuse (SYN) slow, dense, thick,
uncomprehending (ANT) smart,
sharp, quick-witted

obvious (SYN) plain, evident,
perceptible, visible, unmistakable
(ANT) unclear, complex,
inconspicuous, indistinct

obviously (SYN) clearly, discernibly,
naturally, without a doubt (ANT)
perhaps, possibly

occasion (SYN) event, occurrence,
opportunity, reason, cause, prompt

occasionally (SYN) sometimes,
periodically, once in a while, on
occasion, now and again (ANT)
often

occult (SYN) supernatural, mystical,
mysterious, unearthly, magical

occupant (SYN) resident, inhabitant,
dweller, tenant

occupation (SYN) job, profession,
vocation, possession, invasion

occupy (SYN) engage, involve, inhabit,
seize, possess

occur (SYN) happen, develop, come
about, take place, spring to mind,
suggest itself

occurrence (SYN) instance, episode,
appearance, existence, prevalence

odd (SYN) strange, unusual,
unaccountable, quirky,
extraordinary, solitary, spare,
various, random (ANT) normal,
regular, ordinary, natural, even

odds (SYN) probability, likelihood, chances, luck, chance

odious (SYN) offensive, loathsome, detestable, repugnant, repulsive (ANT) attractive, pleasant, appealing, inviting, wonderful

odium (SYN) hatred, enmity, revulsion, antipathy, animosity (ANT) love, affection, attachment

odor (SYN) smell, scent, aroma, fragrance, stench

odorous (SYN) smelly, stinky, reeking, strong

odyssey (SYN) journey, voyage, quest, pilgrimage, trek, crusade

off (SYN) absent, away, wrong, erroneous, cancelled, postponed, remote, distant, (ANT) on, right, illuminated

offend (SYN) insult, upset, hurt, wound, outrage, provoke, affront (ANT) please, placate, praise

offended (SYN) hurt, stung, disgruntled, piqued (ANT) pleased

offense (SYN) crime, transgression, wrong, resentment, indignation (ANT) defense

offensive (SYN) disrespectful, derogatory, distasteful, objectionable, foul, aggressive, combative (ANT) complimentary, decent, defensive

offer (SYN) bid, present, submit, propose, proposal, suggestion,

volunteer (ANT) withdraw, deny, withhold, refuse

office (SYN) workplace, study, division, bureau, position, appointment

officer (SYN) agent, executive, representative, official

official (SYN) legitimate, certified, valid, authoritative, officer, functionary (ANT) unofficial, dubious, questionable, unauthorized

officiate (SYN) preside, conduct, serve, manage

offspring (SYN) child, descendent, heir, young, progeny

often (SYN) frequently, regularly, commonly, on many occasions, generally, repeatedly (ANT) seldom, infrequently, rarely

ogle (SYN) leer, stare

oil (SYN) grease, fat, lubricate

ointment (SYN) balm, cream, lotion, salve, emollient

old (SYN) aged, elderly, mature, antique, dated, former, previous (ANT) young, new, current, modern

omen (SYN) sign, warning, premonition, forewarning

ominous (SYN) threatening, sinister, foreboding, imminent, menacing (ANT) encouraging, promising

omission (SYN) exclusion, oversight, failure, deletion, negligence (ANT) inclusion, addition omit (SYN) forget, skip, exclude, disregard, overlook (ANT) include, introduce, insert, remember

omnipotent (SYN) supreme, almighty, unstoppable, all-powerful (ANT) weak, powerless

omnipresent (SYN) everywhere (ANT) nowhere, somewhere

omniscient (SYN) all-knowing, all-wise

once (SYN) formerly, previously, at one time (ANT) now

ongoing (SYN) continuing, in progress, continuous, under way, unfinished (ANT) finished, complete

one (SYN) single, solitary, (ANT) many, several

only (SYN) sole, lone, unique, barely, just, exclusively

onset (SYN) start, beginning, inception, opening, commencement, outbreak (ANT) end, finish

onslaught (SYN) attack, barrage, assault, charge

onus (SYN) burden, task, load, obligation, blame

onward (SYN) ahead, forward, forth, on (ANT) backward

ooze (SYN) seep, leak, drain, trickle, exude, emanate

opaque (SYN) cloudy, murky, impenetrable, dark (ANT) transparent

open (SYN) ajar, public, accessible, frank, straightforward, unlock, start, initiate (ANT) closed, shut, private, protected, insincere, suppressed, end, close

opening (SYN) gap, hole, door, opportunity, vacancy, launch, outset, initial (ANT) obstruction, closing, final

operate (SYN) work, perform, run, manage, control, function

operation (SYN) process, procedure, action, execution, working, running (ANT) inaction, ineffectiveness

operator (SYN) technician, handler, driver, pilot, operative

opinion (SYN) theory, sentiment, point of view, belief, judgment (ANT) fact

opponent (SYN) adversary, rival, competitor, challenger, enemy, critic (ANT) ally, supporter, comrade

opportune (SYN) timely, apt, convenient, favorable, suitable (ANT) inopportune, ill-timed, unfitting, inauspicious

opportunity (SYN) chance, opening, window, possibility, freedom

oppose (SYN) fight, counter, resist, contest, challenge (ANT) support, concur, approve

opposite (SYN) reverse, contradictory, conflicting, incompatible, different, facing, across from (ANT) identical, like, similar, same

opposition (SYN) disapproval, hostility, resistance, dissent, competition, rival (ANT) agreement, support, endorsement

oppress (SYN) burden, afflict, persecute, wrong, subdue (ANT) aid, relieve

oppression (SYN) persecution, injustice, cruelty, tyranny, ill-treatment (ANT) freedom

oppressive (SYN) merciless, despotic, severe, harsh, stifling, muggy

opt (SYN) choose, select, elect, prefer

optimal (SYN) favorable, desirable

optimistic (SYN) positive, hopeful, encouraged, promising, reassuring (ANT) pessimistic, despairing, negative, depressing, hopeless

option (SYN) choice, possibility, selection, alternative, recourse

optional (SYN) extra, elective, voluntary, discretionary (ANT) mandatory, compulsory, obligatory, required

opulence (SYN) wealth, luxury, riches, plenty, abundance (ANT) poverty, destitution, deprivation

opus (SYN) masterpiece, composition, work

oral (SYN) spoken, verbal, voiced, uttered (ANT) written, printed

orator (SYN) speaker, lecturer

oratory (SYN) rhetoric, eloquence, elocution

orbit (SYN) course, path, trajectory, circle, revolve around

orchestrate (SYN) arrange, coordinate, organize, set up

ordain (SYN) appoint, invest, demand, legislate, determine, designate

ordeal (SYN) hardship, trial, test, trauma, unpleasant experience

order (SYN) instruction, direction, requirement, sequence, structure, discipline, sort, family, society, charge, bid, request, instruct, arrange (ANT) allowance, disorder, chaos

ordinance (SYN) law, rule, decree, regulation, rite, ceremony

ordinarily (SYN) customarily, usually, generally, normally, as a rule (ANT) uncommonly, rarely, occasionally

ordinary (SYN) common, regular, typical, mundane, average (ANT) amazing, remarkable, unusual, exceptional

organic (SYN) natural, living, essential, pure, systematic, harmonious, coherent (ANT) inorganic, extraneous

organism (SYN) being, entity, creature, living thing

organization (SYN) format, arrangement, planning, efficiency, management, group, association (ANT) disorganization, spontaneity

organize (SYN) plan, run, coordinate, catalogue, institute, orchestrate orientation (SYN) direction, bearings, location, familiarization, acclimation, attitude, inclination

orifice (SYN) opening, hole, vent, aperture

origin (SYN) beginning, foundation, start, root, heritage, source, genesis (ANT) outcome, end, conclusion

original (SYN) initial, earliest, archetype, authentic, innovative, seminal, fresh, novel (ANT) unoriginal, derivative

originality (SYN) imagination, creativity, ingenuity, invention, novelty

originate (SYN) pioneer, introduce, create, arise, emerge (ANT) follow

ornament (SYN) decoration, adornment, bauble, trimming, embellish, festoon (ANT) simplicity

ornamental (SYN) decorative, showy, ornate, fancy (ANT) simple, austere

ornate (SYN) elaborate, florid, fancy, adorned, flashy, ostentatious (ANT) plain, unadorned

orthodox (SYN) conventional, traditional, established, sanctioned, strict (ANT) unorthodox, unacceptable, heretical, unconventional, liberal

oscillate (SYN) vary, waver, fluctuate, sway, change (ANT) adhere, decide, resolve

ostensible (SYN) apparent, seeming, displayed, professed

ostentatious (SYN) pretentious, flamboyant, showy, loud, pompous (ANT) humble, reserved, modest

ostracize (SYN) banish, exile, reject, shun, shut out (ANT) welcome, include, accept

other (SYN) additional, further, alternative, different, distinct

otherwise (SYN) differently, or else, if not

ought (SYN) should, must

ounce (SYN) grain, speck, trace, iota, shred, drop

oust (SYN) eject, topple, unseat, expel, overthrow, dislodge (ANT) install

out (SYN) gone, elsewhere, extinguished, finished, ended (ANT) in, present, on

outbreak (SYN) eruption, rash, burst, onset, beginning

outburst (SYN) explosion, blowup, fit, surge

outcast (SYN) exile, abandoned, forsaken, forlorn, friendless

outcome (SYN) result, conclusion, conclusion, end

outer (SYN) external, exterior, exposed, surface, outlying, remote (ANT) inner, internal

outfit (SYN) clothes, ensemble, enterprise, organization, unit, equip, furnish outgrowth (SYN) development

outing (SYN) expedition, trip, excursion, drive

outlet (SYN) release, vent, opening, shop, store

outline (SYN) profile, silhouette, summarize, plan, synopsis

outlive (SYN) survive, outlast

outlook (SYN) attitude, perspective, standpoint, prospect, forecast, prognosis

outrage (SYN) insult, indignity, fury, anger, offend, incense, affront

outrageous (SYN) shocking, unspeakable, atrocious, unreasonable, steep (ANT) appropriate, moderate

outside (SYN) outer, external, exterior, surface, marginal, faint (ANT) inside, inner, internal

outspoken (SYN) candid, direct, unreserved, blunt, frank (ANT) subtle, timid

outstanding (SYN) excellent, superior, impressive, unpaid, remaining, due (ANT) ordinary, common, average, usual, settled, paid

over (SYN) above, upon, beyond, in excess of , exceeding, finished, concluded, past (ANT) under, underneath

overall (SYN) in general, altogether, on the whole, inclusive, comprehensive (ANT) in particular, specifically

overcast (SYN) cloudy, gloomy, dismal, dark (ANT) clear, bright, sunny

overcome (SYN) beat, prevail, triumph, moved, overwhelmed (ANT) surrender, yield

overdue (SYN) late, tardy, delinquent, unpaid, owed (ANT) early, punctual, paid

overestimate (SYN) inflate

overflow (SYN) spill, run over, overabundance, surplus, extra, additional

overhaul (SYN) repair, restore, service, revamp, mend

overhead (SYN) above, aloft, overhanging, elevated, suspended, operating costs, expenses (ANT) below, surface, underground

overlap (SYN) coincide, cross

overlook (SYN) miss, disregard, forget, ignore, excuse, pardon, condone (ANT) note, observe

overseas (SYN) abroad

overseer (SYN) supervisor, boss, foreman

oversight (SYN) omission, mistake, blunder, lapse, failure

overt (SYN) obvious, conspicuous, open, blatant, noticeable (ANT) covert, concealed, disguised

overtake (SYN) catch, outdistance, exceed, eclipse, befall, overcome overthrow (SYN) defeat, conquer, unseat, vanquish, downfall, demise

overture (SYN) introduction, prelude, opening, invitation, proposition

overwhelm (SYN) crush, inundate, trounce, thrash, overcome, stir, affect

owe (SYN) be obligated, be in debt, be under obligation

own (SYN) personal, individual, posses, retain, hold, control (ANT) lack, lose

owner (SYN) possessor, holder, proprietor (ANT) renter

ownership (SYN) possession, domination, title, rights

P

pace (SYN) rate, speed, velocity, tempo, step, stride

pacifist (SYN) conscientious objector

pacify (SYN) placate, soothe, calm, tranquilize, quiet (ANT) stir, antagonize, arouse, incense

pack (SYN) bundle, parcel, load, jam, stuff, group, herd (ANT) unpack, loosen

package (SYN) box, carton, combination, whole, wrap, pack

pact (SYN) agreement, deal, understanding, treaty, alliance

pad (SYN) cushion, stuffing, dressing, notebook, creep, tiptoe, stretch, exaggerate

paddock (SYN) pen, enclosure

pagan (SYN) heathen, polytheist, infidel (ANT) believer

page (SYN) side, leaf, sheet, attendant, squire, messenger, call, summon

pageant (SYN) show, spectacle, display, parade

pail (SYN) bucket, container

pain (SYN) discomfort, ache, suffering, sorrow, grief, effort, sadden, trouble (ANT) pleasure, enjoyment, comfort

painful (SYN) sore, tender, agonizing, distressing, traumatic (ANT) pleasurable, enjoyable

paint (SYN) dye, pigment, coat, color, depict, portray

painting (SYN) illustration, artwork, oil canvas

pair (SYN) couple, duo, twosome, match, combine

pal (SYN) friend, buddy, companion, chum

palace (SYN) mansion, castle, fortress, chateau

palatable (SYN) yummy, appetizing, delicious, appealing, pleasing (ANT) gross, disgusting, unappetizing

palatial (SYN) grand, stately, opulent, sumptuous, regal (ANT) humble, modest, spare pale (SYN) muted, pastel, pasty, ashen, whiten, dim (ANT) flushed, rosy, glow, dark

pallid (SYN) pale, colorless, anemic (ANT) flushed, ruddy

palpable (SYN) clear, evident, unmistakable, obvious, tangible

palpitate (SYN) beat, pound, tremble, flutter, throb, vibrate

paltry (SYN) trivial, insignificant, meager, minor, petty (ANT) important, major, considerable

pamper (SYN) spoil, indulge, baby, coddle

pamphlet (SYN) booklet, brochure, circular, leaflet

pan (SYN) pot, skillet, follow, sweep, track, swing

panacea (SYN) cure all, nostrum, universal solution

pandemonium (SYN) chaos, turmoil, din, uproar, confusion (ANT) calm, tranquility, serenity

pander (SYN) gratify, please, cater to, indulge

panel (SYN) console, controls, instruments, committee, board

panic (SYN) fear, alarm, fright, scare, unnerve (ANT) calm, soothe

pant (SYN) gasp, wheeze, heave, puff, huff

pantry (SYN) closet, storage room

pants (SYN) slacks, trousers

paper (SYN) newspaper, journal, essay, report, document, identification

par (SYN) average, standard, usual, norm

parable (SYN) lesson, allegory, moral tale, fable

parade (SYN) procession, march, display, flaunt, exhibit, strut

paradigm (SYN) ideal, model, example, pattern

paradise (SYN) heaven, utopia, ecstasy, bliss, nirvana (ANT) hell

paradox (SYN) contradiction, incongruity, puzzle, enigma, conundrum

paragon (SYN) epitome, ideal, standard, quintessence

paragraph (SYN) section, part, passage, portion, division

parallel (SYN) alongside, matching, similar, equal, resemblance, similarity (ANT) perpendicular, divergent, different

paralysis (SYN) immobility, incapacity, helplessness, shutdown, standstill

paralyze (SYN) disable, incapacitate, freeze, numb, stun

parameter (SYN) framework, limitation, restriction, specification

paramount (SYN) primary, chief, main, principal, supreme, key paranoia (SYN) delusion, neurosis, insanity, suspicion, fear

paraphrase (SYN) restate, reword, rephrase, gloss

parasite (SYN) leech, passenger

parcel (SYN) package, bundle, box, wrap

parch (SYN) dry, dehydrate, shrivel, wither (ANT) saturate, hydrate, moisten

pardon (SYN) forgiveness, amnesty, absolution, excuse, acquit (ANT) punish, blame

pardonable (SYN) forgivable, minor, understandable, excusable (ANT) inexcusable, unforgivable, unpardonable

pare (SYN) peel, shave, skin, reduce, cut, decrease

parent (SYN) father, mother, procreator, sire (ANT) child, offspring

parish (SYN) church, congregation, community

park (SYN) garden, playground, position, stop, deposit

parley (SYN) consult, conference, debate, talk, discussion, huddle

parliament (SYN) assembly, congress, council, legislature

parlor (SYN) living room, lounge, sitting room

parochial (SYN) provincial, limited, narrow-minded (ANT) open-minded

parody (SYN) satire, spoof, caricature, imitation, mockery

parrot (SYN) repeat, copy, echo, imitate

parsimony (SYN) stinginess, frugality, meanness, selfishness (ANT) generosity

part (SYN) section, component, piece, character, role, divide, split, separate

partially (SYN) slightly, in part, somewhat, up to a point (ANT) wholly, completely

partiality (SYN) bias, preference, favoritism, liking, inclination (ANT) impartiality, fairness, justice

participate (SYN) join, take part, be involved in, share, contribute

participation (SYN) involvement, partaking, contribution, sharing in

particle (SYN) bit, speck, spot, splinter, fragment

particular (SYN) specific, precise, exact, fussy, demanding, detail, specification (ANT) general, indiscriminate

particularly (SYN) notably, especially, uniquely, distinctly, specifically

partisan (SYN) supporter, adherent, partial, interested, biased, factional (ANT) unpartisan, unbiased

partition

partition (SYN) wall, barrier, divide, separate, split (ANT) union, connection

partly (SYN) partially, somewhat, up to a point, to some extent (ANT) wholly

partner (SYN) companion, associate, colleague, collaborator, spouse, mate

party (SYN) gathering, celebration, get-together, celebrate, group, company

pass (SYN) go by, qualify, give, transfer, approve, exceed

passage (SYN) trip, voyage, advance, course, hall, excerpt, quotation

passé (SYN) dated, unfashionable, obsolete, old-fashioned (ANT) modern, current, up-to-date

passenger (SYN) traveler, rider

passion (SYN) zeal, desire, fervor, intensity, enthusiasm (ANT) apathy, calm

passionate (SYN) intense, strong, amorous, loving, heated (ANT) apathetic, cool, dull

passive (SYN) docile, inactive, submissive, resigned, compliant (ANT) active, dynamic, resistant, aggressive

past (SYN) former, previous, background, history, beyond, after (ANT) present, future, now

paste (SYN) glue, cement, adhesive, stick, affix

pastel (SYN) pale, delicate, muted, soft (ANT) dark, bright

pastime (SYN) hobby, diversion, game, recreation, leisure activity, interest

pastor (SYN) clergyman, minister, vicar, reverend

pastoral (SYN) rural, rustic, country, clerical, priestly (ANT) urban, metropolitan, lay

pasture (SYN) field, meadow, grass

pat (SYN) tap, touch, clap, stroke

patch (SYN) spot, bit, scarp, area, mend, repair, reinforce (ANT) break, damage

patent (SYN) copyright, license, obvious, evident, blatant (ANT) unclear, inconspicuous, hidden, covert

paternal (SYN) fatherly, protective, devoted, concerned

path (SYN) way, trail, track, course, route, channel

pathetic (SYN) sad, pitiable, touching, wretched, deplorable (ANT) funny

pathos (SYN) sadness, poignancy, compassion

patience (SYN) endurance, restraint, forbearance, perseverance, composure (ANT) restlessness, impatience, impetuosity

patient (SYN) tolerant, understanding, accommodating, persistent,

205

determined, sick person (ANT) impatient, impetuous, complaining

patriot (SYN) loyalist, nationalist

patriotic (SYN) loyal, nationalistic (ANT) traitorous, unpatriotic

patriotism (SYN) nationalism

patrol (SYN) guard, sentinel, police, vigilance, watching

patron (SYN) customer, client, shopper, supporter, sponsor, champion

patronize (SYN) fund, promote, back, talk down to, condescend, mock (ANT) praise, exult

pattern (SYN) plan, template, model, copy, imitate, motif, sequence

pauper (SYN) beggar, poor person

pause (SYN) stop, break, delay, interrupt, lull, gap, hesitation (ANT) continue

pave (SYN) cover, surface, prepare, lead

pavement (SYN) asphalt, sidewalk

paw (SYN) grab, manhandle, touch

pawn (SYN) puppet, tool, instrument, sell, pledge

pay (SYN) reward, compensate, spend, wages, earnings, income

payment (SYN) installment, premium, pay, salary

peace (SYN) calm, serenity, contentment, accord, armistice, treaty (ANT) agitation, violence, war

peak (SYN) mountain, point, summit, crest, zenith, height, maximum (ANT) bottom, nadir

peal (SYN) chime, ring, blast, resound

peasant (SYN) commoner, rustic

peck (SYN) pick, gig, poke, nibble

peculiar (SYN) strange, odd, unconventional, abnormal, extraordinary (ANT) normal, ordinary, common, regular

peddle (SYN) sell, push, hawk, tout

pedestal (SYN) stand, support, base

pedestrian (SYN) walker, foot-traveler, dull, mundane, routine (ANT) driver, exciting, inspired, imaginative

pedigree (SYN) lineage, ancestry, family, genealogy, descent

peek (SYN) look, peep, glimpse, snoop

peel (SYN) skin, pare, rind

peer (SYN) equal, fellow, contemporary, gaze, inspect, scan, look closely

peg (SYN) pin, dowel, fix, secure, fasten, attach

pejorative (SYN) negative, derogatory, disparaging, degrading (ANT) complimentary, flattering, positive

pelt (SYN) skin, hide, coat, hurl, pepper, strike

pen (SYN) write, draft, compose, corral, coop, enclosure

penalize (SYN) punish, discipline, disadvantage (ANT) benefit, reward

penalty (SYN) punishment, fine, price, sanction, sentence (ANT) prize, reward

penchant (SYN) fondness, liking, taste, tendency, inclination

pending (SYN) approaching, imminent, looming, unsettled, unresolved

penetrate (SYN) enter, stab, puncture, infiltrate, register, click (ANT) withdraw, retreat

penitent (SYN) remorseful, guilty, sorry, contrite, apologetic (ANT) unrepentant, unapologetic

pennant (SYN) flag, streamer, banner

penniless (SYN) poor, impoverished, bankrupt, broke, destitute (ANT) wealthy, rich, well-off

pension (SYN) allowance, retirement, annuity, benefit, support

pensive (SYN) solemn, preoccupied, thoughtful, reflective, wistful (ANT) carefree, unconcerned

people (SYN) persons, individuals, humanity, citizens, population, nation

pepper (SYN) seasoning, spice, sprinkle, dot, bombard, pelt, shower

perceive (SYN) understand, grasp, realize, discern, observe, note (ANT) misunderstand, ignore

perceptible (SYN) visible, obvious, tangible, evident, clear (ANT) undetectable, indiscernible, unrecognizable, imperceptible

perception (SYN) awareness, grasp, impression, feeling, sensation, insight (ANT) ignorance

perch (SYN) resting place, branch, post, balance, alight, rest, land

percolate (SYN) brew, steep

peremptory (SYN) final, decisive, binding, absolute

perennial (SYN) lasting, constant, enduring, persistent, recurring (ANT) ephemeral

perfect (SYN) flawless, ideal, supreme, precise, improve, refine (ANT) damaged, incomplete, flawed

perfection (SYN) precision, excellence, exactness, purity, the ideal (ANT) imperfection, mediocrity

perfectly (SYN) wonderfully, faultlessly, exquisitely, completely, thoroughly (ANT) poorly, badly, partly

perfidy (SYN) treason, disloyalty, betrayal, treachery

perforate (SYN) pierce, puncture, penetrate, breach

perform (SYN) present, stage, enact, accomplish, execute (ANT) fail, refrain, neglect performance (SYN) production, show, rendition, completion, fulfillment, behavior

performer (SYN) actor, actress, artist, player

perfume (SYN) fragrance, scent, aroma, smell, bouquet, eau de toilette

perfunctory (SYN) cursory, mechanical, indifferent, superficial

perhaps (SYN) maybe, possibly, feasibly, conceivably (ANT) definitely, absolutely

peril (SYN) danger, risk, threat, hazard, jeopardy, menace

perimeter (SYN) border, boundary, edge, confines, periphery, limit (ANT) center, heart, middle

period (SYN) interval, span, term, stretch, era, time

periodical (SYN) journal, magazine, paper, publication

peripheral (SYN) external, outside, marginal, secondary, inessential (ANT) central, important

periphery (SYN) edge, border, circumference, boundary (ANT) center, inside, middle

perish (SYN) die, extinguish, expire, pass away, vanish, disappear, rot, decay (ANT) live, survive

perishable (SYN) decomposable, spoilable (ANT) non-perishable

perjury (SYN) lying under oath, giving false testimony, forswearing

permanent (SYN) lasting, enduring, steadfast, stable, indelible, irreversible (ANT temporary, short-lived, brief, changing

permanently (SYN) forever, indefinitely, perpetually, always, irreparably (ANT) temporarily, briefly

permeable (SYN) penetrable, porous (ANT) impenetrable, impermeable, dense

permeate (SYN) pervade, saturate, penetrate, fill, spread through

permission (SYN) consent, approval, authorization, liberty, clearance, blessing (ANT) denial, opposition, ban, refusal

permit (SYN) allow, sanction, pass, license, warrant (ANT) restrict, prevent, oppose

pernicious (SYN) destructive, damaging, harmful, wicked (ANT) beneficial

perpendicular (SYN) straight, upright, on end, at right angles to (ANT) parallel

perpetrate (SYN) perform, enact, commit, execute

perpetual (SYN) endless, repeated, eternal, unremitting, continual, incessant (ANT) temporary, intermittent, momentary

perpetuate (SYN) maintain, preserve, continue (ANT) stop, curb perplex (SYN) puzzle, baffle, confuse, bewilder, mystify

perplexity (SYN) confusion, puzzlement, incomprehension, difficulty, paradox

persecute (SYN) oppress, maltreat, harass, badger, plague

persecution (SYN) affliction, harassment, oppression, harm

perseverance (SYN) endurance, tenacity, resolution, determination

persevere (SYN) continue, keep going, carry on, endure (ANT) give up, quit, stop, cease

persist (SYN) persevere, continue, keep trying, remain (ANT) quit, stop, give up

persistence (SYN) determination, stamina, perseverance, grit, tirelessness

person (SYN) human being, individual, soul, man, woman

personable (SYN) likeable, agreeable, nice, pleasant (ANT) rude, disagreeable, unfriendly

personal (SYN) private, intimate, confidential, unique, disrespectful, offensive (ANT) public, open, impersonal

personality (SYN) identity, individuality, nature, character, disposition

personification (SYN) embodiment, epitome, representation, portrayal

personnel (SYN) staff, employees, workers, people

perspective (SYN) viewpoint, outlook, context, angle, attitude, position, slant

perspiration (SYN) sweat, moisture

perspire (SYN) sweat, swelter, secrete

persuade (SYN) convince, influence, urge, coax, sway, win over, cause (ANT) dissuade, deter, discourage

persuasive (SYN) convincing, effective, influential, sound, compelling, plausible (ANT) incredible, unconvincing

pert (SYN) bold, sassy, impertinent, insolent, cheeky (ANT) humble, reserved,

pertain (SYN) relate, apply, concern, refer, belong

pertinent (SYN) relevant, applicable, appropriate, material, fitting (ANT) irrelevant, unsuited

perturb (SYN) disturb, bother trouble, vex, ruffle (ANT) calm, settle, soothe

peruse (SYN) scan, read, inspect, study, look over

pervade (SYN) fill, penetrate, permeate, infiltrate, spread through

pervasive (SYN) prevalent, extensive, universal, widespread, rife (ANT) uncommon, rare perversion (SYN) distortion, corruption, twisting, deviation, aberration

pervert (SYN) warp, distort, debase, deprave, abuse (ANT) protect, defend, preserve

pesky (SYN) annoying, nagging, irritating, bothersome, vexing

pessimism (SYN) despair, gloom, hopelessness, negativity, dejection (ANT) optimism, cheerfulness, hopefulness

pessimist (SYN) cynic, worrier, defeatist, misanthrope (ANT) optimist, enthusiast

pest (SYN) nuisance, annoyance, blight, bug, scourge, menace, headache

pestilence (SYN) plague, epidemic

pet (SYN) caress, stroke, favorite, cherished, domesticated

petite (SYN) small, delicate, dainty, slight, little, diminutive (ANT) large, huge, heavy

petition (SYN) appeal, request, beg, plead, entreat

petrify (SYN) harden, fossilize, terrify, paralyze, stun

petty (SYN) trivial, small, unimportant, trifling, insignificant (ANT) important, essential, consequential

pew (SYN) bench, seat

phantom (SYN) ghost, spirit, apparition, specter, illusion, hallucination

phase (SYN) stage, period, facet, chapter, step, spell

phenomenon (SYN) incident, occurrence, wonder, marvel, sensation

philanthropic (SYN) charitable, humanitarian, benevolent, kind, generous (ANT) mean, stingy, greedy, selfish

philosopher (SYN) thinker, logician, sage, theorist

philosophy (SYN) outlook, doctrine, world view, reasoning, metaphysics

phobia (SYN) fear, aversion, horror, dread, antipathy, revulsion

phone (SYN) telephone, call, ring

photograph (SYN) picture, snapshot, shoot, record, snap

photographic (SYN) lifelike, graphic, vivid, accurate, precise

phrase (SYN) expression, remark, saying, voice, word, formulate, couch, frame

physical (SYN) bodily, real, tangible, palpable, solid, substantial (ANT) mental, emotional, spiritual, intellectual

physician (SYN) doctor, medical practitioner, clinician, specialist

physique (SYN) body, shape, form, figure, structure

pick (SYN) select, choose, gather, pull, harvest, provoke, preference, decision, best, elite (ANT) refuse, decline, reject

picket (SYN) protest, boycott, demonstration, stake, post, upright

pickle (SYN) predicament, dilemma, quandary, preserve, steep

picture (SYN) image, representation, illustration, impression, visualize, see, envision, depict

picturesque (SYN) scenic, attractive, beautiful, pleasing, lovely (ANT) ugly, grim

piece (SYN) part, segment, slice, work, composition (ANT) whole, total, entirety

pier (SYN) dock, wharf, jetty, column, pillar, upright

pierce (SYN) puncture, stab, penetrate, drill, enter (ANT) retract

piercing (SYN) sharp, shrill, ear-splitting, searching, probing, keen

pig (SYN) hog, swine, sow, boar

pigment (SYN) color, tint, dye, stain, paint

pile (SYN) heap, mound, stack, crowd, jam, fiber, nap, beam, support

pilgrim (SYN) traveler, wanderer, devotee, worshiper

pilgrimage (SYN) journey, expedition, trip, trek, odyssey

pill (SYN) tablet, capsule, caplet, pellet

pillage (SYN) loot, raid, rob, plunder, destroy (ANT) save, restore, repair

pillar (SYN) prop, support, column, post, pier, supporter, mainstay, backbone, champion

pilot (SYN) airman, aviator, fly, navigate, steer, trial, test

pin (SYN) fasten, affix, secure, immobilize, tack, nail

pinch (SYN) squeeze, nip, bit, dash, trace, pain, crisis, difficulty

pine (SYN) long, crave, desire, hanker, hunger

pinion (SYN) fasten, chain, fetter, shackle

pink (SYN) rosy, flushed, reddish, rose

pinnacle (SYN) peak, top, summit, height, crown, zenith (ANT) low point, bottom, base, nadir

pioneer (SYN) innovator, leader, trailblazer, explorer, establish, develop

pious (SYN) devout, religious, reverent, saintly, righteous (ANT) irreligious, unholy, unrighteous

pipe (SYN) tube, duct, hose, conduit, convey, whistle, peep

piquant (SYN) sharp, spicy, zesty, lively, interesting, stimulating (ANT) dull, bland, flavorless

pique (SYN) resentment, displeasure, umbrage, irritation, affront, offend, arouse, excite pirate (SYN) buccaneer, marauder, copy, plagiarize, steal, reproduce

pit (SYN) hole, crater, depression, scar, dent, mark

pitch (SYN) throw, fling, toss, erect, raise, lurch, roll, slope, incline, tone, sound, key, intensity

pitfall (SYN) peril, danger, hazard, snag, trap, snare, risk, stumbling block

pithy (SYN) concise, brief, succinct, terse, pointed (ANT) lengthy, wordy, pontificating

pitiful (SYN) pathetic, heartbreaking, sad, wretched, shabby, contemptible (ANT) impressive, praiseworthy

pittance (SYN) trifle, peanuts, next to nothing

pity (SYN) compassion, sympathy, shame, misfortune, feel sorry for, understand, empathize with (ANT) cruelty, indifference, severity

pivot (SYN) rotate, turn, swivel, axle, rely, depend

pivotal (SYN) crucial, key, vital, decisive, central, focal (ANT) unimportant, minor, insignificant

placate (SYN) calm, appease, pacify, assuage, soothe (ANT) agitate, upset, ruffle

place (SYN) area, spot, location, position, duty, put, deposit, identify, remember

placid (SYN) calm, tranquil, serene, composed, untroubled (ANT) excited, disturbed, agitated, ruffled

plagiarism (SYN) theft, copying, piracy

plague (SYN) disease, infection, epidemic, curse, affliction, bother, torment

plain (SYN) clear, candid, straightforward, bare, stark, ordinary, grassland, prairie (ANT) obscure, ornate, uncommon, extraordinary

plainly (SYN) clearly, evidently, obviously, visibly, frankly (ANT) ambiguously, cryptically

plan (SYN) diagram, design, blueprint, scheme, formulate, organize, intend, aim

plane (SYN) airplane, aircraft, level, horizontal

planet (SYN) orb, globe

plank (SYN) board

plant (SYN) vegetable, factory, foundry, sow, seed, place, introduce (ANT) uproot, dig up

plaque (SYN) tablet, marker

plastic (SYN) pliant, flexible, supple, manageable, docile, artificial, insincere (ANT) rigid, stiff, hard, genuine

plate (SYN) platter, dish, portion, serving, coat, gild

plateau (SYN) highland, mesa, leveling off, stability (ANT) lowland, fluctuation

platform (SYN) stage, podium, policy, objective, party line

platitude (SYN) cliché, banality, truism

platonic (SYN) friendly, unromantic

platoon (SYN) squadron, unit, team, outfit, group

platter (SYN) plate, tray, serving dish

plaudits (SYN) praise, approval, applause

plausible (SYN) credible, believable, likely, persuasive, probable (ANT) incredible, unlikely, implausible, unconvincing, unimaginable

play (SYN) romp, revel, compete, participate, act, drama, show, entertainment, sport (ANT) work, labor

plea (SYN) request, appeal, petition, entreaty, supplication

plead (SYN) beg, implore, ask, claim, allege

pleasant (SYN) enjoyable, agreeable, comforting, delightful, lovely, personable (ANT) unpleasant, disagreeable, irritating

pleasantly (SYN) politely, amiably, genially, cordially, good-naturedly (ANT) unpleasantly, rudely

please (SYN) satisfy, indulge, delight, like, wish, prefer (ANT) annoy, offend, displease, dissatisfy

pleased (SYN) happy, contented, glad, contented, gratified (ANT) unhappy, upset, dissatisfied

pleasure (SYN) bliss, enjoyment, amusement, satisfaction, glee (ANT) unhappiness, displeasure, misery, suffering

pledge (SYN) promise, vow, oath, covenant, swear, give one's word

plenty (SYN) enough, lots, plethora, abundance, profusion (ANT) deficiency, scarcity, drought

plethora (SYN) surplus, excess, abundance, profusion (ANT) deficiency

pliant (SYN) bendable, flexible, lithe, susceptible, impressionable (ANT) rigid, intractable, unyielding, difficult

plight (SYN) trouble, difficulty, predicament, dire straights, jam

plod (SYN) trudge, lumber, stomp, toil, labor (ANT) skip, dance, stride

plot (SYN) plan, conspiracy, story line, devise, intrigue, concoct, tract, acreage, mark, chart

plow (SYN) till, dig, cultivate, crash, bulldoze, press, wade

pluck (SYN) pick, pull, tug, yank, strum, courage, bravery

plug (SYN) stopper, cork, seal, block, mention, promote (ANT) unplug, unblock

plum (SYN) best, choice, prize

plumb (SYN) explore, delve, probe, penetrate, fathom, understand

plume (SYN) feather, quill

plummet (SYN) fall, sink, dive, plunge, drop (ANT) rise, soar, climb

plump (SYN) portly, chubby, round, corpulent, ample (ANT) slim, slender, thin, underweight

plunge (SYN) throw, cast, immerse, charge, dash, descend, tumble (ANT) soar, rise, climb

plus (SYN) and, together with, extra, supplementary, bonus, advantage (ANT) minus, disadvantage

plush (SYN) lavish, lush, luxurious, sumptuous, soft (ANT) austere, simple, stark

poach (SYN) trespass, encroach, intrude

pocket (SYN) pouch, compartment, steal, pilfer, compact, miniature, portable

pod (SYN) shell, husk, hull, case

podium (SYN) platform, dais, stage, stand

poem (SYN) lyric, verse, rhyme, sonnet, song

poet (SYN) bard, lyricist, writer

poetic (SYN) lyrical, expressive, artistic, imaginative, symbolic, creative

poetry (SYN) verse, rhymes, rhyming

poignant (SYN) moving, intense, touching, affecting, piercing (ANT) dull, insipid, trite

point (SYN) tip, end, aim, indicate, essence, meaning, intention, spot, location, moment, instant, score

pointless (SYN) futile, absurd, meaningless, inane, senseless, idle (ANT) valuable, meaningful, useful, relevant, fruitful

poise (SYN) presence, assurance, composure, dignity, grace, elegance (ANT) awkwardness

poison (SYN) venom, toxin, contaminate, pollute, taint, corrupt

poisonous (SYN) lethal, toxic, fatal, noxious, malicious (ANT) harmless, non-toxic, nourishing, benevolent

poke (SYN) jab, nudge, prod, thrust, protrude

police (SYN) law enforcement, patrol, guard, watch, monitor, enforce

policy (SYN) approach, plan, guidelines, stance, position

polish (SYN) shine, buff, enhance, refine, varnish, wax, gloss, sophistication (ANT) roughen, neglect

polite (SYN) courteous, civilized, gracious, respectful, thoughtful (ANT) rude, impolite, discourteous political (SYN) governmental, policy-making, legislative, parliamentary

politician (SYN) legislator, representative, public servant

politics (SYN) government, civics, diplomacy

poll (SYN) question, interview, survey, census, count

pollute (SYN) spoil, contaminate, sully, desecrate, taint (ANT) purify, clean, sanitize, cleanse

pollution (SYN) impurity, contamination, filth, infection, smog (ANT) cleanliness, purity

pompous (SYN) arrogant, showy, pretentious, boastful, haughty, vain (ANT) modest, humble, timid, meek

ponder (SYN) think, consider, deliberate, reflect, muse, dwell on

pool (SYN) puddle, pond, lake, swimming hole, supply, fund, combine, share

poor (SYN) needy, impoverished, deficient, inadequate, inferior, unfortunate (ANT) rich, wealthy, abundant, superior

pop (SYN) burst, bang, crack, explosion, slip, insert

popular (SYN) liked, accepted, common, prevailing, widespread (ANT) unpopular, disreputable, exclusive

popularity (SYN) favor, approval, acceptance, regard

populate (SYN) occupy, settle, inhabit, colonize

population (SYN) people, residents, society, citizens, inhabitants

populous (SYN) crowded, over populated, teeming, dense (ANT) sparsely populated

pore (SYN) opening, hole

porch (SYN) veranda, patio, deck

porous (SYN) permeable, absorbent, penetrable, spongy (ANT) impermeable, impenetrable

port (SYN) harbor, haven, docks, marina

portable (SYN) manageable, movable, wireless, convenient, mobile (ANT) stationary, wired, inconvenient

portal (SYN) door, opening, gate, entryway

portend (SYN) predict, foreshadow, indicate, warn of, herald

portent (SYN) omen, sign, warning, indication, forewarning

portentous (SYN) significant, menacing, ominous, solemn, fateful (ANT) trivial, insignificant, light

porter (SYN) carrier, baggage handler, attendant, skycap

portion (SYN) share, serving, allotment, destiny, luck (ANT) whole, total, entirety

portly (SYN) stout, heavy plump, large, fleshy (ANT) slender, trim, slim portrait (SYN) picture, likeness, image, depiction, impression, painting

portray (SYN) show, represent, impersonate, describe, play

pose (SYN) position, stance, model, ask, raise, feign, masquerade

position (SYN) location, whereabouts, posture, opinion, view, station, occupation, arrange

positive (SYN) decided, affirmative, certain, constructive, beneficial, optimistic, cheerful (ANT) negative, unsure, doubtful, vague, pessimistic

possess (SYN) own, hold, boast, control, seize (ANT) lose, surrender, sell, disown

possession (SYN) ownership, custody, property, asset, thing

possessive (SYN) controlling, dominating, jealous, overprotective, selfish (ANT) generous, sharing

possibility (SYN) chance, likelihood, potential, option, alternative

possible (SYN) likely, feasible, viable, conceivable, plausible (ANT) unlikely, impossible, unattainable, hopeless

post (SYN) upright, support, display, pin up, job, position, station, situate

poster (SYN) notice, advertisement, announcement, bill, sign

posterity (SYN) future, heirs, descendents, children

postpone (SYN) delay, reschedule, defer, put off, suspend, shelve (ANT) confront, engage, proceed

postscript (SYN) P.S. afterthought, addition

postulate (SYN) suppose, hypothesize, assume, theorize, adage, truism

posture (SYN) carriage, attitude, bearing, affect, pose

pot (SYN) pan, vessel, saucepan

potent (SYN) strong, effective, intense, powerful, influential, compelling (ANT) weak, impotent, ineffective

potential (SYN) promise, prospects, capability, possible, future (ANT) current, past

potion (SYN) brew, elixir, draft, concoction

pottery (SYN) earthenware, terracotta, ceramics

pouch (SYN) bag, sack, pocket, purse, compartment

pounce (SYN) spring, jump, attack, leap, lunge, swoop

pound (SYN) beat, hammer, pummel, thump, punch, enclosure, pen

pour (SYN) flow, gush, spew, stream, throng, spill, decant

pout (SYN) sulk, glower, mope

poverty (SYN) want, destitution, hardship, need, scarcity, shortage (ANT) wealth, plenty, abundance powder (SYN) dust, cover, sprinkle

power (SYN) might, force, strength, energy, authority, control, ability (ANT) inability, weakness, incapacity

powerful (SYN) mighty, dynamic, effective, forceful, weighty, dominant (ANT) weak, ineffectual, infirm, inept

practical (SYN) useful, realistic, pragmatic, functional, sensible (ANT) impractical, idealistic, absurd, senseless

practically (SYN) almost, virtually, nearly, essentially, sensibly, reasonably (ANT) nowhere near, impractically

practice (SYN) rehearsal, repetition, custom, ritual, observe

pragmatic (SYN) practical, realistic, utilitarian, down-to-earth, no-nonsense (ANT) impractical, theoretical

prairie (SYN) meadow, grassland, field

praise (SYN) approval, congratulation, commend, applaud, glorify, worship (ANT) criticism, contempt, disapproval, criticize, disparage

prance (SYN) dance, romp, skip, strut, swagger (ANT) trudge, slump, lumber

prank (SYN) practical joke, antic, trick, escapade

prate (SYN) boast, brag, chatter, babble

pray (SYN) beseech, implore, solicit, appeal, supplicate

prayer (SYN) invocation, supplication, request, devotion, litany

preach (SYN) proclaim, teach, lecture, recommend, urge, advocate

preacher (SYN) minister, pastor, clergyman, evangelist

preamble (SYN) preface, forward, introduction, opening remarks

precarious (SYN) perilous, risky, unsteady, uncertain, unpredictable (ANT) safe, sure, sound

precaution (SYN) protection, safety measure, caution, insurance

precede (SYN) introduce, lead, go before, preface, usher in (ANT) follow, come after

precedent (SYN) example, standard, model, criterion

precept (SYN) rule, principle, regulation, statute

precinct (SYN) limit, confine, district, section, zone

precious (SYN) treasured, beloved, prized, valuable, dear, darling (ANT) cheap, common

precipice (SYN) cliff, bluff, crag

precipitate (SYN) accelerate, speed, launch, swift, unexpected

precipitation (SYN) rain, snow, sleet

precipitous (SYN) sheer, steep, high, reckless, hasty, sudden, abrupt

precise (SYN) exact, accurate, specific, meticulous, strict, rigid (ANT) imprecise, faulty, erroneous, inaccurate

precision (SYN) exactness, accuracy, care, scrupulousness, rigor (ANT) imprecision, error, inaccuracy

preclude (SYN) prevent, inhibit, exclude, rule out, impede, thwart (ANT) encourage, aid, promote

precocious (SYN) smart, advanced, bright, quick (ANT) slow, unintelligent, dim

precursor (SYN) predecessor, antecedent, forerunner

predatory (SYN) hunting, predacious, carnivorous

predecessor (SYN) ancestor, forerunner, antecedent, forefather (ANT) successor, descendant

predestined (SYN) fated, predetermined, preordained (ANT) spontaneous

predicament (SYN) dilemma, plight, situation, quandary, emergency

predict (SYN) forecast, foretell, prophecy, portend

prediction (SYN) prophecy, prognosis, forecast

predilection (SYN) leaning, fondness, preference, taste, penchant, weakness (ANT) aversion, distaste

predominant (SYN) chief, leading, primary, main, important (ANT) secondary, minor, insignificant, inconsequential

preeminent (SYN) excellent, outstanding, matchless, incomparable, superior

preface (SYN) introduction, foreword, prologue, open, introduce

prefer (SYN) choose, favor, pick, be partial to, select

preferable (SYN) better, superior, advantageous, recommended, desirable

preference (SYN) favorite, liking, penchant, partiality, priority, precedence

pregnant (SYN) expectant, charged, loaded, suggestive, significant, telling

prehistoric (SYN) early, primitive

prejudice (SYN) bias, discrimination, intolerance, bigotry, influence, undermine

prelude (SYN) overture, introduction, start, beginning, precursor (ANT) ending, postlude, epilogue

premature (SYN) early, hasty, rash, impulsive, impetuous (ANT) overdue

premier (SYN) leading, top, primary, head of government

premiere (SYN) debut, opening night, first performance

premise (SYN) assumption, hypothesis, proposition, thesis

premium (SYN) bonus, reward, payment

premonition (SYN) hunch, suspicion, omen, feeling, intuition, portent

preoccupied (SYN) distracted, immersed, absorbed, oblivious, pensive (ANT) focused

preparation (SYN) planning, readiness, groundwork, arrangements, development

prepare (SYN) make ready, arrange, plan, practice, train, put together

preponderance (SYN) mass, dominance, extensiveness, superiority, weight (ANT) absence

preposterous (SYN) crazy, absurd, ludicrous, ridiculous, foolish, unreasonable (ANT) logical, reasonable, practical

prerequisite (SYN) condition, qualification, mandatory, vital, indispensable

prerogative (SYN) right, privilege, authority, liberty (ANT) limitation, obligation, violation

presage (SYN) bode, foreshadow, portend

prescribe (SYN) advise, suggest, recommend, order, direct, specify

prescription (SYN) instruction, medicine, drug, remedy

presence (SYN) attendance, occupancy, air, personality, charisma (ANT) absence

present (SYN) here and now, attending, current, today, gift, give, introduce, exhibit (ANT) absent, future, past, receive

presentation (SYN) performance, demonstration, speech, giving, awarding, appearance

preservation (SYN) protection, safeguarding, conservation, care, maintenance, sustaining (ANT) destruction, harming

preserve (SYN) defend, protect, shelter, save, uphold, area, domain (ANT) lose, destroy, abolish

preside (SYN) run, govern, manage, command, supervise (ANT) follow

press (SYN) push, crush, flatten, coerce, urge, entreat, news media, journalists (ANT) pull, retract

pressure (SYN) compression, force, influence, stress, tension (ANT) relaxation

prestige (SYN) status, importance, reputation, repute, prominence (ANT) obscurity, notoriety

presume (SYN) assume, infer, surmise, dare, venture (ANT) know, prove

presumption (SYN) assumption, guess, supposition, audacity, boldness (ANT) discovery

presuppose (SYN) imply, presume, take for granted, assume

pretend (SYN) fake, feign, simulate, imagine, make believe, false, mock (ANT) real, genuine

pretense (SYN) show, charade, deception, trickery, fraud (ANT) honesty, truthfulness, sincerity

pretension (SYN) self-importance, conceit, artifice, deception, acting (ANT) humility, inferiority, meekness

pretext (SYN) excuse, guise, ruse, ploy, cover (ANT) reality, truth

pretty (SYN) attractive, lovely, fetching, moderately, somewhat (ANT) ugly, unappealing, very

prevail (SYN) triumph, succeed, win, predominate, abound (ANT) lose, be defeated

prevalent (SYN) common, widespread, popular, frequent, rife (ANT) rare, sporadic, uncommon, peculiar, exclusive

prevent (SYN) stop, thwart, inhibit, avert, interrupt (ANT) allow, support, encourage

prevention (SYN) deterrence, precaution, hindrance, circumvention (ANT) assistance, permission, allowance

preview (SYN) advance showing, trailer

previous (SYN) prior, earlier, preceding, former, aforementioned (ANT) later, following, subsequent, next

previously (SYN) before, formerly, in the past, at one time, earlier (ANT) subsequently

prey (SYN) quarry, game, victim, target (ANT) predator

price (SYN) cost, value, expense, worth, rate

prick (SYN) stab, puncture, jab, lance, sting, prickle, wound, hole

pride (SYN) pleasure, gratification, dignity, satisfaction, vanity, assuredness, ego (ANT) modesty, humbleness, selflessness

priest (SYN) cleric, clergyman, father, vicar, curate

prim (SYN) proper, fussy, demure, fastidious, straight-laced (ANT) informal, laid-back, improper

primary (SYN) main, cardinal, first, paramount, simple, introductory (ANT) secondary, subsequent

prime (SYN) principal, select, choice, peak, height, prepare, make ready (ANT) inferior

primitive (SYN) crude, unrefined, simple, early, rough (ANT) advanced, cultivated, refined, complicated

prince (SYN) monarch, ruler, sovereign

princess (SYN) monarch, ruler, sovereign

principal (SYN) dean, headmaster, headmistress, main, leading, star (ANT) trivial, minor principle (SYN) rule, law, theory, conscience, integrity, virtue, ethics

print (SYN) publish, issue, reproduction, copy, write

prior (SYN) previous, earlier, former, preceding, past (ANT) later, after

priority (SYN) rank, preference, seniority

prison (SYN) jail, dungeon, penitentiary

prisoner (SYN) convict, inmate, hostage, captive, detainee (ANT) captor

pristine (SYN) immaculate, pure, untouched, perfect, spotless (ANT) dirty, spoilt, defiled, sullied

privacy (SYN) seclusion, isolation, retreat

private (SYN) personal, intimate, confidential, reclusive, introverted, clandestine, secluded, concealed (ANT) public, open, social

privation (SYN) hardship, adversity, need, difficulty

privilege (SYN) advantage, entitlement, benefit, right, honor, pleasure

prize (SYN) value, esteem, reward, award, trophy, top, best (ANT) penalty

probability (SYN) odds, chance, likelihood, prospect, expectation

probable (SYN) likely, plausible, possible, presumable (ANT) improbable, incredible, unlikely

probably (SYN) most likely, perhaps, chances are, in all probability, doubtless

probation (SYN) apprenticeship, trial period

probe (SYN) investigate, examine, scrutinize, prod, inquiry, exploration

problem (SYN) complication, obstacle, dilemma, riddle, question (ANT) solution, resolution, explanation

procedure (SYN) method, course of action, system, practice, routine

proceed (SYN) continue, progress, advance, begin, move (ANT) stop

process (SYN) procedure, operation, course, exercise, technique, handle

procession (SYN) parade, march, file, train

proclaim (SYN) profess, declare, announce, state, broadcast

proclamation (SYN) revelation, announcement, decree, notification, pronouncement

proclivity (SYN) leaning, fondness, inclination, tendency

procrastinate (SYN) stall, postpone, delay, hesitate, put off (ANT) rush, hurry

procrastination (SYN) hesitation, dallying, delaying, vacillation, wavering (ANT) efficiency, haste

prod (SYN) poke, nudge, shove, goad, prompt, reminder

prodigal (SYN) reckless, wasteful, extravagant, immoderate, spendthrift (ANT) thrifty, frugal, cautious

prodigious (SYN) massive, giant, immense, vast, staggering, phenomenal (ANT) small, insignificant, ordinary

prodigy (SYN) genius, whiz, mastermind, marvel, talent, wonder (ANT) dunce, idiot

produce (SYN) create, generate, cause, offer, present, fruits and vegetables (ANT) destroy, demolish

producer (SYN) maker, manufacturer, creator, builder, promoter

product (SYN) goods, merchandise, outcome, result, yield

production (SYN) construction, formation, assembly, creation, performance, show

profane (SYN) wicked, sacrilegious, foul, obscene, vulgar, desecrate, defile (ANT) pure, pious, holy, sacred

profanity (SYN) swearing, cursing, obscenity, impiety, irreverence

profess (SYN) assert, vouch, declare, allege, protest

profession (SYN) occupation, job, career, vocation, statement, confession

professional (SYN) accomplished, skilled, competent, expert, appropriate, proper (ANT) amateur, inept, inexperienced, unqualified

professor (SYN) teacher

proffer (SYN) give, offer, extend, tender (ANT) take, receive

proficient (SYN) adept, skilled, capable, competent, efficient (ANT) unable, inept, incompetent

profile (SYN) outline, silhouette, biography, characterization, description

profit (SYN) gain, proceeds, revenue, benefit, help (ANT) loss, disadvantage, lose

profligate (SYN) reckless, wasteful, extravagant, immoral, shameless, wanton (ANT) pure, uncontaminated, blameless

profound (SYN) wise, philosophical, sincere, overwhelming, insightful, extensive, radical, deep (ANT) superficial, shallow, simple, mild

profuse (SYN) prolific, plentiful, copious, abundant, excessive, thick (ANT) meager, scant, deficient

profusion (SYN) surplus, bounty, plethora, wealth, abundance

progeny (SYN) children, offspring, young, descendents, issue

prognosis (SYN) projection, prediction, forecast, foretelling

prognosticate (SYN) predict, project, forecast

program (SYN) schedule, timetable, plan, performance, presentation, arrange progress (SYN) growth, improvement, movement, develop, continue, proceed (ANT) regression, stagnate, relapse, retrogression

progression (SYN) progress, headway, series, sequence, chain

progressive (SYN) liberal, enlightened, forward-thinking, gradual, continuous (ANT) conservative, reactionary, immobile

prohibit (SYN) forbid, bar, prevent, hinder, restrict (ANT) allow, encourage, foster, promote, tolerate

prohibition (SYN) restriction, prevention, embargo, bar, injunction (ANT) permission, allowance, sanction

project (SYN) venture, undertaking, task, estimate, predict, protrude, extend

projectile (SYN) missile, bullet

projection (SYN) forecast, estimation, expectation, ledge, overhang, outcrop (ANT) indentation

proletarian (SYN) working-class, common, plebian

proliferate (SYN) increase, multiply, expand, snowball, burgeon

prolific (SYN) productive, fertile, bountiful, abundant, teeming (ANT) barren, sterile, unproductive

prologue (SYN) preface, introduction, forward, preamble (ANT) epilogue, postscript, conclusion

prolong (SYN) lengthen, stretch, draw out, protract, perpetuate (ANT) shorten, abbreviate, curtail

promenade (SYN) parade, walkway, walk, stroll, saunter, turn

prominent (SYN) famous, notable, renowned, conspicuous, unmistakable (ANT) unknown, unimportant, inconspicuous

promise (SYN) pledge, swear, vow, guarantee, bond, oath, potential, aptitude, indicate, portend (ANT) disavow, deny

promote (SYN) help, boost, forward, raise, advertise, plug (ANT) demote, obstruct, impair

promotion (SYN) rise, elevation, publicity, support, furtherance (ANT) demotion, hindrance

prompt (SYN) provoke, elicit, remind, cue, speedy, immediate, punctual (ANT) avoid, deter, late, slow, tardy

promptly (SYN) punctually, on time, swiftly, immediately, pronto (ANT) later, sometime, eventually, slowly

prone (SYN) apt, inclined, susceptible, face down, prostrate (ANT) immune, resistant, upright

prong (SYN) point, tine, spike

pronounce (SYN) speak, articulate, vocalize, announce, proclaim, decree

pronunciation (SYN) intonation, inflection, speech, accent, enunciation proof (SYN) evidence, confirmation, substantiation, impervious, impenetrable

prop (SYN) support, brace, uphold, pole, buttress, cornerstone, accessory

propaganda (SYN) hype, promotion, disinformation, publicity, advertising

propagate (SYN) publish, spread, circulate, reproduce, multiply (ANT) destroy, extinguish

propel (SYN) drive, push, urge, thrust, fling (ANT) delay, hold, stall, stop

propensity (SYN) tendency, penchant, inclination, bent, disposition

proper (SYN) correct, suitable, acceptable, conventional, formal, polite (ANT) improper, wrong, unorthodox, indecent

properly (SYN) fittingly, correctly, accurately, respectably, politely (ANT) improperly, incorrectly, erroneously

property (SYN) possessions, belongings, effects, land, trait, attribute, feature prophecy (SYN) divination, prediction, augury, second sight, prognostication

prophesy (SYN) predict, foresee, divine, forecast

prophet (SYN) seer, oracle, soothsayer, forecaster, fortune teller

proportion (SYN) ratio, relationship, balance, correspondence, percentage, amount

proportions (SYN) size, magnitude, bulk, capacity, dimensions

proposal (SYN) suggestion, proposition, offer, plan, bid, presentation (ANT) refusal, denial

propose (SYN) submit, motion, present, intend, ask for one's hand in marriage (ANT) withdraw, negate, refuse, reject

proposition (SYN) recommendation, scheme, plan, idea, solicit

proprietor (SYN) owner, possessor, holder, landlord, landlady

propriety (SYN) decorum, etiquette, decency, seemliness, rightness (ANT) impropriety, indecency, impoliteness, unseemliness

propulsion (SYN) push, drive, impetus

prosaic (SYN) unimaginative, everyday, routine, ordinary, mundane (ANT) poetic, inspired, creative

prosecute (SYN) charge, try, arraign, indict, take to court, bring to trial (ANT) defend, acquit

prospect (SYN) expectation, anticipation, promise, possibility, view, sight, seek, explore, survey

prospective (SYN) potential, possible, likely, future, aspiring (ANT) current

prospectus (SYN) synopsis, outline, program, list, brochure, catalog

prosper (SYN) succeed, thrive, flourish, blossom, advance (ANT) flounder, fail, suffer prosperity (SYN) wealth, fortune, affluence, success, ease, opulence (ANT) hardship, poverty, adversity destitution

prosperous (SYN) rich, fortunate, wealthy, thriving, lucrative (ANT) poor, ailing

prostrate (SYN) prone, horizontal, exhaust, drain, kneel, grovel

protagonist (SYN) hero, heroine, main character, principal (ANT) antagonist

protect (SYN) guard, defend, shelter, safeguard, preserve (ANT) harm, expose, neglect, attack

protection (SYN) safety, security, refuge, custody, barrier, shield (ANT) carelessness, vulnerability

protégé (SYN) apprentice, successor, heir

protest (SYN) objection, challenge, dissent, complain, disagree, strike, rally (ANT) approval, support, agree, acquiesce

protocol (SYN) procedure, formalities, ritual, customs, conventions

prototype (SYN) pattern, original, model, standard, template (ANT) successor

protracted (SYN) lengthy, extended, prolonged, drawn out (ANT) short, brief

protrude (SYN) jut, project, extent, stick out

proud (SYN) self-assured, confident, arrogant, haughty, satisfied (ANT) humble, meek, ashamed

proudly (SYN) contentedly, assuredly

prove (SYN) verify, confirm, authenticate, validate, corroborate (ANT) contradict, refute, disprove

proverb (SYN) saying, adage, maxim, aphorism, motto

provide (SYN) supply, offer, give, furnish, render, contribute, reveal (ANT) withhold, deprive

providence (SYN) destiny, fate, fortune

province (SYN) region, area, zone, section, function, responsibility

provincial (SYN) limited, insular, rural, local, rustic, unsophisticated (ANT) national, metropolitan, cosmopolitan

provision (SYN) condition, specification, stipulation, clause, supplying, providing

provocative (SYN) stimulating, confrontational, offensive, inflammatory, incendiary (ANT) calming, soothing

provoke (SYN) incite, prompt, induce, enrage, anger (ANT) pacify, soothe, placate, calm, ally, appease

prowl (SYN) sneak, slink, steal, creep, stalk

prowess (SYN) skill, talent, expertise, proficiency, finesse (ANT) inability, ineptitude

proximity (SYN) nearness, closeness

proxy (SYN) agent, representative, substitute, delegate, surrogate

prudent (SYN) wise, sensible, judicious, shrewd, careful, frugal (ANT) imprudent, unwise, extravagant, reckless

prune (SYN) trim, cut, reduce, clip, snip

pry (SYN) meddle, intrude, interfere, spy, snoop

psalm (SYN) poem, hymn, chant

pseudonym (SYN) pen name, alias, nom de plume

psyche (SYN) mind, self, soul, individuality, personality

psychiatrist (SYN) psychotherapist, therapist, analyst

psychic (SYN) supernatural, paranormal, metaphysical, clairvoyant, medium

psychology (SYN) behaviorism, attitude, mentality, psyche

puberty (SYN) adolescence

public (SYN) civic, open, unrestricted, people, society, community (ANT) private, restricted, personal

publication (SYN) newspaper, book, periodical, printing, distribution

publicity (SYN) press, promotion, advertising, exposure, limelight

publish (SYN) print, reveal, publicize, announce, divulge (ANT) conceal, hide, censor

puff (SYN) blast, gust, gasp, wheeze, inhale

puissant (SYN) potent, powerful

pulchritude (SYN) attractiveness, charm, elegance, beauty, loveliness

pull (SYN) tow, yank, strain, gather, extract, influence, power (ANT) push, repel

pulp (SYN) mush, paste, flesh, crush

pulsate (SYN) beat, throb, palpitate, quiver

pulse (SYN) beat, rhythm, throb, vibrate

pulverize (SYN) crush, grind, defeat, pound, destroy

pummel (SYN) pound, thump, hammer, batter

pump (SYN) force, push, supply, swell, enlarge

punch (SYN) hit, box, blow, jab, perforate, pierce

punctual (SYN) prompt, timely, on time, on schedule (ANT) late, tardy

punctuality (SYN) promptness, readiness

punctuate (SYN) stress, emphasize, intersperse, pepper, sprinkle

puncture (SYN) rupture, gash, perforation, prick, pierce

pundit (SYN) commentator, expert

pungent (SYN) sharp, strong, piquant (ANT) mild, vapid

punish (SYN) penalize, discipline, sentence, chastise, scold (ANT) pardon, reward, exonerate

punishment (SYN) penalty, retribution, sanction, sentence, discipline (ANT) praise, reward

puny (SYN) tiny, feeble, weak, frail, stunted (ANT) mighty, powerful, substantial

pupil (SYN) student, scholar, trainee, novice (ANT) teacher

puppet (SYN) pawn, tool, instrument, doll, marionette

purchase (SYN) buy, acquire, obtain, investment, acquisition (ANT) sell

pure (SYN) perfect, virtuous, wholesome, clean, unadulterated (ANT) polluted, immoral, foul, spoiled

purge (SYN) remove, get rid of, eradicate, elimination, dismiss, cleanse, purify

purify (SYN) cleanse, refine, clarify, disinfect, absolve, sanctify (ANT) dirty, debauch, foul

purity (SYN) innocence, virtue, piety faultlessness, cleanliness (ANT) filth, obscenity, indecency, immorality

purloin (SYN) steal, filch, pilfer, thieve

purpose (SYN) objective, intention, goal, function, persistence, tenacity

purse (SYN) money, resources, pucker, tighten

pursue (SYN) chase, hunt, seek, work towards, perform, practice

pursuit (SYN) search, chase, quest, activity

push (SYN) shove, ram, elbow, urge, persuade, energy, initiative (ANT) pull, discourage

put (SYN) place, deposit, express, state

putrid (SYN) rotten, rancid, decayed, spoiled, disgusting (ANT) fresh

puzzle (SYN) baffle, confuse, perplex, mystery, paradox, riddle

puzzling (SYN) complicated, unclear, enigmatic, problematic (ANT) clear

Q

quack (SYN) fraud, imposter, fake, charlatan

quagmire (SYN) swamp, bog, marsh, mire, morass

quaint (SYN) charming, old-fashioned, curious, peculiar, eccentric (ANT) modern, usual, common, expected

quake (SYN) tremble, shudder, vibrate, shake, rock, convulse, heave

qualification (SYN) attribute, eligibility, fitness, condition, stipulation, provision (ANT) incompetence

qualify (SYN) limit, restrict, be eligible,
count, allow, license (ANT)
disqualify, eliminate, exclude

quality (SYN) caliber, class, merit,
excellence, feature, attribute

qualm (SYN) apprehension, disquiet,
scruple, hesitation, misgiving

quantity (SYN) amount, sum, total,
quota, volume

quarantine (SYN) separation, confine,
isolate

quarrel (SYN) fight, disagreement,
dispute, squabble, clash (ANT)
agree, consent, concur

quarry (SYN) prey, game, objective,
goal

quarters (SYN) accommodations,
lodgings, rooms, home

queen (SYN) ruler, sovereign, majesty,
monarch

queer (SYN) peculiar, abnormal, weird,
eerie, uncanny (ANT) normal,
common, expected

quell (SYN) subdue, suppress, crush,
allay, soothe (ANT) agitate, stir,
incite

quench (SYN) satisfy, satiate, abate,
stifle (ANT) rouse, begin, kindle

query (SYN) question, ask, inquire,
uncertainty, reservation (ANT)
accept, trust

quest (SYN) mission, search, expedition,
voyage, crusade, pursuit

question (SYN) problem, doubt, debate,
inquiry, interrogation, suspect, issue
(ANT) answer, reply, assurance,
certainty

questionable (SYN) dubious, suspicious,
suspect, controversial (ANT) honest,
reliable, certain

questionnaire (SYN) survey, question
form, quiz, opinion poll

queue (SYN) line, chain, file, column,
procession

quick (SYN) fast, swift, rapid, sudden,
astute, perceptive (ANT) slow,
unhurried, deliberate, inattentive

quicken (SYN) hurry, accelerate,
invigorate, energize, revive (ANT)
slow, dull, deaden, impede

quickly (SYN) fast, briskly, promptly,
hastily, soon (ANT) slowly,
unhurriedly, later

quiet (SYN) silent, hushed, tranquil,
undisturbed, reserved, sedate, peace
(ANT) loud, bust, bustling, noisy,
boisterous

quietly (SYN) silently, inaudibly,
noiselessly, softly, calmly (ANT)
loudly, out loud

quilt (SYN) bedspread, coverlet, duvet

quintessence (SYN) essence, nature,
spirit, core

quintessential (SYN) ultimate,
definitive, typical

quip (SYN) jibe, joke, wisecrack, retort

quirk (SYN) eccentricity, habit, oddity, foible, trait

quit (SYN) give up, abandon, leave, exit, resign (ANT) stay, remain

quite (SYN) utterly, completely, altogether, thoroughly (ANT) somewhat

quiver (SYN) tremble, shake, quaver

quixotic (SYN) dreamy, romantic, idealistic, fanciful (ANT) practical, realistic

quiz (SYN) test, question, examine, interview, examination

quota (SYN) ration, allowance, allocation, potion

quotation (SYN) citation, reference, excerpt, estimate, bid

quote (SYN) repeat, cite, refer to, echo, mention, allude to

R

rabid (SYN) mad, irrational, fanatical, extreme

race (SYN) contest, dash, run, hurry, speed, tribe, nation

racial (SYN) ethnic, tribal, race-related, cultural

racism (SYN) bigotry, intolerance, narrow-mindedness

rack (SYN) stand, framework, structure, pain, afflict, torment

racket (SYN) noise, din, uproar, tumult, fraud, scam (ANT) quiet

radiant (SYN) gleaming, luminous, shining, lustrous, ecstatic (ANT) dull, dark, gloomy

radiate (SYN) shed, diffuse, spread, emit, cast, emanate (ANT) gather, concentrate

radical (SYN) extreme, revolutionary, fundamental

rage (SYN) fury, wrath, anger, ire, vexation, indignation (ANT) calm, peacefulness, tranquility

ragged (SYN) shabby, tattered, worn, rough, jagged (ANT) new, pristine, smooth, even

raid (SYN) attack, onslaught, storming, assault, invade, loot (ANT) repair, replenish

railing (SYN) bar, barrier, fence, banister, balustrade

rain (SYN) showers, drizzle, downpour, fall, shower

rainfall (SYN) precipitation, showers (ANT) drought

raise (SYN) elevate, hoist, increase, nurture, cultivate, suggest, introduce (ANT) lower, reduce, cut, lessen, abase

rake (SYN) gather, collect, comb, scrape, rummage, rifle, sift

rally (SYN) gathering, convention, recovery, revival, improve, reunite (ANT) slump, disperse, retreat ram (SYN) force, smash, impact, cram, stuff

ramble (SYN) saunter, stroll, wander, jabber, babble, blither

ramification (SYN) result, consequence, repercussion, outcome, effect (ANT) cause

ramp (SYN) slope, gradient, bank, rise, incline

rampage (SYN) riot, storm, tear, tantrum, rage

rampant (SYN) widespread, prevalent, unchecked, rife, unruly, boisterous (ANT) controlled, calm, mild

rampart (SYN) wall, fortification, defense, bastion

rancid (SYN) rotten, putrid, foul, tainted (ANT) fresh

rancor (SYN) hatred, animosity, acrimony, hostility, spite (ANT) affection, friendliness, affability, goodwill

random (SYN) accidental, haphazard, arbitrary, chance, irregular (ANT) planned, specific, deliberate, systematic

range (SYN) scope, limits, extend, stretch, roam, wander, row, ridge

rank (SYN) status, level, position, group, sort, arrange, foul, disgusting, abundant, dense (ANT) sparse, pleasant

rankle (SYN) annoy, irritate, agitate, anger (ANT) calm, please, soothe

ransack (SYN) search, rummage, scour, raid, loot

ransom (SYN) price, payoff, money

rant (SYN) shout, rave, fume, spout, sound off

rap (SYN) tap, knock, hit, strike, talk, chat

rapid (SYN) fast, swift, sudden, brisk, prompt, immediate (ANT) slow, prolonged, sluggish, labored

rapidly (SYN) quickly, instantly, hastily, hurriedly, pronto (ANT) slowly, deliberately, haltingly

rapport (SYN) relationship, bond, connection, empathy, fellowship (ANT) alienation, isolation, estrangement

rapture (SYN) joy, bliss, euphoria, delight, ecstasy (ANT) misery, woe, sadness

rare (SYN) uncommon, scarce, strange, unusual, exceptional, unique (ANT) common, ordinary, everyday, typical

rarely (SYN) seldom, infrequently, scarcely, occasionally, sparingly (ANT) often, frequently, always, commonly

rascal (SYN) rogue, scoundrel, trickster, villain

rash (SYN) hasty, impulsive, reckless, imprudent, hives, outbreak, eruption (ANT) cautious, careful, observant

rate (SYN) speed, pace, cost, price, consider, evaluate, ratio, proportion rather (SYN) preferably, somewhat, relatively, moderately

ratify (SYN) uphold, approve, authorize, confirm, formalize (ANT) reject, derail

ratio (SYN) percentage, proportion, rate, correlation, fraction

ration (SYN) share, portion, allowance, limit, restrict, conserve, supplies, provisions (ANT) surplus, squander, waste

rational (SYN) wise, lucid, sensible, sound, shrewd, reasoned (ANT) illogical, irrational, unreasonable, erratic

rationalize (SYN) justify, excuse, account for (ANT) admit

rattle (SYN) bang, jangle, shake, jolt, disconcert, unnerve

raucous (SYN) noisy, harsh, grating, discordant (ANT) pleasing, sweet

ravage (SYN) destroy, spoil, demolish, lay waste, ruin (ANT) protect, salvage, rebuild

rave (SYN) gush, enthuse, praise, extol, rant, fume (ANT) criticize, belittle

ravenous (SYN) starving, hungry, famished, voracious, insatiable

ravine (SYN) gulch, gorge, canyon, gully, chasm

raw (SYN) uncooked, fresh, natural, crude, biting, chilly (ANT) cooked, processed, experienced

ray (SYN) beam, flash, shaft, stream, flicker

raze (SYN) flatten, level, demolish, destroy (ANT) erect, build, construct

reach (SYN) extent, scope, attain, accomplish, achieve, contact, grasp (ANT) fail, miss

react (SYN) respond, reply, answer, act, behave

reaction (SYN) reply, response, retort, backlash, rejoinder

reactionary (SYN) conservative, conventional, right-wing, traditionalist (ANT) liberal, open-minded, progressive, radical

read (SYN) peruse, study, scan, interpret, register

readily (SYN) gladly, eagerly, effortlessly, easily, unhesitatingly (ANT) reluctantly, grudgingly, with difficulty

readiness (SYN) ease, facility, preparation, willingness, enthusiasm (ANT) difficulty, unsuitability

readjust (SYN) adapt, fix, alter

ready (SYN) arranged, prime, equipped, inclined, willing, handy, accessible (ANT) unprepared, unavailable, hesitating, delayed

real (SYN) valid, genuine, authentic, sincere, tangible (ANT) false, untrue, feigned, imaginary, imitation

realistic (SYN) practical, sensible, pragmatic, feasible, attainable, accurate, life-like (ANT) idealistic, impracticable, unnatural, fake

reality (SYN) truth, fact, actuality, the real world, existence (ANT) fantasy, imagination, illusion

realization (SYN) comprehension, discernment, recognition, grasp, fulfillment (ANT) unawareness, unconsciousness

realize (SYN) understand, apprehend, register, perceive, accomplish, fulfill (ANT) misinterpret, overlook, misunderstand

really (SYN) actually, truly, genuinely, unquestionably, indeed (ANT) doubtfully, possibly

realm (SYN) kingdom, domain, sphere, territory, field

reap (SYN) harvest, collect, gather, obtain, gain

rear (SYN) back, tail end, hind, last, raise, nurture, loom, tower (ANT) front

reason (SYN) motive, incentive, rationale, logic, judgment, deduce, calculate (ANT) emotion, feeling

reasonable (SYN) wise, plausible, sound, moderate (ANT) illogical, extreme, excessive, impractical

reasonably (SYN) relatively, sufficiently

reasoning (SYN) thinking, analysis, thought, logic

reassure (SYN) comfort, soothe, cheer up, hearten (ANT) discourage, alarm

rebate (SYN) refund, discount, deduction, reduction

rebel (SYN) nonconformist, subversive, revolutionary, maverick, revolt, defy, challenge (ANT) conformist, follow, submit

rebellion (SYN) uprising, revolution, mutiny, defiance, disobedience (ANT) compliance, order, patience

rebellious (SYN) unmanageable, disorderly, unruly, insubordinate, defiant (ANT) loyal, tranquil, compliant

rebound (SYN) bounce, recoil, spring back, ricochet

rebuff (SYN) reject, spurn, snub, refusal, slight, dismissal (ANT) accept, acceptance, welcome

rebuild (SYN) remake, repair, resurrect, restore, fix

rebuke (SYN) scold, reprimand, chide, admonish, reproach (ANT) praise, compliment, reward, absolve

rebuttal (SYN) answer, disproof, invalidation, refutation, contradiction

recalcitrant (SYN) willful, unruly, stubborn, defiant (ANT) manageable, obedient

recall (SYN) recollect, remember, evoke, memory, withdraw, retraction (ANT) forget

recant (SYN) withdraw, disclaim, take back, retract

recapitulate (SYN) summarize, repeat, restate, outline

recede (SYN) ebb, retreat, subside, abate, diminish, subside (ANT) advance, approach, grow

receipt (SYN) proof of purchase, sales slip, receiving, acceptance (ANT) delivery

receive (SYN) be given, obtain, take, experience, sustain, greet, welcome (ANT) give, send, return, inflict

recent (SYN) current, new, contemporary, fresh, up to date (ANT) old, outdated

recently (SYN) lately, just now, not long ago

receptacle (SYN) container, repository

reception (SYN) greeting, treatment, celebration, party, function

recess (SYN) hollow, alcove, niche, break, rest, intermission

recession (SYN) downturn, slump, depression, slowdown (ANT) boom

recipe (SYN) formula, directions, instructions, method, blueprint

reciprocal (SYN) mutual, complementary, corresponding, equivalent (ANT) one-sided

reciprocate (SYN) exchange, trade, requite, respond, swap

recital (SYN) performance, concert, recitation, account

recite (SYN) quote, deliver, recount, repeat, speak, deliver, enumerate

reckless (SYN) rash, careless, irresponsible, foolhardy, impulsive (ANT) cautious, thoughtful, mindful, prudent, careful

reckon (SYN) compute, tally, think, suppose, guess

reclaim (SYN) retrieve, recover, regain, salvage, save, rescue (ANT) neglect, forget, abandon

recline (SYN) lounge, rest, lean, relax, lie (ANT) stand up

recluse (SYN) hermit, solitary, loner

recognition (SYN) acknowledgement, gratitude, commendation, recollection, identification

recognize (SYN) place, recall, grant, accept, pay tribute to (ANT) forget, overlook, ignore

recoil (SYN) shrink, jerk back, repercussion, misfire

recollect (SYN) remember, recall, think back to, think of, reminisce about

recollection (SYN) memory, impression, retrospection, reminiscence (ANT) forgetfulness, oblivion

recommend (SYN) suggest, nominate, advocate, support, urge (ANT) advise against, disapprove, condemn

recommendation (SYN) proposal, endorsement, reference, praise, testimonial

reduce

recompense (SYN) payment, amends, compensation, reward, pay

reconcilable (SYN) fixable

reconcile (SYN) resolve, settle, reunite, submit, yield (ANT) incite, aggravate, upset

recondite (SYN) obscure, mysterious, hidden, profound, concealed (ANT) obvious, clear, apparent

reconnaissance (SYN) exploration, investigation, survey, observation

reconsider (SYN) rethink, reassess, revise, review, change one's mind

reconstruct (SYN) recreate, reenact, renovate, rebuild, restore (ANT) destroy, ruin

record (SYN) document, chronicle, note, log, report, indicate, vinyl, album (ANT) erase

recorder (SYN) historian, scribe, clerk, secretary

recount (SYN) tell, describe, relate, report, communicate

recourse (SYN) option, alternative, way out, remedy, resort

recover (SYN) heal, mend, recuperate, repossess, reclaim (ANT) deteriorate, decline, lose

recovery (SYN) improvement, revival, retrieval, restoration

recreation (SYN) entertainment, amusement, diversion, relaxation, play, pleasure (ANT) work

recrimination (SYN) counterattack, squabbling

recruit (SYN) enlist, draft, enroll, novice, beginner (ANT) dismiss

rectify (SYN) correct, remedy, repair, right, adjust (ANT) damage, destroy

rectitude (SYN) decency, morality, virtue, integrity, goodness (ANT) depravity, evil, wickedness, immorality

recuperate (SYN) recover, mend, improve, convalesce, get better

recur (SYN) persist, happen again, repeat, come back, return

recurrent (SYN) frequent, habitual, periodic, continued (ANT) sporadic, random, rare

recycle (SYN) reuse, save, reprocess, reclaim, salvage, recover (ANT) throw out

red (SYN) crimson, scarlet, cherry, vermilion, rosy

redeem (SYN) absolve, deliver, liberate, atone for, repurchase, recover (ANT) abandon, neglect, ignore, condemn

redolent (SYN) fragrant, perfumed, aromatic, evocative, suggestive

redress (SYN) correct, make amends for, rectify, put right, compensate (ANT) wreck, ruin, damage

reduce (SYN) lessen, decrease, curtail, diminish, degrade, humble (ANT) maximize, increase, magnify, augment reduction (SYN) decrease, lessening, cut, lowering (ANT) increase, growth, enlargement

redundant (SYN) unnecessary, extra, superfluous, repetitious, inessential (ANT) concise, succinct

reek (SYN) stink, smell, odor, stench

reel (SYN) whirl, spin, stumble, lurch

reenact (SYN) perform again, redo, repeat

refer (SYN) mention, cite, allude, consult, send, guide

referee (SYN) judge, arbitrator, umpire

reference (SYN) quotation, citation, source, endorsement, recommendation (ANT) detraction, condemnation

refine (SYN) purify, clarify, cleanse, improve, hone, fine-tune (ANT) dirty, spoil, sully, mix, debase

refined (SYN) pure, clean, sophisticated, discerning, polished (ANT) crude, coarse, uncivilized, uncultivated

reflect (SYN) consider, contemplate, muse, return, echo, mirror, indicate, betray

reflection (SYN) image, likeness, manifestation, evidence, deliberation, meditation

reform (SYN) rehabilitation, amendment, better, revise, revamp (ANT) damage, aggravate

reformatory (SYN) jail, prison

refrain (SYN) chorus, melody, avoid, abstain, desist (ANT) continue, give in

refresh (SYN) enliven, revive, restore, prompt, jog (ANT) weary, tire, exhaust

refreshments (SYN) food and drink, snacks

refuge (SYN) retreat, shelter, sanctuary, protection, asylum (ANT) peril, exposure, danger

refugee (SYN) exile, fugitive, asylum seeker

refund (SYN) return, repay, reimburse, compensate, rebate

refurbish (SYN) overhaul, mend, renovate, recondition, upgrade

refusal (SYN) rejection, denial, no (ANT) acceptance, approval, assent

refuse (SYN) deny, withhold, turn down, waste, garbage, rubbish (ANT) accept, grant, allow

refute (SYN) rebut, negate, disprove, contradict, counter (ANT) support, credit, claim, assert

regain (SYN) recover, retrieve, recoup, repossess, get back

regal (SYN) noble, royal, majestic, imperial, princely (ANT) lowly, common, humble

regale (SYN) delight, entertain, divert, amuse (ANT) bore, weary, bother regard (SYN) mind, consider, rate, view, concern, respect

regarding (SYN) about, concerning, with reference to, relating to, in connection with

regardless (SYN) nevertheless, despite, anyway, even so, heedless, indifferent

regenerate (SYN) renew, revive, reawaken, reestablish, breathe new life into

regeneration (SYN) rebirth, awakening, rejuvenation

regime (SYN) government, system, leadership, administration, command

regimen (SYN) plan, system, order

region (SYN) area, sector, zone, district, division, territory

register (SYN) list, catalogue, file, note, indicate, express

registration (SYN) enrollment

regret (SYN) repentance, remorse, contrition, grieve, rue, feel sorry about (ANT) contentment, satisfaction, welcome

regrettable (SYN) unfortunate, disappointing, sad, distressing, unwelcome (ANT) lucky, favorable, fortunate, advantageous

regular (SYN) ordinary, customary, even, consistent, frequent, perpetual (ANT) sporadic, erratic, occasional, unusual, irregular

regularity (SYN) routine, constancy, fixedness, uniformity, steadiness (ANT) irregularity, unevenness, inconsistency, strangeness

regulate (SYN) control, govern, manage, standardize, adjust (ANT) deregulate, give up control

regulation (SYN) law, rule, standard, supervision, monitoring

regurgitation (SYN) vomiting, throwing up, spewing

rehabilitate (SYN) restore, repair, adjust, reintegrate

rehearsal (SYN) practice, preparation, run-through, drill, training

rehearse (SYN) prepare, practice, train, go over, recite

reign (SYN) rule, influence, prevail, power, monarchy, sovereignty

reimburse (SYN) repay, compensate, pay back, refund, remit

rein (SYN) bridle, harness, restraint, halt, restrict

reinforce (SYN) strengthen, fortify, enhance, stress, emphasize (ANT) weaken

reiterate (SYN) repeat, say again, restate, reinforce (ANT) omit

reject (SYN) deny, refuse, snub, shun, renounce (ANT) embrace, welcome

rejoice (SYN) celebrate, be happy, be glad, delight (ANT) mourn rejoinder (SYN) reply, comeback, retort, comeback

rejuvenate (SYN) refresh, renew, modernize, revitalize, restore (ANT) deplete, age, exhaust

relapse (SYN) backslide, regress, worsen, deterioration (ANT) improve, progress, advance

relate (SYN) link, correlate, apply, pertain, tell, recount

relation (SYN) connection, correlation, bond, kinship, association (ANT) dissociation

relationship (SYN) affinity, connection, rapport, similarity, link (ANT) separation

relative (SYN) respective, proportionate, comparable, kin, family (ANT) disproportionate, unconditional

relax (SYN) rest, unwind, take it easy, calm, soothe, slacken (ANT) tense, tighten, increase

relaxation (SYN) pleasure, leisure, recreation, entertainment, recess (ANT) work, activity

relay (SYN) transmit, communicate, send, transfer, broadcast, circulate

release (SYN) free, liberate, deliverance, discharge, loose, launch, publish (ANT) imprison, restrict, bind, arrest

relegate (SYN) demote, downgrade, lower, put down (ANT) promote, upgrade

relent (SYN) yield, soften, show mercy, subside, abate (ANT) toughen, persevere, harden

relentless (SYN) nonstop, unremitting, persistent, ruthless, implacable, dogged (ANT) merciful, compassionate, lenient

relevant (SYN) pertinent, significant, material, applicable, germane (ANT) irrelevant, unrelated, separate

reliable (SYN) dependable, certain, secure, trustworthy, unfailing, (ANT) irresponsible, unreliable, erratic, questionable

reliance (SYN) faith, belief, conviction, dependence, confidence (ANT) doubt, mistrust

relic (SYN) trace, remnant, keepsake, remains, vestige, antiquity

relief (SYN) ease, remedy, solace, respite, break, help, assistance

relieve (SYN) comfort, reduce, mitigate, alleviate, support, aid (ANT) inflict, aggravate, worsen, intensify

religious (SYN) spiritual, devout, godly, pious, faithful, meticulous, conscientious (ANT) irreligious, impious, profane, secular

relinquish (SYN) surrender, forsake, renounce, abdicate, leave (ANT) retain, continue, resist, keep, hold

relish (SYN) appreciate, enjoy, savor, pleasure, enthusiasm, (ANT) disfavor, dislike, distaste reluctance (SYN) unwillingness, wavering, misgivings, second thoughts, aversion (ANT) inclination, enthusiasm

reluctant (SYN) hesitant, loathe, opposed, unenthusiastic, slow (ANT) willing, eager, quick

rely (SYN) depend, count, lean, confide bank

remain (SYN) stay, linger, abide, endure, wait (ANT) depart, leave, vanish

remainder (SYN) balance, surplus, excess, remnants

remains (SYN) leftovers, remnants, body, corpse

remark (SYN) comment, declare, mention, observe, statement, reflection

remarkable (SYN) notable, striking, extraordinary, uncommon, rare (ANT) normal, inconspicuous, usual

remarkably (SYN) exceptionally, impressively, singularly, notably

remedial (SYN) basic

remedy (SYN) cure, treatment, solution, resolution, rectify, straighten out (ANT) illness, disease

remember (SYN) recall, recollect, bear in mind, commemorate, retain (ANT) forget, overlook, repress, disregard

remembrance (SYN) memorial, recognition, memory, retrospection, monument

remind (SYN) prompt, evoke, jog someone's memory

reminisce (SYN) recollect, remember, hark back, recall

reminiscent (SYN) similar, evocative, suggestive, redolent of

remiss (SYN) careless, negligent, lax, forgetful, sloppy (ANT) responsible, thoughtful, mindful

remit (SYN) cancel, repeal, postpone, pardon, alleviate

remittance (SYN) payment, fee

remnant (SYN) remainder, trace, residue, rest, remains

remonstrate (SYN) dispute, protest, object, grumble, complain (ANT) agree, consent, applaud

remorse (SYN) regret, contrition, shame, repentance, guilt (ANT) complacency, callousness, shamelessness

remote (SYN) isolated, secluded, distant aloof, withdrawn, slight, unlikely (ANT) close, nearby, friendly, distinct

removal (SYN) taking away, transporting, dismissal, expulsion, elimination (ANT) installation, installment, appointment, imposition remove (SYN) take off, move, eliminate, dislodge, dismiss, cut (ANT) insert, replace, appoint

remuneration (SYN) payment, earnings, compensation, income, salary, wages

renaissance (SYN) rebirth, renewal, resurgence, revival, reawakening

rend (SYN) wrench, tear, rupture, separate

render (SYN) make, cause to become, portray, depict, represent

rendezvous (SYN) meeting, appointment, engagement, gather, meet

rendition (SYN) performance, interpretation, version, arrangement

renegade (SYN) traitor, deserter, defector, rebellious, disloyal (ANT) faithful, loyal

renew (SYN) replace, overhaul, refurbish, renovate, revive, extend, continue (ANT) deplete, diminish

renewal (SYN) restoration, fresh start, new beginning

renounce (SYN) give up, quit, abandon, relinquish, waive, disown (ANT) continue, keep, accept

renovate (SYN) repair, restore, recondition, update, refit (ANT) ruin, ignore

renown (SYN) fame, distinction, reputation, esteem, prominence (ANT) notoriety, disrepute, obscurity, anonymity

rent (SYN) hire, charter, lease, tear, slash, rip (ANT) own

repair (SYN) fix, mend, patch, restoration, improve, rectify (ANT) destroy, wreck, damage, demolish

reparation (SYN) atonement, compensation, payment, amends

repartee (SYN) banter, conversation, wordplay

repay (SYN) return, reimburse, refund, reciprocate, retaliate

repeal (SYN) lift, reverse, abolish, rescind, invalidation, cancellation (ANT) maintain, continue, validate, enact

repeat (SYN) duplicate, echo, reiterate, replication, repetition (ANT) stop, cease

repeatedly (SYN) often, frequently, over and over, recurrently, persistently (ANT) once, occasionally

repel (SYN) ward off, rebuff, disgust, offend, repulse (ANT) attract, draw, delight

repellent (SYN) revolting, horrid, sickening, abhorrent, proof, resistant (ANT) attractive, delightful, alluring

repent (SYN) regret, rue, feel sorry, apologize, atone

repentance (SYN) guilt, contrition, remorse, penitence, qualm (ANT) complacency, indifference

repercussion (SYN) consequence, effect, result, backlash

repertoire (SYN) range, list, collection, stock, repository, supply

repetition (SYN) repeating, replication, recurrence, redundancy, tautology (ANT) singularity

repetitive (SYN) monotonous, boring, tedious, routine, mechanical (ANT) unique, varied, changing, exciting

replace (SYN) substitute, supplant, exchange, swap, restore (ANT) remove

replacement (SYN) proxy, substitute, double, stand-in, understudy, alternate

replenish (SYN) refill, restore, reload, replace, supply (ANT) empty, drain, deplete

replete (SYN) full, stuffed, gorged, filled to the max (ANT) empty

replica (SYN) copy, duplicate, reproduction, imitation, model (ANT) original, prototype

reply (SYN) answer, respond, retort, reaction, response, rejoinder

report (SYN) account, story, news, announce, communicate, declare (ANT) suppress, withhold, conceal

reporter (SYN) journalist, correspondent, writer, columnist

repose (SYN) peace, stillness, tranquility, relaxation, composure, slumber, recline (ANT) agitation, excitement, distress, commotion, activity

repository (SYN) vault, treasury, storehouse, warehouse

reprehensible (SYN) disgraceful, shameful, bad, criminal, wicked (ANT) upright, blameless, honest, moral

represent (SYN) depict, portray, embody, personify, speak on behalf of

representation (SYN) rendition, description, portrayal, illustration, likeness

representative (SYN) delegate, emissary, spokesperson, typical, symbolic (ANT) atypical, uncharacteristic

repress (SYN) stifle, curb, inhibit, suppress, quell, subjugate (ANT) express, permit, allow, approve

reprieve (SYN) respite, relief, deferment, pardon, alleviation, spare

reprimand (SYN) blame, censure, scold, admonition, rebuke (ANT) praise, pardon, approve

reprisal (SYN) revenge, retaliation, vengeance, retribution

reproach (SYN) disapproval, condemnation, criticize, disparagement, insult (ANT) respect, applaud, commend

reproduce (SYN) multiply, breed, procreate, copy, replicate, match

reprove (SYN) berate, chide, scold, scorn, punish (ANT) approve, applaud, praise repudiate (SYN) reject, denounce, disown, reject, disavow (ANT) accept, welcome, embrace

repugnant (SYN) disgusting, repulsive, vile, sickening, hideous (ANT) pleasing, pleasant, attractive

repulse (SYN) repel, rebuff, drive back, fight off, spurn (ANT) attract

repulsion (SYN) distaste, aversion, loathing, hatred, detestation (ANT) attraction, pleasure

reputable (SYN) respectable, trustworthy, reliable, honorable, straightforward (ANT) disreputable, dishonest, notorious, corrupt

reputation (SYN) name, stature, esteem, standing, character, prominence

request (SYN) petition, seek, solicit, demand, entreat, implore, supplicate

require (SYN) need, demand, expect, mandate, oblige, force

requirement (SYN) essential, prerequisite, necessity, exigency, condition

requisite (SYN) demand, vital, fundamental, obligatory, indispensable (ANT) inessential, secondary, unnecessary

requisition (SYN) request, demand, summons

requite (SYN) reciprocate, retaliate, avenge, respond, get even

rescind (SYN) cancel, repeal, annul, invalidate (ANT) uphold, maintain, allow, permit, propose

rescue (SYN) save, deliver, retrieve, salvage, recovery, liberation (ANT) hinder, obstruct

research (SYN) investigation, study, exploration, examine, probe, experiment

resemblance (SYN) likeness, similarity, parallel, conformity, congruence (ANT) dissimilarity, unlikeness, difference, distinction

resemble (SYN) look like, mirror, take after, favor, bear a resemblance to (ANT) differ from

resent (SYN) begrudge, take offense at, take exception to, be bitter about

resentment (SYN) bitterness, animosity, rancor, ill will, indignation (ANT) satisfaction, contentment, harmony, goodwill

reservation (SYN) doubt, hesitation, skepticism, unease, qualification, stipulation, reserve, sanctuary

reserve (SYN) hold, keep, set aside, book, prearrange, stock, reservoir, restraint, shyness (ANT) release, give, waste, confidence

reservoir (SYN) lake, pond, store, source, supply

reside (SYN) live, abide, dwell, inhabit, lodge

residence (SYN) home, house, dwelling, quarters, domicile

resident (SYN) occupant, lodger, tenant, inhabitant, native

residual (SYN) unused, vestigial, remaining, leftover

residue (SYN) rest, remainder, surplus, dregs, ends

resign (SYN) quit, step down, succumb, accept, surrender (ANT) stay, remain

resignation (SYN) departure, leaving, stoicism, forbearance, acquiescence (ANT) resistance

resigned (SYN) passive, subdued, fatalistic, uncomplaining, long-suffering

resilient (SYN) strong, hardy, irrepressible, flexible, elastic

resist (SYN) contest, oppose, combat, avoid, abstain from, withstand (ANT) relent, welcome, submit, surrender, comply

resistance (SYN) defiance, struggle, obstruction, refusal, immunity (ANT) susceptibility

resolute (SYN) determined, steadfast, tenacious, unshakable, decisive (ANT) weak, irresolute, vacillating

resolution (SYN) decision, intention, resolve, perseverance, willpower (ANT) indecision, hesitation

resolve (SYN) determine, conclude, intend, answer, solve, firmness, purpose

resonant (SYN) booming, resounding, reverberating, vibrant

resort (SYN) utilize, turn to, hope, alternative, option, retreat

resource (SYN) means, assets, reserves, aid, support

resourceful (SYN) creative, inventive, ingenious, clever (ANT) incapable, dense, incompetent, unimaginative

respect (SYN) admire, esteem, reverence, regard, courtesy, aspect, feature (SYN) despise, disregard, contempt, scorn

respectable (SYN) honorable, decent, reputable, sizeable, considerable (ANT) unworthy, scandalous, unsavory, reprehensible, paltry

respectful (SYN) polite, civil, deferential, gracious, compliant (ANT) rude, disobedient, impertinent

respectfully (SYN) courteously, politely, deferentially (ANT) rudely, impolitely

respective (SYN) individual, own, particular, separate, personal

respiration (SYN) breathing, exhaling, inhaling

respite (SYN) pause, lull, recess, break, suspension, breather

resplendent (SYN) dazzling, brilliant, shining, radiant, glorious

respond (SYN) answer, reply, counter, react, reciprocate

response (SYN) answer, retort, rejoinder, reaction, feedback responsibility (SYN) authority, duty, obligation, blame, fault, dependability, maturity (ANT) irresponsibility, unreliability

responsible (SYN) accountable, dependable, reliable, at fault, culpable (ANT) irresponsible, immature, insensible, not guilty

rest (SYN) remainder, surplus, relaxation, stillness, relax, lean, prop (ANT) motion, commotion, activity

restaurant (SYN) cafe, bistro, diner, eatery

restitution (SYN) amends, compensation, reparation, satisfaction

restless (SYN) unsettles, wired, edgy, nervous, agitated, fidgety (ANT) at ease, relaxed, peaceful, untroubled, tranquil

restore (SYN) renew, mend, repair, revitalize, return, reinstate (ANT) damage, harm, tire

restrain (SYN) inhibit, control, hamper, check, suppress, prevent (ANT) liberate, loosen, release

restraint (SYN) control, limitation, self-discipline, moderation, subtlety (ANT) impetuousness, freedom, ostentation

restrict (SYN) limit, regulate, fetter, obstruct, impede (ANT) allow, permit

restrictive (SYN) confining, inhibiting, constricting (ANT) loose

result (SYN) effect, consequence, product, stem, arise, ensue (ANT) cause, source, origin

resume (SYN) restart, begin again, continue, recommence (ANT) abandon, suspend, quit, halt

resurrection (SYN) rebirth, resurgence, renaissance, resuscitation, renewal

resuscitate (SYN) revive, save, bring round

retain (SYN) keep, maintain, preserve, conserve, employ (ANT) give up, discard, dismiss, surrender

retaliation (SYN) revenge, vengeance, reprisal, reciprocation, counter-attack

retard (SYN) delay, impede, slow, postpone, hinder (ANT) accelerate, speed, hasten, expedite

reticence (SYN) reserve, silence, unresponsiveness, shyness, restraint (ANT) forwardness, expansiveness

retire (SYN) withdraw, depart, go to bed, turn in, stop working

retirement (SYN) seclusion, retreat, solitude, privacy

retort (SYN) response, answer, comeback, reply, counter

retract (SYN) sheathe, pull back, recant, deny, revoke (ANT) affirm, assert

retreat (SYN) sanctuary, refuge, withdraw, flight, departure (ANT) advance, advancement, progress, attack retrench (SYN) save, curtail, economize, reduce (ANT) spend, splurge

retribution (SYN) punishment, justice, reckoning, revenge, vengeance

retrieve (SYN) recover, regain, get back, recoup (ANT) misplace, lose

retrograde (SYN) regress, worsen, backslide, deteriorate, degenerate (ANT) develop, improve, proceed

retrospect (SYN) hindsight, re-examination

return (SYN) come back, reappear, give back, revert, replace, profit, gain (ANT) keep, take

reuse (SYN) recycle, refashion (ANT) discard, abandon

reveal (SYN) disclose, divulge, uncover, expose, display (ANT) hide, keep secret, conceal, cover

revelation (SYN) unveiling, disclosure, discovery, unearthing, proclamation

revelry (SYN) fun, festivity, celebration, party

revenge (SYN) retaliation, retribution, vindictiveness, avenge, repay (ANT) forgiveness, amnesty, forgive, pardon, reconcile

revenue (SYN) income, profits, gain, earnings, yield (ANT) expenditure

reverberate (SYN) resound, echo, vibrate, ring

revere (SYN) venerate, respect, admire, esteem, think highly of (ANT) despise, think ill of

reverie (SYN) daydream, trance, dream, abstraction

reverse (SYN) transpose, alter, revoke, go backwards, turn around, opposite (ANT) continue

revert (SYN) return, resume, relapse, default

review (SYN) commentary, critique, analysis, evaluation, study, rehearse, recollect

revile (SYN) malign, abuse, reproach, smear (ANT) protect, praise, respect

revise (SYN) update, edit, alter, amend, rework, improve

revision (SYN) change, correction, amendment, critique

revolt (SYN) insurrection, mutiny, uprising, rebel, riot, disgust, sicken

revolution (SYN) rebellion, insurgency, transformation, innovation, orbit, circle (ANT) peace, serenity, stagnation

revolutionary (SYN) novel, progressive, unconventional, rebel, agitator (ANT) orthodox, stale, old-fashioned

revolve (SYN) rotate, spin, turn, go round, orbit

revulsion (SYN) disgust, loathing, repulsion, abhorrence (ANT) attraction, fascination reward (SYN) award, prize, bounty, pay, remunerate (ANT) punish, charge

rhapsodize (SYN) gush, enthuse, rave

rhapsody (SYN) enthusiasm, happiness, glee, delight, ecstasy

rhetoric (SYN) eloquence, command of language, fluency, wordiness, pomposity

rhyme (SYN) poem, verse, poetry, ode, sound alike

rhythm (SYN) beat, cadence, tempo, time, pattern, flow

ribald (SYN) rude, obscene, racy, vulgar, suggestive (ANT) polite, appropriate, clean

rich (SYN) wealthy, affluent, abundant, plentiful, sumptuous, succulent, creamy (ANT) poor, destitute, barren, cheap, light

riches (SYN) fortune, treasure, wealth, money, assets, resources

rid (SYN) free, purge, dispose of, eliminate, expel (ANT) acquire, gain

riddle (SYN) puzzle, enigma, conundrum, question, brain-teaser

ride (SYN) mount, travel, drive, excursion, journey, drift

ridge (SYN) hump, crest, mound

ridicule (SYN) mock, deride, sneer, scorn, mockery (ANT) respect, honor, praise

ridiculous (SYN) laughable, absurd, ludicrous, silly, nonsensical (ANT) sensible, reasonable, realistic

rife (SYN) prevalent, widespread, rampant, extensive, ubiquitous (ANT) localized, uncommon, rare

riffle (SYN) rummage, forage, search, ransack, pillage

rift (SYN) split, fissure, crack, breach, quarrel, feud

rig (SYN) arrange, manipulate, equip, outfit, apparatus, equipment

right (SYN) just, lawful, moral, accurate, valid, proper, seemly, claim, privilege, rectify, fix (ANT) wrong, incorrect, bad, left, unfair

righteous (SYN) pure, virtuous, ethical, principled, upstanding (ANT) wicked, depraved, evil, immoral, sinful

rigid (SYN) fixed, unbending, inflexible, stubborn, severe (ANT) yielding, elastic, flexible

rigor (SYN) harshness, strictness, stringency, difficulty, inflexibility

rigorous (SYN) demanding, exacting, uncompromising, severe, careful, meticulous (ANT) lax, mild, gentle

rim (SYN) edge, lip, brim, verge, border

rind (SYN) peel, skin, husk, crust

ring (SYN) band, loop, arena, surround, encircle, group, association, chime, toll, call rinse (SYN) clean, wash, bathe, splash, dip

riot (SYN) tumult, anarchy, disturbance, profusion, show, rampage

riotous (SYN) wild, unrestrained, unruly, lawless, rowdy (ANT) quiet, orderly, controlled

rip (SYN) tear, split, slash, tug, wrench

ripe (SYN) mature, ready, suitable, opportune, ideal (ANT) unripe, young, unfavorable

ripen (SYN) mature, grow, develop

rise (SYN) increase, escalate, mount, get up, ascend, advancement, (ANT) fall, decline, descend, plunge, slump

risk (SYN) chance, gamble, danger, imperil, hazard, venture

rite (SYN) ritual, ceremony, practice, observance, custom

ritual (SYN) act, formality, ceremony, prescribed, routine

rival (SYN) opponent, adversary, competing, equal, match (ANT) ally, friend, teammate, colleague

rivalry (SYN) competition, conflict, contention, opposition (ANT) harmony, cooperation, alliance, partnership

river (SYN) stream, torrent, deluge, cascade, tributary

riveting (SYN) enthralling, gripping, captivating, hypnotic, intriguing

(ANT) boring, dull, uninteresting, humdrum

road (SYN) track, pathway, route, street, thoroughfare

roam (SYN) travel, wander, stray, ramble, traipse

roar (SYN) growl, howl, bellow, shout, thunder, guffaw (ANT) whisper, murmur

rob (SYN) steal from, burglarize, deprive, strip, cheat, swindle

robber (SYN) thief, bandit, burglar, mugger, looter

robe (SYN) gown, cloak, wrap, clothe, dress

robotic (SYN) mechanical, automatic, computerized

robust (SYN) strong, powerful, vigorous, sturdy, resilient (ANT) frail, fragile, feeble, infirm

rock (SYN) stone, boulder, sway, lurch, shake, disconcert, astonish

rod (SYN) stick, cane, shaft, pole, baton

rogue (SYN) rascal, villain, criminal, scoundrel, fraud

role (SYN) part, character, position, function, task, responsibility

roll (SYN) twist, wind, tumble, rock, rumble, flow, run, list, register

romance (SYN) charm, glamour, allure, fairy tale, love story, courtship romantic (SYN) sentimental, amorous, loving, tender, idealist, dreamer (ANT) unromantic, realistic, practical, pragmatic

rookie (SYN) beginner, amateur (ANT) professional, expert

room (SYN) chamber, area, space, capacity, opportunity

roost (SYN) coop, hutch, perch

root (SYN) dig, burrow, stem, source, origin, anchor, moor (ANT) result, fruit

rope (SYN) line, cord, cable

roster (SYN) roll, register, list, census

rostrum (SYN) stage, podium, platform, stand

rot (SYN) decay, decompose, spoil, deteriorate, corruption, blight (ANT) grow, thrive, develop

rotary (SYN) turning, spinning, revolving (ANT) stationary

rotate (SYN) revolve, whirl, pivot, swivel, alternate, switch

rotation (SYN) circulation, orbit, revolution, sequence, cycle

rote (SYN) repetition, mechanization, system

rotten (SYN) festering, decomposing, rank, corrupt, despicable (ANT) fresh, clean, good, honorable

rotund (SYN) round, spherical, plump, corpulent, stout (ANT) angular, lean

rough (SYN) jagged, coarse, unfinished, preliminary, harsh, turbulent, aggressive (ANT) smooth, sleek, refined, sweet, courteous

roughly (SYN) approximately, about, nearly, around (ANT) precisely, exactly

round (SYN) circular, curved, skirt, turn, globe, orb, series, succession

roundabout (SYN) indirect, circuitous, evasive, meandering, tortuous (ANT) straightforward, direct,

rouse (SYN) awaken, excite, provoke, galvanize, stir, stimulate (ANT) calm, pacify, sedate

rout (SYN) defeat, conquer, crush, trounce, vanquish (ANT) surrender

route (SYN) course, direction, path, road, way

routine (SYN) habitual, typical, predictable, method, pattern (ANT) unusual, original, imaginative

row (SYN) line, string, dispute, squabble, uproar, commotion (ANT) harmony, agreement

rowdy (SYN) unruly, noisy, wild, disorderly (ANT) polite, restrained, reserved

royal (SYN) regal, imperial, sovereign, majestic, stately, princely (ANT) humble, low, common

rub (SYN) massage, stroke, polish, chafe, abrade

rubbish (SYN) garbage, waste, litter, trash, nonsense

rubble (SYN) ruins, scraps, remnants

ruddy (SYN) rosy, radiant, glowing, reddish, blushing (ANT) pale, pasty

rude (SYN) vulgar, uncouth, impertinent, uncivil, abrupt, startling (ANT) polite, courteous, dignified, clean

rudimentary (SYN) fundamental, primitive, primary, essential (ANT) advanced, supplementary, developed

rue (SYN) regret, lament, mourn, repent

ruffian (SYN) thug, bully, brute

ruffle (SYN) dishevel, tousle, fluster, irritate, perturb (ANT) smooth, calm

rugged (SYN) irregular, craggy, rough, brawny, sturdy, resilient (ANT) smooth, level, delicate, even

ruin (SYN) demolish, wreck, devastate, collapse, disrepair, destitution (ANT) save, rebuild, protection, restoration

ruinous (SYN) dire, shattering, catastrophic, crippling, obliterating

rule (SYN) law, regulation, principle, command, govern, reign, leadership, prevail, pronounce (ANT) chaos, anarchy

ruler (SYN) measure, yardstick, monarch, leader, sovereign, potentate (ANT) subject

rumble (SYN) thunder, roar, boom

ruminate (SYN) ponder, contemplate, reflect, deliberate, muse, brood

rummage (SYN) root, delve, search, hunt, scour

rumor (SYN) gossip, whisper, speculation, talk, buzz (ANT) fact

run (SYN) sprint, dash, operate, function, manage

runner (SYN) jogger, messenger, courier

rupture (SYN) burst, crack, sever, breakage, leak, fissure

rural (SYN) country, rustic, pastoral, bucolic (ANT) urban, metropolitan

ruse (SYN) ploy, scheme, wile, device, hoax, subterfuge

rush (SYN) hurry, hasten, push, gush, surge, charge, storm (ANT) loiter, delay, procrastinate

rust (SYN) corrode, oxidize, deteriorate, tarnish

rustic (SYN) rural, pastoral, rough, natural, unadorned (ANT) polished, sophisticated, urban

rustle (SYN) crackle, crinkle

rut (SYN) groove, trough, indentation, habit, routine

ruthless (SYN) cruel, savage, merciless, remorseless, callous (ANT) merciful, relenting, lenient, compassionate, sympathetic

S

sabotage (SYN) damage, destroy, subvert, undermine, impair, spoil

sack (SYN) bag, pouch, plunder, loot, pillage, raid (ANT) return, give back

sacred (SYN) holy, divine, sanctified, hallowed, religious, protected (ANT) secular, worldly, profane, blasphemous

sacrifice (SYN) offering, cost, loss, forego, forfeit, offer

sacrilegious (SYN) profane, irreverent, impious, blasphemous (ANT) reverent, pious

sacrosanct (SYN) untouchable, inviolable, sacred

sad (SYN) unhappy, mournful, glum, forlorn, miserable, lamentable (ANT) happy, cheerful, gleeful, joyous

saddle (SYN) burden, load, encumber

sadistic (SYN) cruel, brutal, vicious, ruthless (ANT) kind, gentle, caring

safe (SYN) secure, harmless, protected, unharmed, vault (ANT) insecure, dangerous, risky, hazardous, reckless

safety (SYN) welfare, security, protection, assurance, shelter, refuge (ANT) peril, risk

sag (SYN) droop, sink, dip, slump, weaken (ANT) lift, raise, straighten

saga (SYN) tale, legend, story, epic, myth

sagacious (SYN) wise, shrewd, judicious, sensible

sage (SYN) philosopher, scholar, rational, logical, experienced (ANT) dunce, idiot, naive, foolish

sail (SYN) embark, drift, glide, float, pilot, navigate, cruise

sake (SYN) benefit, interest, behalf, purpose, motive

salary (SYN) income, pay, wages, earnings, earnings

sale (SYN) selling, marketing, transaction, bargain (ANT) purchase

salient (SYN) prominent, noticeable, manifest, conspicuous (ANT) inconspicuous

salubrious (SYN) healthy, hygienic, beneficial, wholesome (ANT) unhealthy, noxious

salutation (SYN) greeting

salutary (SYN) beneficial, advantageous, profitable (ANT) destructive, harmful

salute (SYN) address, greeting, welcome, acknowledge, honor, recognize

salvage (SYN) save, rescue, retrieve, reclaim (ANT) dump, trash, discard

salvation (SYN) deliverance, rescue, redemption, lifeline, savior (ANT) damnation salve (SYN) balm, ointment, lotion, cream, soothe, heal

same (SYN) identical, alike, consistent, unvarying, aforementioned (ANT) different, another, dissimilar

sample (SYN) test, experience, example, model, representative

sanctify (SYN) consecrate, hallow (ANT) desecrate

sanction (SYN) permission, authority, approval, permit, endorse, ban, penalty (ANT) prohibition, prohibit, refuse, forbid

sanctuary (SYN) asylum, shelter, safety, haven, refuge, church, temple (ANT) danger, peril, exposure

sane (SYN) rational, sensible, reasonable, level-headed, lucid, balanced (ANT) foolish, irrational, deranged, mad

sanitary (SYN) hygienic, clean, healthy (ANT) unsanitary, dirty, unclean

sanity (SYN) reason, mental health, lucidity, sound mind, common sense (ANT) lunacy, irrationality, imprudence

sap (SYN) weaken, deplete, exhaust, drain, erode

sarcasm (SYN) irony, derision, scorn, causticity (ANT) civility, courtesy

sarcastic (SYN) cynical, cutting, mocking, satirical, derisive (ANT) pleasant, complimentary, agreeable

satanic (SYN) wicked, evil, demonic, diabolical, infernal, fiendish (ANT) godly, holy, heavenly

satiate (SYN) satisfy, fulfill, gratify, gorge, stuff, overfill

satire (SYN) parody, mockery, sarcasm, ridicule, lampoon, caricature, spoof

satisfaction (SYN) contentment, enjoyment, pride, fulfillment, achievement

satisfactory (SYN) adequate, passable, sufficient, convincing (ANT) unsatisfactory, unacceptable, inadequate

satisfy (SYN) please, content, indulge, fulfill, convince, reassure (ANT) frustrate, displease, tantalize

saturate (SYN) soak, drench, permeate, flood, oversupply (ANT) dry

saunter (SYN) stroll, walk, amble, meander

savage (SYN) wild, untamed, ferocious, violent, brute, monster (ANT) civilized, mild, gracious, benevolent, humane

save (SYN) rescue, deliver, conserve, accumulate, gather (ANT) injure, waste, discard, abandon

savings (SYN) resources, fund, reserves

savior (SYN) liberator, deliverer, redeemer, champion

savoir-faire (SYN) tact, finesse, poise, diplomacy, discretion, social graces savor (SYN) enjoy, delight in, appreciate, enjoy, aroma, flavor (ANT) dislike, reject

say (SYN) speak, declare, voice, articulate, assert, suppose, assume, influence, clout (ANT) suppress, hush

saying (SYN) adage, proverb, axiom, maxim, quotation, expression, phrase

scald (SYN) burn, scorch

scale (SYN) climb, ascend, gradation, hierarchy, range, scope, proportion

scamper (SYN) dart, hasten, scurry, run, scuttle

scan (SYN) skim, look over, browse, scrutinize, sweep, inspect

scandal (SYN embarrassment, disgrace, outrage, shame, affair, gossip, slander

scant (SYN) meager, inadequate, sparse, minimal (ANT) abundant, plentiful, bounteous, ample

scapegoat (SYN) fall guy, whipping boy

scar (SYN) wound, blemish, mark, damage, injure, trauma

scarce (SYN) rare, infrequent, uncommon, insufficient, in short supply (ANT) abundant, plentiful, prevalent

scarcely (SYN) hardly, barely, rarely, seldom

scare (SYN) frighten, alarm, terrify, startle, shock, start, jump (ANT) compose, soothe, placate

scatter (SYN) disperse, dispel, spread, fling, sprinkle (ANT) gather, collect, assemble

scenario (SYN) story line, summary, plot, situation

scene (SYN) setting, location, site, context, backdrop, fuss, commotion, arena, segment

scenery (SYN) landscape, terrain, surroundings, set, backdrop

scenic (SYN) spectacular, picturesque, beautiful, breathtaking, panoramic

scent (SYN) smell, aroma, fragrance, perfume, trail, track, detect, discern

schedule (SYN) agenda, plan, timetable, plan, arrange, organize

scheme (SYN) strategy, plot, intrigue, conspire, devise, blueprint, diagram

scholar (SYN) student, pupil, intellectual, academic

scholarship (SYN) education, leaning, knowledge, grant, endowment

scholastic (SYN) scholarly, academic, learned, pedagogic

school (SYN) academy, college, institution, group, faction, train, coach

science (SYN) discipline, subject, area of study, skill, technique scientific (SYN) systematic, precise, methodical, technical, empirical

scoff (SYN) sneer, scorn, despise, jeer, belittle

scold (SYN) censure, reprimand, reproach, punish, berate (ANT) encourage, compliment, praise

scoop (SYN) ladle, spoon, lift, gather up, hollow, gouge, exclusive, revelation

scoot (SYN) dash, dart, hurry, slide, shuffle

scope (SYN) range, reach, extent, realm, opportunity, liberty

scorch (SYN) singe, burn, sear, parch, wither

score (SYN) tally, count, points, grade, grudge, gain, achieve, mark, scrape

scorn (SYN) ridicule, disparage, flout, spurn, contempt, derision (ANT) praise, extol, compliment, admiration, respect

scoundrel (SYN) rogue, rascal, villain

scour (SYN) scrub, abrade, clean, search, comb, ransack (ANT) dirty

scout (SYN) lookout, spy, investigate, observe, probe, search, reconnoiter

scowl (SYN) glower, frown, glare (ANT) smile, grin

scramble (SYN) struggle, clamber, climb, strive, jostle, race, competition

scrap (SYN) piece, shred, fragment, waste, discard, abandon (ANT) whole, keep, preserve

scrape (SYN) graze, scuff, grate, grind, grating, rasp, cut

scratch (SYN) mark, claw, score, grate, delete, eliminate

scream (SYN) yell, shriek, yelp, cry, howl, squawk

screech (SYN) cry, scream, shriek

screen (SYN) mesh, net, partition, shade, conceal, cover, evaluate, sort (ANT) show, reveal, expose

screw (SYN) tighten, turn, twist

scribble (SYN) write, jot, scrawl, doodle, sketch

script (SYN) lines, dialogue, handwriting, penmanship

scrub (SYN) rub, cleanse, scour, brush

scrupulous (SYN) upright, moral, conscientious, careful, meticulous (ANT) unscrupulous, dishonest, deceitful

scrutinize (SYN) examine, inspect, peruse, survey, check (ANT) overlook, neglect

scrutiny (SYN) analysis, study, inspection, exploration, search

sculpture (SYN) carving, statue

sea (SYN) ocean

seal (SYN) stamp, insignia, close, cork, clinch, secure

seam (SYN) joint, stitching, layer, vein

search (SYN) look, comb, scour, scrutinize, pursuit, quest

season (SYN) period, time of year, term, flavor, salt, spice

seat (SYN) chair, bench, place, settle, accommodate, hub, location

secede (SYN) withdraw, break with, leave, pull out

secession (SYN) withdrawal, resignation

seclusion (SYN) solitude, isolation, retirement, quarantine, hiding (ANT) involvement, association, fellowship

second (SYN) next, following, inferior, lesser, extra, spare, endorse, back, moment, instant, flash

secrecy (SYN) mystery, privacy, confidentiality, stealth, concealment (ANT) openness, clarity, exposure

secret (SYN) concealed, furtive, confidential, private, cryptic, mystery (ANT) apparent, evident, undisguised

sect (SYN) party, faction, group, cult, denomination

section (SYN) portion, fragment, slice, segment, area, district

sector (SYN) part, region, division, branch, sphere

secular (SYN) worldly, earthly, temporal, profane, non-religious (ANT) sacred, religious, holy

secure (SYN) safe, protected, assured, confident, tighten, fasten, obtain (ANT) vulnerable, threatened, jeopardized, loosen, uncertain

security (SYN) precautions, defense, safeguards, safety, care (ANT) insecurity

sedate (SYN) calm, serene, composed, collected, tranquil (ANT) unruly, wild

sedative (SYN) tranquilizer, narcotic, relaxing, calming, soothing

sedentary (SYN) inactive, motionless, seated (ANT) active

sediment (SYN) dregs, deposit, silt, grounds

sedition (SYN) subversion, insubordination, rabble-rousing

see (SYN) view, observe, glimpse, understand, realize, discover, encounter, meet

seed (SYN) grain, egg, germ, origin, beginning, descendents

seek (SYN) pursue, look for, aim, attempt, endeavor, solicit

seem (SYN) appear, look, sound, come across as

seep (SYN) ooze, leak, dribble, drain, trickle, exude

seethe (SYN) fume, rage, simmer, boil, surge, be furious

segment (SYN) section, part, wedge, portion, cut (ANT) whole, entirety, total

segregation (SYN) separation, isolation, division, discrimination, exclusion (ANT) union, connection, integration

seize (SYN) grab, clutch, snatch, capture, apprehend, confiscate (ANT) release, relinquish, return

seldom (SYN) rarely, hardly, infrequently, scarcely (ANT) often, commonly, frequently

select (SYN) choose, pick, single out, choice, exclusive, preferred (ANT) refuse, reject, inferior

selection (SYN) choice, option, preference, range, variety, assortment

self-esteem (SYN) confidence, pride, self-respect, poise

selfish (SYN) greedy, egocentric, self-absorbed, stingy (ANT) generous, charitable, thoughtful, benevolent

sell (SYN) market, trade, peddle, auction, retail (ANT) buy, purchase, obtain

semblance (SYN) appearance, pretense, mask, veneer

send (SYN) dispatch, transmit, convey, propel, fling (ANT) receive, get

senility (SYN) infirmity, decrepitude, weakness (ANT)alertness, youth

senior (SYN) superior, elder, older, advanced (ANT) junior, subordinate, younger

sensation (SYN) feeling, impression, awareness, excitement, thrill, uproar

sense (SYN) reason, wisdom, meaning, thrust, detect, recognize, appreciation, awareness

senseless (SYN) illogical, foolish, futile, pointless, stunned, unconscious (ANT) wise, sensible, reasonable, rational

sensibility (SYN) sensitivity, responsiveness, emotion, feeling, insight (ANT) apathy, indifference

sensible (SYN) intelligent, wise, practical, realistic, mindful (ANT) foolish, irrational, unsound, irresponsible

sensitive (SYN) impressionable, susceptible, delicate, tender, touchy, defensive, tactful, diplomatic (ANT) insensitive, impervious, unfeeling

sensuous (SYN) luxurious, sumptuous, luscious, pleasurable, gratifying (ANT) unattractive, plain

sentence (SYN) penalize, condemn, judgment, verdict, ruling

sentiment (SYN) feeling, attitude, view, emotion

sentimental (SYN) romantic, dreamy, overemotional, cloying, nostalgic, sappy (ANT) pragmatic, practical

sentinel (SYN) lookout, guard, sentry, watchman

separate (SYN) divide, sever, isolate, unconnected, divergent, individual (ANT) unite, link, join, merge, attached

separation (SYN) gap, dissociation, break, division, breakup, divorce (ANT) unity, unison, attachment, fusion

septic (SYN) infected, poisoned, putrid, festering

sepulcher (SYN) crypt, tomb, grave, vault, mausoleum

sequel (SYN) continuation, follow-up, conclusion, outcome, result

sequence (SYN) progression, succession, chain, order, pattern, flow

sequester (SYN) quarantine, isolate, remove, seclude, cloister (ANT) integrate

serendipitous (SYN) fortunate, advantageous

serene (SYN) placid, calm, tranquil, composed, untroubled (ANT) rough, violent, turbulent, chaotic

serenity (SYN) peace, composure, stillness, rest (ANT) agitation, disturbance, excitement, commotion

series (SYN) sequence, string, chain, round, wave, course

serious (SYN) solemn, grave, grim, critical, significant, sincere, genuine (ANT) trivial, superficial, flippant, relaxed

seriously (SYN) severely, critically, earnestly, sternly, honestly, truthfully

sermon (SYN) lecture, homily, address, speech, talk

serpentine (SYN) winding, twisting, labyrinthine (ANT) straight, direct

servant (SYN) attendant, maid, butler, slave (ANT) master

serve (SYN) attend, help, benefit, fulfill, present, deliver, function, suffice

service (SYN) assistance, avail, work, duty, ceremony, ritual, amenity

servile (SYN) lowly, fawning, obsequious, base, menial, subservient (ANT) noble, esteemed

session (SYN) meeting, conference, assembly, hearing

set (SYN) collection, group, place, deposit, arrange, prepare, established, inflexible, equipped, solidify

setting (SYN) context, backdrop, scene, surroundings, locale, environment

settle (SYN) conclude, decide, resolve, quell, soothe, alight, inhabit, straighten out (ANT) waver, confuse, shift, stir up

settlement (SYN) agreement, arrangement, deal, resolution, colony, community

sever (SYN) split, detach, amputate, divide, terminate (ANT) unite, join, link, maintain several (SYN) many, various, some, assorted (ANT) one, none

severe (SYN) strict, rigid, serious, grave, intense, austere, unembellished (ANT) lenient, gentle, mild, ostentatious

severity (SYN) strictness, harshness, rigor, intensity, toughness (ANT) tolerance, kindness, ease, indulgence

sew (SYN) mend, stitch, patch

sex (SYN) gender

shabby (SYN)tattered, worn, threadbare, dirty, squalid, contemptible (ANT) elegant, well-kept, decent

shackle (SYN) chain, bind, fetter, handcuff

shade (SYN) tone, hue, shadow, screen, canopy, hint, suggestion (ANT) light, brilliance

shadow (SYN) darkness, cover, shade, follow, track, silhouette, profile (ANT) light

shaft (SYN) pole, rod, stem, ray, beam, tunnel, passage

shake (SYN) tremble, quake, wiggle, wave, upset, rattle

shallow (SYN) superficial, trivial, frivolous, cursory (ANT) deep, profound, thorough

sham (SYN) fraud, hoax, imitation, lie

shambles (SYN) muddle, disarray, chaos, jumble

shame (SYN) embarrass, dishonor, guilt, humiliation, indignity, pity (ANT) honor, respect, glory, praise

shape (SYN) form, build, outline, mold, develop, condition, health

share (SYN) split, divide, allocate, participate, portion, ration (ANT) hoard, whole

sharp (SYN) pointed serrated, clever, intelligent, clear, distinct, cutting, harsh, acute, intense, precisely, punctually (ANT) blunt, dull, smooth, dim, bland, slow

sharpen (SYN) hone, heighten, grind, file

shatter (SYN) crack, smash, splinter, wreck, ruin, devastate

shave (SYN) trim, crop, shear, scrape

sheathe (SYN) case, covering, sleeve

shed (SYN) shack, hut, emit, spill, slough, cast off, discard

sheepish (SYN) embarrassed, mortified, ashamed, humble, abashed (ANT) brazen, unapologetic, shameless

sheer (SYN) transparent, gauzy, diaphanous, steep, absolute, downright (ANT) opaque, thick, gradual

sheet (SYN) leaf, piece, layer, coat, blanket

shell (SYN) case, pod, hull, casing, framework

shelter

shelter (SYN) sanctuary, refuge, protection, cover, harbor, safety (ANT) exposure, danger, neglect, expose

shepherd (SYN) usher, lead guide, herd

shield (SYN) screen, cover, protect, guard (ANT) expose, imperil, uncover

shift (SYN) move, rearrange, reposition, change, alteration, stint, stretch

shimmer (SYN) sparkle, glimmer, gleam, twinkle, iridescence

shine (SYN) flash, glitter, glow, radiate, buff, polish, excel, luster, brightness

ship (SYN) boat, craft, vessel, send, dispatch, deliver

shiver (SYN) tremble, shudder, quake, start, flutter

shock (SYN) appall, astound, stun, blow, bombshell, surprise, fright (ANT) delight, soothe, calm, allay, bore

shoddy (SYN) inferior, trashy, second-rate (ANT) superior, fine, quality

shoot (SYN) fire, discharge, project, launch, bolt, sprout, sprig, photograph, film

shop (SYN) market, store, boutique

shore (SYN) beach, coast, strand, shoreline, support, brace, buttress

short (SYN) petite, little, concise, succinct, brusque, curt, suddenly (ANT) tall, long, lengthy, protracted, courteous

shortage (SYN) lack, scarcity, want, deficiency, poverty, shortfall (ANT) abundance, surplus, plethora

shorten (SYN) decrease, abbreviate, condense, prune, truncate (ANT) lengthen, expand, extend, prolong

shot (SYN) pellet, bullet, slug, effort, endeavor, crack, bang, photograph

shout (SYN) yell, scream, bellow, holler, call (ANT) whisper, suppress, intimate

shove (SYN) push, thrust, force, ram, shoulder

shovel (SYN) scoop, move, heap, load

show (SYN) exhibit, display, divulge, guide, presentation, performance, pretense, illusion

shower (SYN) rain, heap, lavish, deluge, barrage

shred (SYN) scrap, piece, sliver, tatter, tear, grate, mince

shrew (SYN) nag, vixen, harpy

shrewd (SYN) prudent, astute, cunning, sharp, perceptive (ANT) stupid

shriek (SYN) squeal, scream, howl, yelp, shout

shrill (SYN) high-pitched, piercing, sharp (ANT) low

shrink (SYN) diminish, dwindle, reduce, recoil, flinch (ANT) expand, increase, grow shrivel (SYN) wither, wilt, shrink, parch (ANT) inflate, expand, renew, revive

shroud (SYN) veil, covering, pall, conceal, cloak, mask, obscure

shudder (SYN) shiver, tremble, convulse, tremor, spasm

shuffle (SYN) drag, dodder, scrape, jumble, rearrange

shun (SYN) reject, ignore, avoid, eschew, turn away from (ANT) welcome, embrace, accept

shut (SYN) close, fasten, secure, lock (ANT) open, unlock

shy (SYN) timid, withdrawn, introverted, reserved, cautious, suspicious (ANT) garrulous, extroverted, brazen, self-confident

sick (SYN) ill, unwell, ailing, diseased, nauseous (ANT) healthy, well, vigorous

sickness (SYN) ailment, affliction, illness, complaint, malady

side (SYN) border, edge, perimeter, facet, surface, team, camp, perspective, opinion (ANT) center

sieve (SYN) colander, strainer, sift, strain

sight (SYN) vision, seeing, spectacle, scene, spot, perceive

sign (SYN) indication, clue, notice, symbol, signal, gesture, endorse, autograph

significance (SYN) importance, magnitude, consequence, gravity (ANT) insignificance, pettiness, triviality, worthlessness

significant (SYN) noteworthy, weighty, remarkable, considerable, meaningful, suggestive (ANT) insignificant, trivial, inconsequential

signify (SYN) indicate, denote, portend, suggest, symbolize

silence (SYN) quiet, stillness, quiet, muffle, stifle, suppress (ANT) noise, clamor, cacophony

silently (SYN) quietly, inaudibly, wordlessly, without a sound (ANT) loudly, audibly

silhouette (SYN) outline, profile, shape

silly (SYN) foolish, absurd, senseless, playful, ridiculous (ANT) serious, somber, grave, sensible

silt (SYN) sediment, deposit, sludge

similar (SYN) alike, comparable, resembling, equivalent, corresponding (ANT) different, unlike, divergent, incongruous

similarity (SYN) resemblance, likeness, correspondence, equivalence, uniformity (ANT) difference, variance, dissimilarity

simple (SYN) easy, uncomplicated, elementary, plain, classic, unsophisticated, unpretentious (ANT) complex, difficult, fancy, ornate, affected

simplicity

simplicity (SYN) ease, clarity, straightforwardness, restraint, austerity, modesty (ANT) complexity, difficulty, adornment

simplify (SYN) streamline, clarify (ANT) complicate

simply (SYN) plainly, easily, merely, purely, completely, utterly

simulate (SYN) pretend, act, feign, mimic, imitate, replicate

simultaneous (SYN) at the same time, synchronized, coincident, concurrent (ANT) separate

simultaneously (SYN) together, in concert, in unison, contemporaneously

sin (SYN) misdeed, iniquity, crime, transgress, err, misbehave (ANT) virtue, goodness, righteousness

sincere (SYN) honest, genuine, heartfelt, truthful, candid (ANT) insincere, phony, hypocritical, affected

sincerely (SYN) genuinely, earnestly, honestly, truly, wholeheartedly

sincerity (SYN) candor, honesty, frankness, directness, integrity (ANT) dishonestly, falsehood, deceit

sing (SYN) warble, chant, croon, purr, hum, whine

singe (SYN) burn, sear, char, scorch

single (SYN) solitary, one, individual, lone, distinctive, unmarried, unattached

singular (SYN) individual, separate, exceptional, remarkable, unique, uncommon

sinister (SYN) evil, menacing, threatening, ominous, dark, nefarious (ANT) innocent, unthreatening

sink (SYN) fall, lower, descend, plunge, decline, weaken, stoop (ANT) raise, rise, elevate, float

sinner (SYN) offender, transgressor, evildoer, miscreant

sip (SYN) drink, taste, drop, swallow

sit (SYN) rest, perch, place, deposit (ANT) stand

site (SYN) location, position, spot, setting

situate (SYN) position, place, settle, locate

situation (SYN) condition, circumstances, state, status, office, post

size (SYN) mass, bulk, dimensions, magnitude, volume, proportions

skeleton (SYN) bones, framework, structure, sketch

skeptic (SYN) cynic, doubter, unbeliever

skeptical (SYN) doubtful, disbelieving, mistrustful, dubious, incredulous (ANT) trusting, unquestioning, convinced

sketch (SYN) outline, draft, rough out, drawing, design, plan skill (SYN) expertise, dexterity, knack, prowess, ability, proficiency (ANT) incompetence, ineptitude

skillful (SYN) adept, adroit, professional, accomplished, deft (ANT) incompetent

skim (SYN) scan, glance, brush, graze, glide, float

skimp (SYN) scrimp, be sparing with, cut corners

skin (SYN) hide, pelt, peel, rind, film, coating, scrape, abrade

skip (SYN) prance, caper, omit, overlook, disregard

skirt (SYN) avoid, evade, circumvent

skit (SYN) sketch, parody, play, comedy, performance

skittish (SYN) jumpy, nervous, excitable, fidgety (ANT) relaxed, at ease

skulk (SYN) lurk, prowl, slink, sneak

slack (SYN) loose, baggy, limp, idle, lazy, sluggish, room, leeway

slam (SYN) bang, smash, wham, ram, strike

slander (SYN) smear, defame, defamation, malign, aspersion (ANT) flattery, commendation

slant (SYN) slope, incline, tilt, angle, distort, bias, emphasis, stance

slap (SYN) smack, blow, spank, hot

slaughter (SYN) butcher, kill, slay, murder, massacre, carnage

slave (SYN) servant, serf, labor, toil (AT) master

slavery (SYN) captivity, bondage, enslavement, subjugation (ANT) freedom, liberty

slay (SYN) murder, kill, butcher, exterminate

sleazy (SYN) seedy, sordid, corrupt, immoral (ANT) reputable, moral

sleek (SYN) smooth, glossy, shiny, lustrous, streamlined, graceful (ANT) rough, rugged, bulky

sleep (SYN) rest, slumber, doze, nap, snooze, drowse (ANT) wake, wakefulness, insomnia

slender (SYN) thin, svelte, willowy, lean, scant, limited (ANT) overweight, chubby, stout, plump

slice (SYN) portion, share, helping, cut divide

slick (SYN) smooth, sleek, polished, glib, self-assured (ANT) hesitant

slide (SYN) slip, glide, skim, slither

slight (SYN) small, dainty, measly, remote, snub, insult, ignore (ANT) bulky, enormous, respect, compliment

slim (SYN) trim, narrow, slender, willowy, slight, weak, faint (ANT) plump, wide, flabby, hefty sling (SYN) throw, cast, fling, hurl, suspend

slip (SYN) fall, skid, blunder, err, slide, sneak

slippery (SYN) greasy, glassy, unsafe, devious, cunning, tricky, evasive (ANT) dry, safe, sticky, honest

slit (SYN) opening, split, incision, tear, cut, slash

slither (SYN) glide, undulate, slip, sneak

slogan (SYN) motto, catch phrase

slope (SYN) incline, ramp, rise, gradient, pitch

slot (SYN) slit, vent, opening, hole

sloth (SYN) inactivity, inertia, laziness, idleness (ANT) energy, vigor, activity

slovenly (SYN) untidy, sloppy, disorderly, messy (ANT) neat, pristine

slow (SYN) unhurried, leisurely, gradual, protracted, unintelligent, obtuse, delay, curb (ANT) fast, quick, hasty, bright, accelerate

slowly (SYN) gradually, steadily, little by little, unhurriedly (ANT) quickly, briskly

sluggish (SYN) lethargic, torpid, listless (ANT) active, alert, vigorous

slum (SYN) hovel, ghetto, shanty town

slumber (SYN) sleep, doze, drowse, nap

slump (SYN) sag, slouch, hunch, decline, crash, plunge, collapse, recession (ANT) straighten, rise, boom

slur (SYN) insult, smear, insinuation, mumble, garble

sly (SYN) cunning, clever, devious, stealthy, shrewd (ANT) simple, open, straightforward

smack (SYN) hit, slap, strike, squarely, precisely

small (SYN) little, miniature, petite, minor, insignificant, modest (ANT) large, enormous, major, considerable

smart (SYN) intelligent, bright, astute, sharp, sting, hurt (ANT) unintelligent, slow, dense, foolish

smash (SYN) shatter, break, crush, collide, demolish (ANT) mend, repair

smattering (SYN) bit, modicum

smell (SYN) sniff, aroma, fragrance, stink, stench

smile (SYN) grin, beam (ANT) scowl, frown

smirk (SYN) simper, leer, look smug

smolder (SYN) burn, fume, rage, boil

smooth (SYN) sleek, glossy, level, effortless, well-ordered, persuasive, suave, flatten, press, assuage, appease, mellow (ANT) uneven, rough, difficult smother (SYN) suffocate, stifle, suppress, conceal, muffle (ANT) express

smudge (SYN) smear, mark, blemish, tarnish

snap (SYN) break crack, bite, nip, crackle, pop, sudden, instant

snare (SYN) capture, trap, seize, net, hook, catch

snarl (SYN) growl, bark, tangle, entwine

snatch (SYN) crab, seize, grip, clutch

sneak (SYN) slink, skulk, creep, smuggle

sneaking (SYN) nagging, lingering, persistent, insidious, hidden, secret

sneer (SYN) jeer, mock, disdain, deride, smirk

snide (SYN) malicious, sarcastic, cynical, disparaging

sniff (SYN) inhale, breathe, smell

snob (SYN) elitist

snub (SYN) rebuff, spurn, slight, insult, affront, put-down

snug (SYN) tight, close-fitting, cozy, comfortable, secure (ANT) loose, baggy, voluminous

soak (SYN) douse, steep, drench, immerse, permeate, absorb (ANT) dry

soar (SYN) mount, rise, ascend, glide, hover, escalate, skyrocket (ANT) plummet, sink, crash, descend

sob (SYN) weep, cry, howl, whimper

sober (SYN) serious, rational, moderate, plain, drab, subdued (ANT) drunk, giddy, frivolous, flamboyant

sobriety (SYN) obstinate, moderation, temperance, gravity, solemnity (ANT) drunkenness, frivolity

social (SYN) affable, outgoing, collective, gathering, party (ANT) individual, morose, secluded

society (SYN) public, community, civilization, nation, club, guild, fellowship, upper class

sodden (SYN) soggy, drenched, saturated, sopping (ANT) dry, parched

sofa (SYN) couch, settee, divan

soft (SYN) supple, spongy, velvety, quiet, muted, dim, faint, sensitive, permissive (ANT) hard, firm, harsh, sharp, strict, unsympathetic

soften (SYN) ease, cushion, mitigate, weaken, moderate (ANT) stiffen, harden

soil (SYN) dirt, earth, ground, pollute, sully (ANT) clean, scrub

sojourn (SYN) stay, stopover

solace (SYN) comfort, consolation, relief, succor (ANT) irritation, aggravation soldier (SYN) warrior, fighter, trooper

sole (SYN) single, solitary, lone, exclusive (ANT) numerous, many

solely (SYN) entirely, exclusively, simply, merely, only

solemn (SYN) formal, grave, stately, sedate, staid, genuine (ANT) cheerful, light-hearted, frivolous, insincere

solicit (SYN) beseech, entreat, request, seek

solid (SYN) firm, dense, stable, substantial, convincing, sound (ANT) liquid, flimsy, thin, vulnerable

solidify (SYN) harden, set, congeal

solitary (SYN) single, alone, isolated, reclusive, deserted (ANT) accompanied, sociable, populated

solitude (SYN) seclusion, privacy, isolation, detachment, loneliness (ANT) involvement, exposure

solution (SYN) mixture, compound, answer, explanation, result, key

solve (SYN) resolve, unravel, decipher, explain, answer

somber (SYN) gloomy, sober, dismal, mournful, serious (ANT) bright, happy, joyful

somehow (SYN) one way or another, come what may

sometimes (SYN) occasionally, from time to time, now and then, on occasion

song (SYN) tune, ballad, anthem, chorus, strain, melody

soon (SYN) shortly, before long, quickly (ANT) later

soothe (SYN) calm, allay, pacify, alleviate, reduce (ANT) excite, annoy, agitate, aggravate

sophistication (SYN) worldliness, experience, culture, refinement, elegance

sordid (SYN) base, contemptible, dirty, filthy, unclean, shameful (ANT) pure, decent, upright

sore (SYN) tender, inflamed, painful, cross, resentful, annoyed

sorrow (SYN) grief, misery, heartache, anguish, misfortune, affliction (ANT) happiness, joy, pleasure, solace

sorry (SYN) contrite, penitent, apologetic, remorseful, wretched, pitiful (ANT) unrepentant, unsympathetic

sort (SYN) type, variety, divide, arrange, categorize, classify, resolve, rectify

soul (SYN) spirit, embodiment, essence, person, being, core, vitality

sound (SYN) noise, reverberation, seem, appear, healthy, unimpaired, sensible, logical, deep, peaceful (ANT) silence, unsound, ailing, unreliable, irrational sour (SYN) tart, curdled, acrimonious, bitter, resentful, spoil, harm (ANT) sweet, fresh, agreeable, amiable, improve

source (SYN) origin, beginning, cause, authority, reference (ANT) result, outcome

souvenir (SYN) memento, keepsake, trophy, reminder

sovereign (SYN) supreme, imperial, monarch, ruler, independent, autonomous

sow (SYN) plant, scatter, seed

space (SYN) room, capacity, gap, omission, span, duration, position, arrange

spacious (SYN) roomy, capacious, expansive, sizable, voluminous (ANT) crowded, cramped

span (SYN) extent, reach, distance, period, spell, bridge, link

spare (SYN) extra, reserve, save, forgive, excuse, thin, gaunt

spark (SYN) flash, twinkle, blink, glint, trigger, provoke

sparkle (SYN) shimmer, glisten, glisten, flicker, brilliance, spirit, vivacity

sparse (SYN) scarce, scanty, meager, spare, slight (ANT) abundant, plentiful, bountiful

spasm (SYN) convulsion, contraction, twitch, burst

speak (SYN) talk, communicate, utter, express, articulate

speaker (SYN) orator, lecturer, presenter, spokesperson

special (SYN) exceptional, singular, extraordinary, uncommon, distinctive, specific (ANT) ordinary, general, unremarkable, insignificant

specialist (SYN) expert, authority, professional, master

species (SYN) kind, group, category, breed

specific (SYN) particular, determined, distinct, explicit, precise (ANT) general, vague, indefinite

specify (SYN) indicate, mention, identify, name, stipulate

specimen (SYN) sample, example, model, instance, type

speck (SYN) particle, iota, fleck, spot, dot

spectacle (SYN) scene, sight, marvel, exhibition, performance

spectacular (SYN) impressive, magnificent, arresting, dazzling, memorable (ANT) dull, forgettable, ordinary, boring

spectator (SYN) observer, onlooker, bystander, witness (ANT) participant

specter (SYN) ghost, phantom, apparition, presence, spirit

spectrum (SYN) range

speculate (SYN) surmise, guess, hypothesize, theorize, muse

speculation (SYN) conjecture, supposition, theory, guesswork, opinion

speech (SYN) communication, language, diction, talk, oration, lecture

speed (SYN) pace, velocity, tempo, haste, rush, race (ANT) dawdle, hinder, slow

spell (SYN) indicate, signify, charm, incantation, influence, bout, stretch

spend (SYN) occupy, pass, consume, exhaust, squander, expend (ANT) save

sphere (SYN) ball, orb, globe, realm, scope, territory, area

spherical (SYN) round, globular

spice (SYN) flavor, season, seasoning, excitement, zest

spill (SYN) pour, knock over, upset, overflow, slosh, tumble, fall

spin (SYN) twirl, reel, oscillate, revolve, rotation, turn, angle, slant, trip, ride

spine (SYN) backbone, vertebral column, barb, quill, spike

spiral (SYN) coil, helix, winding, curl, twist, scroll

spirit (SYN) enthusiasm, liveliness, soul, psyche, mood, morale, meaning, essence, ghost, phantom

spiritual (SYN) holy, religious, divine, sacred, incorporeal, non-material (ANT) secular, worldly, material, faithless

spit (SYN) eject, expectorate, dribble, saliva, drool

spite (SYN) malice, animosity, malevolence, upset, wound, hurt (ANT) kindness, benevolence, please

splash (SYN) spray, shower, splatter, touch, burst

splendid (SYN) wonderful, marvelous, magnificent, superb, smashing (ANT) awful, plain, uninteresting

splice (SYN) join, unite, graft

splinter (SYN) fragment, sliver, shard, shatter, split, smash, crack

split (SYN) break, crack, separate, diverge, allocate, distribute, fissure, breach, rift, division (ANT) mend, join, converge, union

spoil (SYN) ruin, damage, overindulge, pamper, curdle, decay (ANT) improve, neglect

spoken (SYN) verbal, oral (ANT) written

sponsor (SYN) patron, backer, benefactor, fund, subsidize, promote, support

spontaneous (SYN) impromptu, unplanned, impulsive, natural (ANT) planned, deliberate, premeditated sporadic (SYN) irregular, intermittent, random, scattered (ANT) regular, consistent

sport (SYN) game, diversion, amusement, athletics, wear, flaunt

spot (SYN) mark, stain, blemish, site, location, sight, detect, observe

spouse (SYN) partner, husband, wife, consort

spout (SYN) shoot, spray, stream, squirt, nozzle

sprawl (SYN) lounge, stretch, slump, loll

spray (SYN) sprig, branch, sprinkle, jet, mist, spout, water

spread (SYN) expand, circulate, increase, proliferation, dispersal, sweep, extent (ANT) fold, collect, gather, suppress

spring (SYN) leap, bounce, bound, buoyancy, flexibility, originate, issue, stem

sprinkle (SYN) scatter, dust, strew, drizzle

sprint (SYN) race, dash, dart, bolt, charge (ANT) walk

sprout (SYN) grow, shoot, bud, develop

spruce (SYN) smart, dapper, trim, neat

spry (SYN) nimble, agile, active, sprightly

spur (SYN) motive, incentive, goad, impel, prompt, urge (ANT) discourage

spurious (SYN) false, bogus, artificial (ANT) authentic, genuine

spurn (SYN) reject, slight, scorn, rebuff, snub (ANT) accept, welcome

spy (SYN) glimpse, notice, observe, detect, agent, mole

squad (SYN) troop, team, company, platoon, detachment

squalid (SYN) filthy, unclean, sordid, neglected (ANT) clean, tidy, well-kept

squander (SYN) waste, misuse, throw away, consume (ANT) save, conserve, preserve

square (SYN) align, level, correspond, agree, resolve

squash (SYN) smash, crush, compress, flatten, suppress, quell

squeak (SYN) peep, squeal, groan

squeal (SYN) scream, yell, shriek, wail

squeeze (SYN) grip, compress, pinch, force, extract, wedge, cram, crowd

squirm (SYN) wriggle, writhe, twist

stability (SYN) soundness, strength, steadiness, durability, permanence

stable (SYN) firm, established, immovable, reliable, staunch, steadfast, balanced (ANT) wobbly, rocky, unbalanced, shaky

stack (SYN) pile, mound, heap, amass, accumulate (ANT) clear staff (SYN) personnel, workers, employees, stick, rod, scepter

stage (SYN) phase, point, level, platform, dais, podium

stagger (SYN) wobble, totter, sway, astound, overwhelm, shock, alternate, overlap

stagnant (SYN) still, stale (ANT) flowing, fresh

stagnate (SYN) idle, languish, rot, vegetate

staid (SYN) composed, sober, solemn, earnest, grave (ANT) joyful, cheerful, playful

stain (SYN) spot, smear, tinge, blot, discoloration, dishonor, shame

stake (SYN) pole, post, chance, hazard, risk, interest, concern

stale (SYN) dry, old, rancid, stuffy, stagnant, overused, banal, unoriginal (ANT) fresh, original, new

stalemate (SYN) deadlock

stalk (SYN) pursue, track, follow, hunt, march, storm, stem

stall (SYN) delay, hedge, procrastinate, coop, pen, corral, counter, booth

stalwart (SYN) strong, staunch, loyal, committed, dedicated (ANT) unreliable, unfaithful

stamina (SYN) endurance, energy, tenacity, perseverance, grit, determination

stamp (SYN) imprint, mark, trample, crush, sign, seal

stampede (SYN) charge, rush

stance (SYN) position, viewpoint, attitude, posture, bearing, carriage

stand (SYN) be upright, rise, endure, tolerate, position, place, opinion, attitude, support, tripod (ANT) sit, lie down

standard (SYN) model, gauge, guideline, average, regular, typical (ANT) unusual, special, uncommon

standpoint (SYN) stance, position, angle, viewpoint

stanza (SYN) verse, line

staple (SYN) principal, fundamental, key, important, basic

star (SYN) heavenly body, celebrity, leading lady, leading man, outstanding, eminent (ANT) minor

stare (SYN) watch, gape, gawk, gaze, ogle

stark (SYN) bleak, barren, austere, absolute, utter, harsh (ANT) lush, ornate

start (SYN) begin, commence, initiate, originate, jump, flinch, inception, onset (ANT) conclude, finish, stop, end, complete

startle (SYN) surprise, scare, frighten, alarm, jolt (ANT) forewarn, calm, soothe starvation (SYN) hunger, malnourishment, deprivation (ANT) gluttony, satisfaction, fullness

state (SYN) condition, situation, express, voice, nation, region, territory

statement (SYN) declaration, account, report, assertion, utterance

static (SYN) still, fixed, unmoving, stationary, motionless (ANT) in motion

station (SYN) post, seat, rank, assign, establish, headquarters, depot

stationary (SYN) immobile, fixed, static, parked (ANT) moving, shifting

stature (SYN) prestige, importance, standing, reputation, height, build

status (SYN) rank, position, place, esteem, eminence

statute (SYN) law, ruling, decree

staunch (SYN) loyal, steadfast, firm, faithful

stay (SYN) remain, linger, tarry (ANT) leave

steadfast (SYN) resolute, unwavering, constant, faithful, steady

steady (SYN) constant, regular, continuous, stabilize, brace, firm, balanced, soothe (ANT) unsteady, shaky, fluctuating, sporadic

steal (SYN) take, thieve, purloin, creep, slink, sneak

stealth (SYN) secrecy, slyness, furtiveness (ANT) openness, directness

steep (SYN) sheer, precipitous, sharp, high, unreasonable, soak, submerge, infuse (ANT) gradual, level, reasonable

steer (SYN) direct, guide, control, pilot, maneuver

stem (SYN) stalk, shoot, branch, stop, curb, originate, arise

step (SYN) pace, stride, stage, phase, action, measure, walk, stair

stereotype (SYN) conventional idea, cliché, label, typecast, pigeonhole

sterile (SYN) disinfected, germ free, hygienic, infertile, unproductive

sterilize (SYN) purify, disinfect, clean

sterling (SYN) excellent, fine, sound

stern (SYN) severe, harsh, rigid, strict, serious (ANT) lenient, lax, genial

stick (SYN) poke, jab, thrust, fasten, affix, branch, twig

stiff (SYN) rigid, inflexible, tense, awkward, formal, reserved (ANT) flexible, pliable, supple, relaxed

stiffen (SYN) brace, tense, harden, reinforce (ANT) soften, relax

stifle (SYN) suppress, smother, restrain, hush, inhibit (ANT) release, encourage stigma (SYN) shame, disgrace, blot, stain, vestige

still (SYN) motionless, tranquil, calm, hush, lull, soothe, however, nevertheless (ANT) moving, active, excite

stimulate (SYN) rouse, incite, encourage, trigger, spark (ANT) discourage, deaden

stimulus (SYN) incentive, spur, motivation, inspiration (ANT) deterrent

sting (SYN) pain, hurt, tingle, prick, smart, burn

stingy (SYN) ungenerous, miserly, cheap, selfish, parsimonious (ANT) giving, generous

stink (SYN) reek, stench, foul smell

stipulate (SYN) specify, demand, require

stir (SYN) mix, beat, agitate, awaken, arouse, commotion, bustle, flurry

stirring (SYN) moving, inspiring, touching, poignant, emotional

stock (SYN) wares, goods, merchandise, sell, supply, assets, investments

stoic (SYN) unemotional, aloof, indifferent, dispassionate (ANT) emotional

stomach (SYN) belly, abdomen, appetite, desire, bear, tolerate, endure

stone (SYN) pebble, rock, pelt

stoop (SYN) bend, crouch, duck, slouch (ANT) straighten

stop (SYN) halt, cease, conclude, hinder, obstruct (ANT) start, begin, initiate

store (SYN) reserve, deposit, stockpile, market, shop

storm (SYN) squall, tempest, gale, attack, charge, rage

story (SYN) tale, account, report, description, floor, level

stout (SYN) heavy, portly, plump, strong, robust (ANT) slender, lean, slim

stow (SYN) store, pack, tuck, stash

straight (SYN) direct, unbent, aligned, upright, vertical, frank, candid, continuous, successive, at once (ANT) bent, crooked, twisting, dishonest

straighten (SYN) arrange, tidy, order

strain (SYN) stretch, tighten, overexert, twist, filter, sift, stress, tension, effort

strait (SYN) channel, sound

strand (SYN) filament, thread, string, seashore, beach, waterfront

strange (SYN) weird, unusual, peculiar, unfamiliar, novel (ANT) typical, average, normal, expected

strangely (SYN) oddly, curiously, abnormally

stranger (SYN) foreigner, outsider, newcomer, guest

strangle (SYN) choke, asphyxiate, throttle, suppress, stifle, inhibit

strap (SYN) belt, tie, fasten, buckle, bind

strategy (SYN) plan, scheme, ploy, ruse, maneuver, approach

stray (SYN) wander, err, digress, deviate, homeless, lost, random

streak (SYN) line, stripe, stroke, speed, hurtle, sprint

stream (SYN) creek, brook, flow, surge, course, spill, cascade

street (SYN) lane, avenue, path, road, boulevard

strength (SYN) might, muscle, force, intensity, vigor, asset, advantage (ANT) weakness, frailty, impotence, disadvantage

strengthen (SYN) fortify, intensify, toughen, reinforce, support (ANT) weaken

strenuous (SYN) demanding, taxing, arduous, difficult, grueling (ANT) easy, effortless, painless

stress (SYN) pressure, tension, anxiety, emphasize, accentuate, importance (ANT) relaxation, ease, downplay

stretch (SYN) extend, reach, spread, strain, time, spell (ANT) contract, shorten

strict (SYN) stern, firm, harsh, precise, meticulous, absolute (ANT) flexible, lenient, compromising, easygoing

stride (SYN) pace, step, march, stomp

strident (SYN) jarring, discordant, grating, screeching, shrill (ANT) melodious, pleasant

strike (SYN) hit, hammer, thump, attack, assail, revolt, walkout, affect

string (SYN) thread, cord, twine, series, sequence, succession

stringent (SYN) rigid, inflexible, strict, tight, exacting (ANT) lax

strive (SYN) attempt, struggle, toil, endeavor, labor (ANT) give up

stroke (SYN) pet, caress, seizure, fit, movement, motion

stroll (SYN) amble, walk, saunter

strong (SYN) powerful, strapping, durable, substantial, compelling, convincing, intense, fierce, drastic (ANT) weak, feeble, mild, gentle

structure (SYN) building, formation, construction, design, arrange, organize

struggle (SYN) work, strive, labor, fight, battle, clash, contend (ANT) overcome

strut (SYN) swagger, parade

stubborn (SYN) obstinate, unyielding, tenacious, adamant, relentless (ANT) flexible, reasonable, yielding

stuck (SYN) fixed, fastened, pinned, immovable, stumped, baffled

student (SYN) pupil, learner, disciple, scholar (ANT) teacher, educator, mentor study (SYN) contemplate, learn, examine, analyze, inspection, scrutiny

stuff (SYN) things, belongings, objects, possessions, cram, force, squeeze

stumble (SYN) trip, falter, stagger, discover, find, unearth, stammer, err

stump (SYN) baffle, confound, bewilder, perplex, mystify (ANT) enlighten

stun (SYN) astound, shock, stupefy, daze, dumbfound

stunt (SYN) suppress, retard, trick, feat, exploit (ANT) enhance, increase

stupendous (SYN) amazing, marvelous, breathtaking, sensational, colossal, giant (ANT) dull, insignificant, minor

stupid (SYN) unintelligent, ignorant, obtuse, foolish, nonsensical, unwise (ANT) smart, intelligent, sensible

stupor (SYN) daze, lethargy, torpor (ANT) energy, feeling

sturdy (SYN) solid, hardy, robust, durable, well built (ANT) flimsy, weak, feeble

stutter (SYN) stammer, falter, hesitate

style (SYN) fashion, design, manner, elegance, sophistication, taste, type, variety, shape, tailor

suave (SYN) slick, smooth, charming, debonair, tactful (ANT) crude, awkward

subdue (SYN) overpower, control, defeat, quell, mellow, soften (ANT) agitate, incense

subject (SYN) topic, matter, issue, subordinate, inferior

subjective (SYN) personal, biased, emotional, intuitive, individual (ANT) objective, fair

sublime (SYN) elevated, glorious, exalted, magnificent (ANT) trivial, unimpressive, insignificant

subliminal (SYN) subconscious

submerge (SYN) immerse, dunk, plunge, sink, dip

submissive (SYN) meek, docile, compliant, passive, obedient (ANT) resistant, intractable, assertive, obstinate

submit (SYN) yield, surrender, comply, tender, present (ANT) resist, withdraw

subordinate (SYN) inferior, subject, lower, junior (ANT) superior, senior

subscribe (SYN) support, endorse, donate, contribute

subscription (SYN) membership fee, dues, contribution, gift

subsequent (SYN) following, later, successive, future, next (ANT) former, earlier, prior, preceding, previous

subservient (SYN) servile, deferential, submissive, obsequious (ANT) superior, forceful subside (SYN) abate, lessen, ebb, diminish, ease, decrease (ANT) intensify, increase, grow

subsidize (SYN) fund, support, back, finance, sponsor

subsidy (SYN) aid, grant, allowance, help, assistance

substance (SYN) material, meaning, essence, significance, reality

substantial (SYN) considerable, sizeable, significant, large, appreciable (ANT) little, meager, minor, miniscule

substantiate (SYN) confirm, prove, verify, authenticate (ANT) disprove

substitute (SYN) swap, replace, exchange, surrogate, sub, alternative, proxy

subterfuge (SYN) deception, ploy, trick, ruse

subtle (SYN) understated, faint, implied, delicate, muted, soft (ANT) obvious, clear, overt, dramatic

subtlety (SYN) refinement, sophistication, ingenuity, cunning

subtract (SYN) diminish, take away, remove, deduct (ANT) add

subversive (SYN) riotous, disruptive, troublemaking, dissident, agitator

succeed (SYN) follow, come after, replace, triumph, be successful (ANT) fail, precede

success (SYN) triumph, fortune, prosperity, accomplishment, achievement (ANT) failure, loss

successful (SYN) thriving, prosperous, booming, flourishing, wealthy (ANT) unsuccessful, unfortunate

succession (SYN) series, sequence, progression, assumption, inheritance

successive (SYN) consecutive, following, sequential, in a row

successor (SYN) heir

succinct (SYN) concise, brief, compact, terse (ANT) long, verbose, prolonged, protracted

succor (SYN) help, assistance, aid

succulent (SYN) juicy, luscious, moist

succumb (SYN) surrender, yield, submit, fold, capitulate (ANT) resist

sudden (SYN) abrupt, swift, unexpected, unforeseen, precipitous (ANT) slow, anticipated, expected, gradual

suddenly (SYN) abruptly, swiftly, all of a sudden, without warning (ANT) gradually

sue (SYN) take legal action, prosecute, summon, take to court

suffer (SYN) endure, undergo, tolerate, hurt, ache

suffering (SYN) agony, misery, hardship, adversity, affliction (ANT) pleasure, joy, celebration suffice (SYN) serve, be enough, be sufficient

sufficient (SYN) ample, adequate, enough, satisfactory, plenty (ANT) lacking, deficient, inadequate

suffocate (SYN) choke, smother, stifle

suggest (SYN) recommend, propose, advise, evoke, imply, indicate

suggestion (SYN) recommendation, hint, proposal, allusion, trace, whisper

suit (SYN) outfit, clothing, befit, become, satisfy, gratify, litigation (ANT) displease, disagree

suitable (SYN) fitting, proper, appropriate, seemly (ANT) unsuitable, improper, inappropriate

suite (SYN) rooms, apartment

suitor (SYN) admirer, beau

sulk (SYN) mope, pout, be sullen

sullen (SYN) moody, morose, cross, bitter, gloomy (ANT) cheerful, upbeat

sully (SYN) tarnish, disgrace, stain, defile, pollute, foul (ANT) clean, purify

sultry (SYN) humid, tropical, muggy, oppressive, stifling, hot

sum (SYN) total, amount, aggregate (ANT) part

summary (SYN) synopsis, overview, outline, review, abstract

summit (SYN) peak, top, pinnacle, zenith, crest, meeting, conference (ANT) bottom, base, nadir

summon (SYN) gather, muster, invite, call, send for

sumptuous (SYN) luxurious, lavish, grand, opulent, splendid (ANT) plain, austere

sundry (SYN) assorted, various, different, miscellaneous

sunrise (SYN) dawn, daybreak (ANT) dusk, sundown

sunset (SYN) dusk, nightfall (ANT) sunrise, daybreak, dawn

super (SYN) great, excellent, outstanding, wonderful

superb (SYN) splendid, superlative, exceptional, admirable, grand (ANT) poor, inferior, unimpressive

supercilious (SYN) arrogant, haughty, contemptuous, disdainful (ANT) modest, meek, lowly

superficial (SYN) shallow, frivolous, surface, casual, hurried, perfunctory (ANT) deep, profound, through

superfluous (SYN) excess, surplus, remaining, unnecessary, redundant (ANT) useful, helpful, necessary

superintendent (SYN) supervisor, director, manager, overseer

superior (SYN) preferred, better, greater, higher, supreme, finest, choice, senior, supervisor (ANT) inferior, lesser, subordinate supernatural (SYN) paranormal, miraculous, unearthly, transcendental (ANT) human, earthly, terrestrial

supercede (SYN) replace, supplant, usurp

supervise (SYN) manage, oversee, look after, guide, administer (ANT) follow

supervision (SYN) monitoring, governance, care, direction, management

supervisor (SYN) boss, foreman, manager

supper (SYN) dinner

supple (SYN) flexible, pliant, limber, lithe, malleable (ANT) rigid, inflexible, stiff

supplement (SYN) addition, extra, extension, augment, reinforce

supply (SYN) provide, contribute, furnish, stock, reserve, ration (ANT) take, receive

support (SYN) brace, prop, maintain, sustain, defend, assist, encouragement, maintenance, upkeep (ANT) hinder, block, neglect, oppose

suppose (SYN) gather, presume, guess, imagine, hypothesize (ANT) know, discover

supposition (SYN) guess, conjecture, speculation, theory, surmise (ANT) knowledge

suppress (SYN) stile, restrain, smother, quell, overpower (ANT) liberate, free, reveal, allow, encourage

supreme (SYN) highest, leading, paramount, ultimate, chief (ANT) insignificant, subordinate, secondary

sure (SYN) certain, assured, confident, positive, inevitable, inescapable (ANT) unsure, unlikely, uncertain, doubtful

surely (SYN) definitely, unquestionably (ANT) perhaps

surface (SYN) outside, exterior, face, arise, emerge, materialize (ANT) inside, interior, dive, disappear

surfeit (SYN) excess, gluttony, superfluity

surge (SYN) rush, flood, gush, wave, swell, heave, increase

surly (SYN) cross, grouchy, uncivil, disagreeable, hostile (ANT) friendly, jovial, cheery

surmise (SYN) suppose, presume, speculate, assumption, guess (ANT) know

surmount (SYN) overcome, triumph over (ANT) succumb to

surpass (SYN) exceed, outdo, eclipse, go beyond, top (ANT) fall short, fail

surplus (SYN) excess, balance, remainder, overage (ANT) lack, dearth

surprise (SYN) shock, stun, amazement, wonder, incredulity, discover, startle surrender (SYN) submit, give up, yield, concede, relinquish, resignation, capitulation (ANT) fight, win, resist

surreptitious (SYN) secret, furtive, covert, stealthy, sneaky (ANT) open, straightforward

surrogate (SYN) substitute, proxy, stand-in

surround (SYN) encircle, envelop, encompass, confine, besiege

surroundings (SYN) setting, environment, backdrop, habitat

surveillance (SYN) watch, observation, scrutiny

survey (SYN) scan, inspect, appraise, measure, inquiry, review

survive (SYN) remain alive, last, outlive, weather (ANT) die, perish

susceptible (SYN) liable, disposed, inclined, vulnerable, impressionable, receptive (ANT) invulnerable, immune

suspect (SYN) believe, speculate, distrust, doubt, questionable, suspicious (ANT) trust

suspend (SYN) hang, dangle, postpone, interrupt, discontinue (ANT) continue, reinstate, renew

suspense (SYN) expectation, anticipation, tension, irresolution

suspension (SYN) break, postponement, deferment, interruption

suspicion (SYN) distrust, wariness, misgiving, hunch, impression (ANT) trust, faith, conviction

suspicious (SYN) dubious, suspect, skeptical, doubtful, questionable, mysterious (ANT) unquestioning, trusting, honest, innocent

sustain (SYN) preserve, maintain, support, uphold, encourage, nourish

sustenance (SYN) food, nourishment

swagger (SYN) brag, boast, parade

swallow (SYN) gulp, consume, eat

swamp (SYN) marsh, wetland, mire, bog, flood, overwhelm, inundate

swap (SYN) trade, exchange, switch, replace (ANT) keep

swarm (SYN) throng, multitude, army, teem, abound, flock, surge

swarthy (SYN) dark

swat (SYN) hit, whack

sway (SYN) lean, rock, roll, teeter, influence, persuade, power, authority

swear (SYN) vow, pledge, testify, curse

sweat (SYN) perspiration, worry, panic, stress, perspire, labor, toil

sweep (SYN) clear, brush, glide, skim, extent, scope

sweet (SYN) sugary, cloying, adorable, charming, fragrant, aromatic, pleasant, agreeable, confection, treat

(ANT) sour, savory, harsh, unpleasant, irritable

swell (SYN) bulge, expand, distend, grow, wave, surge (ANT) shrink, deflate, decrease

sweltering (SYN) hot, scorching, stifling, boiling (ANT) cool, chilly

swerve (SYN) veer, deviate, stray, turn

swift (SYN) rapid, speedy, hurried, fast (ANT) slow, lethargic, leisurely

swindle (SYN) cheat, con, defraud, deceive, trick

swing (SYN) sway, rock, pivot, swivel, fluctuation, oscillation

swirl (SYN) twist, spin, twirl, circulate, revolve

switch (SYN) change, shift, swap, substitution, exchange, button, lever

swivel (SYN) turn, pivot, rotate

swollen (SYN) bloated, distended, enlarged, inflamed

swoon (SYN) faint

swoop (SYN) pounce, dive, plunge, descend, attack

symbol (SYN) sign, emblem, mark, representation, character

symbolic (SYN) figurative, representative, indicative, emblematic (ANT) realistic, actual

symbolize (SYN) denote, stand for, represent, mean, signify

symmetrical (SYN) balanced, in proportion, regular, congruous (ANT) asymmetrical, imbalanced, unequal

symmetry (SYN) balance, order, evenness, proportion, accord (ANT) asymmetry, irregularity

sympathetic (SYN) warm, compassionate, understanding, compatible, like-minded (ANT) unsympathetic, indifferent, apathetic

sympathize (SYN) commiserate, identify, feel, agree, relate to

sympathy (SYN) compassion, pity, sentiment, concern, commiseration (ANT) indifference, intolerance, malevolence

symptom (SYN) indicator, warning, manifestation, mark, evidence, clue

synopsis (SYN) summary, abstract, digest, outline, condensation

synthesis (SYN) unification, combination, joining, merging

synthetic (SYN) fake, artificial, manufactured, imitation (ANT) genuine, real, natural

system (SYN) method, technique, formula, organization, structure (ANT) confusion, chaos, disorder

systematic (SYN) methodical, organized, efficient, routine, standardized (ANT) unstructured, disorderly, random

T

table (SYN) counter, desk, catalog, list, chart

tableau (SYN) picture, scene

tablet (SYN) pad, notebook, paper, block

taboo (SYN) unmentionable, forbidden, prohibited, banned, unspeakable, restrictions (ANT) acceptable, sanctioned, normal, orthodox

tacit (SYN) understood, implicit, implied, unspoken, acknowledged (ANT) spoken, stated, declared

taciturn (SYN) quiet, uncommunicative, laconic, reserved, withdrawn (ANT) chatty, expressive, forthcoming

tack (SYN) nail, pin, fasten, fix, approach, method

tackle (SYN) gear, equipment, attempt, confront, handle, seize, down

tact (SYN) sensitivity, understanding, delicacy, diplomacy, subtlety (ANT) thoughtlessness, imprudence, inconsiderateness

tactic (SYN) approach, move, strategy, scheme, ploy, logistics

tactless (SYN) impolite, rude, brash, indelicate, indiscreet, gauche (ANT) considerate, diplomatic, subtle

tag (SYN) label, tab, sticker, identification, flag, ticket

tail (SYN) follow, shadow, track, watch, end, rear

tailor (SYN) dressmaker, seamstress, clothier, adapt, modify, customize

taint (SYN) contaminate, corrupt, pollute, blemish, tarnish (ANT) clean, purify, improve

take (SYN) obtain, seize, bring, transport, steal, require, necessitate, tolerate, accommodate, presume (ANT) give, return

tale (SYN) story, fable, account, narrative, anecdote, lie

talent (SYN) aptitude, gift, knack, ability, flair

talisman (SYN) lucky charm, amulet

talk (SYN) speak, utter, chatter, converse, communicate, speech, address

talkative (SYN) chatty, glib, conversational, garrulous, verbose (ANT) taciturn, quiet, silent

tall (SYN) soaring, lofty, high, elevated (ANT) short

tally (SYN) score, count, total, match, agree

tame (SYN) train, domesticate, docile, gentle, unexciting, curb, bridle (ANT) fierce, wild, interesting

tamper (SYN) alter, meddle, tinker, interfere

tangible (SYN) real, concrete, palpable, actual, physical (ANT) abstract, theoretical, intangible tantalize (SYN) taunt, tease, torment, tempt, lure, bait

tantamount (SYN) equal, equivalent, synonymous

tantrum (SYN) fit, outburst, frenzy, conniption

tap (SYN) knock, rap, drum, valve, faucet, bug, monitor, utilize

tape (SYN) record, seal, stick, strip, ribbon

taper (SYN) narrow, thin, dwindle, fade, subside (ANT) grow, increase, widen

target (SYN) aim, goal, objective, victim, focus

tariff (SYN) tax, levy, duty, toll

tarnish (SYN) stain, darken, discolor, spot, dirty, blemish (ANT) cleanse, polish, brighten, restore

tart (SYN) pie, pastry, sour, tangy, sharp, scathing (ANT) sweet

task (SYN) assignment, chore, duty, effort

taste (SYN) flavor, savor, sample, experience, fondness, inclination, style, discernment

tasteful (SYN) refined, elegant, aesthetic, stylish, exquisite (ANT) tasteless, garish, gaudy, offensive

taunt (SYN) tease, deride, mock, torment, ridicule, pester (ANT) honor, respect

taut (SYN) tight, tense, rigid, stretched, snug (ANT) loose, relaxed

tawdry (SYN) vulgar, tasteless, flashy, cheap, gaudy (ANT) refined, elegant, expensive

tax (SYN) charge, fee, toll, strain, exhaust, weary

teach (SYN) instruct, educate, train, coach, tutor (ANT) learn, misguide

teacher (SYN) guide, mentor, educator, instructor (ANT) student, pupil

team (SYN) group, squad, crew, couple, match, unite

tear (SYN) rip, rend, shred, rupture, laceration, dash, sprint

tease (SYN) mock, taunt, make fun of, goad, bother, irritate

technical (SYN) scientific, specialized, technological, complicated

technique (SYN) method, manner, system, strategy, craft, proficiency

tedious (SYN) monotonous, dull, boring, repetitive, uninteresting (ANT) amusing, lively, exciting, varied, eventful

tell (SYN) announce, inform, express, order, ascertain, deduce, distinguish (ANT) conceal, withhold

temper (SYN) rage, fury, composure, self-control, cool, moderate, soften

temperament (SYN) disposition, nature, personality, character, personality

temperance (SYN) restraint, moderation, self-discipline, forbearance (ANT) excess, self-indulgence, gluttony

temperate (SYN) mild, pleasant, dispassionate, composed (ANT) stormy, extreme, immoderate

tempest (SYN) storm, gale, squall, hurricane

temple (SYN) shrine, mosque, synagogue, church, cathedral, house of worship

tempo (SYN) beat, rhythm, cadence

temporal (SYN) earthly, transitory, temporary (ANT) eternal

temporary (SYN) brief, fleeting, momentary, ephemeral (ANT) lasting, permanent, abiding, fixed, endless

tempt (SYN) entice, allure, attract, seduce, coax (ANT) discourage, repel, deter

temptation (SYN) enticement, pull, draw, fascination, desire, impulse

tenacious (SYN) determined, persistent, tough, stubborn, resolute (ANT) fragile, yielding

tenacity (SYN) perseverance, steadfastness, obduracy, resolve

tenant (SYN) renter, occupant, resident, inhabitant

tend (SYN) nurture, cultivate, look after, gravitate, incline, lean (ANT) neglect, ignore .

tendency (SYN) inclination, propensity, aptness, likelihood, bent, leaning

tender (SYN) gentle, compassionate, loving, sensitive, vulnerable, submit, propose (ANT) cruel, harsh, callous, rough

tenderness (SYN) affection, compassion, warmth, sentimentality, soreness, inflammation (ANT) severity, insensitivity, heartlessness

tenet (SYN) belief, doctrine, principle, conviction

tense (SYN) edgy, uptight, stiff, nervous, stressful, tight, rigid, brace (ANT) relaxed, tranquil, loose, relax

tension (SYN) pressure, apprehension, stress, anxiety, stiffness (ANT) calm, relaxation

tentative (SYN) anticipated, unsettled, indefinite, unconfirmed, cautious, unsteady (ANT) definite, conclusive, confident

tenuous (SYN) flimsy, dubious, doubtful, sketchy, feeble (ANT) significant, convincing, strong

tepid (SYN) lukewarm, apathetic, indifferent, unenthusiastic, half-hearted (ANT) hot, enthusiastic, passionate

term (SYN) word, expression, duration, period, dub, label, condition, provision

terminal (SYN) station, incurable, fatal, ultimate, last, concluding (ANT) curable, initial, opening, beginning terminate (SYN) end, abort, discontinue, cease, conclude (ANT) continue, start, begin

termination (SYN) ending, finish, cessation, conclusion (ANT) beginning

terminology (SYN) vocabulary, language, jargon, nomenclature

terrain (SYN) land, topography, landscape, countryside

terrestrial (SYN) earthly, worldly

terrible (SYN) awful, atrocious, excruciating, unbearable, appalling (ANT) excellent, great, pleasing, joyous

terrific (SYN) marvelous, dazzling, brilliant, colossal, gigantic, frightening, ghastly (ANT) dull, unimpressive, slight

terrify (SYN) scare, horrify, paralyze, frighten, alarm (ANT) soothe, reassure, appease

territory (SYN) area, region, land, dominion, realm

terror (SYN) fear, fright, horror, dread, alarm, scourge (ANT) security, calm

terse (SYN) concise, brief, pithy, succinct, short, brusque (ANT) lengthy, verbose, rambling, garrulous

test (SYN) check, investigate, trial, examination, evaluation, experiment

testament (SYN) will, last wishes, proof, evidence, demonstration

testify (SYN) attest, state, vouch, swear, witness, corroborate

testimony (SYN) statement, declaration, verification, proof, evidence

tether (SYN) fetter, bind, tie, secure, fasten, rope, leash, lead

text (SYN) words, wording, context, manual, book

textile (SYN) fabric, cloth, material

texture (SYN) feel, surface, grain, finish, fiber, constitution

thank (SYN) bless, show one's gratitude

thankful (SYN) grateful, appreciative, obliged, pleased (ANT) ungrateful

thanks (SYN) acknowledgement, credit, recognition, gratitude, appreciation

thaw (SYN) melt, soften, warm, defrost (ANT) freeze, chill

theater (SYN) hall, arena, playhouse, stadium

theatrical (SYN) dramatic, affected, artificial, stagy, exaggerated, melodramatic

theft (SYN) stealing, robbery, larceny, burglary, shoplifting

theme (SYN) subject, topic, motif, thrust, thread, melody

theology (SYN) religion, doctrine

theorem (SYN) thesis, problem

theoretical

theoretical (SYN) hypothetical, conjectural, speculative, abstract (ANT) proven, certain, practical

theory (SYN) hypothesis, thesis, premise, supposition, opinion, contention

therapeutic (SYN) healing, beneficial, restorative, remedial (ANT) harmful

therapy (SYN) treatment, cure, remedy, counseling

therefore (SYN) so, ergo, consequently, hence, as a result

thesis (SYN) essay, dissertation, theory, hypothesis, argument

thick (SYN) broad, solid, teeming, crammed, bushy, luxuriant, heavy (ANT) thin, slender, sparse, watery

thief (SYN) robber, burglar, criminal

thin (SYN) slim, slender, narrow, lean, gaunt, delicate, sheer, meager, flimsy (ANT) thick, fat, substantial, bulky

thing (SYN) object, entity, article, commodity

think (SYN) ponder, muse, consider, recall, imagine, believe, guess

thirst (SYN) craving, longing, hankering, yearning, appetite

thirsty (SYN) parched, dehydrated, dry, eager, greedy (ANT) satiated

thorn (SYN) spike, barb, spine, prickle

thorough (SYN) complete, absolute, utter, sweeping, exhaustive,

meticulous (ANT) careless, hasty, incomplete, superficial, cursory

thoroughly (SYN) painstakingly, conscientiously, fully, totally, downright

though (SYN) although, while, notwithstanding, still, nevertheless

thought (SYN) reflection, consideration, deliberation, idea, notion, regard, concern

thoughtful (SYN) pensive, contemplative, prudent, considerate, unselfish, accommodating (ANT) careless, indifferent, thoughtless, inconsiderate

thread (SYN) strand, fiber, filament, theme, plot, pass, weave, navigate

threat (SYN) danger, risk, hazard, warning, omen (ANT) reassurance, defense

threaten (SYN) intimidate, menace, bully, terrorize, jeopardize, endanger, signal, indicate, loom (ANT) protect

threshold (SYN) beginning, brink, verge, entrance, doorway, limit

thrift (SYN) frugality, economy, prudence, care, parsimony (ANT) waste, extravagance, imprudence

thrifty (SYN) sparing, frugal, economical, penny-pinching (ANT) extravagant, wasteful, indulgent

thrill (SYN) excitement, pleasure, titillation, stir, electrify, intoxicate (ANT) bore, boredom, numbness thrive (SYN) succeed, prosper, flourish, blossom, boom (ANT) wither, decline, fail, shrivel

throb (SYN) pulsate, vibrate, beat, pulse, pounding

throng (SYN) crowd, mob, bevy, horde, swarm, converge

throttle (SYN) choke, strangle, suppress, garrote

through (SYN) between, past, via, over, finished, completed, during

throughout (SYN) everywhere, all over, all, for the whole of

throw (SYN) hurl, fling, project, cast, confuse

thrust (SYN) push, drive, shove, force, momentum, gist, message

thud (SYN) thump, crash, clunk

thunder (SYN) rumble, boom, peal, resound, bellow, roar

thus (SYN) hence, therefore, so, consequently

thwart (SYN) prevent, frustrate, foil, impede, derail (ANT) help, further, promote

ticket (SYN) slip, voucher, coupon, label, tag

tickle (SYN) please, delight, amuse, entertain

tide (SYN) ebb and flow, course, drift, tend, direction

tidy (SYN) neat, spruce, orderly, trim, straighten, clean (ANT) messy, disorganized, sloppy, unkempt

tie (SYN) bind, secure, attach, link, match, equal, draw, connection, affiliation (ANT) loosen, untie, separate, unfasten, free

tier (SYN) level, rank, stratum, layer, grade, echelon

tight (SYN) snug, stretched, close, even, secured, sealed, tense, cramped (ANT) loose, slack, leaky, relaxed

tighten (SYN) constrict, squeeze, narrow, stretch, strain (ANT) loosen, relax, slacken

till (SYN) work, dig, plow, cultivate, labor

tilt (SYN) slant, slope, incline, angle, lean, pitch

timber (SYN) wood, lumber, logs, planks, trees

timbre (SYN) tone, ring, resonance

time (SYN) period, stretch, duration, occasion, instance, rhythm

timely (SYN) convenient, opportune, appropriate, prompt, punctual (ANT) ill-timed, inconvenient, early, late

timid (SYN) cowardly, hesitant, shy, fearful, apprehensive, shrinking (ANT) bold, fearless, brave, courageous, unafraid

timidity (SYN) fear, cowardice, fright, nervousness

timorous (SYN) bashful, diffident, shy, fearful, faint-hearted (ANT) brave, daring, adventurous

tingle (SYN) prickle, sting, quiver, shiver, thrill

tinker (SYN) meddle, fiddle, play

tint (SYN) color, shade, hue, dye, wash, tinge

tiny (SYN) minute, miniature, little, slight, diminutive (ANT) large, massive, colossal, immense, giant, vast

tip (SYN) gratuity, reward, pointer, suggestion, tilt, incline, end, point

tirade (SYN) outburst, diatribe, tantrum, sermon, lecture, condemnation (ANT) approval, praise

tire (SYN) weary, drain, fatigue, droop, bore, exasperate (ANT) arouse, awaken, enliven

tired (SYN) worn, sleepy, exhausted, fed up, predictable, clichéd (ANT) rested, energetic, fresh, lively, refreshed

titanic (SYN) mammoth, colossal, huge, immense, hulking (ANT) tiny, small, insignificant

title (SYN) name, heading, designation, ownership, possession, championship

toast (SYN) warm, brown, grill, tribute, salute

together (SYN) collectively, in unison, simultaneously, concurrently, practical, efficient (ANT) alone, separately, individually, flighty, disorganized

toil (SYN) labor, work, drudge, struggle, effort, exertion (ANT) lay, leisure, enjoyment, relax, rest

token (SYN) symbol, expression, representation, hollow, superficial

tolerance (SYN) open-mindedness, leniency, permissiveness, endurance, resistance (ANT) intolerance, bias

tolerant (SYN) liberal, understanding, broad-minded, patient, charitable (ANT) intolerant, strict, narrow, inflexible

toll (SYN) ring, sound, peal, strike, charge, fee

tomb (SYN) grave, crypt, vault, mausoleum, sepulcher

tombstone (SYN) gravestone, marker, headstone, monument

tone (SYN) inflection, pitch, mood, temper, color, hue, shade

tongue (SYN) language, dialect, vernacular, speech

tonic (SYN) stimulant, boost, restorative, refreshing, energizing

too (SYN) also, in addition, moreover, overly, excessively

tool (SYN) instrument, implement, appliance, gadget, device

top (SYN) summit, peak, maximum, highest, leading, principal, cover, lead, surpass, exceed (ANT) bottom, base, lowest, minimum

topic (SYN) subject, theme, issue, point, concern

topple (SYN) tumble, collapse, overturn, unseat, bring down

torment (SYN) torture, distress, provoke, harass, suffering, anguish, pain (ANT) comfort, relieve, pleasure

tornado (SYN) whirlwind, storm, tempest

torpid (SYN) lethargic, inactive, sluggish, apathetic (ANT) lively, energetic, active

torrent (SYN) cascade, deluge, rush, downpour, flood

torrential (SYN) bursting, streaming, violent, rushing

torrid (SYN) sweltering, sultry, steamy, passionate, intense (ANT) cool, frigid, indifferent, apathetic

tortuous (SYN) winding, meandering, indirect, complicated, roundabout (ANT) straightforward, direct, clear

torture (SYN) abuse, cruelty, atrocity, agony, misery, torment, afflict (ANT) ease, comfort, pleasure, relief

toss (SYN) flip, throw, fling, shake, thrash, wriggle

total (SYN) complete, entire, absolute, sum, whole (ANT) part, portion, division, lacking

totally (SYN) fully, utterly, completely, thoroughly, one hundred percent (ANT) partially, incompletely

touch (SYN) handle, feel, affect, influence, bit, drop, skill, flair

touching (SYN) moving, affecting, tender, poignant, emotive, stirring

tough (SYN) difficult, strenuous, resilient, durable, strict, severe (ANT) easy, mild, weak, frail, tender

tour (SYN) expedition, journey, visit, explore, travel

tourist (SYN) traveler, sightseer, voyager, visitor, globetrotter

tournament (SYN) contest, competition, championship

tow (SYN) pull, drag, haul, lug, tug

tower (SYN) pillar, column, steeple, soar, dominate

towering (SYN) lofty, tall, overwhelming, imposing, impressive (ANT) short, miniature, small, tiny, insignificant

toxic (SYN) harmful, poisonous, lethal, dangerous, noxious (ANT) harmless, clean, healthy

toy (SYN) plaything, model, play, fiddle, dally

trace (SYN) tinge, suggestion, indication, mark, find, discover, copy

track (SYN) path, trail, follow, pursue, stalk, course, line tractable (SYN) docile, manageable, compliant, loyal, submissive (ANT) intractable, obstinate, unruly, unwilling

traction (SYN) friction, grip, resistance

trade (SYN) swap, exchange, commerce, business, occupation, craft

tradition (SYN) convention, ritual, heritage, institution

traditional (SYN) established, time-honored, customary, classic, standard (ANT) modern, unconventional, revolutionary, innovative

traffic (SYN) trade, commerce, exchange, transport, peddle

tragedy (SYN) misfortune, calamity, disaster, adversity, catastrophe (ANT) comedy, prosperity

tragic (SYN) sad, distressing, painful, devastating, horrible (ANT) happy, joyous, fortunate

trail (SYN) path, route, track, footprints, drag, tow, lag, dawdle, follow, shadow

train (SYN) instruct, educate, prime, study, exercise

training (SYN) preparation, practice, instruction, teaching, discipline

trait (SYN) feature, characteristic, attribute, quality, mannerism

traitor (SYN) betrayer, back-stabber, turncoat, defector, counteragent

trajectory (SYN) course, path, line, track, flight path

tramp (SYN) drifter, vagrant, hike, tread, stamp, plod, trudge

trample (SYN) crush, flatten, squash, stomp, walk over

trance (SYN) daze, stupor, reverie, hypnotic state

tranquil (SYN) peaceful, calm, serene, restful, still, undisturbed (ANT) noisy, agitated, turbulent, excited

tranquility (SYN) repose, stillness, quiet, peace, placidity (ANT) excitement, bustle, frenzy, turmoil, agitation

transaction (SYN) deal, negotiation, settlement, arrangement, agreement

transcend (SYN) surpass, exceed, go beyond, rise above, outdo (ANT) regress

transcribe (ANT) take down, write out

transcript (SYN) copy, record, reproduction, duplicate

transfer (SYN) move, relocate, reassign, transport, shift, carry

transform (SYN) alter, change, convert, rebuild, modify, revolutionize, overhaul

transgression (SYN) sin, offense, violation, crime, misdeed

transient (SYN) temporary, fleeting, ephemeral, passing, short-lived (ANT) lasting, permanent, immutable, changeless transit (SYN) movement, passage, transportation

transition (SYN) change, progression, shift, metamorphosis, conversion, alteration, development

transitory (SYN) brief, short, impermanent, momentary (ANT) unending, permanent

translate (SYN) interpret, decipher, transform, paraphrase

translation (SYN) interpretation, rendition, version

transmission (SYN) transfer, spread, broadcasting, sending, program

transmit (SYN) convey, impart, carry, disseminate, relay

transmute (SYN) change, convert

transparent (SYN) clear, sheer, diaphanous, obvious, evident, plain (ANT) opaque, dark, obscure, ambiguous, convoluted

transpire (SYN) happen, come about, arise, occur

transplant (SYN) transfer, move, relocate, uproot

transport (SYN) haul, bring, shipment, enchant, delight, bliss

transpose (SYN) switch, interchange, swap, exchange

trap (SYN) catch, ensnare, trick, ambush, lure, ruse, deception

trash (SYN) garbage, rubbish, litter, demolish, ruin, trounce, nonsense

traumatic (SYN) disturbing, upsetting, painful, stressful, harrowing (ANT) comforting, pleasurable

travail (SYN) misery, torment, suffering

travel (SYN) journey, roam, globetrot, trip, excursion

traverse (SYN) cross, span, go over, pass

treacherous (SYN) treason, betrayal, infidelity, unreliable, evil (ANT) loyal, steadfast, reliable

tread (SYN) step, walk, stamp, pace

treason (SYN) disloyalty, betrayal, subversion, rebellion, deception (ANT) devotion, fidelity, allegiance, loyalty

treasure (SYN) riches, wealth, fortune, cherish, prize, value (ANT) trash, detest

treasury (SYN) bank, storehouse, vault

treat (SYN) regard, handle, tend, nurse, entertainment, thrill, indulge, luxury

treatise (SYN) essay, thesis, dissertation

treatment (SYN) therapy, remedy, care, handling, management, conduct

treaty (SYN) pact, contract, covenant, alliance, entente

trek (SYN) hike, odyssey, expedition, rove, walk

tremble (SYN) vibrate, shudder, quiver, shake, wobble

tremendous (SYN) huge, immense, formidable, splendid, outstanding, brilliant (ANT) tiny, small, insignificant

tremor (SYN) shake, quiver, quake, shock

trench (SYN) ditch, trough, gutter, furrow, rut

trenchant (SYN) scathing, pointed, acerbic, potent, forceful

trend (SYN) tendency, flow, inclination, fashion, rage

trepidation (SYN) uneasiness, disquiet, apprehension, fear, dread (ANT) bravery, courage, assurance, confidence

trespass (SYN) intrude, invade, encroach, breach, infringe

trial (SYN) litigation, hearing, test, experiment, affliction, hardship, adversity

tribe (SYN) clan, people, race, family

tribulation (SYN) sorrow, woe, agony, grief, suffering (ANT) delight, elation, joy

tribunal (SYN) court, panel, committee

tribute (SYN) recognition, accolade, salute, homage (ANT) criticism, condemnation, admonishment

trick (SYN) swindle, deceive, dupe, prank, ploy, illusion

trickle (SYN) seep, dribble, spill, leak, ooze (ANT) gush, pour

trifle (SYN) bauble, triviality, toy, play

trifling (SYN) trivial, insignificant, unimportant, petty, inconsequential (ANT) weighty, important, major, essential, momentous

trigger (SYN) set off, activate, spark, produce

trim (SYN) crop, prune, spruce, tidy, fit, svelte, decoration, adorn (ANT) disorderly, messy, overweight, heavy

trio (SYN) threesome, trinity, triumvirate

trip (SYN) journey, voyage, jaunt, stumble, slip, fall

trite (SYN) stale, unoriginal, dull, wearisome, banal (ANT) imaginative, novel, fresh, stimulating

triumph (SYN) success, victory, pride, jubilation, overcome, prevail, rejoice (ANT) lose, fail, defeat, failure

triumphant (SYN) victorious, exultant, prevailing, celebratory, gleeful (ANT) defeated, unsuccessful, vanquished, despondent

trivia (SYN) details, minutiae, froth, trifles

trivial (SYN) meaningless, worthless, frivolous, insignificant, petty (ANT) important, significant, serious, consequential

troop (SYN) band, group, company, squad

trophy (SYN) prize, award, cup,
souvenir, token

tropical (SYN) sultry, hot, steamy,
humid, sticky (ANT) cold, arid, dry

trot (SYN) canter, jog, lope, run

trouble (SYN) distress, inconvenience,
bother, worry, disturb, nuisance,
burden, impose on

trounce (SYN) crush, thrash, beat

troupe (SYN) cast, company, band

trousers (SYN) slacks, pants

truant (SYN) absentee, delinquent

truce (SYN) peace, respite, ceasefire, lull

true (SYN) factual, accurate, authentic,
legitimate, valid (ANT) wrong, false,
untruthful, erroneous

truism (SYN) axiom, platitude, cliché

truly (SYN) really, actually, indeed,
correctly, faithfully, sincerely

trumpet (SYN) horn, bugle, proclaim,
broadcast, announce

trunk (SYN) chest, box, crate, stem,
body, torso, snout

trust (SYN) faith, confidence,
conviction, expect, assume, commit,
believe in, bank on (ANT) doubt,
skepticism, mistrust

truth (SYN) accuracy, validity, honesty,
precision, veracity (ANT) deception,
hypocrisy, lies, falsehood, fiction

try (SYN) attempt, strive, appraise,
sample, endeavor

trying (SYN) taxing, bothersome,
annoying, demanding, frustrating
(ANT) easy, pleasant

tryst (SYN) rendezvous, meeting,
appointment

tuck (SYN) fold, gather, pinch, push,
insert

tuft (SYN) clump, knot, cluster

tug (SYN) pull, yank, jerk, draw, tow
(ANT) push, shove

tuition (SYN) education, teaching,
training, instruction, lessons

tumble (SYN) fall, topple, stumble,
plunge, spill

tumult (SYN) confusion, agitation,
commotion, upheaval, riot (ANT)
peace, tranquility, quiet, order

tumultuous (SYN) wild, rowdy, chaotic,
noisy, turbulent (ANT) calm,
peaceful, settled, stable

tune (SYN) melody, song, pitch,
regulate, adjust

tunnel (SYN) passage, channel, shaft,
underpass, burrow, dig, mine

turbid (SYN) cloudy, muddy, dark,
obscured, murky (ANT) clear

turbulence (SYN) instability, confusion,
chaos, anarchy, unrest (ANT) calm,
peace, tranquility

turbulent (SYN) rough, choppy, raging, stormy, tumultuous (ANT) clam, quiet

turmoil (SYN) disarray, commotion, disorder, pandemonium, agitation (ANT) order, peace

turn (SYN) rotate, spin, deviate, bend, shift, chance, opportunity

tutor (SYN) teacher, instructor, educator, coach, mentor, guide

tweak (SYN) adjust, fix, pinch, squeeze

twig (SYN) branch, stick, sprig, shoot

twilight (SYN) dusk, sundown, sunset, evening (ANT) morning, sunrise, dawn

twin (SYN) duplicate, copy, double, math, pair, link

twine (SYN) string, cord, coil, loop, encircle

twinge (SYN) pang, stab, prick, spasm

twinkle (SYN) sparkle, gleam, shine, flash, flicker, shimmer

twirl (SYN) spin, rotate, turn, pivot, rotation, pirouette

twist (SYN) wind, wrap, contort, swivel, development, surprise, arc, bend (ANT) straighten

twitch (SYN) jerk, spasm, convulse, shudder, shiver

tycoon (SYN) mogul, magnate, businessman, businesswoman

type (SYN) category, sort, variety, species, print, lettering

typical (SYN) common, usual, average, normal, representative (ANT) unorthodox, atypical, peculiar, deviant, exceptional

tyranny (SYN) oppression, cruelty, fascism, despotism, subjugation, totalitarianism

tyrant (SYN) dictator, bully, oppressor, autocrat, authoritarian

U

ubiquitous (SYN) universal, omnipresent, everywhere, pervasive, global (ANT) rare

ugly (SYN) unattractive, hideous, unsightly, unpleasant, disagreeable (ANT) beautiful, appealing, handsome, pleasant

ulterior (SYN) hidden, covert, undisclosed, shrouded, secret (ANT) open, clear, obvious, plain

ultimate (SYN) final, concluding, absolute, extreme, utmost, quintessential (ANT) first, beginning, initial

ultimately (SYN) finally, eventually, in the long run, sooner or later

ultimatum (SYN) condition, choice

umbrage (SYN) anger, bitterness, resentment, outrage, indignation (ANT) pleasure, contentment, harmony umpire (SYN) referee, judge, arbitrator

unable (SYN) incapable, powerless, impotent, incompetent, unqualified (ANT) adequate, qualified, effective

unalienable (SYN) fixed, immutable, permanent, unchangeable

unanimous (SYN) united, in agreement, harmonious, agreed, concurrent (ANT) discordant, divided, varied

unanimously (SYN) without exception, as one, in concert

unassuming (SYN) unassertive, modest, unpretentious, reserved, unobtrusive (ANT) vain, arrogant, haughty, showy

unavoidable (SYN) certain, inevitable, fated, inescapable, obvious (ANT) avoidable, preventable, needless

unaware (SYN) ignorant, uninformed, oblivious (ANT) knowledgeable, informed, conscious

unbearable (SYN) intolerable, agonizing, insufferable, distressing (ANT) bearable, tolerable, easy

unbecoming (SYN) unfit, improper, indecent, unflattering, unsightly (ANT) becoming, seemly, suitable, appropriate

unbelievable (SYN) incredible, astonishing, implausible, amazing (ANT) convincing, probable, believable

unblemished (SYN) spotless, flawless, perfect, innocent, clean (ANT) blemished, stained, dirty, marred

unbridled (SYN) unchecked, excessive, unrestrained, wanton (ANT) temperate, moderate

uncanny (SYN) weird, mysterious, eerie, exceptional, remarkable (ANT) normal, usual, common

uncertainty (SYN) doubt, ambiguity, confusion, vagueness, ambivalence (ANT) certainty, clarity, faith, conviction

uncivilized (SYN) barbaric, primitive, wild, savage, uncouth (ANT) civilized, cultivated, refined, courteous

unclear (SYN) vague, obscure, nebulous, unsettled, indefinite (ANT) clear, evident, straightforward

uncomfortable (SYN) awkward, harsh, distressing, anxious, embarrassed (ANT) comfortable, easy, relaxed, untroubled

uncommon (SYN) rare, infrequent, strange, exceptional, distinctive (ANT) common, typical, normal, ordinary

unconcern (SYN) apathy, indifference, nonchalance, detachment (ANT) interest, concern, anxiety

unconditional (SYN) absolute, unwavering, complete, entire, wholehearted (ANT) limited, reserved, qualified, restricted, conditional

unconscionable (SYN) unscrupulous, devious, immoral, underhanded, unprincipled (ANT) honest, ethical, honorable, reputable

unconscious

unconscious (SYN) senseless, out cold, unaware, oblivious, unintentional, unwitting (ANT) conscious, alert, aware, voluntary

uncoordinated (SYN) clumsy, awkward, graceless, ungainly (ANT) coordinated, graceful, synchronized

uncouth (SYN) rude, uncivilized, rough, coarse (ANT) civilized, cultured, polite, mannered

uncover (SYN) expose, reveal, unearth, discover, detect (ANT) hide, cover, conceal

under (SYN) below, beneath, less than, subject to, governed by (ANT) over, above, greater than, higher

underestimate (SYN) minimize, miscalculate, undervalue, misjudge (ANT) overestimate, overrate

undergo (SYN) experience, face, go through, suffer, sustain, withstand

underground (SYN) buried, subterranean, covert, hidden, subversive (ANT) above ground, open, conspicuous, overt

undergrowth (SYN) scrub, brush, briars

underline (SYN) underscore, mark, stress, emphasize, highlight

underlying (SYN) primary, basic, intrinsic, fundamental, central

undermine (SYN) weaken, sabotage, shake, threaten, compromise (ANT) support, strengthen

underrate (SYN) underestimate, belittle, devalue (ANT) overrate, overestimate

understand (SYN) comprehend, grasp, know, realize, acknowledge (ANT) confuse, misunderstand, misinterpret, ignore

understood (SYN) implied, unspoken, inferred, assumed, accepted

undertake (SYN) try, attempt, tackle, embark on, contract, vow (ANT) quit

undertaker (SYN) funeral director, mortician

undertaking (SYN) endeavor, venture, task, promise, commitment

underwear (SYN) undergarments, lingerie, underclothes

underwrite (SYN) fund, finance, back, insure, sponsor

undesirable (SYN) unpleasant, objectionable, unattractive, disagreeable, distasteful (ANT) wanted, pleasant, welcome, desirable

undignified (SYN) improper, informal, dishonorable (ANT) dignified, fitting

undo (SYN) unfasten, loose, reverse, cancel, invalidate, wreck, shatter (ANT) fasten, tighten, bind, enhance

undoubtedly (SYN) surely, definitely, indisputably, undeniably, clearly (ANT) perhaps

undulate (SYN) wiggle, swerve

unearth (SYN) find, discover, come across, excavate, dredge up

uneasy (SYN) anxious, on edge, nervous, apprehensive, troubled, fraught (ANT) calm, relaxed, comfortable, secure, steady

unemotional (SYN) composed, dispassionate, cold, reserved, unexcitable (ANT) demonstrative, emotional, expressive, passionate

unemployed (SYN) jobless, out of work, laid off, redundant

unequal (SYN) different, unmatched, disparate, disproportionate, irregular (ANT) equal, balanced, even

unequivocal (SYN) clear, certain, explicit, utter, sharp (ANT) unclear, indefinite, ambiguous

unerringly (SYN) precisely, exactly, accurately, infallibly (ANT) erringly, incorrectly

unethical (SYN) wrong, dishonest, immoral, corrupt, unscrupulous (ANT) ethical, right, moral, proper

uneven (SYN) rough, bumpy, irregular, asymmetrical, inconsistent, patchy (ANT) even, flat, regular, consistent

uneventful (SYN) boring, ordinary, routine, dull, tedious, monotonous (ANT) eventful, exciting

unexpected (SYN) unforeseen, surprising, abrupt, sudden, startling (ANT) anticipated, expected, predictable

unfair (SYN) partial, biased, unjust, prejudiced, unethical, dishonest (ANT) just, impartial, balanced, reasonable

unfaltering (SYN) constant, steadfast, constant, abiding (ANT) faltering, wavering, inconsistent, changing

unfasten (SYN) undo, detach, separate, disconnect, remove, unlock (ANT) fasten, join, lock, attach

unfavorable (SYN) negative, adverse, unfortunate, hostile (ANT) satisfactory, positive, advantageous, lucky

unfinished (SYN) incomplete, undone, unrefined, natural (ANT) complete, finished, done, refined

unfit (SYN) unqualified, inappropriate, incapable, incompetent, unhealthy (ANT) fit, suitable, skilled, equipped, adequate

unfold (SYN) open, unfurl, spread out, develop, occur, disclose (ANT) fold, collapse

unfortunate (SYN) unlucky, regrettable, adverse, disastrous, lamentable (ANT) fortunate, opportune, advantageous, prosperous, auspicious

unfounded (SYN) false, groundless, baseless, unjustified (ANT) justified

unfriendly (SYN) unsociable, hostile, inhospitable, chilly (ANT) friendly, congenial, warm ungainly (SYN) awkward, clumsy, uncoordinated, graceless (ANT) elegant, graceful

ungrateful (SYN) unappreciative (ANT) thankful, appreciative, mindful

unhappy (SYN) sad, downcast, melancholy, morose, unsatisfied, displeased (ANT) happy, cheerful, content, joyous

unhealthy (SYN) harmful, destructive, sick, ailing, infirm (ANT) healthy, fit, well, beneficial

uniform (SYN) outfit, suit, steady, constant, invariable, equal (ANT) varying, irregular, inconsistent, unmatched, changeable

uniformity (SYN) similarity, regularity, evenness, dullness, monotony (ANT) variance, difference, irregularity

unify (SYN) unite, join, merge, integrate, combine, fuse (ANT) separate, split

unimaginative (SYN) predictable, uninspired, ordinary, dull, banal (ANT) creative, visionary, inspired

unimpeachable (SYN) righteous, blameless, honorable

unimportant (SYN) minor, insignificant, irrelevant, trivial, petty (ANT) important, critical, consequential

uninhibited (SYN) free, unrestrained, liberated, relaxed, unbridled (ANT) inhibited, controlled, restricted

unintelligible (SYN) muddled, incoherent, meaningless, unclear, garbled (ANT) intelligible, lucid, cogent, articulate, comprehensible

unintentional (SYN) accidental, unintended, inadvertent, unplanned (ANT) intentional, planned, purposeful

union (SYN) association, alliance, joining, mixture, agreement, synthesis (ANT) opposition, divergence, separation, parting, discord

unique (SYN) single, distinctive, exceptional, original, unrivaled, unparalleled (ANT) common, normal, customary, typical

unison (SYN) harmony, agreement, concert, accord

unit (SYN) section, group, measure, component, element

unite (SYN) combine, link, cooperate, band, mingle (ANT) divide, separate, segregate, split

unity (SYN) solidarity, unison, federation, oneness, consensus (ANT) division, discord

universal (SYN) common, general, widespread, global, broad (ANT) localized, rare, narrow, individual

universe (SYN) space, nature, cosmos, creation

unjust (SYN) unfair, one-sided, wrong, partial (ANT) just, deserved, right, impartial unkempt (SYN) disordered, shaggy, tousled, messy, disheveled (ANT) neat, tidy, groomed

unkind (SYN) cruel, mean, malicious, unpleasant (ANT) kind, charitable, agreeable, sympathetic

unknown (SYN) anonymous, obscure, unfamiliar, hidden, undisclosed, strange (ANT) known, identified, explored, named, discovered

unlike (SYN) different, distinct, opposite, dissimilar, in contrast to (ANT) like, equal to, similar to

unload (SYN) empty, unpack, lighten, dump, remove (ANT) fill, load

unlucky (SYN) unfortunate, hapless, doomed, ominous, disappointing (ANT) lucky, blessed, fortunate, favorable

unmentionable (SYN) taboo, scandalous, shameful, indecent

unmistakable (SYN) obvious, clear, evident, manifest (ANT) ambiguous, unsure, unclear, indistinct

unnatural (SYN) abnormal, unusual, extraordinary, artificial, false (ANT) natural, common, normal, genuine

unnecessary (SYN) needless, uncalled for, pointless, unwarranted, optional (ANT) necessary, essential, required, indispensable

unobtrusive (SYN) inconspicuous, subdued, unassuming, low-key (ANT) conspicuous, blatant, forward, disruptive

unpleasant (SYN) bad, displeasing, disagreeable, offensive, nasty (ANT) pleasant, nice, likeable, appealing

unprecedented (SYN) unheard of, novel, original, remarkable (ANT) ordinary, commonplace, expected

unpredictable (SYN) random, erratic, variable, chance (ANT) consistent, predictable, unchanging

unprepared (SYN) unaware, taken off guard, surprised, spontaneous (ANT) prepared, ready, aware

unravel (SYN) untangle, undo, untwist, solve, clarify (ANT) entangle, twist

unreasonable (SYN) excessive, undue, outrageous, illogical, biased (ANT) rational, reasonable, moderate, warranted

unreliable (SYN) irresponsible, undependable, uncertain, deceptive (ANT) trustworthy, reliable, accurate, sound

unrest (SYN) agitation, rebellion, discontent, discord, strife (ANT) harmony, contentment, peace

unruly (SYN) wild, willful, uncontrollable, disobedient, defiant (ANT) docile, manageable, orderly, acquiescent

unsafe (SYN) dangerous, treacherous, risky, hazardous, high-risk (ANT) safe, secure, harmless, protected

unsatisfactory (SYN) unacceptable, insufficient, poor, disappointing, mediocre (ANT) favorable,

unscrupulous

sufficient, good, pleasing,
satisfactory

unscrupulous (SYN) corrupt, dishonest,
unethical, devious, disreputable
(ANT) honest, moral, principled,
honorable

unseemly (SYN) improper,
inappropriate, undignified,
unsuitable (ANT) becoming, proper,
decorous, dignified

unsettle (SYN) disturb, agitate, upset,
ruffle, fluster (ANT) soothe, calm,
pacify

unsightly (SYN) ugly, unattractive,
grotesque, revolting (ANT) attractive

unsophisticated (SYN) simple,
unrefined, naive, natural, unaffected
(ANT) sophisticated, worldly,
complicated, cunning

unsteady (SYN) precarious, wobbly,
shaky, volatile, fluctuating (ANT)
stable, steady, firm, settled, constant

unsuitable (SYN) unfit, inapt,
unacceptable, unbecoming (ANT)
suitable, fitting, eligible

unsure (SYN) insecure, doubtful,
hesitant, skeptical (ANT) sure,
convinced, confident, assured,
positive

untenable (SYN) groundless, weak,
indefensible (ANT) sound, logical

untidy (SYN) cluttered, messy, scruffy,
disorganized, disordered (ANT) neat,
tidy, orderly

untie (SYN) unfasten, loosed, free,
unlace (ANT) tie, knot, lace

untoward (SYN) irritating, troublesome,
annoying, inconvenient, adverse,
unexpected (ANT) welcome,
favorable, fortunate

untrue (SYN) false, incorrect, invented,
concocted, disloyal, unfaithful
(ANT) true, correct, accurate,
trustworthy

unusual (SYN) abnormal, infrequent,
curious, singular, unconventional
(ANT) common, ordinary,
unremarkable, prevalent

unveil (SYN) reveal, expose, uncover
(ANT) hide, shroud, conceal

unwell (SYN) sick, ill, ailing, unhealthy
(ANT) well, healthy, fit

unwieldy (SYN) unmanageable,
cumbersome, bulky, awkward

unwilling (SYN) reluctant, loath,
resistant, grudging, involuntary
(ANT) willing, keen, eager

unwind (SYN) uncoil, unravel, relax
(ANT) wind, twist

unwise (SYN) foolish, rash, imprudent,
reckless, senseless (ANT) wise,
shrewd, judicious

unwitting (SYN) chance, inadvertent,
accidental, unintentional,
unsuspecting, innocent (ANT)
knowing, conscious, aware,
intentional

upbeat (SYN) cheerful, happy, positive, optimistic, hopeful (ANT) negative, pessimistic, downcast

upbraid (SYN) admonish, scold, blame, reprimand, criticize (ANT) praise, commend, approve

upheaval (SYN) turmoil, disorder, disturbance, disruption, confusion (ANT) peace, calm

uphold (SYN) support, champion, endorse, preserve, sustain (ANT) oppose, overturn, fight, deny

uplift (SYN) raise, elevate, inspire, rouse, hearten, improvement, advancement (ANT) lower, depress

upper (SYN) higher, high, top, eminent, greater (ANT) lower

upright (SYN) straight, vertical, ethical, principled, virtuous (ANT) dishonest, unethical, crooked, flat, horizontal

uprising (SYN) rebellion, mutiny, insurrection, revolt

upset (SYN) topple, disturb, bother, agitate, distress (ANT) calm, reassure, placate, pacify

urban (SYN) city, metropolitan, municipal, suburban (ANT) rural

urbane (SYN) cultivated, sophisticated, polite, refined, civil (ANT) unrefined, boorish, inconsiderate

urchin (SYN) gamin

urge (SYN) insist, persuade, recommend, desire, yearning, itch (ANT) dissuade, discourage, allow

urgency (SYN) importance, gravity, seriousness, pressure, crisis

urgent (SYN) pressing, critical, imperative, dire, compelling, high-priority (ANT) unimportant, trivial, insignificant

usage (SYN) use, handing, control, method, convention, custom

use (SYN) utilize, employ, consume, exploit, expend, application, purpose

used to (SYN) accustomed to, familiar with

useful (SYN) helpful, valuable, worthwhile, functional, handy (ANT) impractical, useless, inconvenient

usual (SYN) normal, regular, standard, routine, familiar, expected (ANT) unusual, exceptional, atypical, uncommon

usually (SYN) normally, frequently, customarily, as a rule, mainly, on the whole, in general (ANT) rarely, occasionally

usurp (SYN) seize, posses, take, assume, claim (ANT) relinquish, abdicate

utensil (SYN) tool, device, contraption, instrument

utility (SYN) usefulness, value, practicality, convenience, efficacy utilize (SYN) use, employ, take advantage of, occupy, avail

utmost (SYN) greatest, paramount, most, maximum, supreme

utopian (SYN) heavenly, blissful, perfect, ideal

utter (SYN) express, say, voice, complete, absolute, sheer

utterance (SYN) words, statement, remark, speech, articulation

utterly (SYN) fully, completely, totally, absolutely, entirely

V

vacancy (SYN) opening, opportunity, position, emptiness

vacant (SYN) empty, void, available, uninhabited, thoughtless, blank, unresponsive (ANT) full, occupied, expressive, engaged

vacate (SYN) leave, evacuate, resign from, relinquish (ANT) occupy, take up

vacation (SYN) holiday, leave, trip, break

vacillate (SYN) sway, hesitate, fluctuate, vary, oscillate (ANT) act, decide, persist

vacuum (SYN) emptiness, space, void, gap, chasm

vagabond (SYN) beggar, vagrant, itinerant, drifter, nomad

vagrant (SYN) hobo, nomad, wanderer, roaming, rootless, unsettled

vague (SYN) hazy, indistinct, obscure, ambiguous, nebulous (ANT) clear, defined, precise, sharp, certain

vain (SYN) arrogant, conceited, futile, pointless, unproductive (ANT) modest, unassuming, meek, successful, effective

valet (SYN) groom, attendant, manservant

valiant (SYN) brave, heroic, courageous, daring, gallant (ANT) timid, cowardly, weak

valid (SYN) legitimate, genuine, sound, logical, defensible (ANT) invalid, irrational, unreasonable, erroneous

validate (SYN) confirm, substantiate, support, confirm, prove (ANT) invalidate, contradict

validity (SYN) legitimacy, right, weight, strength, cogency

valley (SYN) gorge, canyon, rift, gully, ravine

valor (SYN) courage, boldness, heroism, bravery (ANT) fear, fright, cowardice

valuable (SYN) expensive, costly, treasured, useful, beneficial, important (ANT) cheap, worthless, useless, undesirable

value (SYN) price, worth, evaluate, appraise, revere, esteem

vanish (SYN) disappear, fade away,
evaporate, dissolve, evaporate
(ANT) appear, emerge, materialize

vanity (SYN) pride, arrogance,
narcissism, boastfulness, cockiness
(ANT) modesty, humility, reserve,
self-effacement

vanquish (SYN) trounce, defeat,
conquer, overwhelm, crush (ANT)
lose, surrender, cede

vapid (SYN) dull, boring, insipid,
uninspiring, trite (ANT) novel,
innovative, fresh, interesting

vapor (SYN) mist, fog, steam, haze

variable (SYN) mutable, unstable,
shifting, irregular, fluid (ANT)
steady, invariable, constant,
unchanging

variance (SYN) disagreement,
divergence, incongruity

variation (SYN) deviation, modification,
departure, contrast, fluctuation
(ANT) uniformity, balance,
continuity

varied (SYN) assorted, mixed, diverse,
disparate, miscellaneous (ANT)
similar, unchanging, homogenous

variety (SYN) diversity, range, array,
selection, category, type (ANT)
similarity, homogeneity

various (SYN) several, assorted,
differing, sundry, motley (ANT)
singular, similar

varnish (SYN) polish, gloss, lacquer

vary (SYN) differ, disagree, swing,
fluctuate, alter, adjust (ANT) steady,
establish, maintain

vast (SYN) huge, immense, colossal,
boundless, massive (ANT) tiny,
diminutive, small, limited, miniscule

vault (SYN) bound, leap, clear, safe,
depository, crypt

veer (SYN) swerve, shift, turn, deviate,
change course

vegetate (SYN) stagnate, languish, idle

vegetation (SYN) plants, flowers, foliage

vehement (SYN) intense, strong,
forceful, fierce, passionate (ANT)
cool, calm, quiet

vehicle (SYN) transportation, means,
channel, medium

veil (SYN) cover, cloak, screen, hide
disguise, shield, swathe, envelop

vein (SYN) course, stripe, stratum,
mood, attitude, manner

velocity (SYN) speed, pace, tempo, rate

vendetta (SYN) quarrel, feud, bad blood

vendor (SYN) merchant, salesman,
peddler

veneer (SYN) guise, pretense, facade
appearance

venerable (SYN) esteemed, respected,
sage, wise, revered

veneration (SYN) worship, adoration,
respect, reverence

vengeance (SYN) revenge, retaliation, retribution, requital (ANT) forgiveness, pardon

venom (SYN) poison, toxin, malice, bitterness, spite

venomous (SYN) lethal, poisonous, fatal, dangerous, savage, hostile (ANT) harmless

vent (SYN) opening, duct, outlet, emit, expel, express

venture (SYN) project, endeavor, attempt, hazard, volunteer, presume

venue (SYN) location, scene, place

veracity (SYN) honesty, truthfulness, fidelity, sincerity (ANT) deception, dishonesty, lying

verbal (SYN) spoken, oral, vocal, stated, said (ANT) written

verbatim (SYN) exactly, precisely, literal, word for word, to the letter (ANT) summarized, paraphrased

verbose (SYN) wordy, long-winded, garrulous, circumlocutory (ANT) succinct, terse, brief, to the point, concise

verdant (SYN) lush, green, leafy, flourishing (ANT) barren

verdict (SYN) decision, finding, judgment, ruling, sentence

verge (SYN) edge, brink, threshold, border, approach (ANT) center, inside

verify (SYN) confirm, prove, authenticate, affirm, uphold (ANT) refute, weaken

verity (SYN) truth, reality, fact

versatile (SYN) adaptable, flexible, multifaceted, resourceful, adjustable (ANT) one dimensional, unchanging

verse (SYN) poem, lyric, line, stanza

version (SYN) account, interpretation, rendering, side, variety, type

vertical (SYN) upright, standing, erect, perpendicular, on end (ANT) horizontal, flat

verve (SYN) liveliness, sparkle, animation, vitality, spirit

very (SYN) highly, extremely, profoundly, thoroughly, actual, precise, mere (ANT) slightly

vessel (SYN) ship, boat, container, basin, jug, receptacle

vestibule (SYN) foyer, lobby, hall

vestige (SYN) trace, remnant, legacy, reminder, echo

veteran (SYN) experienced, old, seasoned (ANT) novice, beginner, apprentice

veto (SYN) forbid, reject, ban, disallow, negate, deny (ANT) approve, pass

vex (SYN) irritate, annoy, bother, provoke, anger, exasperate (ANT) soothe, mitigate, please vexation (SYN) frustration, displeasure, chagrin, problem, nuisance (ANT) pleasure, gratification

viable (SYN) feasible, workable, practical, realistic, (ANT) impracticable, impractical

vibrant (SYN) alive, dynamic, energetic, vivid, striking (ANT) lifeless, dull, pale, somber

vibrate (SYN) shake, pulsate, tremble, shudder, throb

vibration (SYN) tremor, quiver, pulsation, shake, reverberation

vicarious (SYN) indirect, substituted, surrogate

vice (SYN) sin, wickedness, depravity, offense, corruption, fault, shortcoming (ANT) virtue, innocence, strength

vicinity (SYN) neighborhood, proximity, district, neck of the woods

vicious (SYN) fierce, cruel, malevolent, vindictive, brutal, callous (ANT) kind, gentle, admirable

victim (SYN) casualty, sufferer, sacrifice, prey, survivor (ANT) culprit, criminal

victorious (SYN) triumphant, successful, wining, conquering, champion (ANT) losing, unsuccessful, vanquished, defeated

victory (SYN) success, win, conquest, triumph, coup (ANT) loss, defeat, failure

victuals (SYN) food, provisions, sustenance

vie (SYN) contend, compete, struggle, fight, battle, jockey

view (SYN) sight, scene, perspective, outlook, opinion, sentiment, observe, scan, regard

vigilance (SYN) watchfulness, observance, alertness, attentiveness, wariness (ANT) inattentiveness, negligence

vignette (SYN) scene

vigor (SYN) energy, strength, vitality, drive (ANT) lethargy, inactivity, weakness

vigorous (SYN) robust, healthy, strong, strenuous, aggressive (ANT) feeble, weak

vigorously (SYN) forcefully, energetically, passionately, briskly

vile (SYN) repulsive, disgusting, despicable, horrid, foul, nauseating (ANT) pleasant, appealing

vilify (SYN) abuse, slander, malign, defame, revile (ANT) praise, honor, protect, applaud

village (SYN) town, community, hamlet (ANT) city

villain (SYN) criminal, rogue, crook, felon, devil

vindicate (SYN) clear, exonerate, absolve, justify, prove

vindictive (SYN) vengeful, spiteful, malicious, unrelenting

vintage (SYN) classic, historic, timeless, antique, quality (ANT) modern, new, current

violate (SYN) desecrate, profane, break, disregard, infringe (ANT) respect, uphold, protect

violence (SYN) brutality, savagery, force, roughness, severity, vehemence (ANT) weakness, impotence, tenderness

violent (SYN) intense, threatening, ferocious, powerful, strong, unbridled (ANT) gentle, mild, weak, tame

virgin (SYN) pure, perfect, undefiled, pristine, spotless, clean

virile (SYN) masculine, manly, strong, macho, bold (ANT) weak, feminine, effeminate

virtue (SYN) merit, excellence, goodness, integrity, asset, benefit (ANT) vice, failing, disadvantage

virtuous (SYN) moral, honorable, righteous, upright, incorruptible (ANT) evil, depraved, wicked

visage (SYN) face, appearance, countenance

visceral (SYN) internal, gut

viscous (SYN) thick, syrupy, gelatinous, sticky

vise (SYN) grip, clamp

visible (SYN) apparent, observable, evident, discernable, plain (ANT) invisible, imperceptible, obscured

vision (SYN) seeing, sight, dream, hallucination, foresight, intuition, image, innovation, creativity

visionary (SYN) idealistic, speculative, unworkable, utopian, prophetic

visit (SYN) see, drop in, stop by, chat

visitor (SYN) guest, caller, company (ANT) host, hostess

visual (SYN) optical, ocular, visible, perceptible, observable (ANT) acoustic, tactile

visualize (SYN) picture, imagine, conjure, call to mind, see

vital (SYN) essential, imperative, critical, alive, vigorous (ANT) dispensable, unnecessary, trivial, unimportant, listless

vitality (SYN) life, animation, exuberance, vivacity, vigor

vitiate (SYN) debase, pervert, degrade, adulterate

vitriolic (SYN) scathing, withering, bitter, hateful, caustic (ANT) friendly, kind, considerate, obliging

vivacious (SYN) upbeat, bubbling, sprightly, ebullient (ANT) lethargic, lifeless

vivid (SYN) bright, rich, colorful, graphic, evocative, stirring (ANT) dull, vague vocabulary (SYN) words, language, glossary, lexicon

vocal (SYN) outspoken, forthright, expressive, candid, oral, voiced (ANT) silent, inarticulate

vocation (SYN) career, job, occupation, profession, trade, calling

vogue (SYN) fashion, trend, rave, style, mode

voice (SYN) sound, speech, intonation, utter, speak, air, express

void (SYN) emptiness, gap, hollow, cancel, reverse, invalidate, vacant, blank (ANT) valid, full, engaged

volition (SYN) free will, choice, discretion, decision, wish

volley (SYN) shower, storm, barrage, torrent, burst

volume (SYN) capacity, amount, mass, quantity, sound, loudness, book, publication

voluminous (SYN) roomy, ample, cavernous, immense, vast

voluntary (SYN) willing, unforced, deliberate, intentional, elective (ANT) compulsory, involuntary, required, compulsory

volunteer (SYN) offer, extend, come forward (ANT) withdraw

voluptuous (SYN) buxom, shapely, sensual, curvy (ANT) skinny

vomit (SYN) retch, heave, throw up, regurgitate

voracious (SYN) greedy, insatiable, hungry, ravenous, uncontrolled

vortex (SYN) whirlpool, maelstrom

vote (SYN) opt, elect, poll, ballot

vouch (SYN) confirm, support, guarantee, certify

voucher (SYN) token, coupon, ticket

vow (SYN) oath, promise, pledge, swear, covenant, commitment

voyage (SYN) journey, passage, cruise, expedition

vulgar (SYN) crude, indecent, tasteless, unrefined, filthy, obscene (ANT) decent, tasteful, elegant, polite

vulnerable (SYN) exposed, unguarded, defenseless, in danger, at risk, susceptible (ANT) safe, protected, invulnerable

W

waddle (SYN) shuffle, wobble, totter, toddle

wade (SYN) splash, plough, labor, toil

waft (SYN) float, drift, glide, sail

wag (SYN) wave, swish, shake, wiggle, flourish

wage (SYN) pay, fee, earnings, pursue, conduct, carry out

wager (SYN) bet, stake, gamble, risk

wagon (SYN) carriage, buggy, cart

waif

waif (SYN) orphan, stray, urchin

wail (SYN) cry, lament, howl, groan, bawl (ANT) murmur, whisper

wait (SYN) pause, tarry, linger, stay, remain, delay, interruption (ANT) proceed, leave, expedite

waiter (SYN) server, attendant

waive (SYN) renounce, relinquish, surrender, sacrifice, ignore

wake (SYN) arise, rouse, kindle, stimulate, vigil, funeral, waves, trail (ANT) sleep

walk (SYN) stroll, amble, traipse, gait, step, stride, path, trail (ANT) run, stand

wall (SYN) screen, partition, fence, obstacle

wallet (SYN) purse, case, pouch, billfold, pocketbook

wallow (SYN) relish, delight, bask, glory, splash around

wand (SYN) stick, rod, baton

wander (SYN) drift, meander, roam, stray, deviate, digress

wane (SYN) diminish, ebb, weaken, fade, decrease, shrink, wither (ANT) wax, grow, increase

wangle (SYN) contrive, manipulate

want (SYN) desire, covet, fancy, need, lack, shortage (ANT) abundance

wanton (SYN) deliberate, senseless, arbitrary, gratuitous, immoral, lewd, shameless

war (SYN) fighting, battle, clash, combat, enmity (ANT) peace, armistice, truce

warble (SYN) sing, twitter, chirp, trill

ward (SYN) charge, minor, dependant, department, unit, division, repel, deflect

warden (SYN) superintendent, guardian, caretaker, keeper

wardrobe (SYN) closet, cupboard, armoire, clothing, attire

wares (SYN) goods, products, merchandise, stuff

warehouse (SYN) storeroom, stockroom, depot, magazine

warily (SYN) cautiously, suspiciously, with care, watchfully, gingerly (ANT) recklessly, imprudently, rashly

warm (SYN) tepid, balmy, temperate, snug, cordial, affectionate, reheat (ANT) cold, chilly, hostile, insensitive, chill

warmth (SYN) heat, coziness, tenderness, amiability, love (ANT) cold, coolness, unfriendliness, ill will

warn (SYN) notify, alert, inform, advise, urge

warning (SYN) caution, alarm, omen, sign, example, deterrent, reprimand, censure

303

warp (SYN) twist, distort, buckle, contort, pervert, deprave (ANT) straighten

warrant (SYN) permission, authorization, license, deserve, justify, sanction

warranty (SYN)guarantee, contract, pledge, promise, agreement

warrior (SYN) soldier, fighter, combatant

wary (SYN) careful, distrustful, prudent, heedful, suspicious (ANT) inattentive, trusting, careless, reckless

wash (SYN) clean, launder, scrub, bathe, swell, wave (ANT) soil, dirty, sully

waste (SYN) misuse, squander, exhaust, garbage, loss, consumption, atrophy, shrivel (ANT) conserve, save, preserve

wasteful (SYN) extravagant, reckless, destructive, excessive, prodigal, lavish (ANT) frugal, thrifty

watch (SYN) observe, scrutinize, regard, mind, look after, vigil (ANT) ignore, neglect

water (SYN) spray, soak, irrigate, douse

wave (SYN) ripple, breaker, flood, surge, beckon, signal, flutter, flap

waver (SYN) flicker, falter, dither, hesitate, vacillate, fluctuate (ANT) decide, commit

wax (SYN) increase, enlarge, swell, grow (ANT) wane, diminish, reduce

way (SYN) method, means, technique, route, track

wayward (SYN) erratic, unpredictable, disobedient, rebellious, unmanageable (ANT) obedient, compliant, submissive

weak (SYN) frail, infirm, feeble, faint, unconvincing, flimsy, timid, watery (ANT) strong, powerful, forceful

weakness (SYN) shortcoming, fault, imperfection, frailty, delicacy (ANT) strength, resoluteness, power, potency

wealth (SYN) riches, affluence, means, prosperity, abundance, profusion (ANT) poverty, want, dearth

wealthy (SYN) prosperous, well-to-do, rich, loaded, affluent, moneyed (ANT) poor, destitute, needy

wear (SYN) don, sport, display, clothes, attire, erode, deteriorate, grind, damage, abrasion

weary (SYN) fatigued, tired, exhausted, discouraged, jaded, drain, sap (ANT) energized, fresh, effervescent, rested, refresh, rejuvenate

weather (SYN) conditions, climate, forecast, withstand, endure, overcome

weave (SYN) knit, intertwine, plait, create, spin, zigzag, wend

web (SYN) cobweb, network, tangle, mesh, gossamer

wed (SYN) marry, unite, join, merge, espouse (ANT) divorce, split, separate

wedding (SYN) marriage, union, nuptials

wedge (SYN) lodge, force, cram, block, triangle

weep (SYN) cry, sob, lament, mourn, whimper, blubber, wail (ANT) laugh, rejoice, smile

weigh (SYN) ponder, consider, balance, juxtapose, tip the scales at

weight (SYN) poundage, mass, impact, consequence, significance, load, burden

weird (SYN) strange, peculiar, eerie, uncanny, eccentric (ANT) normal, natural, conventional, common

welcome (SYN) reception, salutation, greet, receive, acceptable, desirable, embrace, appreciate (ANT) unwelcome, resent, object to

weld (SYN) fuse, solder, bond, connect, splice, attach

welfare (SYN) well-being, interest, health, safety, benefit

well (SYN) healthy, fit, pleasantly, satisfactorily, deftly, thoroughly, spring, shaft, gush, spill (ANT) sick, ill, poorly, badly, negligently

welt (SYN) mark, contusion, blister

wet (SYN) moist, drenched, waterlogged, saturated, rainy, soak, dampen (ANT) dry, parched, arid

wetlands (SYN) swamps, marshes

wharf (SYN) pier, dock, harbor, jetty, quay

wheedle (SYN) cajole, coax, persuade

wheel (SYN) disk, roller, turn, twirl, rotation

whereabouts (SYN) location, position, site, spot, address

whet (SYN) stimulate, kindle stir, sharpen, hone

whim (SYN) urge, impulse, fancy, caprice, inclination

whimper (SYN) whine, snivel, weep

whimsical (SYN) fanciful, playful, wondrous, arbitrary, curious (ANT) ordinary, dull, serious, sober

whine (SYN) cry, complain, grumble, mewl, carp, drone

whip (SYN) lash, cane, beat, defeat, whisk, electrify, goad

whirl (SYN) spin, pirouette, reel, confusion, daze, bustle, flurry

whisk (SYN) beat, whip, fluff, sweep, speed, hurtle

whisper (SYN) murmur, rustle, sigh, confide, gossip (ANT) shout, yell

white (SYN) pale, ashen, pasty, chalky, washed out, ghostly (ANT) flushed, rosy

whittle (SYN) trim, carve, shave, reduce, erode

whole (SYN) entire, total, undivided, intact (ANT) partial, divided

wholesome (SYN) nutritious, beneficial, moral, respectable, good (ANT) unhealthy, harmful, noxious

wick (SYN) fuse, string

wicked (SYN) evil, fiendish, villainous, vile, malevolent, mischievous, naughty (ANT) virtuous, good, decent, noble

wide (SYN) broad, vast, sweeping, extensive, comprehensive (ANT) narrow, thin, limited

width (SYN) breadth, girth, scope, span, diameter

wield (SYN) brandish, wave, flourish, exert, exercise

wife (SYN) souse, mate, partner, bride

wiggle (SYN) squirm, writhe, shimmy, twitch

wild (SYN) untamed, savage, unruly, natural, turbulent, excited (ANT) cultivated, calm, disciplined, domesticated

wilderness (SYN) wilds, desert, wasteland

will (SYN) determination, resolve, wish, preference, testament, bequeath

willful (SYN) stubborn, obstinate, strong, inflexible, intentional, conscious(ANT) submissive, flexible, reasonable, accidental

willing (SYN) ready, compliant, game, consenting (ANT) reluctant, hesitant

willowy (SYN) slender, lithe, svelte, slim, graceful (ANT) hulking, cumbersome, bulky

wilt (SYN) droop, wither, languish, flag, slouch, sag (ANT) flourish, thrive

wily (SYN) cunning, crafty, shrewd, sly (ANT) artless, gullible, unassuming

win (SYN) triumph, succeed, prevail, achieve, procure, victory (ANT) lose, loss

wince (SYN) grimace, flinch, cower, start

wind (SYN) air, breeze, breath, talk, coil, spiral, snake, meander (ANT) unwind

windfall (SYN) jackpot, godsend

window (SYN) portal, pane, casement

wing (SYN) arm, section, faction, fly, soar, clip

wink (SYN) blink, bat, twinkle, glimmer, sparkle, flash

winnings (SYN) profits, spoils, proceeds, gains, takings, purse

winnow (SYN) sift, sort out, separate, divide

winsome (SYN) charming, agreeable, engaging, peasant (ANT) off-putting, unpleasant, standoffish, aloof

wipe (SYN) swab, clean, brush, erase

wire (SYN) connect, stimulate, electrify

wisdom (SYN) insight, acumen, enlightenment, sense, prudence, scholarship (ANT) foolishness, folly, stupidity, ignorance, irrationality

wise (SYN) sage, clever, judicious, erudite, sensible, profound (ANT) foolish, stupid, ignorant, simple

wish (SYN) want, hope, yearn, aspiration, intention, will

wispy (SYN) thin, flimsy, fine, delicate

wistful (SYN) dreamy, pensive, thoughtful, contemplative, longing (ANT) realistic, cynical

wit (SYN) cleverness, ingenuity, intelligence, humor, repartee (ANT) sobriety, slowness

witch (SYN) sorceress, crone, hag, enchantress

withdraw (SYN) remove, extract, recall, rescind (ANT) introduce, enter, insert

withdrawn (SYN) introverted, shy, distant, reserved (ANT) extroverted, social, communicative, forthcoming

wither (SYN) decay, shrivel, perish, fade, languish (ANT) grow, flourish, thrive, refresh

withering (SYN) scornful, hurtful, devastating, humiliating, scathing, stinging

withhold (SYN) suppress, hold back, refuse, refrain, hide, check (ANT) release, yield, give

witness (SYN) bystander, observer, notice, see, watch

wizard (SYN) sorcerer, magician, warlock, genius, marvel, expert

woe (SYN) grief, misery, anguish, sorrow, distress (ANT) glee, happiness, mirth, gladness

woman (SYN) lady, female

wonder (SYN) awe, amazement, ponder, gape, curiosity, phenomenon

wonderful (SYN) superb, magnificent, astonishing, staggering, sublime

wondrous (SYN) glorious, fantastic, sensational, outstanding

wont (SYN) likely, apt, accustomed

woo (SYN) court, pursue, romance, entice, wheedle

wood (SYN) timber, lumber, forest, woodland, grove

wool (SYN) fleece, yarn, coat

word (SYN) term, name, message, information, oath, pledge, phrase, couch

work (SYN) effort, labor, employment, task, function, operate, creation (ANT) play, relax, recreation

world (SYN) earth, globe, realm, domain, environment

worldly (SYN) urbane, sophisticated, cultured, secular, materialistic, earthly (ANT) naive, unrefined, spiritual, immaterial worn (SYN) tattered, frayed, ragged, shabby, used, tired, weary (ANT) new

worry (SYN) trouble, fret, brood, apprehension, unease (ANT) soothe, peace of mind, contentment, peace

worsen (SYN) aggravate, exacerbate, decline, sink, degenerate (ANT) improve

worship (SYN) exalt, praise, venerate, cherish, respect, devotion, glorification (ANT) curse, despise

worth (SYN) value, estimation, price, merit, importance

worthless (SYN) useless, vile, despicable, unimportant, pointless, vain (ANT) valuable, meaningful, worthy

worthy (SYN) deserving, admirable, meritorious, laudable (ANT) unworthy, reprehensible, disreputable

wound (SYN) injure, hurt, pierce, offend, sting, gash, laceration (ANT) mend, heal

wrap (SYN) envelop, package, bind, swathe, cape, cloak (ANT) unwrap, open, unpack

wrath (SYN) rage, fury, anger, indignation, resentment (ANT) praise, commendation, happiness, pleasure

wreath (SYN) garland, crown, ring, circlet, loop

wreck (SYN) destroy, demolish, ruin, devastation, destruction (ANT) preserve, protect, fix

wrench (SYN) jerk, yank, tear, ring, wrest, pry

wrest (SYN) seize, take, grab, extract

wrestle (SYN) battle, grapple, scuffle, struggle

wretched (SYN) pathetic, miserable, desolate, tragic, sordid (ANT) cheerful, comfortable

wriggle (SYN) writhe, squirm, slink, maneuver, jiggle

wring (SYN) twist, squeeze, extract

wrinkle (SYN) crease, furrow, rumple, pucker, gather (ANT) smooth, straighten, iron

write (SYN) record, scribble, inscribe, jot down, compose, draft

writer (SYN) author, scribe, wordsmith

writhe (SYN) thrash, wiggle, twist, squirm, struggle

wrong (SYN) incorrect, inaccurate, unwise, criminal, nefarious, transgression, offence, awry, amiss, mistreat, harm (ANT) right, correct, just, good

wry (SYN) dry, ironic, sarcastic, uneven, twisted

X

xenophobic (SYN) intolerant,
prejudiced, bigoted, jingoistic

Y

yank (SYN) pull, tug, jerk, wrench

yarn (SYN) thread, wool, filament,
story, tale, fable

yearn (SYN) long, crave, hunger, pine,
wish, covet, ache

yell (SYN) shout, scream, cry, shriek,
howl, yelp, wail

yen (SYN) longing, passion, thirst,
hankering, itch

yes (SYN) certainly, affirmative,
absolutely, gladly, sure (ANT) no

yet (SYN) however, nonetheless, still, so
far, up to now

yield (SYN) defer, succumb, surrender,
produce, generate, deliver, profit,
gain

yonder (SYN) distant, faraway

young (SYN) youthful, juvenile,
immature, junior, new, early,
offspring, children (ANT) old,
ancient, senior

youngster (SYN) youth, kid, lad, lass,
child

youth (SYN) childhood, adolescence,
immaturity, adolescent, next
generation (ANT) adulthood, old age

youthful (SYN) young, childlike, spry,
vigorous (ANT) elderly

Z

zany (SYN) wacky, comical, goofy,
eccentric, bizarre, quirky (ANT)
conventional, sensible, sober

zeal (SYN) enthusiasm, spirit, verve,
devotion, energy, gusto (ANT)
apathy, indifference, reluctance

zealous (SYN) devoted, eager, fanatical,
enthusiastic

zenith (SYN) height, apex, pinnacle,
summit, top, high point (ANT)
depth, nadir, low point

zephyr (SYN) breeze, draft, wind

zero (SYN) none, nothing, nil, bottom

zest (SYN) relish, exhilaration,
enjoyment, thrill, delight

zone (SYN) section, area, region,
territory, quarter

zoo (SYN) menagerie

zoom (SYN) zip, speed, race, dash,
hurtle, fly

Dinosaur Facts

The word dinosaur comes from the Greek words for "terrible" (dino) and "lizard" (saur). English paleontologist Sir Richard Owen coined the term in 1842. Paleontologists are scientists who study fossils to learn about the history of life on Earth. Using fossils, paleontologists discover details about the lives of extinct animals, such as dinosaurs. The largest complete dinosaur skeleton ever discovered belongs to a Brachiosaurus. It measures as long as two school buses and as high as a four-story building! (Bonus fact: Blue whales are larger than any dinosaur on record!) Not all dinosaurs were towering giants. One of the smallest dinosaurs discovered to date, the Compsognathus, was roughly the size of a chicken.

Dinosaurs existed Earth during the Mesozoic Era, which is divided into the Triassic, Jurrasic, and Cretaceous periods. It is believed that dinosaurs roamed the Earth for approximately 165 million years! Dinosaurs have been extinct for about 65 million years, since the end of the Cretaceous period. The word extinct is used to describe plants or animals that have died out, leaving no living representatives. (Bonus Fact: Synonyms for extinct include gone, vanished, and deceased. Antonyms include living, alive, existing, and current.)

Dinosaurs were land-dwellers. The marine reptiles that co-existed with the dinosaurs were Plesiosaurs, Mosasaurs, and Ichtosaurs, and the flying replies of the time are referred to as Pterosaurs. Archaeopteryx, classified as a bird from the Jurrasic period, is frequently offered as evidence to prove a link between dinosaurs and birds. While possessing a dinosaur-like skeleton, Archaeopteryx also had feathers like modern-day birds. Dinosaur bones have been found on every continent. Within the United States of America, dinosaur bones have been found in 35 states. The world's largest and most complete Tyrannosaurus Rex skeleton, named Sue, is on display at the Field Museum in Chicago, Illinois. Sue's skull alone weighs 600 pounds!

The Names of 792 Dinosaurs

Aachenosaurus	*Alectrosaurus*	*Anchiceratops*
Abelisaurus	*Aletopelta*	*Anchisaurus*
Abrictosaurus	*Algoasaurus*	*Andesaurus*
Abrosaurus	*Alioramus*	*Angaturama*
Acanthopholis	*Aliwalia*	*Animantarx*
Achelousaurus	*Allosaurus*	*Ankistrodon*
Achillobator	*Alocodon*	*Ankylosaurus*
Acrocanthosaurus	*Altirhinus*	*Anodontosaurus*
Actiosaurus	*Altispinax*	*Anoplosaurus*
Adasaurus	*Alvarezsaurus*	*Anserimimus*
Aegyptosaurus	*Alwalkeria*	*Antarctosaurus*
Aeolosaurus	*Alxasaurus*	*Antetonitrus*
Aepisaurus	*Amargasaurus*	*Anthodon*
Aetonyx	*Amazonsaurus*	*Antrodemus*
Afrovenator	*Ammosaurus*	*Apatodon*
Agathaumas	*Ampelosaurus*	*Apatosaurus*
Aggiosaurus	*Amphicoelias*	*Aragosaurus*
Agilisaurus	*Amtosaurus*	*Aralosaurus*
Agnosphitys	*Amurosaurus*	*Archaeoceratops*
Agrosaurus	*Amygdalodon*	*Archaeopteryx*
Agustinia	*Anabisetia*	*Archaeornithoides*
Alamosaurus	*Anasazisaurus*	*Archaeornithomimus*
Albertosaurus	*Anatosaurus*	*Archaeovolans*
Albisaurus	*Anatotitan*	*Arctosaurus*

Argentinosaurus
Argyrosaurus
Aristosaurus
Aristosuchus
Arrhinoceratops
Arstanosaurus
Asiaceratops
Asiamericana
Asiatosaurus
Astrodon
Astrodonius
Atlantosaurus
Atlasaurus
Aublysodon
Aucasaurus
Austrosaurus
Avaceratops
Avalonianus
Aviatyrannis
Avimimus
Azendohsaurus
Bactrosaurus
Bagaceratops
Bagaraatan
Bahariasaurus
Bainoceratops
Bambiraptor
Barapasaurus
Barosaurus
Barsboldia
Bathygnathus
Becklespinax
Beipiaosaurus
Bellusaurus
Belodon
Betasuchus
Bienosaurus
Bihariosaurus
Blikanasaurus
Borogovia
Bothriospondylus
Brachiosaurus
Brachyceratops
Brachylophosaurus.
Brachypodosaurus
Brachyrophus
Bradycneme
Brasileosaurus
Breviceratops
Brontosaurus
Bruhathkayosaurus
Bugenasaura
Byronosaurus
Caenagnathasia
Caenagnathus
Calamosaurus
Callovosaurus
Camarasaurus
Camelotia
Camposaurus

Camptosaurus
Campylodoniscus
Carcharodonto-saurus
Cardiodon
Carnotaurus
Caseosaurus
Cathetosaurus
Caudipteryx
Caudocoelus
Caulodon
Cedarosaurus
Cedarpelta
Centemodon
Centrosaurus
Ceratops
Ceratosaurus
Cetiosauriscus
Cetiosaurus
Chaoyangsaurus
Charonosaurus
Chasmosaurus
Chassternbergia
Cheneosaurus
Chialingosaurus
Chiayusaurus
Chienkosaurus
Chilantaisaurus
Chindesaurus
Chingkankousaurus
Chirostenotes
Chondrosteosaurus
Chuandongocoelurus
Chuanjiesaurus
Chubutisaurus
Chungkingosaurus
Cionodon
Citipati
Cladeiodon
Claorhynchus
Claosaurus
Clasmodosaurus
Clepsysaurus
Coelophysis
Coeluroides
Coelurus
Colepiocephale
Colonosaurus
Coloradisaurus
Compsognathus
Compsosuchus
Conchoraptor
Corythosaurus
Craspedodon
Crataeomus
Craterosaurus
Creosaurus
Crichtonsaurus
Cristatusaurus
Cryolophosaurus
Cryptodraco

Cryptosaurus
Cryptovolans
Dacentrurus
Dakosaurus
Dandakosaurus
Danubiosaurus
Daspletosaurus
Dasygnathoides
Datousaurus
Deinocheirus
Deinodon
Deinonychus
Deltadromeus
Denversaurus
Deuterosaurus
Dianchungosaurus
Diceratops
Diclonius
Dicraeosaurus
Didanodon
Dilophosaurus
Dimodosaurus
Dinheirosaurus
Dinodocus
Dinotyrannus
Diplodocus
Diplotomodon
Diracodon
Dolichosuchus
Doratodon
Doryphorosaurus
Draconyx
Dracopelta
Dravidosaurus
Drinker
Dromaeosauroides
Dromaeosaurus
Dromiceiomimus
Dromicosaurus
Dryosaurus
Dryptosauroides
Dryptosaurus
Dynamosaurus
Dyoplosaurus
Dysalotosaurus
Dysganus
Dyslocosaurus
Dystrophaeus
Dystylosaurus
Echinodon
Edmarka
Edmontonia
Edmontosaurus
Efraasia
Einiosaurus
Elachistosuchus
Elaphrosaurus
Elmisaurus
Elopteryx
Elosaurus

Emausaurus	*Goyocephale*	*Jaxartosaurus*
Embasaurus	*Graciliceratops*	*Jeholosaurus*
Enigmosaurus	*Gracilisuchus*	*Jenghizkhan*
Eobrontosaurus	*Gravitholus*	*Jiangshanosaurus*
Eolambia	*Gresslyosaurus*	*Jingshanosaurus*
Eotyrannus	*Gryponyx*	*Jinzhousaurus*
Epachthosaurus	*Gryposaurus*	*Jobaria*
Epanterias	*Guaibasaurus*	*Jubbulpuria*
Epicampodon	*Gwyneddosaurus*	*Kaijiangosaurus*
Epidendrosaurus	*Gyposaurus*	*Kakuru*
Equijubus	*Hadrosaurus*	*Kangnasaurus*
Erectopus	*Hallopus*	*Kelmayisaurus*
Erliansaurus	*Halticosaurus*	*Kentrosaurus*
Erlikosaurus	*Hanssuesia*	*Kentrurosaurus*
Eshanosaurus	*Haplocanthosaurus*	*Khaan*
Eucamerotus	*Harpymimus*	*Klamelisaurus*
Eucentrosaurus	*Hecatasaurus*	*Koparion*
Eucerosaurus	*Heishansaurus*	*Kotasaurus*
Eucnemesaurus	*Heptasteornis*	*Kritosaurus*
Eucoelophysis	*Herbstosaurus*	*Kulceratops*
Eugongbusaurus	*Herrerasaurus*	*Kunmingosaurus*
Euhelopus	*Hesperosaurus*	*Labocania*
Euoplocephalus	*Heterodontosaurus*	*Labrosaurus*
Eupodosaurus	*Heterosaurus*	*Laevisuchus*
Eurolimnornis	*Heyuannia*	*Lamaceratops*
Euronychodon	*Hierosaurus*	*Lambeosaurus*
Euskelosaurus	*Hikanodon*	*Lametasaurus*
Eustreptospondylus	*Histriasaurus*	*Laosaurus*
Fabrosaurus	*Homalocephale*	*Laplatasaurus*
Ferganasaurus	*Hongshanosaurus*	*Lapparentosaurus*
Frenguellisaurus	*Hoplitosaurus*	*Leaellynasaura*
Fukuiraptor	*Hoplosaurus*	*Leipsanosaurus*
Fukuisaurus	*Hortalotarsus*	*Leptoceratops*
Fulengia	*Huabeisaurus*	*Leptospondylus*
Fulgurotherium	*Huayangosaurus*	*Lesothosaurus*
Galesaurus	*Hudiesaurus*	*Lessemsaurus*
Gallimimus	*Hulsanpes*	*Lewisuchus*
Galtonia	*Hylaeosaurus*	*Lexovisaurus*
Gargoyleosaurus	*Hylosaurus*	*Liaoceratops*
Garudimimus	*Hypacrosaurus*	*Liaoningosaurus*
Gasosaurus	*Hypselosaurus*	*Libycosaurus*
Gasparinisaura	*Hypsibema*	*Ligabueino*
Gastonia	*Hypsilophodon*	*Liliensternus*
Genusaurus	*Iguanodon*	*Lirainosaurus*
Genyodectes	*Iliosuchus*	*Lisboasaurus*
Geranosaurus	*Ilokelesia*	*Loncosaurus*
Giganotosaurus	*Incisivosaurus*	*Longosaurus*
Gigantosaurus	*Indosaurus*	*Lophorhothon*
Gigantoscelus	*Indosuchus*	*Loricosaurus*
Gilmoreosaurus	*Ingenia*	*Losillasaurus*
Giraffatitan	*Inosaurus*	*Lourinhanosaurus*
Glyptodontopelta	*Irritator*	*Lourinhasaurus*
Gobipteryx	*Isanosaurus*	*Lucianosaurus*
Gobisaurus	*Ischisaurus*	*Lufengocephalus*
Gobititan	*Ischyrosaurus*	*Lufengosaurus*
Gojirasaurus	*Isisaurus*	*Lukousaurus*
Gondwanatitan	*Itemirus*	*Lurdusaurus*
Gongbusaurus	*Iuticosaurus*	*Lusitanosaurus*
Gongxianosaurus	*Jainosaurus*	*Lusotitan*
Gorgosaurus	*Janenschia*	*Lycorhinus*

Macelognathus
Macrodontophion
Macrophalangia
Macrurosaurus
Magnirostris
Magnosaurus
Magyarosaurus
Maiasaura
Majungasaurus
Majungatholus
Malawisaurus
Maleevosaurus
Maleevus
Mamenchisaurus
Mandschurosaurus
Manospondylus
Marmarospondylus
Marshosaurus
Masiakasaurus
Massospondylus
Megalosaurus
Megapnosaurus
Megaraptor
Melanorosaurus
Mendozasaurus
Metriacanthosaurus
Microceratops
Microcoelus
Microhadrosaurus
Micropachycepha-
losaurus
Microraptor
Microsaurops
Microvenator
Minmi
Mochlodon
Mongolosaurus
Monkonosaurus
Monoclonius
Monolophosaurus
Mononykus
Montanoceratops
Morinosaurus
Morosaurus
Mussaurus
Muttaburrasaurus
Mymoorapelta
Naashoibitosaurus
Nanosaurus
Nanotyrannus
Nanshiungosaurus
Nanyangosaurus
Nedcolbertia
Neimongosaurus
Nemegtosaurus
Neosodon
Neovenator
Neuquensaurus
Nigersaurus
Niobrarasaurus

Nipponosaurus
Noasaurus
Nodocephalosaurus
Nodosaurus
Nomingia
Nothronychus
Notoceratops
Notohypsilophodon
Nqwebasaurus
Nuthetes
Ohmdenosaurus
Oligosaurus
Olorotitan
Omeisaurus
Onychosaurus
Opisthocoelicaudia
Orinosaurus
Ornatotholus
Ornithodesmus
Ornitholestes
Ornithomerus
Ornithomimoides
Ornithomimus
Ornithopsis
Ornithosuchus
Ornithotarsus
Orodromeus
Orthogoniosaurus
Orthomerus
Othnielia
Ouranosaurus
Oviraptor
Ozraptor
Pachycephalosaurus
Pachyrhinosaurus
Pachysauriscus
Pachysaurops
Pachyspondylus
Palaeoctonus
Palaeopteryx
Palaeosauriscus
Palaeoscincus
Paleosaurus
Panoplosaurus
Paralititan
Paranthodon
Pararhabdodon
Parasaurolophus
Parksosaurus
Paronychodon
Parrosaurus
Parvicursor
Patagonykus
Patagosaurus
Patricosaurus
Pawpawsaurus
Pectinodon
Peishansaurus
Pekinosaurus
Pelecanimimus

Pellegrinisaurus
Pelorosaurus
Pentaceratops
Phaedrolosaurus
Phuwiangosaurus
Phyllodon
Piatnitzkysaurus
Picrodon
Pinacosaurus
Pisanosaurus
Piveteausaurus
Planicoxa
Plateosauravus
Plateosaurus
Platyceratops
Pleurocoelus
Pleuropeltus
Pneumatoarthrus
Podokesaurus
Poekilopleuron
Polacanthoides
Polacanthus
Polyodontosaurus
Polyonax
Ponerosteus
Poposaurus
Prenocephale
Priconodon
Priodontognathus
Probactrosaurus
Proceratops
Proceratosaurus
Procerosaurus
Procheneosaurus
Procompsognathus
Prodeinodon
Prosaurolophus
Protarchaeopteryx
Protiguanodon
Protoavis
Protoceratops
Protognathosaurus
Protohadros
Protorosaurus
Proyandusaurus
Psittacosaurus
Pteropelyx
Pterospondylus
Pukyongosaurus
Pycnonemosaurus
Pyroraptor
Qantassaurus
Qinlingosaurus
Quaesitosaurus
Quilmesaurus
Rajasaurus
Rapator
Rapetosaurus
Rayososaurus
Rebbachisaurus

Regnosaurus
Revueltosaurus
Rhabdodon
Rhadinosaurus
Rhodanosaurus
Rhoetosaurus
Rhopalodon
Ricardoestesia
Riojasaurus
Saichania
Saltasaurus
Saltopus
Sanpasaurus
Santanaraptor
Sarcolestes
Sarcosaurus
Saurolophus
Sauropelta
Saurophaganax
Sauroplites
Sauroposeidon
Saurornithoides
Saurornitholestes
Scansoriopteryx
Scelidosaurus
Scipionyx
Scleromochlus
Scolosaurus
Scutellosaurus
Secernosaurus
Segisaurus
Segnosaurus
Seismosaurus
Sellosaurus
Serendipaceratops
Shamosaurus
Shanshanosaurus
Shantungosaurus
Shanxia
Shanyangosaurus
Shenzhouraptor
Shenzhousaurus
Shuangmiaosaurus
Shunosaurus
Shuvosaurus
Shuvuuia
Siamosaurus
Siamotyrannus
Sigilmassasaurus
Silesaurus
Siluosaurus
Silvisaurus
Sinocoelurus
Sinornithoides
Sinornithomimus
Sinornithosaurus
Sinosauropteryx
Sinosaurus
Sinovenator
Sinraptor

Sonorasaurus
Sphaerotholus
Sphenosaurus
Sphenospondylus
Spinosaurus
Spinosuchus
Spondylosoma
Squalodon
Staurikosaurus
Stegoceras
Stegopelta
Stegosaurides
Stegosaurus
Stenonychosaurus
Stenopelix
Stenotholus
Stephanosaurus
Sterrholophus
Stokesosaurus
Strenusaurus
Streptospondylus
Struthiomimus
Struthiosaurus
Stygimoloch
Stygivenator
Styracosaurus
Succinodon
Suchomimus
Suchoprion
Supersaurus
Symphyrophus
Syngonosaurus
Syrmosaurus
Szechuanosaurus
Talarurus
Tangvayosaurus
Tanius
Tanystrosuchus
Tarascosaurus
Tarbosaurus
Tarchia
Tatisaurus
Taveirosaurus
Tawasaurus
Technosaurus
Tecovasaurus
Tehuelchesaurus
Teinurosaurus
Telmatosaurus
Tendaguria
Teratosaurus
Texasetes
Teyuwasu
Thecocoelurus
Thecodontosaurus
Thecospondylus
Therizinosaurus
Therosaurus
Thescelosaurus
Thespesius

Tianzhenosaurus
Tichosteus
Tienshanosaurus
Timimus
Titanosaurus
Tochisaurus
Tornieria
Torosaurus
Torvosaurus
Trachodon
Trialestes
Triassolestes
Triceratops
Trimucrodon
Troodon
Tsagantegia
Tsintaosaurus
Tugulusaurus
Tuojiangosaurus
Turanoceratops
Tylocephale
Tyrannosaurus
Udanoceratops
Ugrosaurus
Uintasaurus
Ultrasauros
Ultrasaurus
Unenlagia
Unquillosaurus
Utahraptor
Valdoraptor
Valdosaurus
Variraptor
Vectisaurus
Velocipes
Velociraptor
Velocisaurus
Venenosaurus
Volkheimeria
Wakinosaurus
Walgettosuchus
Wannanosaurus
Wuerhosaurus
Wyleyia
Xenotarsosaurus
Xiaosaurus
Xuanhanosaurus
Yandusaurus
Yaverlandia
Yimenosaurus
Yixianosaurus
Yunnanosaurus
Zalmoxes
Zanclodon·
Zapsalis
Zephyrosaurus
Zigongosaurus
Zizhongosaurus
Zuniceratops
Zupaysaurus